Community Schools in Action

ELSIE RIPLEY CLAPP

Principal, Roger Clark Ballard Memorial School
Jefferson County, Kentucky, 1929–1934

Director of Arthurdale School and Community Activities
Arthurdale, West Virginia, 1934–1936

Editor *Progressive Education*, 1937–1939

NEW YORK

The Viking Press

1939

FIRST PUBLISHED IN DECEMBER 1939

COPYRIGHT 1939 BY ELSIE RIPLEY CLAPP

PRINTED IN U. S. A. BY THE VAIL-BALLOU PRESS, INC.

DISTRIBUTED IN CANADA BY THE MACMILLAN

COMPANY OF CANADA, LTD.

IN APPRECIATION

Without the records and diary notes made by the staff of the Ballard Memorial School and the School at Arthurdale, this account of *Community Schools in Action* would not have been possible. Specifically: Chapter IV is based on the diary notes of Mary Elizabeth Sedman and the report written by Ethel Wadsworth, the heads of the Arthurdale Nursery School, and the whole chapter was edited by Jessie Stanton, the director; Chapter V on "Cultural Resources and Opportunities" was written mainly by Fletcher Collins, the director of Drama and Music; and Chapter VI, "A Rural High School," was written by George Beecher, head of the Arthurdale High School.

In this account, names of all the children and, in the chapters on Arthurdale, of the older people also, are fictitious.

The work which is here described is itself a tribute to John Dewey, whose philosophy and whose vision of the school as a social institution prompted our efforts to create a community school and to participate in community education. Although he is in no way responsible for what was done, everything that we have learned from our experiences in this attempt we learned in a special sense from him. The work and the book which records it are to be counted among the numberless expressions of appreciation in this country and abroad of one of the greatest thinkers of our times.

Few professional educators have seen so fully and clearly the opportunities for the social functioning of education as Eleanor Roosevelt. In the work at Arthurdale, her special gifts of sympathy, insight, fairness, and courage in the face of obstacles held us true to the purposes of serviceableness to the people of the community and of helpfulness to other rural schools, for which the Arthurdale School was established.

Acknowledgment is made also of the educational vision of the parents of the Ballard Memorial School and the Jefferson County

IN APPRECIATION

Board of Education; and of the generous co-operation of the Honorable W. W. Trent, State Superintendent of Schools in West Virginia, and of the teachers and the Superintendent of Schools of Preston County.

The book is dedicated to the children, the boys and girls, and to their families, with whom and for whom the schools were established.

Elsie Ripley Clapp

FOREWORD

By John Dewey

From the viewpoint of this book and of the work it represents introductory words by me are superfluous. The trite saying about "speaking for itself" applies in full measure. Nevertheless, I have welcomed as a pleasure the opportunity to write a few words. It is a pleasure because reading the book has vividly recalled to me many stimulating conversations with its author in which the two schools were mentioned, and because of a most enjoyable visit to one of them, that at Arthurdale. But my greatest pleasure would come if anything I may say would advance the cause of education by calling the attention of others to the extraordinary significance for education of the work reported in this book. Education is itself a continuing process. Administrators and teachers will add to their own education by becoming acquainted with the work of these schools, and thereby the larger educative process be promoted. I am happy to have the chance to act as an intermediary, however incidental, in the continuing process.

If I said the book is a record of a highly significant undertaking in the field of community education, it would sound as if schools had in addition some other field of operations. In fact they do not have. Miss Clapp remarks that "A great deal is said in calling a school a community school." If the school lives up to that name, everything is said. The present book portrays what is involved in terms of schools that do fulfill their function. The portrayal is so adequate that I can but underline some points. A great deal is now said about the social function of schools; more is said than is done. In this book we have an account of something actually done and of how it was done. Perhaps the first lesson it teaches us is that schools function socially only when they function in a community for community purposes, and communities are local, present, and close by, while "society" at large is something vaguely in the distance. The reason, I believe, why more is said and written than done about the social function of schools is that "society" is taken as a kind of sociological and academic entity, instead of as the lives of men, women, boys, and girls going on right around us. Under such circumstances, writing becomes pale and shadowy—abstractions dealing in remote language with an abstraction. The neighborhood is the prime community; it certainly is so for the children and youth who are educated in the school, and it must be so for administrators and teachers if the idea of socially functioning schools is to take on flesh and blood. There is no occasion for fear that the local community will not provide roads leading out into wider human relations if the opportunities it furnishes are taken advantage of.

This, then, is one point I would underscore. Here is one report of one of the small number of schools in our country which have made a reality out of theories about the social function of schools, and which has done it by creating a school to which Lincoln's words about democratic government apply: a school not only for, but of and by the community; the teachers being leaders in the movement, since they are themselves so identified with the community.

An important aspect of this point is that those who were teachers in the schools prepared themselves for their work by becoming citizen members of the community in the most intimate way. They became acquainted with their neighbors by being part of the neighborhood. They knew the other members in a face-to-face way. They kept up all the time they were there this process of educating themselves as to the community's needs and resources, its weaknesses and strong points; they learned that only in this way could they engage in further education of the community. They did not "survey" the community; they belonged to it. Results proved the immeasurable value of this phase of community education. It was not just a question of staying "after school"—which is a part of the duties of many teachers. There were literally hardly any hours of night or day that would be said to be *after* school work—that is, educative work—was finished. In spite of the tax on time and energy that was involved, no one can read about the school without getting the feeling that teaching in it was free from the drudgery and monotony that often attend teaching. It was a continuous experience, enlivening as well as enriching, a process in which the joy of discovery and growing was never absent.

The way in which subject-matter to be taught was selected and the way in which methods for teaching it grew directly out of knowledge of community conditions are so concretely reported in the pages of the book that I hardly need to underline the point. I do wish to add from personal knowledge, however, that the vital responsiveness of the members of the community, young and old, to the school as a center of its own life is understated rather than exaggerated in the pages which follow. Closely connected with the warmth and extent of the response is the fact, I believe, that the community was a rural community. For I am convinced it is a mistake to believe that the most needed advances in school organization and activities are going to take place chiefly in cities—especially in large cities. From the viewpoint of genuine community education, country districts provide the greatest opportunity as well as exhibit the most crying need—the most vocal even if not in fact the deepest.

The connection of school activities with out-of-school activities is indirect in the city. It is immediate, close at hand, in villages where there are gardens, shops, and a variety of household activities to meet family needs. First-hand acquaintance with nature, which is the background of scientific study, is obtained with great difficulty in the city. It exists as a matter of course in country districts, and yet is rarely taken advantage of for educational purposes. The completeness with which the study of science in the Arthurdale School was a study of the community has value sufficient to make its record worth study, even were it, as it decidedly is not, the only significant achievement of the school. And while in speaking of rural districts we think first of their needs, the report given of both schools indicates the resources, the positive values, that are there in tradition, in history, in folklore and music, indeed in all the conditions out of which the arts grow when their development is healthy.

Even at the risk of stating the obvious, I conclude by pointing out how central are the problems of health, recreation, and of occupations carried on for a livelihood in any community; how conspicuously these problems stand out in a rural community where they offer themselves as direct personal issues. But I want to point to the book as evidence of how the school as well as the community gains when these basic interests of life are made fundamental in education. I might also say that it is surprising how many alleged pedagogical problems relating to such matters as "discipline and freedom, motivation," etc., either vanish or are greatly reduced when a school is a living part of a community. I do not know that there is much danger that the social function of education will be thought of exclusively as the question of what schools could and should do for the community. But if there is any danger at all, the schools here reported upon show that the relation is a two-way process. They prove what the community can do for schools when the latter are actually centers of community life. Here are cases in which communities develop themselves by means of schools which are the centers of their own life. In consequence, there is no detail of the following report which will not repay study. The report is a demonstration in practice of the place of education in building a democratic life.

CONTENTS

FOREWORD by John Dewey — vii

I: A RURAL SCHOOL IN KENTUCKY — 3
    THE ROGER CLARK BALLARD MEMORIAL SCHOOL — 4
    BEGINNING THE EXPERIMENT IN RURAL EDUCATION — 6
    HEALTH NEEDS — 10
    STAFF MEETINGS AND STUDIES — 14
        Kentucky — 15
    THE PROGRAMS — 21
        Farms and Farming: First Grade — 24
        Study of a Village: Second Grade — 26
        Pioneer Living in Kentucky: Fourth Grade — 28
        Kentucky Life in 1840: Eighth Grade — 32
        Coming to Kentucky by Trail and River: Fifth and Sixth Grades — 35
    THE HEALTH PROGRAM — 40
        Health Work, 1930–31 — 40
        The Ballard Country Fair — 42
        Extension of Health and Social Work in 1931–32 — 43
    THE SCHOOL A RECREATION CENTER FOR THE COMMUNITY — 46
    FORMULATION OF THE CONCEPT OF A COMMUNITY SCHOOL AND OF SOCIAL STUDIES — 47
        Social Studies — 48
        Mathematics Reviewed — 49
        Review of Language — 51
    DEVELOPMENTS IN PROGRAMS AND STUDY OF RESOURCES, 1931–34 — 53
        Further Study of Resources of the Environment — 53
        New Developments in the Programs — 56
    A COMMUNITY SCHOOL'S RELATIONS WITH ITS FAMILIES — 61

The Social-Education Work of a Rural Community School 62

II: COMMUNITY EDUCATION: ARTHURDALE—A SCHOOL 66

Section 1: Building a Community School at Arthurdale, 1934–35 66
Community Schools in Rural Areas 66
The First Step in the Educational Program 68
Plans for the "New School" at Arthurdale 71
   Plan for the School at Arthurdale Drafted by the West Virginia Advisory School Committee 72
   Arrangements for the Establishment of the School 75
   Preparing Buildings at Arthurdale for School Use 77
   Prerequisite Conditions for Community Education 80
   Scott's Run and Arthurdale 81
Shared Living and Working 86
What Is Community Education? 89

Section 2: Community Activities in 1934–35 89
The Arthurdale Health Problem 89
   Physical Condition of the Children 93
   The Older People 94
   Dental Repairs 96
   The Babies on the Project 96
Resources for Recreation and Enjoyments 99
   Square Dances 100
   The First Christmas at Arthurdale 101
"Night School" for the Older Boys and Girls 103
Summer Activities, 1935 107
Early Problems in Farming 110
   The First Farm Co-operative 110
   School Gardens and School Lunches 111
The People: Education in Homestead Work and Living 114
   The Men's and Women's Clubs: Social and Civic Instrumentalities 118
Community Education—Learning by Living 123

CONTENTS

III: THE SCHOOL AT ARTHURDALE — 125
- ENVIRONMENT AND EDUCATION IN RURAL AREAS — 125
- "MAKING BRICKS WITHOUT STRAW" — 128
- EDUCATIONAL USE OF ENVIRONMENT — 131
  - Farming on the Homestead: First Grade — 132
  - Building the Village of Arthurdale: the Second Grade — 136
  - Pioneers in West Virginia: the Fourth Grade — 142
- COUNTY TEACHERS IN A COMMUNITY SCHOOL — 151
  - The Third Grade Studies Indian Life — 153
  - Fifth and Sixth Grade Problems of Adjustment — 154
  - Colonial Study: Fifth Grade, 1935–36 — 156
  - The Sixth Grade in 1935–36 — 158
  - Study of West Virginia: Combined Fifth and Sixth Grades, 1935–36 — 158
  - County Teachers Become Interested in Community Education — 161
- THE THREE R'S IN RURAL SCHOOLS — 165
- STUDY OF LANGUAGE IN LIVING AND LEARNING — 167
- TEACHERS LEARNING IN COMMUNITY EDUCATION — 169
- NEW ELEMENTS IN OUR UNDERSTANDING OF ENVIRONMENT — 170
- SOCIALLY FUNCTIONING STUDIES TESTED IN ACTION — 170

IV: THE ARTHURDALE NURSERY SCHOOL — 172
- SECTION 1: THE NURSERY SCHOOL IN 1934–35 — 172
  - Starting a Nursery School in a Rural Community — 173
  - First Problems of Health and Adjustment — 176
  - Working Problems of Heating and Cooking — 178
  - The Children in Arthurdale — 180
  - The Arthurdale Environment — 181
  - Home Economics at the Nursery School with High School and "Night School" Students — 183
  - The Workmen and Parents Appraise the Nursery School — 184
  - Toy Making by Parents for Christmas — 185
  - The Nursery School at Mid-Winter — 185
  - First Parents' Meeting — 186

CONTENTS

"Visitin'" on the Homestead . . . 187
Children's Progress in March, April, and May . . . 187
First "Well Baby Clinic," May 1935 . . . 189
Visitors: the Nursery School Used as an Observation Center . . . 190

SECTION 2: THE NURSERY SCHOOL IN 1935–36 . . . 192
The New Nursery School Building . . . 192
Children's Improvement in the Fall . . . 194
The Nursery School from January through July 1936 . . . 197
  Parents' Visits to Nursery School . . . 197
  Visits to Families . . . 197
  Use of the Environment . . . 198
    The Playground in the Woods . . . 208
    Earlier Life in the Mines Reflected in Dramatic Play . . . 209
  Relations with the Community . . . 210
  Baby Clinics in 1936 . . . 212
  Physical Examinations . . . 214
The Nursery School a Source of Community Education at Arthurdale . . . 215

V: CULTURAL RESOURCES AND OPPORTUNITIES . . . 217

THE SCHOOL THE CENTER OF CULTURE IN RURAL AREAS . . . 217

CULTURAL RESOURCES AT ARTHURDALE . . . 218
  The Scotch-Irish Traditional Culture . . . 218
    Square-Dancing . . . 220
    Fiddling . . . 222
    Fiddle-Making . . . 223
    Balladry . . . 226
    Children's Songs . . . 232
    Mouth-Harping and Jig-Dancing . . . 239
    Gospel Songs and White Spirituals . . . 240
    Music Festivals, Summers of 1935 and 1936 . . . 242
  Quilt-Making . . . 248
  Furniture-Making . . . 249
  Historical Tradition . . . 251
  Art and Painting . . . 253

Drama	256
Communication	268
"The News" and School-Community Life	268

VI: A RURAL HIGH SCHOOL — 273

Section 1: An Account of the Beginnings of the Arthurdale High School, 1934–35 — 273

Where We Must Begin	273
School Opens	275
Point of Departure	276
Beginning Afresh	278
Organization of Work in the High School	279
High School Groupings	279
Mobilization of Interests in the Seventh and Eighth Grades	282
English	286
The Beginning of a Library	289
Science	291
Work in Botany	291
Development of Work and of Interests	294
Teachers and Curriculum	297

Section 2: The School as the Center of Resources and of Understandings — 298

The New School Buildings	298
The High School in 1935–36	305
The Problem of the Older Boys and Girls	305
Work at the High School in 1935–36	306
Music: Instrument-Making	307
Science in Study of the Environment	309
Understanding and Researches	315
Mathematics Discussed	323
History	324
Research in Language	326
Bringing the Community into the Work of the School	331

VII: COMMUNITY AND SCHOOL LIFE, 1935–36 — 333

Adult Education	333
Agencies of Adult Education Used at Arthurdale	337
Education of Young Adults	342

CONTENTS

Industrial Arts at Arthurdale ... 342
Problems of the Older Boys ... 343
High School and Post-High School Work ... 347
Proposed Studies of Chief Local Problems ... 348
Study of Economic Resources of the Environment ... 350

THE COMMUNITY IN 1935–36 ... 355
  The Second Year a Transitional Phase ... 356
  Growth and Development of the School and Community Library ... 366
  Health Work in 1935–36 ... 368
  Summer Activities in 1936 ... 376
  School and Community Living ... 384
    Arthurdale Not "An Island Community" ... 384
    Relations with Other Towns and Cities ... 385
  Arthurdale a Preston County School ... 388
  Purpose of This Report ... 391

APPENDICES ... 395

INDEX ... 417

ILLUSTRATIONS

facing page

MINE SHACKS IN SCOTT'S RUN   86
Photograph by Farm Security Administration, U.S. Department of Agriculture

VIEW ON THE HOMESTEAD AT ARTHURDALE, WEST VIRGINIA   87
Photograph by Evans, Farm Security Administration, U.S. Department of Agriculture

A FAMILY IN SCOTT'S RUN   102
Photograph by Farm Security Administration, U.S. Department of Agriculture

CHILDREN AT ARTHURDALE   103
Photograph by Farm Security Administration, U.S. Department of Agriculture

FIRST GRADE AT RECESS   110
Photograph by Johnson, Farm Security Administration, U.S. Department of Agriculture

MOTHERS PREPARING THE SCHOOL LUNCH   111
Photograph by Farm Security Administration, U.S. Department of Agriculture

BUILDING THE VILLAGE OF ARTHURDALE, SECOND GRADE   142
Photograph by Farm Security Administration, U.S. Department of Agriculture

PIONEER FAMILY LIFE IN THE LOG CABIN, FOURTH GRADE PLAY   143
Photograph by Farm Security Administration, U.S. Department of Agriculture

HEALTH INSPECTION AT THE NURSERY SCHOOL   178
Photograph by Farm Security Administration, U.S. Department of Agriculture

ILLUSTRATIONS

	facing page
THE NURSERY SCHOOL AT MID-WINTER, 1934–35 *Photograph by Harry Carlson*	179
THE NEW NURSERY SCHOOL BUILDING, 1935–36 *Steward Wagner, Architect Photograph by W. J. Miller*	202
"THE SCHOOL WAS, IN EFFECT, A LITTLE VILLAGE IN ITSELF" *Steward Wagner, Architect Photograph by W. J. Miller*	203
HIGH SCHOOL QUARTERS IN 1934–35 *Photograph by Harry Carlson*	302
ASSEMBLY HALL AND DISPLAY ROOM AT THE TOWN CENTER *Eric Gugler, Architect Photograph by Farm Security Administration, U.S. Department of Agriculture*	302
NEW HIGH SCHOOL BUILDING, 1935–36 *Steward Wagner, Architect Photograph by Locke, Farm Security Administration, U.S. Department of Agriculture*	303
ELEMENTARY SCHOOL BUILDING *Steward Wagner, Architect Photograph by W. J. Miller*	334
SCHOOL CENTER BUILDING *Steward Wagner, Architect Photograph by W. J. Miller*	335
SCHOOL AND COMMUNITY RECREATION BUILDING *Steward Wagner, Architect Photograph by W. J. Miller*	335

COMMUNITY SCHOOLS
IN ACTION

CHAPTER I

A RURAL SCHOOL IN KENTUCKY

IT WAS in Kentucky that we came to an understanding of the nature and functioning of a community school. In Arthurdale, West Virginia, we built a community school and used it as an agency in community education.

It was the work in a public rural school of Jefferson County, Kentucky, and our experiences there in answering the needs of the children and families of that school district, that brought us the realization that a public school in a rural area is necessarily a socially functioning school. So it will perhaps be clearer to rehearse this realization before describing the work at Arthurdale, because that story starts with a school group already familiar with the activity of a community school. To review the experiences by which we grew into the conception of a school as a community school may be of assistance to those who are moving, as we did, from a realization of the social implications of active learning and group enterprises, and of the educational use of environment, to an acceptance of the school as inherently a social institution and the consequences and responsibilities that acceptance entails.

It was in Kentucky that we first made acquaintance with the life and problems of a remote rural area. Where we became familiar with rural people, their nature, interests, habits of thought, feelings, and aspirations. Where we discovered the rich educational opportunities a countryside affords, and learned how to use them educationally. Where we came to understand the importance for educational purposes of teachers' identification with the life and interests of the community. Where we learned fully the needs for health measures, recreational facilities, and cultural enrichment which a remote rural area presents. Where the reorganization of subject matters for use in a rural school, and the use of these in interpreting to the children their lives and surroundings, led us into the conception of a socially functioning curriculum.

By the time we went to West Virginia we were at least familiar with these conditions and responsibilities and opportunities. We understood what a community school was, what it did, and something of its procedures and practices. Had it not been for what our experiences in Kentucky taught us, the work at Arthurdale would not have been possible.

To Kentucky we brought a background of experience in private progressive schools in the East. But a rural district and country children from small farms were new to us. New to us, too, was the State of Kentucky—"the north of the South," as Kentuckians call it. Unfortunately, or fortunately, we knew nothing of rural education. All this we had to learn. At the time, we felt our ignorance to be a great disadvantage and handicap but, now that the period of adjustment and intensive learning is past, I think perhaps we were, by reason of our very unfamiliarity and different background, especially aware of conditions, and sensitive to impressions. Contact with the problems and life of a remote rural area was a revealing and poignant experience which penetrated our accustomed ways of thought and action, and impelled us into a different kind of endeavor and another mode of feeling and thinking.

The Roger Clark Ballard Memorial School

In 1909 Mr. and Mrs. Thruston Ballard gave to the Jefferson County Board of Education a piece of land from their estate and offered to help build a school on it. The County Board of Education sold the sites of two one-room schools near by and gave the proceeds to the building. Neighbors contributed an equal amount, and Mr. and Mrs. Ballard bore the major part of the building costs. A school building was erected with stone from Mrs. Ballard's estate, and in memory of her little son was called "The Roger Clark Ballard Memorial School." The children from the discontinued one-room schools —about 35 in number—and the children of Mrs. Ballard's friends and neighbors attended the new school, perhaps 50 in all. Some fifteen years later, Mrs. Ballard and the neighbors added a gymnasium ("The Thruston Ballard Memorial Hall," in memory of Mr. Ballard) and also several classrooms. These friends, most of them young married people who had moved out from Louisville to live along the Ohio River, decided, instead of starting a private school for their children, to send them to this public school with the country children who were their neighbors. The parents who had contributed in the beginning continued to donate time and effort and money to the school, bearing the cost of repairs and upkeep, supplying additional teachers, helping with school lunches and health work and occasionally with entertainments and plays.

We were attracted to the situation because it offered an opportunity to deal with public education in a rural area; because the school was in the country and in a countryside still largely agricultural, yet only a few miles from a city—the city of Louisville; and especially because its pupils, 75 percent of whom were the children of small farmers and farm "tenants" and 25 percent the children of prosperous old Kentucky families, had been going to school together for twenty years. This situation, together with the fact that the school was, and always had been, a center of the community's interest and effort, seemed to offer an opportunity to develop the educational use of environment and active learning in a public rural school, and a chance to continue and possibly extend the community's interest in the school.

Beginning the Experiment in Rural Education

The beginning of the experiment in rural education had its roots in a dream of what this school might be and do for its community that I outlined to a parents' committee that came north in 1928–29 to find a new principal for the school. It was agreed that the sum of $10,000, which it would be necessary to add to the school's budget for such an experiment, should, if it was to have significance, be contributed in equal amounts by parents and the County Board of Education. The committee returned to Kentucky, and it was they who made the dream a reality. As parents they had for many years helped the school with personal effort and money, and when they called on each member of the County Board and told him that a new and better sort of education could be had for the children of Jefferson County, each Board member believed these good neighbors of his and trusted what they said. So the realization of the dream was made possible by the vision and effort of a group of parents and of a rural County Board of Education of the State of Kentucky.

Although it was our expectation and desire to have on the staff local teachers as well as teachers experienced in progressive education, and though the local school authorities encouraged this idea, the teachers, afraid of losing promotion rating and unsure of a new and strange group and enterprise, declined our offers; so, perforce, the staff was entirely new. Of the three older teachers, two were experienced in progressive work and one in formal work; of the younger teachers, three were from progressive schools, one from a formal school, and three were fresh from college. Two student teachers were Kentucky girls.

Rural schools in Jefferson County open the week after the

State Fair. We all went down a week early to get the School in readiness and to use the opportunity the Fair offered for gathering information about the products and the occupations and interests of the place to which we had come. Quite unexpectedly, the fact that we "came down a week early without pay" and rolled up our sleeves and cleaned the School proved to the neighborhood our interest in the work and counted in our favor with the country people. The job of cleaning the School building and arranging the equipment for our use, of supplanting—with the County Board's help— the screwed-down desks in the youngest classrooms with movable work tables and posture chairs, and of finding ways and means of providing the necessary school supplies in a community not rich in cash, crowded the first week.

The School is not far from Louisville but out in the real country, built on small wooded hills that rise abruptly three meadows back from the Ohio River. Close by are woods, creeks, and meadows, and surrounding the School smaller and larger farms and estates. A "Toonerville" trolley runs out this way along the River, below the palisades. The school district is a long section of territory too spread out for a school bus service. So the children who do not come in cars or ride to school on ponies make their way somehow down to the car line, which lands them at the foot of the School steps. Some of the people live up and down the River Road and the lanes that branch off from it. Others live back up on the higher farm lands, still others in the woods or back of the cornfields, one family across five creeks. One hundred and twenty-three families sent their children to the School in 1929.

Arranging for a wholesome hot lunch for all the children in the school was the first enterprise. This proved to be as good an issue as any on which to get acquainted. With one of the parents, I called on all the country mothers who could not get in to the school. They were confident of their ability to "pack" a lunch for their children of "whatever they had in the house" and had been accustomed to give the children a nickel to "get something at the store," but thought it would be a good idea for the children "to get something hot." The wealthier group found it harder to adjust to a hearty midday lunch for their children—the Kentucky custom being a light lunch and a heavy dinner at night, even for children. However, after a number of parent-teacher meetings, arrangements were finally made.

We set out conservatively to find out what the children knew about the Three R's. Many proved to be far behind the achievement standard for their age and grade, partly owing to irregular school attendance. Meanwhile, the Shop got into action. Miss Lawton, the Shop teacher, herself an adept at equipping a shop, wisely waited to do this until the children had arrived. With them she scraped the worn benches, and rearranged and conditioned the Shop. The children made the tool racks and, as chance had it, it was the older girls who received and unloaded the first order of lumber, and did a good job, too. To meet immediate needs, Miss Lawton appointed any of the older boys or girls who showed aptitude to the honorary job of School carpenter. They built shelves in the schoolrooms, made letter boxes for the office and a telephone shelf, and repaired around the School the things that they had, I dare say, themselves earlier broken. By the time this work was done, the children were ready to defend the Shop and shop work against all comers. It was theirs; they had made it. Slowly, as the programs tentatively planned the summer before began to get under way, the Shop started to function in connection with them. By November, six weeks after the opening of School, we were at work actively learning and living together. The children turned to a different way of learning naturally and with surprising ease, all things considered. Adjustment to a different and more demanding type of study from books proved more difficult.

There was much for the staff of teachers to learn—a new

locality, new conditions, new kinds of people. We had constantly, as we worked, to discover the fundamental as well as the obvious needs of the people; to catch their aspirations as well as their expressed ambitions and desires; to know their springs of interest as well as to understand the form in which these were expressed. At times we understood quickly; at other times we were slow to grasp their viewpoint and slant on life. Many of the necessities were familiar to us as teachers dealing with children; many were unknown and unimagined. The work was one of education—our education—and of interpretation. It was also a work of integration and organization—of schedules, finances, staff, and parents.

The work turned out, of course, to be something that could be attempted only with the help of everyone—parents and neighbors and children, as well as the County Board of Education. The job of becoming acquainted with the locality and the needs of the people of both groups, and of adjusting the curriculum and the school procedures to meet those needs, both rectified and expanded our first "idea" of a school-in-a-community. And this idea gained body and trenchancy as it became the shared enterprise of all the people engaged in it.

We could bring to the problem experience gained in school work elsewhere. We had been used to working co-operatively with people; to working together for ends we all desired; to using, turning to account, whatever happened; to exchanging and sharing. We had in progressive schools been accustomed to seeking really to know and to understand the children. We had known what it was to use children's interests and the things children were familiar with as starting points. We had been accustomed to learning actively, using and testing what we learned as we learned it. This manner of working unexpectedly gave us a common denominator of understanding with the people among whom we had come. "Dewey?" said one of our County Board. "I know him. He's the fellow who said that living was learning, and I guess I know that."

Health Needs

The visits we had made to the homes in connection with school lunches, other visits, and our daily contact with the children in School brought very vividly home to us the health and social needs of the country children.

Through the generosity of several parents, we were able to get from one of the army stores in the city folding army cots and blankets, which we cut in two and hemmed. Twenty-three dollars sufficed to provide each of the children in the First Grade with a cot and blanket of his own. Later in the year, we were able to make the same provision for the Second Grade children, and we had the satisfaction of making it possible that every one of the children in these grades at least once in the twenty-four hours slept soundly stretched out to his full length by himself in a bed. Fully one-half of the children, we found, usually slept at night with two, three, or four other children in a double bed, side by side like so many forks or spoons. The State Tuberculosis Association felt, I know, that this added rest was perhaps the most important thing we did for the children.

Morning recess periods were established for every class, and an afternoon supervised play period was started. The children as a whole were lethargic and showed no initiative. The girls liked best to sit on the School steps or to play desultory games of hop scotch in the shade. A few boys in both groups had a consuming interest in football and baseball. Aside from these games, their inclination was to play with their pets at home or to "play" with each other in a rough and tumble fashion, very much as dogs and kittens do. Not many years before we arrived it had been held immodest for the girls even to watch the boys playing in the gymnasium. It seemed to us that here, as in so many other respects, the needs of the two groups were not dissimilar. The child of well-to-do parents, whose life held so many *things* and so much service and who was so frequently inert and often overweight, needed the quickening and invigoration, the discipline and resource of exercise and sports. The child of the farms, who came to us in the morning after three or four hours of farm chores and who did these again at night after school was over, needed, we felt, to have different muscles called on and to know the fun and relaxation of out-of-door games. By the end of the year a fairly large group of boys had played basketball, baseball, and football and the younger children had become happily active in recess periods. The older girls were finally drawn in, and the month of May saw girls as well as boys on the practice baseball teams. Later the girls formed their own basketball teams.

For many years before we came, perhaps for all the years of the School's life, the parents had done a great deal on matters of health. They had co-operated with the County nurse and had helped put through vaccination against smallpox and diphtheria and typhoid. They had strongly espoused the work of the Louisville Tuberculosis Association, which each year, with the co-operation of the School Board, gave examinations and awards for excellence of physical condition and personal health habits. In cases of individual need, the parents had done everything in their power to get help for the child and to put him in touch with city agencies for medical assistance. As mothers, they realized the importance of these things.

The older people, brought up, like most older people everywhere, under a regime of gold stars and prizes, had unlimited faith in the power of awards to stimulate desirable health habits. To forgo this kind of stimulation, and the according of the blue and gold ribbons on May Day, to them appeared a surrender of the very things they had so long striven for. So we continued this practice the first year, co-operating to the best of our ability with the Association which had this in charge. It seemed to us, however, that the children whom this was designed to help were the very ones whose health habits it did not and, we felt, could not touch. Because of the numbers of children and the necessarily general nature of the competitive examination designed for all children and for every school, the physical examination was superficial and intentionally was made very simple. It represented not so much what the Association thought desirable as what it believed to be feasible and what it felt could be given to everyone.

All through the year, as we went into the homes and lived intimately with the children day by day and came to know the families and the conditions under which they lived, we ardently longed for the opportunity to get more complete physical data about every child in the School. At the end of the year, with the help of Mrs. John Moore, the President of the Parent Teachers Association, we broached with the Tuberculosis Association a plan that was more suited to our particular needs at Ballard, for a thorough physical examination for each child in the School. The Association generously assented, and Mrs. Moore worked through the summer to gain the understanding and approval of all the local authorities.

The School was able, through County agencies and those of the city, to make appointments at dental and eye clinics, and to arrange for hospital care or service. Through the generosity of parents and teachers with cars, we were able to take the children in to these centers. The one County nurse, whose duties covered our large district, was most co-operative. In the spring, a dentist from the County Office came and did work at the School for the country children.

These health measures met the baffling obstacle of ignorance and tired indifference, of distance and carfare and the absence of health ideals. The obstacles were, more fundamentally still, problems of living conditions. In the one- and two-room houses in which many of the children lived, the families had of course little or no privacy. They rarely undressed for the night, rarely had bed sheets or pillow cases. If it was cold they got under an old "coverlid." Dressing, like going to bed, was a quick affair. One washed at the sink or at a bench on the porch, both in public. The scanty water from the well or spring, often brought from a considerable distance, had to do for the whole family. You didn't, if you were considerate, throw it out unless it was really dirty. When the nurse was questioning the children about brushing their teeth, their replies were: "Yes, I guess I brushed them this week; I can't just remember. Perhaps it was last week. Anyway, it was two times lately." As we came to know their homes better we found that they did not have toothbrushes, many of them. We bought these, and hooks with them, and ourselves saw them hung up. But it was the children and the families who had, in the conditions of living I have described, to acquire the habit of using them.

The houses of the poorest type had no inside toilets and some of them no outside toilets. For the first and second grade children just entering school, the proper use of toilets, the use of a basin and stopper, the mystery of a shower bath, were a most imperative part of our teaching. We seemed often to ourselves to be teaching "civilization." "It's all right for you-all to teach me about settin' a table and all that," one of the older girls of a very self-respecting family said, "but at my house we ain't so fancy, we just eats standin' up."

In trying to picture these conditions, I have left out one group of families—the skilled workers and those who ran small farms or dairies. The fathers—expert gardeners, painters, carpenters, or farmers—worked hard and were thrifty. In their houses one found the conditions of any intelligent working people of small means. Their tables were covered with good substantial food and their hospitality was generous. The mothers were excellent cooks and good managers. These parents wanted all the advantages for their children. They constituted only a small proportion of the school families—perhaps 10 percent—although they were a strong and helpful group in our enterprise. They, as much as we, wanted to help the others, contributing food for community suppers and, in cases of need, to other poorer families.

In ways such as these the School and the parents together met the pressing health and other needs of its families. The teachers' main contribution, perhaps, was to supply, from their constant and intimate knowledge of the children and their families, much more information about them than the parents were able themselves to have. As school teachers who "worked too," we were always welcomed in the homes without causing any of the embarrassment and self-consciousness that visits from the well-to-do mothers produced. We came to know all the families well. Once assured of our concern and interest, they increasingly turned to the School for help in time of trouble—in sickness or at birth or death. They were proud, but they were sure the teacher would help. It was their needs and our attempts to meet these, that widened the work of the School to include social services and that pried our eyes open to the responsibilities of a school in a rural area.

Staff Meetings and Studies

The weekly meetings of the staff consisted of either study courses, reports on the work of the different groups and classes, or formulations of the meanings, as we gained them, of the work as it progressed. These meetings form an intrinsic part of the history of our realization of education as socially functioning.

My Year-End Report in May of the first year recalled to the staff that they had first seen the undertaking as an opportunity to establish a progressive school in a rural area, and to make it a demonstration school for the County. It reminded them that they had known it would be an experiment in democracy—

specifically in the mutual adjustments of the several groups of children—and recalled their hope that the School would come to be a recreational and intellectual center of its area. The surprises, it stated, had been to discover that the work was of a *social-educational* nature, and what Kentucky was like. Before describing the work of the School on programs and its educational use of environment, it would perhaps be well to put down the early information the staff had gained of the State, its resources, products, and industries, its ways of life, and something of its development.

KENTUCKY

The State of Kentucky is still largely agricultural. Louisville, with a population of 307,745, is the largest city. Next in size are: Covington, with a population of 65,252; Lexington, the chief city of earlier days, with 45,736; Paducah, 35,541; Newport, 29,744; Ashland, 29,074. Following these are seven cities—among them Frankfort, the State capital—whose populations run between 10,000 and 25,000; and sixteen cities between 5000 and 10,000. Outside of these centers, the State is characterized by towns and villages, many of them unincorporated, and by many settlements and hamlets.

The newcomer notices the prevalence of widely scattered groups of houses, single cabins and shanties, innumerable fields and meadows; and the number of horses and mules, the herds of cows, flocks of sheep, the pigs and the chickens. One finds roads and lanes turning right-angle corners among the fields, many streams and rivers with low bush-bordered banks, countless creeks and runs, low folded hills, still forest and trees everywhere. It is a land of fertile soil, unused spaces, wide pastures, luxuriant foliage, great beauty of contour and coloring. Game is still plentiful; cottontail rabbits dart across the road, possum are seen at night hanging from the trees along the highways. In the fields are grown chiefly corn and some potatoes and, of course, hay. Occasionally, on the shelf-deposits of the Kentucky River, hemp is raised. Little or no flax or cotton is grown now in the State.

It is still possible to see existing side by side today illustrations of almost all the stages of Kentucky's history. Driving along its roads one sees log cabins, houses of puncheon boards and of hand-made clapboards, next to modern houses of either the ready-to-use or the individually built type. Houses of stucco, of stone and brick, intermingle with the wooden houses of the simple kind. Driving along the road one passes men on muleback, horses with two or more riders, high spindling buggies with quaint floral patterns on their sides, and old Ford cars, as well as modern cars of every description. In one field a modern tractor at work, in the next an ancient hand-plow and harrow.

On the Ohio River steam packets built on lines practically unchanged since 1840, ply under modern bridges of steel and concrete. The old canoes and flatboats are gone, although the houses of the river-boat people who live along the shores of the Ohio are reminiscent of earlier days. An occasional modern motor boat or sailboat is seen, but the old steam packets, with their tall black smokestacks well forward, their great side wheels or stern drum wheels, still dominate the Ohio River as they have done for the past ninety years.

There are still in Kentucky people who live under conditions very similar to those of the first pioneers, on small clearings, in rude houses, at the creek bottoms, in the hill valleys and hollows, separated from each other, each eking out for himself a hard-won existence, the fathers hunting for food, the women and children raising corn and a few 'taters. Or the whole family works in a small tobacco patch planted on the side of a hill around stumps still left in the ground. They make their own soap, often their own dyes from tree bark or nuts or vegetables. Near the house in the yard stands a kettle for making soap or for dyeing. Inside the houses, in the one or two rooms, bought furniture usually replaces the hand-hewn beds and tables, though crude log stools and board benches still abound. In the place of the old fireplace, usually a cook stove. In one room a table, a dresser, perhaps a rocking chair with a board nailed across for a seat, clothes on pegs around three of the walls; in the other room, one or two double beds for all the family.

Now more than formerly the wool that is raised, the tobacco or corn that is grown, the chickens and hogs, are taken over better roads to more distant and bigger markets. The men and women who in their youth wore "jeans" and dresses of homespun, shirts of hand-raised and hand-woven linen, hats of plaited straw, bonnets of calico, who used for bed coverings skins and furs and hand-woven blankets, now buy their clothes and their comforters ready-made in the nearest town or city. As children, the old people saw at night by the light of the fire or candle or betty lamp. Now they use kerosene, although still they often make dip candles.

On many of the larger farms and on the estates, also, the life of the 1850's and '60's still goes on—hunting, farming, riding, hospitality, entertainment. The houses are fairly large, with high-ceilinged rooms. In them one finds the furniture that prevailed among the gentry in the last century. Often the façade of the house has the long pillars and the two-story doorway—the upper part consisting of shutters and perhaps a balcony—characteristic of the South. Usually the houses are built of wood, sometimes of red brick. In the newer real estate developments, there are "country houses," small or pretentious, of the up-to-date country-life variety.

The two kinds of homes—small cabins and shacks and larger, more ample houses—exist close to each other. On the great estates or the large stock farms, one can hardly believe in the existence of the cabins close by, behind the cornfields, in the woods, up a creek, or in back of the little hills.

Still the slow-moving, slow-running life of the smaller towns goes on much as it has done for the past sixty or seventy years—the large Grain and Merchandise Store, the buggies at the curb, the horses tied to hitching posts by the courthouse. Even in Louisville one sees the indolent loading by hand of steamers lying along the shore where the Ohio River laps at the bank and the paved landing stage. Yet spanning the River are great modern bridges, and beside them steam derricks, stone crushers, grain elevators, gas plants and power houses, railroad yards, warehouses and factories. In Louisville, whose streets are crowded with the cars of the rich and the Fords of the farmers, interspersed with the flower carts and old clothes wagons of the darkies, there are miles and miles of the detached, heavy, large homes of the 1880's. Miles also of small frame houses with tall narrow doors and long windows reaching to the floor, little yards and a gate. Among these, modern chain stores, shops, hotels, garages, movie houses, handsome auditoriums, hospitals, school and government buildings. The main business streets wear the aspect of a large modern city. The wholesale business districts, there as elsewhere, hold some look of the past. Nowhere else, perhaps, is there a greater mingling of the old and the new, the past and the present.

In a very special sense, Kentucky's past is her present. Tradition, stories, memories, and reminiscences prolong her past. Its ways of life still persist. Its deeds and heroes are still a present interest.

She is a young State and settlement, and a very old dwelling place. Here it was, in this very territory, that to our knowledge dwelt the very early Americans—the cave dwellers and mound people, the pre-Indians, whoever they were. Today children hunt and play in the caves, finding relics and reminders of the long-ago people who used them. Here, of course, as we know, hunted and camped the Shawnees and Cherokees and one of the Iroquois tribes. Plowing today still turns up countless flints and arrowheads and occasional stone implements or grinders of Indian or pre-Indian occupation. Here it was probably that the ocean once flowed. The Ohio River bed today holds fossils of sea shells and sea animals.

Less than 200 years ago, then, the pioneers came exploring into a land long known and used. In 1750, the white men first looked over the mountain ranges down into this country full of wild game, lying green and beautiful and fertile before them. Not till 1790 was Kentucky a State. How fast she has lived! Before she was well grown and settled, there entered by river and trail steam-driven boats and trains bearing manufactured goods and machinery from the older East. Through the gateway of Pittsburgh and over the Wilderness Trail, to the lonely cabins, the forts, the great estates and their houses, the East sent its manufactured goods and its imported goods from across the seas. The slower growth of town settlements, the discipline of town meetings, the gradual development of skill in household arts and crafts, invention and the use of machinery, Kentucky did not know. She had to leap from forts to cities, from the cabins of the hunter to settled farms and stations. In her youth, her adolescent years, before she matured and was yet full-grown, she was called on to act as a State and to assimilate the fruits of manufacturing and steam power.

So she remains young—and old, too—still using, and now herself manufacturing and making, new articles, but clinging also to ways of life of the "olden days," as they are called.

This fact it is, among others, that makes her so rich educationally. Her children can understand in terms of the things about them, the things in their own life, the whole history of the State's growth and, through it, the history of the nation. For she is—Kentucky was—the crux of pioneering. To her came men and women from the Eastern colonies, as they had come to these from over the seas. From Pennsylvania, from New Jersey and New England, from North Carolina, Maryland, or

Virginia, they came into Kentucky by trail and river. From her went again some of the pioneers to lands farther west. Through her passed many on their journey, some going through, others to stay. She knew the western advance in all its movements and phases—the dream of fertile land unexplored and inviting; the hardships of the trail, river, and forest; the attacks of Indians who fought with the settlers for their hunting grounds; the loneliness and grind of bare existence, the renewed impulse to wander, departures and returns and desertions; the pride of possession and hard-won ease; the bitterness of neglect and indifference of legislatures; the eagerness and excitement of pleasant and individual living; the slow growth of community thinking and social sharing. Kentucky it was that helped wake the conscience of the country to its frontier people. It was Kentucky that underwrote the country's plans for western advance, by giving assurance to the enlarging Republic of lands of plenty for the taking.

In her today is still a kind of comradeship and neighborliness, a sort of friendly intercourse and exchange, a consciousness of herself and her people, a belief in the State, its life and its future. Her inherent individualism is joined with a sense of the State and the relation of each person to it.

Kentucky is at the place now where for her own interest she begins to seek ways to live better. She sees that, if you wish to farm advantageously, you must know facts about soils and rotation of crops, about forestry, about transportation and roads, about—education. To some who have recently known her, it seems that she has—that she might have—a special role in this country. Not predominantly industrial yet, her descendants of pioneers and of the gentry of Virginia and Maryland think quite simply and straightforwardly about life for their children—life in the State, life in the country. In Kentucky, industries are still in relation to resources on the one hand—rich resources still unexhausted—and to the people and their needs on the other.

If she desired it, Kentucky could maintain and use for her children her special and unique conditions and resources. She is well fitted to educate her children into social living with a completeness and variety not possible to many other States and places. The growing industries, the fertility of the land, and the unexhausted natural resources, the inter-relation of her past and her present, the close ties of the people through the bonds of kinship and marriage—all are facts of great importance to her educationally. The idea of a social school seems especially to fit Kentucky. Carried out there, if it can be, completely and richly, such a school could reveal to other States and places opportunities and responsibilities.

The Programs

The programs which we had tentatively planned for use in the School were based mainly on different phases of Kentucky life and history. We sought at every point to engage in study of the environment and to make educational use of our surroundings. Our purpose in this was to gain with the children a basis for the understanding of their lives. We built better than we knew, for these enterprises proved to be a bond of interest with the parents and neighbors. One community service which these programs rendered was to call forth help from all the parents. The country people were happy to find that they had things which we valued and could use in the School; the wealthier people were interested in lending many of their family treasures, and old books and journals from their libraries. Another use of these programs in our community venture was the widening acquaintance they gave us with the interests and pride and memories of the people. Dealing with the life of the earlier days in Kentucky, we surprisingly found ourselves interpreting the present also.

At the end of the year, the staff discussed the programs, testing them by our more intimate knowledge of the children and the families, to see how far they met the needs of the children. We were especially interested in their interpretive value. They were in summary as follows:

A farm study for the First Grade. A study of village communities for the Second Grade. After these first two years' studies of the world about them, the Third Grade studied the life of the Indians who had used Kentucky as a hunting and camping ground, and of the pre-Indian people who had lived in the caves near by. The Fourth Grade relived the experiences of families coming into Kentucky: their settlement in the wilderness, clearing the land, building and furnishing their log cabins, and all the processes of daily life in a pioneer home. For the Fifth Grade we had planned a study of transportation today and in early times, intending to follow the trails and roads and river ways by which the early settlers came into this land, and to trace these people back to the settlements from which they came. The children, it proved, knew very little about the colonists and asked if they might the first year find out about the settlements on the coast and the countries overseas from which these people came. They did this, and that program turned into a two-year piece of work. Our original plan for the Sixth Grade was a study of the coming into this region of the English, French, and Spanish peoples. The teacher of this group felt unfamiliar with this material, and tried instead a study of Greece and Rome. This did not go well at all; the children had no interest in or connection with these far-away and long-ago people. So in mid-year we changed the plan, and worked instead on the lines of this group's passionate interest in aviation.

The Seventh Grade was to study the first stretch of the history of the State. Convinced that "there never was no Indians outside of Kentucky," they began with studies designed to correct that impression and busied themselves throughout the year with an extensive study of Indian tribes and cultures in America, including a detailed investigation of a Wisconsin tribe, studies of Southwest Indians and pueblos, an excursion into Mayan civilization, and settled down in the spring to a long piece of work on the Southeast Indian tribes who had roamed over Kentucky. This was a restless group, not addicted to book learning. They got a great deal out of this study, not only interest and satisfaction and release for their energies, but also an amazing directness of approach and a genuine interest in getting hold of facts. They were, surprisingly, well prepared the year following for a study that made use of many reference books.

The Eighth Grade planned to work on the period of Kentucky history that began with the introduction of power—steam and electricity—and its application to machinery. This led them into a piece of work on the geological resources of the State. They finally entered deeply into all phases of the period of 1800–50.

We were not sure, when we planned for the School, whether there was to be a Ninth Grade, but ninth graders appeared on the opening day of school. We consulted with the Louisville schools which they would enter the following year and informed ourselves about requirements. At their own request, the ninth graders studied ancient history, which was not required, and took the necessary work in first-year Latin and in Mathematics and English. They built a large model of the Parthenon, and wrote and produced a Latin play—*Villa Sabini Horatii*. The life of the Roman villa was, of course, the life of a self-sustaining farm, and the ceremonial of the spring festival on the Sabine farm presented features that were not unknown in Kentucky. It may be seen that, in the studies of Latin and of Roman History, we sought—as in the History studies with the younger classes—a common denominator of understanding. With the boys of both the Eighth and Ninth Grades we began a preliminary course in Industrial Geography and, with the girls, a course in Home Economics.

Only the First, Second, Fourth, and Eighth Grade programs and the two-year program of the Fifth-Sixth Grade, which proved to have the most interpretive value and to give the more basic understanding, are discussed here. The description is designed to illustrate the use made of the rural environment, and the ways in which these programs drew upon and extended the children's knowledge of their own State and their surroundings.

FARMS AND FARMING: FIRST GRADE

A large number of the children lived on farms. They all lived in the country and knew something about farm life. So it seemed to us that our special work here was to bring out the meaning of their lives and surroundings to them. We had the advantage of using with the children the model farm on Mrs. Ballard's estate which adjoined the School. The model dairy there was excellent for this purpose, both because everything there was done just the way it should be and because it was small enough to be within the children's comprehension and near enough to permit repeated visits. A great many of the families had cows. Some of the families ran small dairies; some had large farms and dairies. These also were available for study and comparison.

The children not only studied about milk and the proper care of it, but they themselves made butter and cooked in their classroom the various things that are made from milk that are good for children to eat. They found out about the feeding of cows and they went into the matter of grains, experimenting a little with raising winter wheat and oats and barley, and did some simple cooking of cereals (the program reinforcing what the School was doing along the lines of nutrition and health). Stables, barns, silos, pig and sheep pens, chicken houses—in fact, the whole barnyard and its arrangements and construction came in for a good deal of attention. The first year the block building centered about dairies, chicken houses, and stock farms. The children brought us back word of home discussions of these matters which they were learning about in school. To our surprise, three of the families changed the location of their well when they learned from the children how disadvantageous it was to have it in the center of the barnyard where the seepage drained into it. This was more than we had hoped for, and opened our eyes to new possibilities. The second year we were able to raise vegetables. In the spring the First Grade planted an early spring garden in the enriched ground which Mrs. Ballard lent the School for this purpose. Three of the fathers, who were themselves farmers and gardeners, generously came to the School at their noon hour and showed the children how this should be done.

The first year, the First Grade children were very much subdued at School. Some of them never spoke above a whisper. They were all very passive and many of them very shy. They did nothing at first but sit, and for practically the first half of the year did not respond to any sort of stimulus. The children of the cabin homes were commonly moved into the corners out of the way of their busy mothers, or played with the animals outside and saw only the other children of their own families, or perhaps of their nearest neighbors. To a great many children the big School building, the presence of so many little children together, the School wash basins and toilets, and the lunchroom were strange and bewildering. Nothing in their lives had prepared them for these experiences. They did not know what to do with the stopper in the basin or how to turn the water on or off, how the toilets worked, how to eat conventionally, or how to live with so many people. To the more privileged children these things were, of course, familiar, but they had been waited on and knew how to do very little for themselves. Block play proved releasing—and so did music. It was to music, in fact, that the children gave their first response.

The second year, in some unexplained way, the situation was entirely different. The group seemed to come to School with happy anticipation the first day. Probably they had learned "about school" from their older brothers and sisters. This second group took in the fact that the School was beside the Ohio River and were very much interested in the boats that plied up and down, in discussing what they carried and where they loaded and unloaded their cargoes. The block building of the second year consisted of more complete farms, and of farms in relation to the River. The children built a great many boats, which loaded or unloaded at the farms, docks, and warehouses; they built houses in connection with the barns, silos, and chicken houses. It was this group that raised the vegetable garden.

STUDY OF A VILLAGE: SECOND GRADE

The Second Grade made a study of a small simple community. This program, like that of the First Grade, was designed to interpret and enlarge the children's knowledge of their own world. The first year, the class was surprised and delighted that they could study a village. They knew villages. There was Harrod's Creek two miles away that had two grocery stores—and a postoffice in one of them—a trolley station stop, and a garage. A few of the children lived there. Several of the children lived at Prospect, a village a little farther away, where there was a bank as well as a grocery store and postoffice, and more houses. With large packing cases the children built their own village on a piece of ground outside their classroom. It, too, had a grocery store and a garage, a postoffice, a bank, houses, and also a church and a school. It also had a vegetable garden. In the winter the children took the buildings indoors and worked on their furnishings. They took the buildings out again in the spring, and were very active planting shrubs and flowers and sowing grass seed—"making the village pretty, as it ought to be."

September of the second year found us all suffering from the drought of the summer which had devastated the State. The Second Grade planted a late fall garden and made irrigation ditches, and in this connection went into the subject of irrigation. They found, to their surprise, that a good many people in other places had to face the problem of what to do when there was little or no water. They gained, I think, a real and enlarged understanding of the drought situation.

Both years the Second Grade villagers got ready for the winter by preserving and drying fruits and vegetables, and by burying some of the vegetables in the ground. The children experimented with all these methods and were especially successful in making preserves. The parents co-operated by supplying the fruits and vegetables. I want to emphasize again the ways in which these programs educated the younger children about foods. Food studies do a great deal for children—young as they are—and through them reach into the homes. Children, we felt, should come up through the School as familiar with foods as they were with other matters. When this is done in schools we shall have a good basis for more significant work in health and nutrition in the older classes.

For the second year, Ethel Carlisle, the teacher of the First Grade, and I decided to make use of our three seasons—fall, winter, and spring—in the work of the village. The fall was used for the location of buildings, for planning and settling boundaries. This town planning discussion brought out the subject of individual rights and social responsibilities. As in Kentucky one is able to be outdoors through November, the children accomplished before cold weather all the big structural work on the houses. They cut the doors and windows, and this second year roofed the buildings with shingles instead of tar paper, doing a very creditable job, too. When the houses came inside for the winter, village life went on in dramatic play, which included trucking and transporting of goods, people, milk, and food.

Miss Carlisle planned a series of trips that would give the children more information along these lines. As the class was large, she took a committee only and made the trip after school hours. Parents helped with cars and almost always some mothers went along. The class decided which children were to go, selecting the ones who especially needed the information the trip would give. The committee that went had a great deal to tell the class on their return. The trip showed them things that they were familiar with, sometimes things they had not seen or had not noticed before. They had gone to Harrod's Creek and to Prospect in the fall. They went also to Lyndon, where there is a freight station and a greenhouse. Later, they went into Louisville to watch the loading of foodstuffs and building materials on one of the Ohio River boats, and also to see the wholesale markets. They made these trips as a matter of study, and they took the trip at the time they were ready for it.

PIONEER LIVING IN KENTUCKY: FOURTH GRADE

The Fourth Grade program by its very nature is based [wrote Miss Sheffield in her Year-End Report, 1929–30] upon this environment and of necessity has found factors in it to be of great use. It is not only because we have studied Kentucky pioneer life that it has so close a connection with things about us, but because we have studied processes that still exist, or have a counterpart, in this community.

We have received much help from the places, people, and things of the countryside. A corner of the Stone Quarry and some poles served for our lean-to. A deaf and dumb man in Harrod's Creek gave us some forked sticks for the outdoor fireplace. Katey Bradford, who lives at the foot of the School lane, loaned us her big black pot. At the State Fair I saw gourds exhibited. I took the man's address and found his farm, and he gave us the few gourds he had left. We hollowed those out, and later one of the children brought more in. We saved the seeds and planted them this spring; some of the children planted seeds at home also. Early in the fall, Mr. Eifler, the head gardener, took us on a trip over Mrs. Ballard's place, and we collected walnut, hickory, and maple barks and hickory nuts, to use in dyeing. When we first whittled spoons and made brooms, we found the wood right outside our door. It was one of the children who knew which kind of wood to use.

The passion of many of the wealthier families for collecting old things, and the relics handed down from one generation to another in the country families, the loan of a spinning wheel, a churn, pieces of linsey-woolsey, and the black pot, have aroused interest and made pioneer life real. Several trips also served as stimulation: the trip to Fort Harrodsburg, to the Belknap farm to see the sheep, and to Wolfpen Mill where corn is still ground by water power, and to the worsted mill in Louisville.

The familiarity of some children with farming helped make real the problem of flax-raising. The freshet in the meadow was used to ret our flax. We put it on the side of the creek where the pigs were not nosing around. When we were preparing the ground in the Quarry for our first flax patch we did some experiments on germination and soils. From flax pulled right from the fields we made thread—hackling, scutching, braking, and finally spinning and weaving it.

Since sheep are so abundant down here, there was a great deal to call on in our wool study. John owned two sheep and Brian's grandfather had them on his place. We were able to examine them closely at the Belknap farm. We learned about sheep: how they differed in other countries; how they are cared for, etc. After going through the processes of washing, sorting, carding, spinning, and weaving wool, we took a trip into Louisville to the American Woolen Company's worsted mill. The man who showed us around showed us the Kentucky wool and how it differed from the foreign wool. We saw it go through machine processes similar to those we had done by hand. We saw it all packed and ready to be sent to the weaving mill. The children in Shop had made a study of the evolution of looms. So that through their own work and experiences they made the connection between sheep—the processes—yarn and cloth.

Our latest study has been of corn, so familiar to them and yet so lacking in any meaning except as cattle food. Mrs. Ballard gave us a fertile piece of ground in which to plant corn. She also gave us corn to plant, and the Sawyers gave us corn to grind. We made meal by pounding and grinding the corn with stones; over an outdoor fireplace we made this into "journey cakes." We also parched corn. However simple, the process of making corn into meal has a wealth of historic, economic and industrial, scientific, and even literary associations. We made a sweep and mortar mill, talked of the hand and horse power stamp mills, and visited the old Wolfpen Mill which is driven by water over an overshot water wheel. Half of our garden in the Quarry has been planted with corn, after studying what conditions would be good for it.

So you can see that in a simple and active way we have been dealing with agriculture and industry. We have done the hand processes, and they have enabled us to understand the machine processes. We have revealed to the children, I am confident, the dependence of industry upon agriculture. Our School is situated between the complicated modern industrial city and the simple, somewhat primitive, agricultural country. Each child feels both influences, some more of one, some more of the other. Our task has been to try to interpret and give meaning to both. By our vegetable dyeing we showed the use of bark, berries, and nuts commonly met in the country. We have also tried out crude mordants, which are at present a matter of scientific research.

This material seemed to be exactly right for children of this age in Kentucky. They lived it out with complete absorption. Somehow it is very satisfying to children to share in all the things that have to be done in such a home. They like to wash and prepare wool, card it, spin it, and weave it; to ret, hackle, and brake the flax, spin and weave it; to make soap, dip candles, and dye with nuts and tree bark and vegetables. They enjoy the job of making the pegged log stools and half-log benches.

The old journals of the early travelers proved a great source of interest to the children. The kinds of things that the travelers noticed and the sort of events they recorded are very much the same kinds of things which the children would have noticed and recorded. Although the strange spelling of the diaries amused the children, the language seemed natural to them. They quickly identified themselves with the whole experience. It was something like their own lives, with the meanings brought out, stripped of hardship and tinged with romance. They showed an amazing power to absorb and use the facts that reconstructed the experience of pioneer living.

The adventures of a pioneer family coming to Kentucky were relived by the children in dramatic play, and by November of the first year the Fourth Grade enacted for the other classes in the School *A Night at the Old Lean-To,* out in the old Stone Quarry behind the School.

The play opens in front of a trapper's lean-to. One trapper is cleaning his gun; the other is looking for his scraper, which has not been seen since he used it to scrape a buffalo hide a few days before. They hear the sound of voices. The travelers prove to be Daniel Boone, his wife and children, and Squire, his brother, who have come from North Carolina through Virginia and over the Wilderness Trail to Kentucky. They are weary and hungry, and the men decide to go hunting for food. Mrs. Boone sends one of the boys to the spring for water, and Hannah, one of the girls, goes in search of berries for supper, cautioned, however, by her mother to take one of the other children with her and not to wander far. A meal is made of the mush Mrs. Boone has cooked and the squirrel the men have brought in. Israel, the boy, returns with the news that the old Jersey that they brought along with them has a calf, and they decide to stay a few days until it is strong enough to travel and Mrs. Boone has had a chance to do some washing. Night draws on, and the women and children settle down to sleep on the leaf beds in the lean-to, while the trappers volunteer to keep watch. During the night the child Hannah gets up to get a drink of water. Finding none in the bucket, she takes the dipper and goes to the spring alone. Consternation runs high when Mrs. Boone, aroused, discovers she is missing and Daniel and his brother Squire go off to find her. Daniel follows her tracks along a creek to an Indian encampment and, waiting his chance until the Indians are asleep, he rescues his daughter, and Mrs. Boone gives them all breakfast on their return.

The older spectators at the play, which held the School's absorbed attention from start to finish, felt poignantly the fact that it depicted only too well the daily cabin life some of the children knew; the pioneer life was their life still.

KENTUCKY LIFE IN 1840: EIGHTH GRADE

For the purposes of contrast and comparison, the description of the work of an older class follows that of the Fourth Grade. It is quoted from the account written by George Beecher of the High School, which was published with that of Miss Sheffield under the title: "Plays in a Kentucky Public School." [1]

The Eighth Grade was studying the period in American History between the settlement of Kentucky and 1840, when Kentucky was an active participant in the development of the Middle West. The emphasis of the study was on the Jacksonian era, which saw the rise of western democracy, the growth of rail and river boat communication, and the opening of the Mississippi Valley. Since the Ohio River runs in front of the School, only a few hundred yards away, and the old type sternwheel packets still steam up and down, the phase of history was already well fixed in the minds of the children. The River and, in addition, the still rural character of the life of the people in this community, offered a setting out of which dramatic activities could easily spring.

Without having in mind the possibilities of drama, the class studied intensively the period between 1830 and 1840, confining its attention largely to the Ohio Valley, except where necessity made reference to other regions. In studying the building of the first railroad in Kentucky, the members of the class who were writing reports on the mechanical problems had to extend their vision to the East, where the Baltimore and Ohio Railroad had preceded the Kentucky builders by several years. In reporting on

[1] *Progressive Education,* January 1931, p. 35.

river boats, likewise, attention had to be given to Eastern shipbuilders.

Various phases of the period were worked out by other members of the class to make the picture of 1840 life as real as possible. One or two children, who were totally unsuited to making useful research, found themselves gradually in the history program through painting scenes which would contribute to the class project as a whole. One boy, in particular, was fond of an old mill, several miles up in the country, where grain had been ground for an unknown number of years. He was not sure at first what value a painting of the scene would have. For a long while, he was disgruntled at his work. But when a drama began to take shape out of the diverse ideas of the class, he felt a growing pride in his scene of the mill. It was developed into the setting for the first act of the play.

Stories by the other members of the class, who exercised some choice of subjects on river life, costumes of the period, conversation, the political campaigns and stories of feuds, all reached the stage of vividness and relish which would be unified at one stroke for the whole class by the writing and production of a play. The character of the life of the period, scarcely less rough than the pioneer, though intermixed with civilization, appealed to the Eighth Grade as strongly as pioneer or Indian life to the Fourth Grade; and a cast of plantation owners, river men, blustering adventurers, independent farmers, cultured ladies, was eagerly supplied.

When the slow process of composing the four-act drama under the title of *The Old Mill Feud* was completed, immediate steps were taken to produce the play. The setting for the first act was almost entirely managed by the painter of the mill scene, who had so long hesitated to share in the activities. The second act and the third required a scene along the Ohio River, which was painted by the girls of the class. The second act and the third required the forepart of an actual river boat, because the action revolved around the landing of a packet at the Louisville stage. The third act required the representation of an 1840 train, which was to bring the campaigners for Harrison and Tyler. The difficulties of providing these two vehicles of transportation were already partially solved by a previous study of the evolution of American transportation which the boys had made in the Shop. Several models—a flatboat, a Conestoga wagon, and early trains—had been drawn or worked in wood. Transferring the ideas onto beaver board was a difficult but only slightly more advanced project for the boys. The setting for the fourth act was provided by a girl who was interested in the domestic architectural styles of 1840 and in the new antique furnishings of the interior. Costumes for the girls proceeded from a combination of history research and practical sewing work, which was part of the girls' home economics course. The costumes for the boys demanded outside help.

The play was enlivened by contention between two rival mill owners for water rights, by campaign speeches and songs, by a party given in honor of a visiting congressman and governor, by humorous byplay of Negro servants, by the romance of an engagement, and by a race between two steam packets, *The Diana* and *The Eclipse,* won by the latter through the assistance of an old lady, a passenger. This incident was authentic. The children discovered it in their reading and were delighted to use it in the play. In the scene at the Louisville landing stage, the old lady, in response to the proud captain's invitation, tells the story to the crowd gathered to watch the end of the race:

The first day I was on board, I went to the Captain and said: "Now, Captain, I am going to the city with my produce. I don't want you to do any racing, young man, while I'm on this boat, but after I get off you can speed as fast as you please." But as we went a little slow, there was a boat that wanted to get ahead of us. I told the Captain it would be all right to go a little faster; I hated to see that other old boat get ahead of us. The Captain said: "We are going as fast as we can on the fuel we have, Madam." I then said: "Captain, you take the ten barrels of lard down on the main deck. Take 'em, Captain, and use 'em for fuel, but don't you dare let that other boat beat us."

The play acted well; only one line of the script had to be changed when it was put in rehearsal.

COMING TO KENTUCKY BY TRAIL AND RIVER: FIFTH AND SIXTH GRADES

After a comparison of the way in which the younger classes studied farms, villages, and pioneers in Kentucky with the work of the Eighth Grade in their study of the period of 1830–1840, it may be interesting to see how a middle class—the Fifth and Sixth Grades—dealt with their material. This class presented a difficult learning situation, not because of the great divergence in their abilities and achievements, though this existed, but because the morale of the group was poor when we first came to know them. The class had, before we came, been one of the most unruly in the school, frequently dividing into clans and cliques which made their own excitement by various kinds of feuds and wars. When Mr. Howard began to live and work with this group, he was wise enough from the outset to let in plenty of air on all matters under discussion. To quote from his Year-End Report for 1929–30:

The outstanding characteristics of the group, as I saw them in September, were an overwhelming vigor and an inordinate desire for self-expression through the spoken word. It was pretty clearly indicated that the past history of the class was represented by unsuccessful attempts to repress both of these assets. My problem was to make use of them. The record of the present fifth grade year has been, more than anything else, a contribution to the art of living together.

In the first year of his work with the class, Mr. Howard spent a great deal of patient effort in teaching the children how to read understandingly; how to get information from books; and how to report and share this with others. So the class approached its second year of work well equipped along these lines.

In the fall of 1930, Mr. Howard described to a group of parents the work of the group in its second year:

One half of the class is making a special point of finding out about Daniel Boone and the other families who lived near him on the Yadkin River in North Carolina.

The children have a trail over the hillside back of the School which leads to the top of the cliff over the Stone Quarry. This trail was worked out by one of the boys who is taking the part of Daniel Boone. When he comes back home, the neighbors from far and near gather to hear about his trip. He has many wonderful things to tell them about the new country through which he has gone, and especially about the fine, rich land which he has seen from a high cliff along a beautiful river. Some of the men want to go with him the next time. Many of the women are afraid to have their husbands take what they think is a very dangerous journey; but the men, most of them, are eager to go. They tell about the high taxes which they have to pay, and how this keeps them always poor even though they work hard on their little farms. At last, Daniel and five men make the trip again; this time they go farther into the new country. When they come back they finally decide to move to Kentucky with their families. Then comes the actual journey over the trail, following the blazes on the trees that Daniel and the men have made, and the building of homes in the new lands.

The other half of the class is taking the part of settlers who reached Kentucky by coming down the Ohio River on flatboats. They live in different parts of the East: New Jersey, New York, Connecticut, Massachusetts, Pennsylvania. They are all sorts of people, in all sorts of businesses, although some are farmers, too. They keep hearing about the new lands down the Ohio River where large pieces of land can be bought very cheap. These lands are said to be so rich that they will grow wonderful crops. Living is cheap because the woods are full of game and wild fruits and nuts.

Finally a town meeting is called in one of the Eastern towns, and the whole matter is talked over. Like their neighbors of North Carolina, some think it a fine idea to move to the new lands; some do not. But, finally, a large group decides to set out for Kentucky. They take with them what they can of their household goods. They have to cross the whole of the State of Pennsylvania before they come to the Ohio River and the flatboats that will carry them to their new homes.

When the pioneers reach Pittsburgh, or Redtown, or Wheeling—as the case may be—they either themselves build, or buy, a boat for the rest of the trip. It is a flatboat or an "ark," and is often called "a Kentucky boat." They buy a copy of Zadock Cramer's *Guide to the Ohio River,* so that they will know how to keep their boat off the shoals and banks and islands when the water of the River is high, and where the settlements are along the River where they may buy flour, meat, fruit, bacon, etc. They fit up the inside of the boat so that it is something like a house, put their cows and horses on board with the family, and begin floating down the Ohio.

They have many adventures on the way. Like the people on the Wilderness Trail, they are in constant danger from Indians. Finally, however, they reach Maysville, where some of them land; others go on until they are stopped at the mouth of Beargrass Creek [2] because of the falls in the Ohio River which are dangerous to pass. They set up homes for themselves in little settlements or forts. Gradually they get in touch with other settlements in Kentucky. More and more people arrive.

Everybody in the class is working on the two big topics, but at the same time each boy or girl is working on something of his or her own. Some of the Ohio River group are taking the part of farmers back East before they set out for Kentucky; some are fishermen, one is a blacksmith, another a captain of a sailing ship, one is a storekeeper.

As the children worked upon topics they had themselves selected, they began to identify themselves with these people. The boy who looked up surveying began to think of himself as a surveyor living at this time; the boy who investigated land speculation came to see himself as Henderson; the girl who studied Mrs. Boone's life almost believed that she was Mrs. Boone. As they studied into these times, they found a great many things and people that were in their own circle of acquaintances: river men and farmers, hunters, traders, mill owners, inn keepers, planters, fathers, mothers, and children. They personally knew all these kinds of people.

They were interested in all they could find out about salt and the salt licks, and the trading that went on there; about

---

[2] Beargrass Creek, familiar to all the children, was on the School side of Louisville.

lumbering, farming, tailoring, and the clothes of the time; about a blacksmith and a miller; about flatboats, river navigation, and river pirates. In this study every possible source of information was drawn on: books of all kinds, some bought or borrowed by the School, others lent by parents; agricultural bulletins, statistics—anything at all that gave the children the information they sought. Family treasures and relics, museum collections, and the duplicate of an old fort at Harrodsburg to which the class took a trip, all served to make what they read real to them.

The class did an excellent piece of research work. And it had added vitality because it was research into matters that were still of absorbing interest to both older and younger Kentuckians. Their work was the kind of work that eleven- and twelve-year-olds are able to do. It was not the kind of research that either the fourteen- and fifteen-year-old students of the Eighth Grade or the nine- and ten-year-old children of the Fourth Grade would have done. It was typical of a sixth grade capacity; but, in the amount that they accomplished, in the quality of the work and the vigor of it, their study far outstripped a usual sixth grade performance. The very characteristics that had made the class formerly unruly and unmanageable proved to be invaluable when they were redirected. The class had many able members; this, of course, is practically always true of unruly classes.

The play given by the Sixth Grade at the end of the second year—*Big River—Little Trail*—was exclusively the work of the children themselves, down to the costumes, which were planned and made by the four girls of the class. The scene on the Trail, with Daniel and his brother Squire hacking at the vines and bushes to clear a path, while the party waited for another family traveling through to catch up with them, was very convincing; as was also the scene on the flatboat with some of the party engaged in steering and directing the course down the River, and others whiling away the time by dancing a shakedown on the roof to the fiddle tune of "Turkey in the Straw," and all hands ducking below at an Indian attack from the shore. At the mill by the salt lick a great deal of trading went forward, and much gossip and exchange of news passed back and forth. But it was in the scene at the Town Hall in Philadelphia where the land speculator and the surveyor sold lots in "Kentuckee" to a fur merchant, a blacksmith, a farmer, a lumberman; where the trapper agreed to consider the matter but the printer, the shipbuilder, and the miller turned down the proposition and were inclined to think it "was all a fraud," that the children did the best piece of individual characterization. The scene was replete with humor.

Not long ago [Mr. Howard reported to the parents] a few boys were acting out the scenes of the Boones on the Trail. Little Jimmie Boone pretended that he had tripped over a log and hurt his leg. Someone suggested that mullein was something the pioneers might have used for a sore leg. The children said they would have found it growing on the hillsides.

The next day four people brought to School mullein which they had growing near their homes. They talked about the kind of ground it likes to grow in, how tall it grows, about its flower stalk. One of the girls had talked to her grandfather, eighty years old, who had told her that the leaves could be dipped in hot water and placed between cloths, and tied around the place of the sore, bruise, or pain. I said that perhaps someone would like to make a picture of the mullein stalk. One of the boys liked the idea. He said there were other plants which the pioneers had used for medicine. He wants to find these, and write an account of how each was used.

He did so. The information and illustrations were made into a book called *Dr. Johnson's Medicine Book* (after the author), and contained descriptions and recipes and illustrations of such herbs as horehound, ginseng, mullein, jimson, castor bean, everlasting, slippery elm, boneset, peppermint, calamus, tobacco, fennel, catnip, May apple, and sumac. This was one of the country boys and his information came as much from his neighbors and classmates and their families as from any reading on the subject. This study revealed to us how much a knowledge of herbs and their use as medicine was still current in the countryside today, and gave us one more insight into the people's lives.

The foregoing programs illustrate the use of environment in a school's study of subject matters, and the ways in which it added to our knowledge of the community, and to the community's sharing in what the School taught. The programs that have been described, or their equivalents, could be carried out in any rural school interested in a study of the background and lives of its people, and in the educational use of material at hand.

The Health Program

HEALTH WORK, 1930–31

Physical Examinations and Nutrition Needs

Through the help of Mrs. Moore, President of the Parent Teachers Association, the plans made in the spring for a thorough physical examination of each child in the School began to be realized in the fall of 1930. A questionnaire was drafted, to be filled in by the mothers at home and by the physician who examined the child. Every family was urged to have its own physician make the examination, if possible. Out of the 208 children in School, 140 were not able to have this done by their family doctor. Through the Medical School of the University of Louisville, of which Dr. Moore, one of our parents, was the head, we were able to engage two well-trained pediatricians by the hour. The Parent Teachers Association, by means of a community supper at which the Sixth Grade's play, *Big River—Little Trail*, was presented, raised the money for this work. We turned first the School office and later the stage of the gymnasium into an examination clinic room. Our parents arranged so that a mother was always present to give the children reassurance and to help the doctor with the record.

Out of the 140 children examined, 109 were found to have some kind of bad posture, 73 were discovered to be suffering from malnutrition. Of these, 42 were reported as needing attention for bad tonsils and 30 were listed as tuberculosis suspects. These examinations gave us also further information about eyes and teeth. The School and the parents set to work to deal as rapidly as possible with these facts. Whatever was done had to be done by teachers who already had a full-time job on their hands and by parents who, although devoted and generous, were themselves busy mothers of families. As an approach to the problem of bad posture, Mrs. Moore arranged for two of the teachers to be taught by a doctor in Louisville simple exercises for the correction of typical posture defects. The two teachers in turn taught the other members of the staff. Arrangements were made for the posture group in each class to work at these exercises with the teacher. In the younger classes the exercises were so popular that everyone wanted to do them. An effort was also made to teach the exercises to their parents.

The parents, who were in the second year running the School lunchroom, planned to meet the nutrition needs through the lunch. One of the mothers, who had a large dairy farm, gave the School extra milk, and we also served mid-morning cocoa and crackers to all the undernourished children and to the tuberculosis suspect cases. These last were examined by the State Tuberculosis Association and the families instructed regarding rest routines, etc. Work in Home Economics had been added through a fund raised by the Parent Teachers; the cooking classes stressed nutrition, and one of the younger teachers took over the work of advising mothers at home about their food problems.

Six families of especially undernourished children were selected for special help. It had been in our minds that we might be able to plan with the mothers more nourishing suppers and breakfasts. It turned out that the help that they needed was, first of all, in buying. The mother of nine children was spending $1.75 a week for staple groceries. We found that we could spend it for her to much better advantage. It was apparent that this was the kind of help needed in the five other families also. Buying for these six families, she was able to buy flour by the sack, cereals in large quantities, crates of onions, tomatoes, and cabbages, etc. In this way, the School was able to save the families package costs, and also had the opportunity to introduce the kind of cereals and flour and vegetables that were beneficial dietetically. The mothers were greatly relieved by the help and very glad to have her do it. This experience opened our eyes to all sorts of possibilities in the way of co-operative buying, and suggested also the plan of canning and preserving surplus fruit and vegetables from the larger farms and estates during the summer under the direction of some of our competent country mothers.

THE BALLARD COUNTRY FAIR

In the spring we were able to carry out a plan, conceived by one of the mothers, for a School Country Fair. For some years past the School had held an annual Horse Show. It was proposed to hold a Fair with this which would exhibit some of the work and interests of the School children and adults. The first year, we encouraged everyone—the children and the adults, the neighbors and the people who lived anywhere about as well as the parents—to enter their sheep and chickens and cows and dogs and horses and pets, requiring only that the animals be in good condition. The year following we were able, with the help of the State and local agricultural agent and 4H groups, to make plans for the breeding of better stock and for instruction in the proper ways of tending it. Mrs. Ballard lent the School a field of rich soil, and we started class gardens of early vegetables, the farmer and gardener fathers assisting us in teaching the best ways of planting and cultivating them.[3] Some of the vegetables from the children's School gardens were exhibited at the Fair. The First Grade walked off with one of the first prizes.

The Fair gave everyone a good time, and was most successful. There were all kinds of booths and sideshows and a barbecue. Breads, cakes and pies, dresses, quilts, and fancy work were exhibited. The Booth of Kentucky Antiques, conducted by some interested parents assisted by Miss Lawton and Miss Sheffield, aroused great interest. There were a great many entries of household treasures by people from the countryside all around. Later an Art Booth was added which displayed work done by both the older people and the children.

In ways such as these the teachers and the parents together tried to meet the community's most urgent health needs. The School was used as the center for all these enterprises and its work expanded into unanticipated activities. We began to try to make out the meaning of these facts.

EXTENSION OF HEALTH AND SOCIAL WORK IN 1931–32

Woman's Food Exchange

In 1932, a co-operative market was started in the form of a "Woman's Exchange," at which chickens, eggs, milk, cream, pumpkins, mincemeat, sausages, cottage cheese, crullers, pies, fruit cake, jams, and preserves were sold. This was held on Fridays at the School to catch the week-end buying. In connection with it, we also ran a small "labor bureau." Carpen-

---

[3] To about fifty children in the School—the undernourished group—we gave, with the help of the Parent Teachers Association, seeds to raise at home. Ninety percent used them.

ters, painters, farm hands and outside men, plumbers and mechanics were numbered among the country fathers who needed work, and the School sought to connect them with jobs to be done. This practice grew up from instances of requests for such services from the wealthier group.

Follow-Up of Physical Examinations

Because of the fact that one of the student teachers, herself the daughter of a physician, was especially interested in health work, the health program was put on a firmer basis and moved ahead, if not as rapidly as the needs and our desires would have it, at least more steadily and systematically than before. Miss Hutchins's Report for the Year notes diphtheria shots given 16 children, and smallpox vaccinations given 14 new children by the County nurse in the fall; a mid-year examination by the County nurse of every child in School for weight, height, and defective teeth and tonsils; the visit of the County dentist, who treated 40 children at the School; and typhoid shots administered in the spring to 68 children. Regarding the tuberculosis suspects Miss Hutchins writes:

Last December, the nurse from the Tuberculosis Dispensary gave the skin test to 13 children who had not before had it. Eight of the children, who had positive reactions and took X-rays last year, have been on a routine of extra rest and nourishment this winter. The nurse has done a great deal of follow-up work with families at the School's request. . . .

Seven children have been fitted with glasses; 4 have been taken in to have their tonsils and adenoids removed (8 others had this done at home); 4 children have been taken in to the City Clinic; 15 were taken in to the City Hospital for re-examination and for an X-ray at the Tuberculosis Dispensary.

Her report makes no mention of the number of visits to these families that were required to put through a tonsil case, for instance: two or three visits to the home to gain the parents' consent and co-operation; another call to take the child to the hospital; a visit to the child in the hospital and a call on the home to report progress; another trip to bring the child home, followed by one or more visits to the home to check on care, nourishment, etc. In all, perhaps six to eight calls in the interests of parent health education.

In the third year, results began to tell. Miss Hutchins reports:

> Dr. Nicholson will have examined 145 children here at School by the end of this week (May 1). This means that for every child in School we now have two records—one of last year and one of this spring—for comparison.
>
> Dr. Nicholson tells me that he is finding fewer cases of very poor posture and real malnutrition, and that he feels that the health level of the whole School is better this year than it was last year.

Miss Hutchins made a routine of placing beside the child, for the doctor's consideration during the physical examination, a full report of the home conditions, together with any relevant material from the School's full analytical reports on the child by all his teachers.

Pre-School Clinics

On April 18, a child Health Conference was held here at the School by the State Board of Health for mothers and pre-school children. Twelve families were represented and 23 children. Seven mothers came with their babies to watch the examinations and to talk with the doctor about their children. The teachers and other mothers helped with cars for transportation.

Last summer, the Parent Teachers Association conducted a summer round-up of children who were to enter School in the fall.

This year, Dr. Veech of the State Tuberculosis Association is anxious to have a survey of *all* the pre-school children in the Ballard district.

Dr. Veech's desires were realized, and it became possible for preventive health work to start with the babies.

Hygiene Classes for Older Girls and Boys

We have started [Miss Hutchins reports] an elementary Hygiene Class this year with our Ninth and Tenth Grade girls. We have been studying how our bodies are made, how they work, and how we can best take care of them. We have begun to use the microscope, and have made a trip to the State Board of Health Laboratory.

Arrangements were made the next year for Hygiene classes for both boys and girls of Grades Six to Twelve with a man and a woman physician, respectively.

A Healthy Assembly Program

Another feature of the health work in 1931–32 was added by students, who in a May Day Health Assembly put on a program for their parents. The students gave talks on exercise and athletics, expressing their own convictions about their bearing on health; School gardens and the School Country Fair; the 4H Club they had formed; and Domestic Science. The youngest children demonstrated the putting-up of cots for midday rest, and posture exercises. It was a revelation to many of the parents. Clearly, the health program had now become the children's own enterprise.

The School a Recreation Center for the Community

BASKETBALL GAMES AND MOVIES

The May Day Assembly expressed realizations about health that had been gained in athletics and the recreation program, which had gone steadily forward each year. Out of the School's active recess-period games and the afternoon supervised sports had developed basketball teams, which in time played teams from other County high schools and neighboring towns and villages. These games came to be a feature of Saturday evenings, and drew an increasingly large crowd. In 1932–33 we experimented with occasional movies. The reception they met made us desire them as a weekly event. The next year Mrs. Ballard set up a revolving fund of $20; and two of our parents arranged for the films and brought their own projector and ran it for us. The admission charge was 5 cents for children and 10 cents for adults, with a generous number of passes for those who could not muster even the 5 cents. The size of the audiences—100 or more at the movies, and another 100 to 200 at the basketball games following—proved that these Saturday night entertainments filled a need in the neighborhood. The players held an annual Athletic Dinner, at which sweaters earned by the teams and bought by proceeds from game admissions were awarded by the fathers, and whose feast was prepared and served by the girls and the mothers.

In addition to the games and movies, the Parent Teachers annual harvest supper and entertainment, the spring School Fair, and also the class assemblies and the School's plays provided recreational opportunities for the neighborhood. The School kitchen and dining room, and the stage and assembly-gymnasium, were frequently used by non-school groups, such as hiking clubs of Louisville and the country parents' Homemakers Club, etc.

Formulation of the Concept of a Community School and of Social Studies

The next and third year of the School's work was marked by certain developments in the work of the classes. It witnessed also attempts to formulate our conception of a community school.

During the first year, the staff had studied subject matters as interests of men through the ages, and had especially reviewed History and Mathematics. In the second year, the staff course received university rating from the University of Louisville and dealt particularly with the principles and practices of progressive education. The staff continued its study of Mathematics and began a study of Language.

Some of the realizations about socially functioning subject matters to which our work had brought us, and which I had formulated in the summer of 1931, are reported here because they forecast trends in the work of the School for the next three years and because they further help to fill in the understanding of a socially functioning school.

The idea of a community school had, with us, been born of the opportunity that the Ballard School and situation seemed to offer. It was, at the outset, an idea only of what such a school might be and do, arising partly from a longing that education really function in people's lives, and partly from a growing feeling about America, and an interest in using its cultures and resources and its regional differences. With us it needed the experiences of work in a rural community to quicken our understanding of the conception of the school as a social institution that John Dewey had expressed forty years before. In a sense we learned it from Kentucky, or from attempting to bring it to pass in Kentucky.

SOCIAL STUDIES

What is meant by social study is study for enterprises essentially social in character of facts and subjects required for their execution. In a school of a community, a socially functioning school, the plan is to have educative experiences that will direct children's growth and enable them to participate intelligently and actively in the life of their community. The school uses the life at the school, the shared enterprises and the learning that results from them, as a means of interpreting to the children the meaning of their lives and of working together for common ends. In the work at school, which is a part of the work and life of the community, programs of classes, units of work, subject matters, are used instrumentally; and knowledge is sought about the problems and resources of the community.

A socialized school uses all the means of learning which a progressive school anywhere employs—but definitely for social ends. These ends change and vary, but they are usually specific, now focused at some one point, and now widened to cover more ground. Arrived at, they open up new leads. The undertakings of the school are characteristically shared by older people as well as children. There are undertakings where children do most of the learning; others where older people do nearly all; but in most social studies undertaken by a community school both children and adults learn—sometimes the same thing, sometimes different and complementary things. The enterprises are calculated to encourage growth and to accomplish something fairly definite, whose importance is more or less granted. Occasionally the school has to take the lead in meeting a need not yet commonly recognized.

These undertakings call on whatever anyone knows or can find out that will help—any relevant facts or ideas. From this angle, subject matters are resources, ways of finding out, methods to use, places to look for information. From a personal point of view, subject matters are men's interests. From a social point of view, they are usable facts that are available. Learning is, of course, always personal, and can be individualistic. But a community school has social ends of some sort in view, and arranges its plans and activities and gathers data for these. Social study would be, then, the selecting and organizing of data for use—for use by people for certain ends. Useful study—socially useful.

MATHEMATICS REVIEWED

We began to ask ourselves, what would Mathematics be as a social study? Mathematics, socially speaking, is a tool, a means. Just because it abstracts from a given situation, can express it in symbols and formulas, manipulate these, proceed to make equations, develop these, translate terms, deal with and express relationships, and, having reached its conclusion, its solution, return with it by substituted values to an actual situation—it can deal with situations which in concrete particular form suggest no solution or remedy. This leverage it is which today gives mathematics its practical importance. It functions in our human operations. Many situations may be expressed in mathematical terms. Reactions, motion, activity and interactivity, as well as time, measures, and money are susceptible of mathematical treatment.

Speaking individually, mathematics is an interest, an absorption, an enterprise. Functionally, it is social as well as logical. It deals, we thought as we studied it, with certain conceptions basically: such ideas as proportion, part and whole relations, groupings, equation, and substitution. As we went into these conceptions, we found them expressed also in daily happenings: practically, in carpentry, cooking, and building; culturally, in art and music; socially, in medicine, for instance; economically, of course, in industry; and, equally of course, logically, in science. These practical operations and forms could be used, we thought, in developing ideas basic to mathematical operations and thinking. From this point of view, mathematics became one mode of expression—a distinctly instrumental one—a method—a technique.

From another angle, we found that symbols, measures, counting, and such groupings as addition, subtraction, multiplication, and division, had their own histories, which are still in the making. The devices and instruments for these activities one could gather and collect and make. When the children made these mathematical instruments, which are also scientific and practical, and used them in situations where they needed them, they understood better, we found, the principles and processes they represented and accomplished.

All this was a matter of our own illumination, but it enfreed us to a more fundamental use of mathematics as a social instrumentality for use in education.

REVIEW OF LANGUAGE

We began the study of another one of the subject matter interests of men—language. Language is, of course, intrinsically social in its function, a means of sharing, of voicing, of recording. As a form of experiencing, it is itself, in a special sense, history—present or past. It testifies to man's inherently social nature as well as his individual existence. We were, in our study of language, bogged down for a time in our thinking in the morass of correct form in speech and writing. But presently we began to get a glimpse of the particular kind of expression that language is—shared meanings of experiences, relationship of ideas and feelings.

We considered ways to share these realizations with students. We felt as teachers largely responsible for attitudes and predispositions, for practices and conceptions, that withheld us from sensing the intrinsically social character that language has, and from making full use of its social function. We saw that we could make of expression and communication an art—a social art.

The study of history today which seeks facts regarding the activities of men and the conditions in which they lived—in rocks, trees and clay, fossils, bones, relics, tombs, mounds, caves, utensils, etc., as well as in manuscripts and pictorial records—we found extended our conception of language and its forms. So did also musical notation and mathematical symbols. We began to understand that the student of language had been held within *words* away from experiences that engendered them. Our initial study of language persuaded us to closer identification with *experiencing,* to actual occurrences of thinking and feeling and communicating, and to the impulses and enterprises of recording and recounting. On the psychological side, discovery of the uses of language for emotional release of the solitary and shy adolescents in our rural situation, and instances of clarification of judgments and action through language expression, as well as the language of children in dramatic play, illuminated our understanding of what language does and what may be its effects.

From these studies we began to wonder if perhaps we in education would not pass *through and out of* the phase of considering subject matter interests as different aspects or elements or emphases of man's living, *to* a study of life, including nature and society, *for different purposes*—a study which would be organized varyingly—now for an understanding of man's work, or of his relations with others; now of his curiosities and discoveries; now of his expression in art and music and language and drama; now of his use of resources and conditions; now of his methods of measuring and computing. Particular needs and shared purposes might counsel now this, now that, organization of material. Studies such as these would be social, not only because socially motivated and used, but also intrinsically, being aspects or emphases of a social whole. We do not need to debate the point that so-called "pure" studies, however methodologically removed and aloof and cherished for their own sake, are human enterprises after all and function socially within living.

By following out these ideas to see where they would lead us we were impelled to the belief in subjects as organizations of experience, and in education as functioning experiences social in nature.

This excursion into the realm of ideas is given because it was basic to, at least preliminary to, our understanding and use of studies as socially functioning, on which our work for the following years in Kentucky, and later in Arthurdale, was based.

Developments in Programs and Study of Resources, 1931-34

By 1931, the School's relations with the University of Louisville had resulted in courses for city and county teachers which I gave at the University on the principles and practices of progressive education, and in work with these teachers individually on the reorganization of the content and procedures of their own curricula and schools; also in a course given by Miss Lawton, the Shop teacher, on the use of Industrial Arts in active learning, and in the use of the Ballard School Shop as a working center for the graduate students. Out of these connections grew the University's practice of using the School as an observation center for their students in Education, and of assigning to the School several of these students for practice teaching. These contacts gave us a realistic acquaintance with the problems of teachers in the country and city schools about us, and made it clear how we could be of service to them.

FURTHER STUDY OF RESOURCES OF THE ENVIRONMENT

Through Mr. John Beard, a member of the University class, we gained more information and a vivid picture of early days in the district in southern Indiana in which he lived. Mr. Beard's mother had been a well-known weaver and spinner; Mrs. Beard's family had kept a roadside inn on what was now one of the main highways across the State. They had seen the evolution of this highway from a trail and log road to a dirt road and, finally, to a paved highway. An old teacher of Mr. Beard had come out to this territory in a covered wagon, a duplicate of which he had made and kept in his barn. Mrs. Martin, Mr. Beard's sister, was willing to let the School have an old hand loom that belonged to her family, and came over to help us set it up. Mr. Beard talked with the Fourth Grade about pioneer days, and brought to them pieces of linsey-woolsey and of hand-raised and hand-woven linen. Miss Sheffield, the teacher of the Fourth Grade, and I visited the farm home of Mrs. Martin, who was president of a historical society and was interested in the old land grants, diaries, and letters, which she had among her family treasures. With her we visited some famous weavers, driving down a muddy lane in a farm wagon hitched to farm horses, fording a stream, passing under the trees of a great beech woods and near a salt lick, and finally coming to a clearing and the cabin of the two sisters, now well on in life, who had brought "coverlids" with them from North Carolina, and who had spent their lives spinning and weaving. The Beards and their friends were typical of many of the country families in the region.

The staff became better acquainted, also, with the cultural resources of the city of Louisville: with its Art Museum, its Arts Club, and its socially functioning Art Center; with its library and forums; and with all the interests and stimulation of its University, its Woman's Club, and its important and helpful historical society—the Filson Club.

Our explorations through the State revealed to us a historical interest, an awareness of historical tradition, which nothing but active investigation on foot and by car would have discovered. These experiences opened our eyes to the indigenous culture of remote rural regions. They, I know, influenced our thinking and our later enterprise in another rural region of the neighboring State of West Virginia. More than that, they made clear to us the degree to which country people themselves value and wish to preserve their past. We found exhibits of early utensils, farm implements, lights and early lamps, costumes, and some earlier furniture in the most unexpected places: in a house in a small river town in southwestern Kentucky along the Ohio, and in the old mills in southern Indiana, for example.

From an antique dealer in Madison, Indiana, I learned of the restoration by the State Indiana Historical Society of Spring Mill Village. This had been an early Indiana village of craftsmen situated beside a rushing stream which was led down from the ravine above it by a kind of aqueduct to turn the great overshot wheel of the mill that ground corn into meal, and to turn a stationary sawmill. The Historical Society was slowly restoring the stone houses and the log cabins of the weaver, the spinner, the hat-maker, the miller. Still standing were the old postoffice and the apothecary's shop, with its old counters and the drawers marked with the names of medicinal herbs and spices. The Society was re-equipping this shop with the medical charts and the weights and measures with which it had originally been furnished. I came upon the Village after hours of search just at dusk when the new moon lighted the tall stone house-chimneys, caught the glint on the rushing stream, and flooded the inner garden of herbs and flowers and little fruit trees. Almost it seemed as if the weaver and his wife, the miller, and the hat-maker might step from their doors for an evening's chat. Although we visited the Village many times afterward and watched the slow and faithful assembling of furniture and the utensils of daily living in the restored houses, and often came to look at the collection of lights and lamps housed on the upper floors of the great mill, which illustrated the history of lighting as well perhaps as any collection in this country, I never recaptured the spirit of the place as completely as on that cold fall moonlit night.

On March 28, 1931, an Old Fiddlers' Concert was held in Jefferson County at the Eastwood School. The players competed on fiddles, banjos, guitars, the piano, and the French harp. The program included also yodeling, jigging, blowing of the fox horn, and hog-calling. The events were by name new to us: "Fiddler Coming Greatest Distance," "Fiddler with Largest Family," "Best-Looking Fiddler," etc.; but we soon felt the excitement of the audience and the performers and realized that judgment was passed upon points of excellence not always clear to us laymen. Individuals and business concerns had offered prizes of one or two dollars; other prizes consisted of 24 pounds of flour, 2 pairs of silk hose, cakes, and a dozen baby chicks. Correspondence a few days later with the Eastwood principal elicited the names and addresses of the contestants, and questioning of the Ballard School children brought out the fact, unrealized by us before, that a good many fiddlers and performers of various sorts were numbered among our fathers and the friends of our families. We communicated with a number of them and later ourselves gave an "old fiddlers' concert" as part of a Parent Teacher entertainment. It was, however, not until we were in West Virginia that we really came to know the musicians of the countryside, participated in their music with them, and gathered them together in a Music Festival; and in the School, under the tutelage of a back-country fiddle-maker, commenced to make fiddles ourselves. But it was the Old Fiddlers' Contest at the Jefferson County school in Kentucky, and the later gathering together of some fiddlers for a concert at the Ballard School, that opened our eyes to the cultural opportunity these arts afforded.

NEW DEVELOPMENTS IN THE PROGRAMS

Among the factors in the development of the material we used with the children at the School were: the opportunities, expanding under our widening acquaintance with the countryside, to use our rural Kentucky environment educationally; our consideration of what might constitute a rounded and complete "education" for the children; the increasing demand for material and studies fundamental to an understanding of regional conditions and opportunities; and our changing conception of the function of subject matter in a community school.

Economic Geography

Further understanding of the educational import of the environment came with an investigation of resources in a study made with the older boys and girls in what we called Economic Geography; and in the way our Shop class in "Home Repairs" seemed to touch off vocational needs.

The boys studied first their own farms—division of the land into pasture, cultivated fields, and woodland; the crops raised, and the ways of marketing them. They discussed fertilizers, the rotation of crops, and stock raising—this by way of considering together in class problems with which they were intimately familiar. They sought help from agricultural stations and Government bulletins. They studied the relative importance of different crops raised in Jefferson County, charting their acreage and value. One of the boys, who had for years been going to market with and for his father, charted the sources of the Louisville markets' supply. The class studied the importance of Louisville as a manufacturing and marketing center. Members of the class each took a county in the State to report on: one in the coal mining section, one in the Burley tobacco region, one in the district producing dark pennyroyal tobacco, one in the Paducah district.

The girls studied especially foods and garden produce; planting, cultivation, and rotation of crops; co-operative marketing; and textile handicrafts. They studied soils intensively and particularly investigated corn. Of great help in the soil experiments was one of the fathers who was an expert gardener; and in the corn study the class's work was greatly assisted by a father who was a graduate of Berea College.

Home and School Repairs

The older boys had by 1931-32 a regular class in "Home Repairs," which was a natural outcome of the practice that had obtained from the beginning of our work at the School of appointing as repair-carpenters students who had a special aptitude for this work. They began by mending broken cupboard doors and making shelves and bookcases the School needed, and took on enterprises from time to time in answer to current needs—like a garden tools rack, baseball bleacher benches, scenery for plays, etc. As we came to know the community better, and realized how useful such skill was on the farm and in the houses (always in need of repairs), and how it increased the value of a handy man to be able to do such jobs well, Miss Lawton felt that the School would be evading its obligations not to offer such a course for the boys. In 1932-1933, the class also did some work in plumbing and electrical repairs, with the help of one of the men teachers, Harry Carlson, which saved the County a considerable amount of money.

The boys gained a good deal of proficiency in this work. They became increasingly able to direct themselves, and enjoyed their own competency. In 1933-34, the dinginess and disrepair of the old School buildings impressed all the children. With the assistance of these older boys and the men teachers, all the classes took hold and repainted their own classrooms and the School hallways, repairing broken plaster, etc., as they went along.

Building the Log Cabin

In 1930-31, the Seventh and Eighth Grades, studying the earlier stretch of Kentucky history as part of an American history program and stimulated by visits to an old fort at Harrodsburg, decided to build a log cabin in the Quarry, where so many of the School's enterprises took place. It was decided to make the cabin 11 by 13 feet—a little smaller than the birthplace of Abraham Lincoln—and a sheltered spot under the cliff was selected for it.

The next fall, when the cabin was finished, the parents and School friends were invited to a housewarming. The Fourth Grade, dressed in pioneer costumes, joined with the older children and enacted around the cabin all the activities of a pioneer home. One group was engaged in washing, sorting, carding and fluffing, spinning, and weaving wool; another group in braking, hackling, scutching, spinning, and weaving flax. A group of boys over a fire were pouring lead into a bullet mold; some women were cooking over an outdoor fireplace; and a group was grinding corn at the hominy block. An old settler sat in the cabin doorway smoking his corncob pipe. The scene was convincing, and the parents learned a great deal from sharing in it.

After this event, the cabin served as a museum. It had been furnished with pioneer furniture and utensils made by the younger classes and with rugs which the older girls had woven for it. It was used by the Fourth Grade for reliving pioneer experiences and was the scene of many plays. The countryside was greatly interested in it, and people from round about visited it Sundays as well as weekdays.

A Community Magazine and Weekly News Sheet

Class magazines and School journals had been produced since the first year by the older classes. Even the students who found writing hard were interested in the telling of stories. The upper classes wrote special reports and articles, and mimeographed a monthly magazine of poems, stories, and articles. For two years the older students had studied the History of Records, in both the Shop and the classroom. By 1933–1934, the Tenth Grade magazine was called *A Community Magazine,* and the Ninth Grade, with the purchase by the School of a second-hand printing press for $16, started a weekly news sheet. It began with a one-page edition, increased in its third issue to two pages and in its fifth to four pages, as the printers' skill developed. In the fourth issue and thereafter, a vigorous editorial appeared always on the last page. The sheet carried reports of the work of all the classes, athletic news, and general School information.

The paper was read by parents and neighbors and, since the School news was so much the news of the events of the community, it had a large sale in the grocery stores of the next villages. We learned a good deal ourselves about the technique of issuing such a newspaper, and saw all kinds of possibilities in a community paper.

It will be seen, then—though I have perforce used only a few illustrations—that we had been trying out in the programs enterprises that might have interpretive value in the children's lives, as well as learning about the ways of life and habits of thought and action of country people.

One side of the work, along more strictly cultural lines, I have omitted here. It would be interesting to disclose how great an aptitude untutored children in a rural district, many of whom had had no contact with the usual cultural agencies, showed in appreciation and in scholarship. All the basic elements of "culture" are, of course, to be found in the country. Country people, more perhaps than the city dweller, understand the sun and the seasons, seedtime and harvest, the stars and the rocks, the rain and the rivers, the trees and the flowers, and the effects of heat and cold. If understandings are built with them upon what they know and have experienced, there is nothing in the arts and the sciences, in history or literature, that they cannot grasp. And when they grasp these facts and ideas, they can bring to their apprehension a depth of understanding and a wealth of experiences in the fundamentals of living that make of astronomy a vital experience, of botany a familiar practice, of history a matter of reliving men's problems and enjoyments. We had no difficulty in sharing with them our cultural interests. There was more to be done, I think retrospectively, in discovering and fostering their own. I have instanced how we began to glimpse possibilities in music and historical tradition. In West Virginia we went much further in finding and fostering indigenous cultural resources.[4]

A Community School's Relations with Its Families

There is a great deal said in calling a school "a community school." It is a *public school,* and therefore the school of the people of that district. The Ballard School of Jefferson County is a school to which both poor and rich children go. For twenty-odd years children of the three groups of families—the owners of estates, business and professional men; the farmers, dairy owners, gardeners, and mechanics; the farm tenants, truckmen, and handy men—have all gone to school together, and parents of all these groups have worked in the School and given to it. It is therefore a community's school in very fact, and itself a democracy.

Teachers as neighbors. The teacher in a community school has a real function in the community. The teachers at the Ballard School live near it, most of them close by, either with families or in cottages on the farms and estates. We know our parents as neighbors. We live our lives in the community. We belong there. The work at School is part of our living. Our living is part of the School.

The parents share in the work of the School. They run the lunchroom, buying the food, planning menus, superintending its finances. Extra milk for mid-morning cocoa for undernourished children, and extra milk and soup in cases of illness,

---

[4] See Chapter V, "Cultural Resources and Opportunities," pp. 217 ff.

are given by some of the mothers. The money which enables the School to have the children examined by a trained pediatrician is raised by the mothers, as are also the funds for Domestic Science and for courses in Hygiene given to the boys and girls by a man and woman physician. Mothers, with teachers, are hostesses at the Saturday night basketball games. The movies preceding the games are run by two of our parents. Several mothers run the School's fiction lending library, on Fridays for the children, and on Saturday nights for the adults. The Woman's Exchange was the idea of one mother, as was also the annual School Country Fair. It is a parent—also our County Trustee—who lends the School his meadows as playing fields.

Our relations with the parents are those of intimate daily contacts. The health and social work of the School takes us constantly into the homes of those parents who cannot get down to the School. And the work at the School that the parents do brings many of them to School daily at all hours. The mothers are always taking some of the children into the city clinics or going with the classes on trips. Teachers and parents do many enjoyable things together—suppers and picnics, walks and rides, concerts, forums, and plays. The School is a co-operative enterprise. Its work is sustained by funds contributed by the County Board of Education, by parents, by teachers, and also by friends and neighbors who have no children in the School. We—the families and the teachers and the children—share belief in the School's work and ideals.

The Social-Education Work of a Rural Community School

Typically, the School began by answering needs and by using its facilities to this end. It faced immediately the need for including health measures in its activities. The dominant features of this work were prescribed by the needs of the children and families in the underprivileged homes. The effort to meet these needs took the School into unexpected lines of endeavor—beyond wholesome lunches to School gardens and help in co-operative buying for families, and on to a Country Fair, to forming a 4H Club, and to launching a Woman's Exchange; beyond classes in sewing and cooking to efforts to better living conditions; beyond routine County health examinations and inoculations to individual examinations by a physician and the establishment of a recurring clinic for mothers and babies.

The leads from this work extended in every direction. No extra assistance for these services was supplied. They were done under the School's direction, now by a student teacher, and now by the wife of a staff member, assisted in every possible way by parents and teachers and by the County and city health agencies. Therefore it was an enterprise demanding effort mainly and a little money—about $250 a year, which was raised by community entertainments given by our Parent Teacher organization. This any community—country or city—could, if it wished, probably duplicate.

Another need the School faced was that of recreation. The games and sports, started as a health measure, became a source of entertainment and enjoyment to the whole neighborhood. The movies, School plays and assemblies, community suppers, and the Fair were welcomed by the children and the families. "Somewhere to go on a lonesome night," one of the girls put it. The only other recreational facilities in the neighborhood were pool rooms, beer and ice cream parlors, dance halls, and, occasionally, church suppers and entertainments, and the not always desirable talk among the men lounging at night in the grocery stores and garages. Recreational facilities, where they are not otherwise supplied, become the responsibility of a school—and its opportunity.

The school is a natural center for social-education work. The families know and trust the school, and it therefore has the chance to connect them with sources of expert help. Not in all places would the school have to supply so many kinds of help. In many places, social agencies exist which can be used, and there the school's task is to co-operate with them. Even with us in our rural district, there were health and social agencies within driving distance, although not in our midst. We could not only help people to reach these centers, but—more necessary still—teach them the need of using them. This the School, by reason of its relation with the families, was especially able to do. It may be every school's responsibility.

The social services of a community school are continuous and intentionally informal. Their basis is the principle of sharing. There is in the country a wholesome self-respect, a "good-as-you" feeling, a pride and reticence that will take from—as it will give to—friends and neighbors. With country people, as with all people everywhere, it is a question of how the thing is done and the purpose and spirit behind it. Life in a countryside makes natural neighborly interest and help, and makes of it a mutual exchange. If social services are in part the self-initiated activity of a school, they are also in part the outgrowth of the school's relations with the community. From the identification of the teachers and the principal with the life and problems and interests of the community comes the intimate knowledge of people and conditions that is needed to direct social work intelligently, and that can give it relevancy and significance and effectiveness. Also, the fact that teachers live their lives in the community and belong there unlocks resources to them and promotes understanding and joint endeavor. It makes sharing natural and mutual help an incident of living, not a matter of formal arrangement.

From our experiences in Kentucky we learned that education is intrinsically a social process; that it is, as a matter of fact, set in the larger process of educating which includes many elements and agencies and influences, and is tantamount to what we call living. A socially functioning school is a school which assumes as an intrinsic part of its undertaking co-operative working with the people of the community and all its educational agencies on community problems and needs with reference to their effect on the lives of the children and of the adults. Its special concern is with the process of growth and development.

CHAPTER II

COMMUNITY EDUCATION: ARTHURDALE—A SCHOOL

Section 1: Building a Community School at Arthurdale, 1934-35

COMMUNITY SCHOOLS IN RURAL AREAS

AT the end of five years' work in Kentucky, we began to glimpse what might happen if a school made clear to itself the possible changes it could effect in its neighborhood and community—that is, saw itself as a factor in the life of its region; learned what it could contribute, what the region and the people could supply; and, working with the people of the neighborhood, sharing their life and interests, discover what joint effort could accomplish.

What the staff had learned regarding a community school in a rural area was summarized by me as Director of the School in the fourth year of the work in Kentucky: [1]

A school in a rural district has a unique opportunity to function socially. In the country there is a community, a neighborhood, linked by common interests and by intimate informal friendly intercourse. A rural school shares those interests and enters into them. As the neutral and often the largest place of the village or the countryside, the rural school is used for neighborhood gatherings of all kinds, for local clubs, sometimes for church services, for entertainments, lectures, concerts. The school's own assemblies and suppers and meetings provide a community inter-

---

[1] *Progressive Education*, March 1933, p. 123.

est in a way unknown in cities. To the school in a rural community, families turn for help in time of sickness and trouble, as well as for help in daily difficulties. They feel sure that the teacher will understand, they are sure that she will care and that she will help them. On the other hand, they will lend the school any help they have. The school can count on assistance from the families for whatever it is doing.

A community school forgoes its separateness. It is influential because it belongs to its people. They share its ideas and ideals and its work. It takes from them as it gives to them. There are no bounds, as far as I can see, to what it could accomplish in social reconstruction if it had enough wisdom and insight and devotion and energy. It demands all these, for changes in living and learning are not produced by imparting information about different conditions or by gathering statistical data about what exists, but by creating by people, with people, for people.

One's imagination is captured by the idea of how such a schoolhouse could be made lively and colorful, teeming with activity and interest; how it could be made the means of gaining for that locality health and recreation and acquaintance with all the events and lands and peoples of the world; how it might enliven the lives and homes of the families, becoming *their* school and the center of their interests.

Because we had been captured by this imagining, we had worked in Kentucky. There we found that what we had suspected was true, that since this process of vitalizing is a process of education, a school is an instrumentality shaped for the purpose. We found that a school which made health and recreation part of its business of learning, and constituted itself the center of the happenings and activities of the neighborhood, did, as a matter of fact, make of that neighborhood a different place.

When the Federal Government began its momentous undertaking of building communities with and for people who had been stranded industrially, an opportunity was presented at Arthurdale, West Virginia, to determine how effective a social instrumentality a school might be in this enterprise, how useful in developing community life and in the restoration of people in and through it.

It was on a piece of active research, then, that we undertook the work at Arthurdale, in West Virginia. We hoped to discover the answers to these questions. As we worked, we found out many things about community education which we might never have learned in any situation less exigent and compelling.

THE FIRST STEP IN THE EDUCATIONAL PROGRAM

The story of Arthurdale really begins with the work of the American Friends Service Committee, assisted by the social agencies and people of Morgantown, West Virginia.

As a result of the surveys and deliberations of "The White House Conference on Child Welfare," called by ex-President Hoover in 1930, the distress and suffering of large numbers of families in the coal fields of northern West Virginia was brought to the Conference in such a way as to stress the malnutrition and lack of opportunity for growth and development of the children of the miners' families. . . . As early as 1931, the children in the eleven counties in the Valley showed marked symptoms of malnutrition, and the menace of disease increased as employment for their fathers decreased.

At that time, Mr. Hoover had in his hands the remainder of a fund provided for the feeding of Belgian and French children during and after the World War. This money was placed at the disposal of the Friends Service Committee of Philadelphia for the feeding of the children in the coal fields of the Monongahela Valley.

That Committee at once made a survey of the needy counties. In Morgantown they found already organized a strong council of Social Agencies which had been valiantly trying to meet the need with very meager local contributions. This seemed the logical place to locate the headquarters of the feeding program, and the work was soon started. By the time the funds were exhausted, the hungry and undernourished children of the eleven counties had been fed more than a million meals, and many volunteers had been enlisted to assist. . . .

As the months of the feeding program passed . . . and the workers learned to know the distressing living conditions of so many people, it became more and more apparent that it was not enough to try to fill only the physical needs of those they were trying to help. The months of lack of proper food had caused a mental lethargy which all workers felt must be combated. To arouse a desire to better their own conditions seemed a task almost as gigantic as the problem of providing food and medical care.

The first effort to develop community initiative was made in Pursglove [2] by the organization of the first Community Council. This organization included the presidents of Parent Teachers Associations, Miners Union, Garden Club, and all social and religious groups. . . .

The first approach to the problem was through a recreation program, including the establishment of two playgrounds. . . .

The forty-two Garden Clubs of the County, with their two thousand members, are also the outgrowth of community initiative; and several of the Clubs function in sponsoring Canning Clubs, Mothers' Clubs, recreational activities, nutrition work and adult education classes.

Public Health Nursing as a branch of the work carried on under the Relief Administration, was started in Monongalia County in . . . 1932. . . .

Nursery Schools are being conducted in seven centers with an average attendance of 25 children each. Four are in mining camps, two in industrial centers . . . and one in the poorest district of Morgantown.[3]

The workers whom the Friends Service Committee sent in to feed children were Alice Davis and Nadia Danilevsky. Miss Davis became the County Relief Administrator and, later, the Federal Relief Administrator. Nadia Danilevsky, who was a specialist in child care, interested herself in establishing a health program and in creating the nursery schools. The work

---

[2] Pursglove was one of the mine camps in Scott's Run.
[3] Introduction to *Report and History of Service and Special Projects of Monongalia County Relief Administration for Year Ending April 1, 1935* (mimeographed report).

that was done by this group awoke hope in the unemployed miners and maintained their morale during "the dark days." The workers set up sewing, weaving, and mattress-making groups for the women, and with the men started making furniture—stools to "set" on in the bare shacks that were stripped of everything but rags in the corner for a bed. This latter enterprise developed later into the Mountaineer Craftsmen Co-operative Association, which produced handmade furniture, reproducing good old American patterns, and made the furniture for the houses on the homestead. The workers had even begun to "homestead" in a small way, acquiring small tracts of land and moving some of the families out onto them.

The activities of this group and the vision of Alice Davis and Nadia Danilevsky created the first design, worked out the first steps in the social-educational process of rehabilitation. The pattern and purpose of community education had been fashioned. Whatever the School later attempted was only a sequel to the work of this group. The basis of community education is characteristically laid by other than school agencies. From the point of view of a socially functioning school, this basis is the first step in the educational program. The second was the creation of a community school center for the use and learning of the homestead community.

In the late summer of 1933, Mrs. Roosevelt had visited the abandoned mine camps in this area and the families of the miners, as a friend of the people who were working there with them. In September, the Federal Government purchased for a homestead the land belonging to Mr. Arthur—Arthurdale. Architects and engineers arrived in October, and in November work was started making roads and clearing the land. The men who had applied for a homestead and who had been tentatively accepted lived in "barracks" at the old Arthur Mansion and began the work of building the village. So desperate was the need for better housing of their families, who were still dragging out an existence in Scott's Run, that ready-to-use houses were ordered. These houses of the three-rooms-in-a-row shack type proved to be too small for the size of the families, which were found to average seven; and the first task of the architects—a thankless one—was somehow to enlarge them. This was a difficult job, calling for ingenuity and resourcefulness.

PLANS FOR THE "NEW SCHOOL" AT ARTHURDALE

When those interested in organizing the homestead community faced the problem of a school, various people in education were called in to advise. As Chairman of a Committee on School and Community Relations,[4] which had offered advisory assistance to various Government agencies, I was asked to go to Arthurdale to make suggestions on the basis of the work I was then directing in Kentucky. I sought first to know the people for whose children the school was to be established, and spent several days in the Relief Office among the men and women who came in for help, and with the nurses and case workers went in and out of the shacks of the mine camps in Scott's Run, seeing there the families who were coming onto the homestead. I visited the project, climbing around in the deep snow to see where they were thinking of locating the school; inspected a model of the school which the architect had designed; and discussed with him a kind of school quite different from the one contemplated.

As I became acquainted with the group of people in the locality who were thinking and planning for the school, I found that they had, each and every one, dreamed a dream of a new school for this new homestead, and had written down the dream. The group comprised the County Superintendents of Preston County, where Arthurdale was located, and of Monongalia County, which adjoined it; a supervising teacher;

---

[4] A Committee of the Progressive Education Association.

several members of the Department of Education of the University of West Virginia in Morgantown; and Alice Davis, the Relief Administrator. I attended the all-day session of this committee,[5] whose purpose was to put all the dreams into a plan to be submitted to Mrs. Roosevelt, who was coming down for a week-end conference at Arthurdale. After Sunday dinner with the men at the Mansion barracks, the committee read the plan to Mrs. Roosevelt and the group of homesteaders. The group passed on it paragraph by paragraph, and discussed ways and means.

The Plan is reproduced here, because it embodies the co-operative thinking of a local group who envisioned a "new school" and illustrates the fact that a community school is the result of a community's planning.

PLAN FOR THE SCHOOL AT ARTHURDALE DRAFTED BY THE WEST VIRGINIA ADVISORY SCHOOL COMMITTEE

It is proposed that just as the organization of this community represents an experiment seeking to discover means of needed adjustment in our social and economic life, likewise let this be a new school, providing for its citizens of all ages richer and more adequate educational opportunities.

It is believed that the character and success of this school will depend on the philosophy of life which is to dominate all the activities constituting the curriculum and other phases of the school program, including pre-school and adult education. It is proposed therefore that the following statement of principles be accepted as a point of departure for the organization of an educational program in the Arthurdale community.

PHILOSOPHY

1. Faith in democracy and confidence in the ability of an enlightened people to govern themselves in economic and political affairs will be accepted as a fundamental doctrine. Consequently,

---

[5] See footnote p. 387, Chapter VII, for list of members of this Committee.

democratic procedures will predominate in the administrative and instructional activities of the school.

2. The school should emphasize the fact that democracy and freedom are challenges to a self-realization, and that real progress with any people results from their own initiative and resourcefulness.

3. The child is to be regarded as an individual with unlimited possibilities, ever capable of learning in "paying"[6] quality and quantity. "Learning" in this connection is to be understood as acquisition of moral and spiritual values rather than those usually associated with schools and commonly expressed in terms that have bookish and academic implications. It will be understood as implying right attitudes and appreciations for all kinds of useful labor and a sincere regard for moral and social virtues.

4. Since it is desirable that we have a citizenship that presents considerable variation in emotional, intellectual and personality traits, the school should, therefore, aim to conserve such individuality in pupils as will admit of a harmonious adjustment to community life. Consequently, the school should cultivate a toleration of, and an appreciation for, individual differences in intellect, emotions and personal habits.

5. At all times and in all school activities the pupils should be living completely and happily. This aim, it is believed, will be achieved through extensive opportunities for creative expression by individuals and especially the co-operative efforts of groups charged with responsibility. It will follow that children and adults will be to a large extent engaged in doing those things that they desire to do.

Curriculum

1. The school program should provide for a three-way set-up: (1) nursery-kindergarten, (2) elementary school, including grades like 8 (or 9),[7] and (3) adult education classes. An adequate program for adult education and adult activities is strongly recommended.

2. *The curriculum should be adapted to the special needs of the community. It should not be hampered by traditional and formal courses of study,* nor by standardized grading and grouping of pupils.

---

[6] A term used in mining.
[7] Later changed to include a full High School.

3. *The community activities will constitute the laboratory through which the children will get their educative experiences*—the grade projects and other agricultural activities—the social activities and civic projects, the care of the home, all will be shared by the school children under the guidance and leadership of the teachers.

This means that the real learning experiences of the school will come chiefly through the vocational life of the community. Industrial arts, specimens of living animal life, museums, library, applied art, home economics, music, elementary science, citizenship problems, will constitute the core of all school activities. *Lifelike problems will constitute the curriculum material, rather than the conventional school subjects.*

Administration

1. The school should be so planned that it may best demonstrate a truly progressive and efficient type of educational procedure. The school organization should grow out of pupil and community needs rather than from traditional heritages.

2. The school should not be established at excessive costs. *It should demonstrate that it is possible in West Virginia, or any other State, that a more desirable rural school is possible without any unreasonable investment of money in the program.*

3. *The type of school buildings recommended is not the traditional type, but rather simple buildings of two or three units, which will be homelike in character and allow the maximum amount of sun and air. The dimensions and arrangements of these buildings to be designed for the kind of work activities described under curriculum No. 3.* It is desired that the parents of the Arthurdale families do part of the work of construction, under direction, and that the greater part of the equipment be planned and made by the boys and girls in the school shop, assisted by the fathers and the school teachers. *It is hoped that the buildings will still be in process of completion when school opens, as they offer an opportunity for investment of parent and student work and interest.*

This group of school buildings can be grouped together on school grounds, which should include also space for playgrounds, school gardens and some land or woods for the children's creative activities out of doors. . . .

5. The principal and teachers . . . should live in the commu-

nity and be identified with the community life at all times. . . .[8]

6. . . . The selection of a faculty should be left to the principal.[9] This person should be largely responsible, with other co-workers, including the advisory committee of local residents, for the planning of the school plant.[10]

This Plan expresses very clearly and explicitly a vision of a community school, and reveals the fact that the committee had thought through many of the conditions and arrangements favorable to its development: a curriculum adapted to the special needs of the community and based on its life and activities, and the identification of its teachers with community life and interests.

The Plan foretold fairly accurately the nature of the work that later went forward in the Arthurdale School. The recommendations about the school buildings were closely followed in both design and location, and the hope expressed that the fathers share in their construction and that the students have an opportunity to watch their completion and participate in the making of equipment was later fulfilled.

ARRANGEMENTS FOR THE ESTABLISHMENT OF THE SCHOOL

Establishing a regular public school on a Government homestead presented all kinds of technical difficulties, and it was five months before all the arrangements could be completed. The situation appeared to be without precedent in this country. It was necessary to confer with members of the West Virginia State Legislative Education Committee and with the State Superintendent of Education to discuss ways and means of making this new school a public County school. The fact that a West Virginia committee of educators had made the plan for the School made it easier to work out ar-

---

[8] See Chapter VII, p. 336.
[9] See Chapter VII, p. 389.
[10] From the *Dominion News* for February 12, 1934, Morgantown, West Virginia.

rangements with the State and County authorities. By May it had been agreed tentatively that the Arthurdale School be a free, independent State school, with freedom in curriculum to meet the special needs of its community; that it be sustained by State funds for basic salaries for the West Virginia teachers who were assigned the School,[11] and with supplementary salary assignments by the County; that provision for the Nursery School be made through the FERA; and that salaries of additional teachers trained in community education work be supplied through private funds.

Discussion of these plans with the authorities in the State and with Federal representatives in Washington continued throughout the summer into September. Before arrangements could finally be made, it was necessary to form and incorporate an association which, as a corporation, was able to draw up an agreement with the State. The legal steps involved took many weeks. It is noteworthy that the legal document of the agreement drawn up among the County, State, and the association declares that "these schools be devoted to the teaching of a new economic and social freedom under American ideals, and to the conducting of an experiment in modern education looking forward to the development in the individual child of his willingness to work and co-operate with others."

In the formation of the "new school," ideas of the State and County officials had their determining and idealistic share. The public-education function of a community school became clarified in these discussions and plans.

Further clarification and definition of community education were achieved through the detailed planning of the school buildings. The conception of the function of a community

---

[11] Teachers in West Virginia are assigned a school on the basis of pupils' average daily attendance for the last three months of the previous school year. As only 87 children of families on the project had been in Preston County schools in 1933–34, only three teachers could be given to the School the first year.

school was involved, not only in decisions as to the general character of the buildings, but also in such questions as: what activities each building was to house; what kind of Science room, classrooms, Library and Nursery School we were to have; and where provision was to be made for the recreational activities, the health program, the kitchen and canning units, and the several playgrounds. No smallest confusion survived this attempt to construct buildings that should serve the needs of a community school.

In all the early stages of the work, the flexibility and open-mindedness of the architect, Eric Gugler, were a great assistance. He had, before I visited the project in February, tentatively planned a school building of the better conventional type. However, he was interested in remodeling this in accordance with the different needs of a community school.

The summer of 1934 was spent between Washington, where Miss Stanton and I planned the buildings for the School, and Arthurdale, where we worked on equipment. There was constant need of introducing the idea of a community school to numberless adult persons to whom the word "school" meant one thing only—the school in which they themselves had been educated twenty or more years before. These discussions were, of course, another means of clarifying the conception of a community school.

Preparing Buildings at Arthurdale for School Use

Meanwhile, despite our hopes that the School buildings would be erected that summer—a hope that seems fantastic now in retrospect—it became clear, one never-to-be-forgotten hot July day in the Town Center at Arthurdale, that they were *not* going to be constructed that summer, and that then and there a decision must be reached as to where in the buildings that already existed school might be held.

When the staff arrived at the project the first of September, exactly nothing had been done to prepare the buildings chosen for school use. So everybody pitched into the task of reconditioning the old Arthur Mansion, which had been used temporarily as a barracks by the men working on the homestead, and attempted to clear it of the accumulation of many years' living. Game-cock pens and barrels of sauerkraut were moved from the cellar; the dirt floor was limed and covered with cinders; coal and wood bins, preserve closets, and potato bins were made; the walls of the rooms were covered with cartridge paper obtained in the wholesale paper district in Pittsburgh; and, eventually, the Mansion was washed and scrubbed and painted until it was fit for children's use.

One shed at the Town Center, used for building supplies, was cleared for the School Shop and lined with wall board. Another, a stock room, had a mezzanine introduced at the top of its ladder staircase, and was made water-tight—more or less —for the High School's use. Both had toilets added and drinking fountains. A room beside the Assembly Hall at the Town Center was used temporarily as a staff headquarters. In the words of a teacher's diary for that week:

> While this work was going on, the School Office was opened in the Community Center in what is now the Mountaineer Craftsmen's display room. There the secretaries set up their typewriters, one of the men teachers made a mail box and a row of shelves, some homesteaders moved in three chairs and two rickety tables, and the Office of the Arthurdale School was established.

From this "office," the staff went about reconditioning the buildings for school use. At the start, we decided to keep exactly the same working hours as the men on the project. That is, we began our day with them. It finished, those first days, only at bedtime, however.

The School opened on time! About three days before, none of the carefully planned equipment having arrived, by the authority of a visiting Washington official, benches of the oldest American school pattern were knocked together by the men on the project. The benches and the floors and the toilets were completed together—Sunday, the day before School opened. At seven o'clock Sunday evening, the big project trucks unloaded the benches to the waiting teachers before an audience of at least a hundred people who had come up from Reedsville to see what was going on. Wrapping paper for blackboards, some books, tests, paper and pencils, were placed in the rooms for the morning. At nine-thirty, weary, I started to go home—only to discover that the painters had left several windows *out* in the back of the house. For the first time I was disheartened, with all the books and school materials lying around. "Go home and rest you easy, Miss Clapp," said a father and an older boy. "We'll watch the night."

For two weeks we had all together—fathers, teachers, mothers, children—worked at everything. The School was a reality at last and it was ours—the community's school. Fortunately the schoolhouse had been the men's house. They had lived in it. My office had been their office. They felt at home in the building and continued to feel that it was theirs. Everyone, although it had been hard work fixing it, liked the way it had been made fresh and clean for the children, and the idea that nothing was too good for them.

On the architect's plans for the Town Center appeared, in place of a fence that connected the two sheds, a long four-room building with windows on both sides. The very place for the Nursery School! Everyone fell to and, incredible as it sounds, the building was finished in ten days. Exactly one week after the "Big School," the Nursery School opened, its equipment—which had been made and collected during the summer months—filling the rooms as fast as they were finished.[12] By good fortune (and quite contrary to our educational preconceptions), the building was over the Supply Shed

---

[12] Chapter IV, pp. 173-4.

and Garage, where project trucks roared in and out all day. By good fortune, for the Nursery School was in the midst of everything that went on. Mothers who worked in the canning kitchen near by stopped on their way home, flattening their noses against the windows to see how it was "coming on." Other mothers and teachers washed the windows. It was everybody's business. The Nursery School began before it opened! I recall arriving at the homestead Sunday afternoon with two five-gallon jars of distilled water in the back of the car obtained from a reluctant filling station in Morgantown and unloading these with the help of all the older boys who were standing around the square. So great was their interest that they stayed on to help distribute wheel barrows and blocks and little irons and dolls among the rooms. Everyone contributed —lumber yards, five-and-ten-cent stores, schools, grocery stores, sand and gravel companies. The city of Morgantown was involved, to say nothing of Washington and New York.

This is, in part, what community education is. A community school is everyone's school. They make it, for their children, with your help. Together you make it; it isn't ready-made, whether you build it, or refashion it.

PREREQUISITE CONDITIONS FOR COMMUNITY EDUCATION

Another thing that must be said is that someone has to know how to do it—just what to do. That the Nursery School could come into being like a miracle was due to Jessie Stanton's expert knowledge, imagination, and creative ability. That an eight-grade school could capture an old mansion used as a barracks, and a High School emerge from a room and two sheds used for supplies, was due to the enterprise and inventiveness of a group of teachers experienced in the creation of a school. Had it not been for our experience in Kentucky, it would not have been possible to construct a community school on a homestead and to use it as an agency in community education. After five years' work in Kentucky we knew what responsibilities such a school carried, we understood at least the kind of curriculum needed, and were familiar with the ways and means of working with a community.

Perhaps the condition we made of being ourselves members of the community, and the responsibilities and relationships and activities into which this membership brought us, revealed to us more than any other one thing the meaning of community education. Kentucky had taught us the value of neighborliness as an educational asset. At Arthurdale, we shared in the common problem of adjustment to new conditions and, like the other homesteaders, ourselves had to cope with problems of food, heat, and shelter. It was extremely difficult that first fall to find places in which to live while we were waiting, like so many of the other people, for houses to be built. The teachers finally scattered through the adjoining towns and villages—Reedsville, Masontown, and Kingwood—living in rooms, bungalows, and boarding houses, as they could. Only I was able, that first year, to find lodging on the project. But this necessity, although inconvenient, was probably fortunate. Arthurdale was, at the outset, regarded by the surrounding district with some mistrust and skepticism. Neighborly contacts with its teachers and the witnessing of their labors and enthusiasms were, I am confident, factors in bringing about a better understanding and greater sympathy with the project.

SCOTT'S RUN AND ARTHURDALE

A few miles outside the city of Morgantown lies Scott's Run, a gulch in the hills about ten to twelve miles long, in which are situated a number of mine camps, only one or two of which were running part-time when the work on the project started. To prevent destruction of the mine shacks the companies allowed the families to continue living in them. Water and light were shut off when the mines closed down, and no repairs had been made on the houses since then. The miners who came out to live on the Arthurdale homestead had been out of employment for a period varying from three to seven years.

On visits to West Virginia in February 1934, and in April and the summer following, I saw in Scott's Run, I think, all the families who later came from there to the project. I remember helping a woman whose hand, blue with cold, clutched the handle of a heavy basket as we climbed a steep hill of snow and ice to her house. I recall a pause one broiling July day beside the narrow piazza of a long dirty one-story house onto which doors opened from rooms, each one of which housed a family, while the district nurse I was with examined a baby, dying, covered with flies.

One could add such pictures without number: a pregnant mother with disheveled hair, four children clinging to her skirts, another in her arms, beside a stove—the only furniture in the room—saying: "I think I'd die happy if I could have enough water for just one day."

I had spent an afternoon in Scott's Run with a relief worker [wrote one of our educational visitors] and seen whole families living in two squalid rooms with rain leaking so that pails stood on the beds to catch the water. Drainage from privies seeped through the soil of the steep hillsides into the stream at the bottom, which was the only source of water supply, and typhoid had been rampant.

A woman with a four-weeks-old baby, whom we visited, had papered her rooms with clean newspapers to make them a little more sanitary, and was heartbroken to see her efforts ruined by the leaking rain. A man sitting outside was staring dumbly at 21 cents, held out in his hand—his whole earnings for the week.

One went back to Arthurdale with a quickened appreciation of the rush with which the work there was going on. For there is a school at Arthurdale, a school that is heart and center of the whole community, a school whose main objective is not the teaching of a graded syllabus, but the meeting of the needs of the children and young people and adults who make Arthurdale.[13]

Some knowledge of the conditions of life in the abandoned mine camps of Scott's Run was, we felt, essential to understanding the nature of the problem of establishing the School on the homestead. One of the members of the staff wrote down her impressions of the Run and of Arthurdale in the early stages of its development:

Scott's Run

I had always rather begin with Scott's Run. Coming from there is really what gives Arthurdale meaning.

Take the valley as a whole—camp after camp, abandoned tipple after abandoned tipple, slag heaps, no trees; steep hillsides made barren, black, ugly, with flimsy dilapidated shacks, worse almost than those crowded along the highway, perched high on their sides; unkempt joints, empty stores with broken glass fronts, rickety porches and worn-out advertisements, dirty under-stocked little stores, trash everywhere; listless, smutty-face men, raggedy sweet-faced children, and maimed curs. Or, take any single camp, built on a cinder heap, not a tree, families living in long shacks in a room or two, foul privies behind. The school, such as it is, with forty children to a room, sitting in desks from nine to four, perched on the hillside high above.

There is Nadia talking to the men who are laying pipes for city water. They are going to have water. Certainly that will help. But no amount of water can wash away the utter, awful ugliness, nor the listless, hopeless attitude.

Whether you remember the valley as a whole, rotting shell left from the boom days, or the details of any of the abandoned camps, you can't help feeling outraged that people should be obliged to exist under such miserable circumstances. What should be done? Well, that is the point of Arthurdale.

Arthurdale

Stand at the crest of G Road Hill. The hills stretch back toward

---

[13] From an unpublished account written by Leila V. Stott of the City and Country School, New York City, who visited the project in the spring of 1935.

the distant mountains. The textures and the colors of the different sods and grains and earth and the patches of trees make a lovely pattern, especially with the little white houses and barns sprinkled around. Reedsville is a toy village on a hill a mile off to the right. And so much sky overhead. The grotesque yet charming Mansion overlooks it all.

But the heart of the community is "The Center." The old church which stood on the main highway near Masontown and where the people of the vicinity gathered for worship and blessing before leaving for the Civil War, is the very center. It is flanked by rooms, used temporarily as schoolrooms, and the Craftsmen's show rooms and forge, and the project office. The orchard still grows in the Center square.

The people. They are not as I expected. I knew what Scott's Run was like and expected a different kind of person from that background. I thought naturally they would be ignorant and rough.

Elsie asked me to stop on my way home from school the Wednesday before Thanksgiving. I supposed she wanted me to get her something at the store. It wasn't that. She had a Thanksgiving basket for Miss Clapp. Some of everything—corn, beets, pickles, even cookies and mince pie. Mrs. Shelby it was who had no layette for her coming baby. It was hard to take because they needed the food more than we. That is the way the Shelbys are. They love to give. I knew poignantly how much easier it is to give than to receive. I accepted, of course. She loved so giving it.

Nor are these people ignorant. Look at the way Mrs. Carter keeps house. The Carters have a cold closet where jars shine bright—red or orange or dark green—for row on row. There are sections for the amount to be used each month of the winter. The bins below the shelves are filled with potatoes and turnips. Mrs. Carter knows about the latest ways of canning. She has a home-made screen drier rigged up over the stove. Oh, they are not all so efficient and capable, but they do not seem like people who have been forced to live under conditions described above.

Their new homes, attractive modern cottages with furnaces, running water, bathrooms, electricity, beds enough for everybody, enough rooms so the boys and girls can sleep separately, attractive handmade furniture, are a great pride to them. Mrs. Mills said to me: "Yes, ma'am, I was saying to the Mister yesterday, I like my house better'n anything." And Mr. Bruce said about his house: "It's just a dream come true."

COMMUNITY EDUCATION: ARTHURDALE

I believe when we came in the fall, when the houses were so brand-new, that their worship of their homes was uppermost. Always Arthurdale has meant to them all a new chance. They had heard plans for a long time of a specially good school, and they craved it for their children. Education, in the conventional sense at least, means a tremendous amount to these people.

Perhaps you wonder how people from a background of Scott's Run have such idealism and vigor. Remember, that sort of a life was something they were caught in—nothing that they degenerated into. I have visited several of the grandmothers and grandfathers. They are those sturdy, clear-eyed farmers who get along with practically no money by endless labor—the kind of people we like to think of as real Americans.

These are the people as we found them when we came the first day of September 1934. And my first impression was like that of most people—how fine they were, how much more attractive than most people I had ever met before. They seemed more real because their problems were how to get enough food to eat and enough clothes to wear, and their lives were natural family lives.[14]

Location and Make-Up of Arthurdale

Arthurdale is one mile from Reedsville. You drive through Reedsville in order to reach Arthurdale. Reedsville is a small village with a population of about 500. The homesteaders buy their groceries and clothing from the stores there. They get their mail from the Reedsville postoffice.[15] There is a barber shop in this neighboring village, a bank, a garage, and a restaurant. So far, Arthurdale has no stores of its own.

When you get on to the homestead you pass new houses being built. Beyond these is the "Town Center," which is really a center in every sense. The Nursery School and High School are located there, and the Assembly Hall, where meetings, dances, games, and plays are held. A forge, blacksmith's shop, garage and the supply sheds, the Mountaineer Craftsmen's workshops and metal forge surround the square in the Center.

Just across the road on a hill is "The Mansion" or Arthur house. This was the home of the people who owned the property before the Government took it over. At present, the Elementary School,

---

[14] Half-Year Report, January 1935, written by Elisabeth Sheffield, teacher of the Fourth Grade.
[15] By the summer of 1935, Arthurdale had its own postoffice.

grades one through eight, is housed there. The doctor and the nurse have their offices in the Mansion also.

Arthurdale is not an isolated village. Masontown, which is a little larger than Reedsville, is five miles down the road, and Morgantown, seventeen miles. To the east, seven miles, is Kingwood, the County Seat of Preston County. Fifteen miles east of here is Terra Alta, where the passenger station of the Baltimore and Ohio Railroad is located.[16]

It is not possible longer to halt events at the point of first impressions, so mixed are these with many-sided activities. Description inevitably becomes a narrative of the events and the means by which the School was organized, and of the ways it assisted in the building up of the new community.

SHARED LIVING AND WORKING

MAKING FRIENDS

We became acquainted rapidly, getting to know our neighbors and entering into everything that happened. Before school began the teachers called on the families of the children. Needs everywhere present, and our common purpose of making a school for the children, drew us into every conceivable activity. The diary of the School executive secretary, Alice Bowie, gives an account of the ways acquaintance grew in and through the School Center:

Contacts with the homesteaders were made as occasion arose. Some have been brought about by my own particular job, such as the census taken in November, which took me into the homes of all the families living near the project but not yet occupying homestead houses.

Another means of acquaintance was the enrollment of the children on the first day of school, getting to know some of the parents who came along with them, and finding out through them the information required on the enrollment sheet—their educational background, the composition of their family group (num-

---

[16] Ethel Carlisle, First Grade Teacher: Half-Year Report, January 1935.

MINE SHACKS IN SCOTT'S RUN

ber of brothers, sisters, their ages, others living in the home besides parents), and a few facts about their physical history (diseases, immunizations, and condition of eyes). Later I copied from the records of the project nurse the physical examinations that had been made as part of the application data for homesteads.

In the beginning, the fact that the homesteaders themselves were on the job of fixing up the Arthur house for School quarters; that they made temporary benches for the first days of school before regular desks, chairs, and tables arrived; that they later hauled and installed the new furniture—gave them a primary interest in the School, which had become the focal point in the community.

They became acquainted with the School and familiar with it as they shared our rooms and we shared theirs. Clinics for vaccinations and immunizations were held at the Arthur house; mothers' meetings with the nurse took place in the classrooms; canning demonstrations in the School kitchen. And School assemblies were held in the Assembly Hall at the Town Center.

When members of the School staff were recognized also as members of the community (I believe the first formal introduction was made at a meeting of the homesteaders to discuss harvesting and crops), when the Men's Club had elected the masculine part of the group to membership, and when the women had organized and included the women teachers and the wives of the men teachers as well, it was time to begin working together in earnest. Committees formed to serve refreshments at the Hallowe'en celebration included people from both home and School.

People interested in acting met together and found that teachers also wanted to be in plays. We could enjoy doing things with the parents, and they with us. There was much less reticence than anyone might have expected, and there was a sharing of genuinely pleasant experience.

I emphasize these contacts, because through them we have the opportunity to form friendships.

Mothers Prepare School Lunches

The teacher of the First Grade, Ethel Carlisle, who, because she was gifted in domestic science, helped with school lunches the first year, writes of the way in which we all attempted to solve that problem the first winter:

Last summer, a large amount of vegetables was raised in the gardens: corn, soy beans, buckwheat, and potatoes. There was a community patch that the men took turns in caring for during the summer. The women worked in the community kitchen a certain number of hours a week. A good deal of the food that had been canned had not been used, also a great many potatoes. After other means of obtaining a hot lunch for the children failed, it was decided to use this extra food. Work was slack at this time—midwinter—and packing lunches for all the children cost the families quite a bit.

The mothers come, each one day a week, to do the cooking and dishwashing. Several unmarried girls help, too. They have all been very dependable, and have done an excellent job. They like to help in the School and like to get together; very often the women drop in and help, or just visit, when it isn't their day to work.

They have been very generous about donating any extra canned goods or vegetables that they have, for they value the hot lunch for the children. It is meager, as far as a well-balanced lunch goes, consisting of potatoes and one other vegetable, bread and milk. Even so, it is much better for the children than the sandwiches, pickles, pie, and cake that they have been bringing. All the children in my room now get milk.

One may recognize in the preparation of school lunches, in the women's meetings in the schoolrooms with the nurse and for canning demonstrations, and in the co-operative working together in plays and on entertainments, the beginnings of "Adult Education" in its natural functioning.[17] Quite contrary to conventional procedure, the learning by adults was at the outset a by-product of a living and working and playing together, rather than a planned program put across by the School. This fact was our deliberate choice of a procedure that suited best, we felt, the situation and the people we were dealing with.[18]

---

[17] See Chapter VII, pp. 332–42.
[18] See also Chapter IV, "The Arthurdale Nursery School," pp. 210-2, and Chapter V, "Cultural Resources and Opportunities," p. 243.

WHAT IS COMMUNITY EDUCATION?

Just what is community education? How do you start a community school? What is it and what does it do?

The story of how the community school at Arthurdale was born has been told to bring out the fact that community education is itself a growing idea, born in the interaction of thinking and doing, shaped in part by events. A community school is made *with* the people whose school it is. In the making, teachers lead as fellow-workers. As members themselves of the community, they are citizens as well as teachers, sharing common problems and interests.

What does a community school do? First of all, it meets as best it can, and with everyone's help, the urgent needs of the people, for it holds that everything that affects the welfare of the children and their families is its concern. Where does school end and life outside begin? There is no distinction between them. A community school is a used place, a place used freely and informally for all the needs of living and learning. It is, in effect, that place where learning and living converge. Some means must be had whereby these enterprises can go forward. But these means may be made, or loaned, or given. If the need is urgent and interest high, ways will be found and invented.

Section 2: Community Activities in 1934-35
THE ARTHURDALE HEALTH PROBLEM

A situation like that of Arthurdale—which is similar to other remote rural areas, and not dissimilar to many villages and small towns—reveals the fact that the problem of health in all its aspects must be a dominant concern and function of a community school.

In Preston County, West Virginia, there are no clinics, no district nurses, no school dentists. This is a condition which, I am told, exists in some hundreds of counties in this country. The homestead health problem was definitely clinical in character, since the people had moved there from especially unhealthy living conditions, after years of lack of proper food and adequate medical care. Yet we came to know that their condition did not differ materially from that of the families on the small farms and in the countryside around us. An energetic and co-operative County Board of Health was situated at Kingwood, seven miles away. Their services, however, had to be stretched to cover a large area whose scattered population is connected mainly by unpaved country roads almost impassable six months of the year. They were, therefore, necessarily largely confined to regulative measures and inoculations. To many people in the area good medical care cannot be available, because of isolation and the cost of private medical treatment.

From Federal and State Health Departments help may be had in epidemics, in problems of sanitation and water supply, in regulations, in demonstrations, in analysis (urine analysis, Wassermann tests, etc.), in informational bulletins—prompt, efficient help generously administered. But all such help fails to meet individual and family health needs in illness, accidents, and childbirth, in home sanitation, nutrition, and health habits. The problem of individual and family health rehabilitation is, moreover, not met by either standardized work in public health, however admirable, or research centers, although these render great assistance.

At Arthurdale, it was from the beginning clear that the medical demand created by malnutrition, neglect, disease, accidents, and childbirth could not be ignored. These needs drove us into rapid action. Other agencies to meet them were

COMMUNITY EDUCATION: ARTHURDALE

not present locally. There could be no debate as to whether or not the School should undertake them.

After an unsuccessful search for a doctor who, as member of our supplementary staff, would undertake family health restoration on the homestead, I returned to the project. Fortunately, I found there a nurse employed by the Government construction unit against possible accidents who had interested herself in a wider assistance to families and in delivery cases. The work of the daily inspection at School of children, which caught incipient cases of cold, sore throats, skin troubles, infectious diseases, and cut infections, was, in the fall of 1934, heavy and burdensome, owing to their previous poor living conditions and lack of medical care. In the month of November, for instance, the total number of children examined in 17 school days was 1625—522 in the Nursery School, and 1103 in Grades 1 to 12. The construction nurse found this work, which she carried on unaided, overwhelming and resigned after months of faithful and able work. Happily we were able to get in touch at once with another nurse, Miss Plummer, who had been a member of the Henry Street nursing group in New York and who had special training and an interest in social service. So the nursing care continued without a break. We used whatever medical services were available through local doctors, but it was in reality the nurse who sustained the health program until the middle of the year. It was necessary for her to organize her day and distribute her time among inspection of children at School, accident cases, and nursing—including prenatal, delivery, and postnatal care.

It was February before our continued efforts to find a physician, well trained and imbued with social vision, were rewarded. Then we were so fortunate as to have Dr. Harry Timbres join the staff of community workers. He was with us on the project until October 1936, when he left to continue research at Johns Hopkins. The project owes him a great debt of gratitude, not only for his generous services and human understanding, but for the plans and procedures of social medicine which he instituted. He was succeeded by another able physician, Dr. M. L. White, who spent the months of his leave of absence from the mission field with us; and he in turn by Dr. Wills, whose interest lay in the field of pediatrics.

Starting from the background of mine camps where wages are commonly docked for the services of indifferent company doctors and continuing through months and years of no medical care at all, the people accepted sickness and death as inevitable. They had little confidence in doctors and did not expect health. It was thought best to make good medical services available on the project until there was a recognition of the need and value of medical care. This was done deliberately for several reasons: from what the Friends Committee had found in their work in Scott's Run, it was evident that the people could not succeed in the new chance offered on the homestead without health rehabilitation; the amount of health work to be done was extremely large and needed the services of a trained and experienced physician and nurse—services for which the people, just emerged from destitution, could not pay. The medical program was sustained during this first period by the same private funds that furnished the supplementary community educators. It was expected that as soon as possible a plan would be worked out for a health co-operative, a kind of health insurance plan, that would cover needs when they became more normal. The start of such a plan was made the following year.[19]

The work for the first months was definitely clinical in character. Dr. Timbres estimated in the early spring that the cost of operations urgently needed, X-rays, hospital care, tonsilectomies that should be done at once, would come, at local prices, to about $2400. Some part of this was donated as a revolving fund.

---

[19] See Chapter VII, p. 374.

Physical Condition of the Children

We had, of course, with the children first of all to meet and counteract, by medical treatment, better food, and health routines at School, the effects of the privations and bad living conditions they had suffered. The different ages of children had, we found, been variously affected.

A large number of the children in the Nursery School had, in the first year, either scabies or impetigo.[20] This condition yielded slowly to treatment, to better food, to baths and physical routines, but it was spring before it was finally eradicated. After that time, only sporadic cases appeared. The Nursery School children in the fall of 1934 were wan and listless in appearance, thin, pale, with pinched faces. However, they improved rapidly and became, by spring, well and rosy. The right food, milk, cod-liver oil, warmer clothing, fresh air, a midday rest, and the proper handling under happy conditions in the Nursery School made the difference. Whenever a child was kept at home for several weeks, however, the improvement had to be made all over again. The nurse that first year treated a very large number of infected cuts on feet and legs; at home the children ran barefoot in the house and outdoors.

The children of the primary grades seemed, on the whole, better than either the Nursery School babies or the boys and girls of the elementary grades, although there were outstanding cases of malnutrition among them. They had been born and had had their start in life before their fathers were out of work, and had not reached the hungry, growing years of middle childhood.

Bad living conditions and insufficient food for the preceding three to seven years had especially affected the children of ten to fourteen, physically and also psychologically. They had been old enough during "the dark days" to share the family's anx-

---

[20] See Chapter IV, "The Arthurdale Nursery School," pp. 177–8.

ieties and to feel the strain and know the fears. They were less stable emotionally and more lethargic than the children of the primary grades.

Of the older children, the boys and girls of High School age had largely escaped the effects of what they had been through. They had attained their early growth before the bad times came, and had—most of them—been in school. But the group of boys of sixteen to twenty-five who had left school in the fifth to seventh grades and had hung around the mine camps for the five to fifteen years following, were in poor condition. During 1934–35 they steadied somewhat in occasional work, and under better living conditions they filled out and became, most of them, husky and well physically, showing gains psychologically but never recovering entirely from the harm they had suffered.[21] The girls of this older group were in somewhat better shape, although they were less stable than the High School group of girls.

The Older People

Almost all the women showed malnourishment and strain. A number needed surgery and suffered from complaints aggravated by the exhausting and never-ceasing demands that their lives had made on them. Dr. Timbres wrote in a report in the summer of 1935:

There are four women, averaging 59 years, who are doing far harder work than their disabilities should allow them. They suffer from varicose veins, high blood pressure, hardening of the arteries, chronic kidney diseases, and weak and insufficient hearts. These are not the only persons suffering from these conditions, but they are the ones that suffer the most. The risk to their lives is serious at all times. Surgery would not benefit them, but they could be made much more comfortable in their physical state, and their lives could doubtless be prolonged, by occasional short periods of rest and freedom from responsibility.

---

[21] See Chapter VII, pp. 343–7; also this chapter, pp. 103–7.

COMMUNITY EDUCATION: ARTHURDALE

It was the need for such rest periods for the women, as well as the many tonsilectomy cases, and the frequent need of a quieter place for deliveries than the crowded houses afforded, that counseled the use of one of the houses as a cottage hospital. Arrangements for this were made and, under Dr. Timbres's direction, equipment for it obtained the year following.[22]

Regarding the men, Dr. Timbres reported:

> None of the bread-winners is in urgent need of major surgical treatment. The elderly husbands of the four women mentioned above have suffered quite as much as their wives from the ravages of age and hard work, and would benefit also from periods of rest.
>
> In addition, there are three or four younger men whose physical state, while not preventing them from engaging in ordinary work, may at some not far distant date necessitate surgical interference or hospital care in order to make them capable of continuing to bear the responsibility of supporting their families.

At the end of the first year, however, everyone who had not a chronic disease was markedly improved. Both the men and women are characteristically vigorous and have an astonishing energy and ambition and industry. Many of the men themselves declared that their health "was better since they moved up on the project." It was. Life in the open, above ground, without strain or despair, with rising ambition and growing satisfaction, acted as a tonic on their inherent muscular strength and latent vigor. A number of them had been hurt in the mines, perhaps a dozen somewhat injured in the World War. The majority of the men, more than the women, bore the scars, not only of the period of hunger and discouragement, but also of unfavorable mine camp conditions. The full effects on the older people of these strains and hardships did not appear for several months after they came onto the homestead. It was in the winter that illness on the project

---

[22] The cottage hospital is now in use and is the center of the medical work on the project.

showed an increase. The psychological effects appeared more slowly still, and persisted longer. In the second year they were somewhat more evident than in the first.[23]

Dental Repairs

So harmful to the health of the children and the older people were decayed and neglected teeth, that dentistry became a major health need of pressing importance. During the summer of 1935, we secured the services by the month of a dentist who had been used by the relief workers in Morgantown. He brought his own instruments; we provided supplies and pledged a nominal salary for the period of his work. The homesteaders paid for the work at minimum charges: 30 cents each for extractions, and 80 cents each for fillings, cleanings, and root fillings. In all, 240 persons in 80 families received dental treatment; 645 extractions, 451 fillings, 56 cleanings, 9 canal fillings, and one repair of crown were necessary. The mouths of the children and adults were, because of malnutrition and neglect, in such bad shape that more extractions than fillings needed to be done. This wholesale removal of decayed teeth brought beneficial results almost at once.

The Babies on the Project

Perhaps the most dramatic improvement in health was in the babies. The babies born just before their parents came onto the homestead, and those born on the project during the first months, showed what their mothers had suffered. Slowly, the better living conditions, better food, release from strain and worry, together with the prenatal and delivery and postnatal care of mothers, began to tell, and we began to have "beautiful babies," as Miss Plummer said. In the spring of 1935, we held a "Well Baby Clinic" [24]—so named to bring out

---
[23] See Chapter VII, pp. 355–64.
[24] See Chapter IV, pp. 189–90 and 212–4.

the fact that at Arthurdale we expected to have our babies well and to keep them well. The babies of these families are much loved and much handled. At first, they were closely housed, dressed over-warmly, kept up late, and fed tea and coffee and bits from the table. In the summer of 1935, the nurse made a routine of a slowly increasing exposure to the sun—and the improvement was remarkable. The mothers, even the older mothers, appreciated the nursing care, and noticed the results of the child care at the Nursery School, and were willing and interested to learn the best modern methods of care and feeding. Gradually the desire for health was born, and the old fatalistic acceptance of death and illness, born of misery and poverty and ignorance, vanished. In the mine camps one had not called in a doctor unless one was near death; and in "the bad times," except for what help the district nurses from the Relief Office could render, there was no medical care at all. Here on the project, there were a good doctor and nurse and people concerned to help one become well and keep well.

Especially interesting and helpful to mothers were the conferences at the Nursery School, where the results of child care were so apparent in the children's improvement. More than any other one agency, the Nursery School revealed to the mothers the right conditions for children's wellbeing: in the selection, preparation, and serving of food, in eating habits, in rest routines, in toilet habits; in the physical provision made for the children's welfare in space, materials, arrangements, clothing, and exercise; in the handling of emotions and in right conditions for their activity and learning. Constant visits to the Nursery School by mothers, and the presence of fathers in and about the buildings at their work, kept everyone in close touch with every development. Everyone on the homestead was sure of the help and value to the families of the Nursery School.

A new mother on the homestead sitting next but one to me

at the square dance started to ask me some questions. "Does she want to know about the Nursery School?" asked Mrs. Regan in between us. "Leave me tell her. Guess I'm the one to know."

Dr. Timbres gave talks before the Women's Club in the summer of 1935 on problems like "summer complaint" and the ways to preserve food in hot weather. The Club formed a "Sick Committee," which consisted of a group of women, one on each road, who volunteered to assist the doctor if need be, and in cases of illness to give her neighbor a helping hand with the cooking and washing. Some of the women, the first year, helped in the nursing, and one of them, especially intelligent in the care of babies, assisted in certain feeding cases. That year few, if any, cows were kept on the project, and we had to concentrate our efforts on procuring milk for babies and expectant mothers.

Certain features of the Arthurdale health program: the School's program of exercise and rest periods, hot lunches, child care routines, daily school inspection and treatment by nurse and doctor, work in nutrition, etc., will be found in the best private and public schools. But the support which the School was able to give to the homestead health program went, of course, far beyond the usual lessons in hygiene of the County schools or the medical help available to them. Yet many of the health measures used by the School could, we believed, also be used by other schools in rural districts. This fact was recognized by the Preston County Board of Education. In the fall of the next year, 1935, they asked us to speak in a series of radio talks for Preston County on features of the health work at Arthurdale that the Board desired for all its schools.

The health program, so difficult to start because its purpose of family health restoration came under neither "public health" nor "private practice" categories, when it finally got under way, seemed so entirely "right," to all of us at least, that it appeared to form a category of its own, one imperatively

COMMUNITY EDUCATION: ARTHURDALE

needed in remote rural areas. The experience at Arthurdale, that first year, in instituting this program persuaded us that the school is a useful co-operating agency in health work. The experiences of the second year [25] convinced us that a school may be an essential assistant in a community health program.

In the first year the difficult beginning was made, and although we were tormented by all that needed to be done, the effects of what we were able to do were immediate. These strengthened our determination to go on, past obstacles, with the difficult task of overcoming the effects of the privation, the lack of medical care, and the living conditions of the mine camps of Scott's Run; of creating expectation of health instead of sickness, and changing poor habits of personal and family hygiene.

RESOURCES FOR RECREATION AND ENJOYMENTS

Besides the organization of a health program, the year 1934–35 saw also the provision of recreational facilities, of "good times," of athletics and supervised play; the establishment for the out-of-school young adults of "Night School"; the formation of a farm co-operative; the appointment by the Men's and the Women's Clubs of committees representing community interests; and the establishment by the School of "summer activities."

Have you perhaps been in a mine camp? Have you been in an abandoned mine camp? Have you gone in and out of the shacks clinging to the sides of the hills or squatting close together in dingy rows at the mine openings? Have you inspected the public privies, learned where the people get their water? Visited the store and saloon and brothel? Stood around the roads and street corners with the idle groups? Looked for a

---

[25] The development of the health program throughout the second year, 1935–36, is told in Chapter VII, pp. 368–76.

space to play ball, or plant a garden? Made real to yourself what you would do there after dark in the evenings? Considered what would be your chance to get out into the world and make a decent living? Looked for comfort or beauty or inspiration?

If you have, you will know that neither hope nor ambition, nor a decent living, nor recreation, nor enjoyment, is possible. Fetid, crowded, steaming heat in summer; bitter, desolate, paralyzing cold in winter.

"The people are hungry," Miss Davis said to me when I came, "not for food now—they can be fed—but for other things."

"Why," I asked a worker who had lived in the mine camps, "are we so impatient at Arthurdale? We can't wait for anything to happen." "Probably," he answered, "because they've been waiting all their lives."

No wonder, then, that the pace was so fast—Labor Day, square dances, Hallowe'en, plays, singing groups, basketball games, Club meetings, Christmas. We initiated and furthered "good times" because it seemed to us that they were essential to recovery. We knew that they would help the homesteaders to forget "the dark days" and reassure them of the happier present. In them we all came to know each other well, and from them a part of our recreational program was born.

Square Dances

A square dance every Saturday night was going on when we came. Miss Sheffield, one of the teachers in the School, describes it:

The Center is lighted, and cars—mostly "has-beens"—are parked closely around the square. Music comes strumming through the closed doors of the Assembly Hall. You open the door and push past the doorkeepers into a crowded hall where the scuffle of feet almost drowns the twanging orchestra. A square dance is going on.

"Swing your partner. That's nice, do it twice. Now, hokey-pokey back to place," Mr. Rogers, the Caller, bellows seriously through a megaphone. The orchestra fiddles madly. The dancers swing and turn, forming and breaking patterns constantly. Chris glides and swings nonchalantly in perfect time. Laughton scuffs and bends his knees, keeping his back poker-stiff. Ben Webb, fat and genial, twirls lightly while his partner can hardly keep feet on the ground. Old man Webber hops and skips, while Johnnie MacDonald clumps sure-footed in his clumsy boots.

One of the women teachers and I were always there and chaperoned the girls, so the mothers who were careful began to let them come. The question came up at the Men's Club —how much admission should we charge? And what about the boys out of work, should they pay too? And should the dance be public, or on invitation? Why have them, anyway, they would ask when the matter seemed insoluble. "For the boys and girls," I said; "they need a good time."

Everyone who came, as a matter of fact, had a good time. The young people danced, the older people danced. Mothers and babies and children watched from the benches around the sides of the Hall. The teachers who liked to dance and the wives of the men teachers came. Two of the men on the staff, Mr. Collins and Mr. Beecher, took a hand in the dance orchestra.[26]

The First Christmas at Arthurdale

At the square dance one night Mrs. Hogan was talking to me as we sat on the bench along the wall watching together.

"Hain't I never told you about last Christmas?" she said. "We was living in a house hadn't got no windows—just a door and big cracks in the walls that the snow come through something terrible. Had to stop up the cracks, they was that wide, with sacks. There wasn't nothing to eat but carrots and them

---

[26] See Chapter V, pp. 220–2.

without salt. And of course I hadn't nothing for the children. I hated to tell them. But they said: 'It must be *some* kind of a day, Mother. People are getting presents.' "

That story brought us our Christmas. We bought at wholesale toy stores, with money given by a friend, toys for all the children from a month to twenty-five years old. In a classroom one cold night up at the Mansion a group of men and women met with me to plan our Christmas. On the blackboard we wrote down the committees we thought of and assigned everyone a part in the preparations.

Those of us who were there that first Christmas will never forget it: the day the men brought in, trailing behind the big truck, a great hemlock from the forest; the anxiety lest the ground pine for the wreaths be buried beneath the snow; the evenings in the Mansion kitchen, when women and men and teachers and children made popcorn balls; the days in the High School shed when all the older boys painted scenery and properties with me for the Christmas play—a dramatization of the carols we had been practicing;[27] the day when Miss Stanton arrived from New York with the Christmas tree ornaments, and half the community turned out to await her coming at the Center; the snowy nights when we all trooped over to the Assembly Hall and made the wreaths and decorated the tree. "My, ain't we having fun! I've been out every night this week," one of the women said. "Turn on the lights just once more, Brooks," they would beg one of the men whose electrical knowledge entitled him to wire the tree. And with the room dark, the Tree would appear, sparkling with lights—red and white and blue and yellow—before we went back home through the snow.

"There ain't never going to be anything like it—our first Christmas at Arthurdale," they would say over and over. We borrowed chairs from the State University seventeen miles

---

[27] See Chapter V, p. 259.

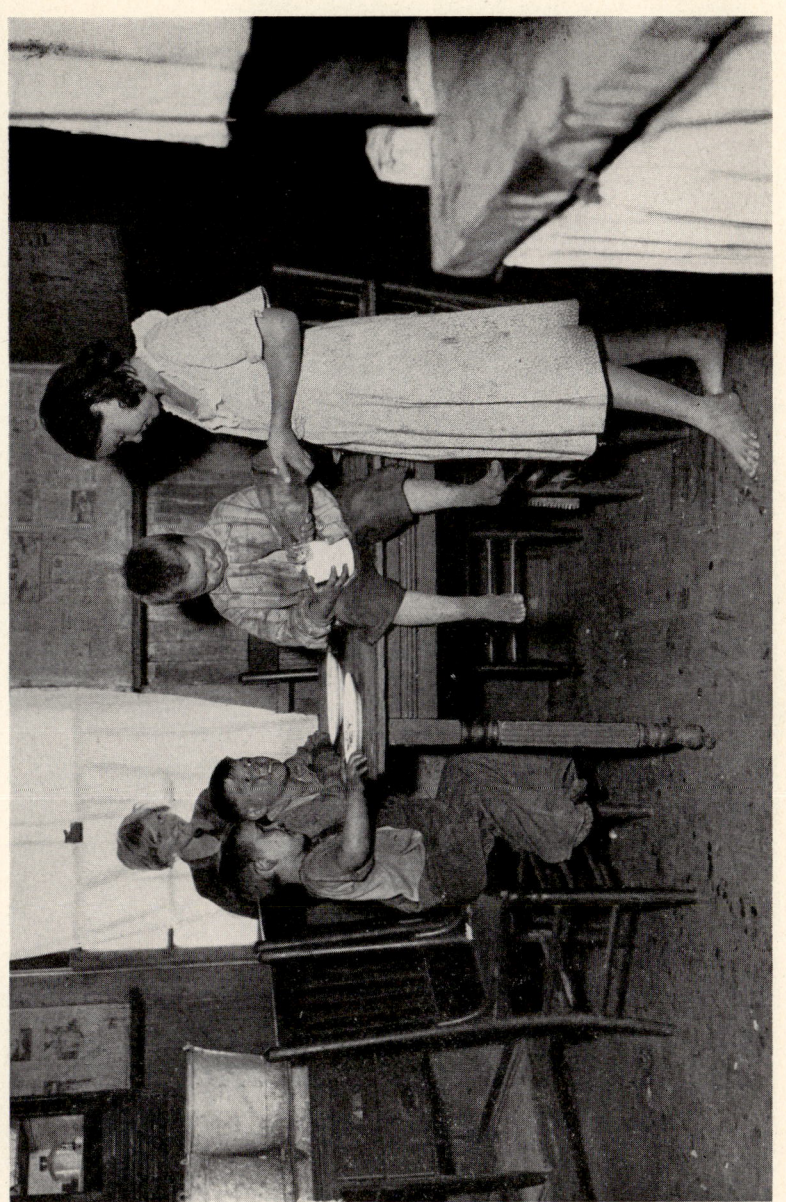

A FAMILY IN SCOTT'S RUN

away, and lights for the Christmas play were lent by the movie house in Morgantown.

Late in the afternoon on Christmas Eve, word came that a child of one of the families was ill with pneumonia. Every doctor for miles around was out. Baffled at the telephone, I finally, with the help of the doctor's wife, traced one who was out rabbit-hunting. The gathering in the crowded hall, packed with all the members of all the families, the carols led by a guitar played from under the branches of the great Tree, the shepherds under the stars, the march of the Kings through the crowd, the discovery of Mary and the Child bathed in light and glory—these were shot through with anxiety for the little girl. Finally, passed up by the crowd of men and boys at the back of the hall, came the word that the doctor had come and would return again later that night.

It was, I truly think, in the joys and the emotion of that Christmas Eve that the spirit of the community was born.

So overflowing were the people's satisfactions, that Christmas morning brought early to my door men who had come for Miss Stanton and Miss Sedman to go with them to collect from the families food, extra canned goods, and toys they could spare, for other people in the neighborhood less fortunate than they.

The pleasures we had shared in Christmas preparations prompted a common desire "to go on having good times together," and gave rise to other gatherings during the year. These shared enjoyments welded the project together. The "dark days" began to recede and the people dared to believe in their good fortune.

"NIGHT SCHOOL" FOR THE OLDER BOYS AND GIRLS

An unforeseen result of getting ready for Christmas was an acquaintance with the needs of the older boys, who all these busy days followed us around and happily did any and every thing that was to be done, glad for some activity and occupation, of whatever sort.

The nurse was one day caring for a mother and baby in a large household. A tremendous clatter sounded from the cellar. "Goodness, Laughton," she called down, "what's happened?" "Nuthin'," Laughton said, "just the furnace door came off the hinges. Somethin' to do, anyhow."

When School reopened after the holidays, the staff and I put our minds on what could be done for the thirty-two older boys and girls whose problems we had postponed, as it were, until classes and activities on the project had got under way. We could, we decided, each of us offer some work in the afternoon and evening, and we drew up a kind of schedule, deciding, however, first to find out what the boys and girls themselves wanted. They were asked, but did not know, really. It was finally planned to hold classes for all the older boys and girls on the homestead who were not enrolled in School, after regular school hours, between three and nine o'clock.

We tentatively arranged courses in woodworking and electricity in the School Shop; in English (reading and writing); in athletics (basketball practice); in mathematics (simple processes and accounting); and, if desired, in History (reading of newspapers and periodicals, discussion of current events) and in Science (soils, biology). "Night School," they called it. Most of the boys had left school between the fifth and seventh grades and had been hanging around the mine camps since, unemployed a good part of the time. One had left school after the third grade. Three had entered High School before they quit. Tests revealed them *all* [28] as of fifth to seventh grade level in reading, arithmetic, and spelling. For the girls, we offered work in Home Economics at the Nursery School, and in pottery. They shared the boys' classes in English and typing.

---

[28] Except for the third grade student, and one other.

They all liked the idea, but found it almost impossible to come regularly after so long a period of doing nothing. With the co-operation of the Government project manager, occasional work, when the supply of FERA labor gave out at the end of each month, was arranged for the boys. It was given only to those whose attendance and work in "Night School" had been satisfactory. This coercion was deliberately planned, for it was soon clear that above all else they needed to be held to something until the habit of daily working was re-established. Even with coercion, regularity in attendance proved difficult for them.

Shop was a popular choice in courses, but in the beginning the boys' interest span was half an hour only. Then they were exhausted and had to sit down and rest and smoke. Their mental and physical muscles were flabby from disuse. Requirements of standards in work floored them; making anything well, redoing a piece of work, irked them almost beyond endurance. Resulting emotional upsets had to be straightened out. Yet they could, some of them, walk three miles from where they still lived and back again once or twice a day. The carpentry group ran around nineteen years of age. It had, perforce, to get acquainted with tools and materials, but it tackled such needs as bookshelves for the library and work benches for the Nursery School. During the spring these boys helped the men reconstruct an old bus for School use, working under the direction of the Shop teacher, Harry Carlson.

All the boys who took work in carpentry also worked on electricity. They studied the wiring of houses (work then going on in the project), and the safety measures connected with the use of electricity; something of the theory and the uses to which electricity can be put (electro-plating, radios, amplifiers); also, in some degree, motors and generators. Arrangements were made so that their work in construction on the project carried out the work that they did in the School Shop. One worked on the electric gang, eight as carpentry helpers, thirteen on roads and excavation, three in the concrete gang, and five as mason helpers.

Two Mathematics groups were formed: one learned to read and write numbers, add, substract, multiply and divide; the advanced group worked on methods of farm bookkeeping, on the arithmetic involved in building construction—using the blueprints of the architect as a basis—and on arithmetic related to the electrical shop work.

For the other classes: discussion of current events and newspaper articles proved difficult; Science was elected by one boy only, though a number hung around the Science room at night; typing classes included seven, four of whom proved very teachable.

Basketball practice was well attended (twenty-two out of thirty-two) all winter. In the spring, the boys made somewhat fitful and half-hearted attempts to put the baseball diamond into shape.

English was elected by fifteen boys and girls. Writing was popular and so was being read to, although it was difficult to find stories within their understanding that held their interest. They tried a tale of adventure by Cornelia Meigs, *As the Earth Turns* by Gladys Carroll, *Horses* by Lucy Sprague Mitchell, *Lorna Doone,* and, by spring, various magazine articles. "Miss Sheffield, she must pretty near know that there book by heart, because when I was readin' she'd know the word I missed, just in a flash, without lookin'," one of them told me admiringly.

They worked on spelling and questions of grammar, "sayin' it just right," and "writin' a good fist." Two members of the group were so handicapped and embarrassed before the others that "tutoring" was arranged for them separately with one of the primary teachers. They began with her on third grade material, improving rapidly to fifth grade level in a few weeks. "I'm gettin' on pretty well," one of these boys said. "I can read pretty nearly every tolerable reasonable hard word now."

The group wrote business letters, in which they had keen interest, and individual long stories which they greatly enjoyed writing and hearing read.

The girls, perhaps because of their home duties in cooking and caring for younger children, or because no pressure was put upon them for these reasons, attended less well than the boys their own special classes in pottery and Home Economics at the Nursery School.[29]

What they all learned at "Night School" amounted to little, except the reacquiring of the habit of working again. However, it is not possible to over-emphasize the importance for them of this reacquisition. By May, the boys were doing six to eight hours' work a day on the project construction and carrying night school with it—an outcome which even we, in our optimism, had hardly expected. The money they earned yielded them clothes—and self-respect. It was a satisfaction to see them at the dances in new pants and shirts, sunburned and heavier, invigorated and erect.

I came home one night for supper to find Donald there on some errand. He lingered, turning his cap round and round. "It seems like before you all came, there warn't no place in the world for us," he said—and bolted.

SUMMER ACTIVITIES, 1935

Having evacuated the Mansion on June 3 in expectation of its removal to make room for the proposed inn, the School, while its new buildings rose slowly from the ground, was again homeless. It reverted to rooms at the Town Center for my office and the doctor's office and concentrated the work in Science and Shop and the summer library in the High School Shed, which was still left us. George Beecher stayed to

---

[29] However, two of these girls assisted in preparing and serving lunches at the Nursery School, and later became first student teachers and then teachers there.

guide work in these fields and to help in the organization of the first farm co-operative,[30] and in the work on the School gardens. Fletcher Collins met drama groups, and worked on the Music Festival.[31] We had decided to make use of the summer months for health work, and the doctor, nurse, and dentist worked from dawn to dark.

Athletics

Carleton Saunders, the director of Athletics, who took charge of the summer athletic program, was assisted by two college students, James Myers, Jr., and Barbara Myers, who were visiting on the homestead. At dusk everyone came out and played ball—children, boys and girls, and the women. Those who were not playing sat around on the grass and watched. We got then our first sense of our new School grounds, this evening use of the playing fields seeming in some way to give them to us. Mr. Saunders writes in his account of the summer's work:

The girls and women formed a group varied in ages as well as in co-ordination of muscles and ability to play games. One of the mothers came up to me after what I should have called the strenuous game of mushball and said: "I'm so glad you have these games for us women because I feel so rested now. I've been working in the garden all day and it gets so tiresome." And she was a grandmother, too! The women took their games in much more of a leisurely way than the men did, and it was not so much a matter of beating someone as of getting some fun and relaxation.

The decision to foster a full athletic program this first summer sprang out of our realization that the people needed to learn to play, and to play themselves, not merely watch others play. This was not easy to accomplish. We found not only that it was necessary to make it possible for these people to have relaxation, but that their inertia and lack of familiarity with

---
[30] See this chapter, pp. 110–1.
[31] See Chapter V, "Cultural Resources," pp. 242–8.

games and of any habit of playing had to be overcome, and that individuals had to be inducted into the enjoyment of sports. This was done by friendly calls at the houses, fraternizing with groups at the Center after work hours, and personally getting one person after another to come out and try it. This particular kind of effort is often required in launching any enterprise. James Myers reports the success of this effort as follows:

In fostering athletic activities for the summer months we were primarily up against a more basic and elementary problem than the mere administration of games.

While school was going on, athletics were a regular part of the school day and accepted as such. Without the drawing card of the School, the problem was to get the boys to come out as regularly as possible and get worked into their systems the habit of getting out for games in which everyone took part. The only effective way is to see them personally and get a few to come out and have a good time. They learn by experience, and it all takes time.

The small boys turned out and played a great deal of mushball, a little baseball; they jumped vigorously into the new sawdust-filled pits, threw horseshoes, played kickball and dodgeball.

The older boys came out en masse in the evening for the Mushball League. In fact this whole group turned out regularly and fully, proving that if anything interests them, it's athletics.

The men's baseball team was composed mainly of Reedsville and neighboring towns' boys. Arthurdale was represented by three or four players. They called themselves "Arthurdale," however, and Mr. Saunders coached them. They practiced and played most of their games in Reedsville, owing to our lack of a diamond.

Work on the diamond was heartbreakingly slow—fitful labor by the boys alternating with very occasional help from Government rollers and steam shovels. But by mid-summer, crowds of people and cars thronged the field—such as it was —on Sunday afternoons. It was especially the homesteaders' pleasure to watch "a good game," and whole families came from adjoining towns and from the country around. We found at Arthurdale, as we had in Kentucky, that games provided the most popular neighborhood recreation.

By the summer's end, it is not too much to say that games belonged to everyone and were not simply part of a school program, or wholly a matter of passive watching and vicarious exercise.[32]

EARLY PROBLEMS IN FARMING

All through the early spring of 1935 we struggled with the problems of clearing the remainder of the land (about 72 acres) that was still covered with stumps and bushes and of planting the gardens. The first year on the project the clearing of land, grubbing, plowing, and planting had been sustained in large measure by the Government; the agricultural work was directed by Bushrod Grimes, who had organized State Garden Clubs in which some of the men had worked before they came to Arthurdale. By mid-winter of 1934-35, a proposal to form a farm branch of the Mountaineer Craftsmen Co-operative was discussed, and estimates were made with the aid of a Washington farm official, and revised under advice from the Agricultural Department of the State University in Morgantown regarding the West Virginia climate and the Arthurdale soil. Advice on the clearing of the homestead land was given by an agricultural adviser from Washington, and a good deal of grubbing was accomplished by FERA labor.

THE FIRST FARM CO-OPERATIVE

George Beecher, the head of the High School, who helped in the organization of the first farm co-operative, writes:

A co-operative, known as the Reedsville Branch of the Mountaineer Craftsmen Co-operative Association, was organized during the winter with a membership of the large majority (86) of the homesteaders. An application was made for a grant or loan from the Government to the Farm Branch.

---

[32] The development of the interest in athletics during the next year is described in Chapter VII, pp. 378-81.

FIRST GRADE AT RECESS

Using Nursery School Playground beside the Mansion Which Housed Grades 1 to 8 in 1934–35

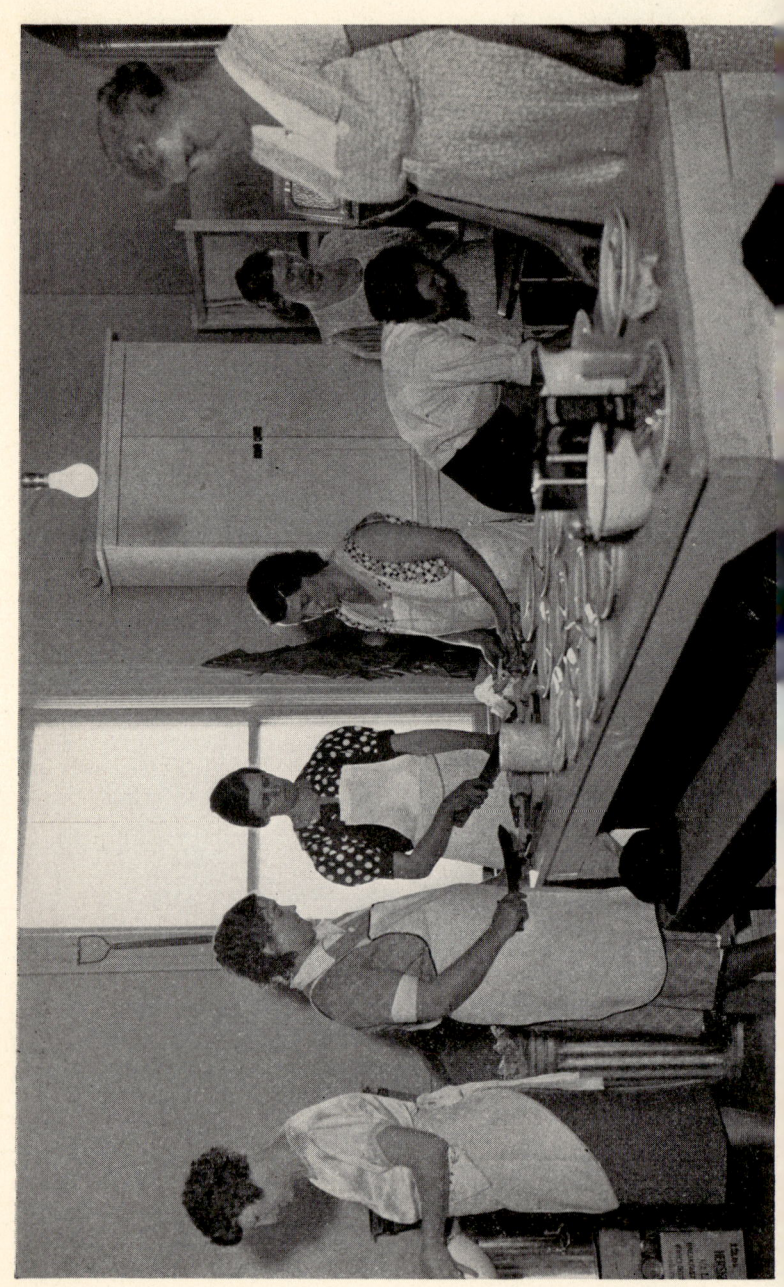

COMMUNITY EDUCATION: ARTHURDALE

In the meantime, the season was advancing, and farm work had to begin with uncertainty as to how the homestead could finance its large seed and fertilizer requirements. A little over a week ago the news came that the Co-operative had been granted a loan.

The Farm Co-operative [Mr. Beecher reports, May 1] has begun active work this week on the purchase and distribution of farm seeds and fertilizers. The newly organized Co-operative has been under heavy pressure in trying to manage a smooth and quick distribution of the incoming materials.

Almost before the Co-operative organization was in running order, the plowing and disking of homestead land was well along toward completion. The cost of operating the tractors is being borne by the homesteaders, and much of the work is being done by them after regular hours of work. For the last two weeks, tractors have been running until dark during fair weather.

The gardens were planted finally, with only such assistance as could be obtained through the State University's Agricultural Department in demonstrations of the best methods of planting and cultivating potatoes, etc. They prospered fairly well, really remarkably well considering that they had, necessarily, been made without expert help.

The School group participated in these problems of farming because at that time no other assistance was available. It was July before an agriculturalist was appointed to the project.

School Gardens and School Lunches

The School, faced with the problem of providing school lunches in 1935–36 for a still larger enrollment of children (estimated at 350 as against 246 of the first year), became a member of the Farm Co-operative, and bought through it fertilizer and seeds. Fifteen acres of land were used for the School garden: five acres of unassigned land for vegetables, and ten acres for potatoes—the latter given by Mr. Beecher and myself from the plots we occupied. It was proposed to plant and cultivate this garden by labor volunteered by the fathers, the School supplying the seeds and fertilizer. This enterprise proved difficult. No official agriculturalist yet being on the project, the organization of the work fell on Mr. Beecher. He reported, June 1:

> The last meeting of the Men's Club was fairly frank about the School garden.
> One man said his own land was getting out of control but he would help later on. Another said he was too old to work after hours (which is true). Others said they would help although, living five miles away, they had a hard time doing their own farming and then helping in the School garden, too, before getting home to supper. Another said there was no use beating about the bush—that there was plenty of labor available, if the men took the interest to come out.
> The meeting thus went on—only a fifth of the homesteaders present—and before long the men accepted the point that careful arrangements, with shifts of six men for one evening in two weeks, would be agreeable to them and would keep the School garden supplied with labor. Before the meeting was over, one man was to bring along his pony to do the plowing, and the men who couldn't come would in their turns send their sons.
> It all sounded perfectly simple, and the enthusiasm was at a pitch. Actually, there is a terrific difficulty in notifying each man of his turn to work, and of explaining how it is that some men work while others refuse or think up an excuse.

This enterprise was difficult, not only because of the slowly developing sense of community responsibility, but also because, for homesteaders who lived in houses on the project, working in the School garden meant finding the time that could be spared from their own gardens and walking to and from the School garden plots, a distance of half a mile to a mile and a half. For the homesteaders who still lived off the project, it meant going without supper in order to work in both their own and the School garden, and then walking the two to five miles back home.

Finally, with the welcome help after the middle of July, of the newly appointed agriculturalist, Mr. Pharr, the crop was harvested. And the women, as soon as their own canning was under way, gave whatever time they could spare to the School canning. All that fall, in the kitchen of the dismantled Mansion, mothers and teachers valiantly coped with the huge task. That about 60 percent of what had been planned was finally canned, and that enough potatoes to carry the School through the winter were brought in from the fields, was really better than could be expected, although not all we had hoped for. This food did, however, provide the children with school lunches.

Shared work of this kind is especially difficult. It is done by women whose own work at home and in their gardens takes all their time and energy—work on which their own family's food for the winter depends. Perhaps two-fifths of the women were kept at home by babies or young children; so the work fell on the other three-fifths, who felt that not everyone did her share. They, the women and men, both, are generous and capable. It is difficult to express how hampering is their disappointment over others' failure to do what they feel is their share. Whether the complainers live up to their own obligations, or not, this disappointment is felt and is expressed. It is in part virtuous indignation and, in part, some sense of harm done to an ideal of co-operation. In any case, this disappointment keeps back from full functioning those who need the release of everybody's participation. In spite of this, a great deal of work was given willingly, if sporadically, especially if the men and women were not worried by too grave and too pressing a responsibility.

The foregoing analysis of the difficulties encountered in canning states the problems which were met also in the mothers' preparation of School lunches, and, in fact, in any and all co-operative working together on the project—a kind of working, it must be recognized, that was new to them.

THE PEOPLE: EDUCATION IN HOMESTEAD WORK AND LIVING

It is clear that it is *the education of people in a growing community,* through the agency of a school, which is being recounted here. On the homestead, *the community needs and activities were the means of education.*

It was the needs of the people individually and collectively that prescribed what, of all the things we might have done, was done. Certain of these needs, such as health and recreation and farming, were apparent on the face of the situation. Others soon appeared, like the women's need for help in canning and cooking, planning and buying, and the men's need of assistance in managing money and in learning to work together. Everyone faced new problems in the adjustment to living in new good houses, with the responsibilities and opportunities this entailed—a far cry from merely existing in dirty, broken shacks with public privies, no lights, and no water. They had to learn how to plant gardens and raise and can vegetables, raise pigs and chickens, take care of cows and milk, kill pigs and cows, and cure and can meat. Back of their lives in the mine camps were childhood memories of life in the country, on "farms"; for some of them occasional experiences in small farming, and, for a few, brief work in the Garden Clubs instituted by Miss Davis's group.

Life in the mine camps had, however, almost obliterated their memories of farm life. Buying out of the mine store, eating out of cans, careless living in company houses, periods of inactivity and anxiety whenever the mines closed down, had constituted their life since childhood; and, after 1931, long months and years of living in whatever way they could, picking up an occasional temporary job, and between times existing on relief allowances of food and coal.

How difficult and how demanding were the new conditions of life and work at Arthurdale, we shall never know. The adjustment was a strain, because it was adjustment along every line at once. At fifty and forty and thirty years of age,[33] the men had to learn new and different trades. They had all come from a long period of inactivity, with its paralyzing physical and psychological effects. Back of their idleness lay their highly skilled and technical work as miners—hazardous, underground.

Some features of this work may have helped them in their adjustment to new and different jobs, as did also perhaps their experiences in casual and varied jobs picked up in the lean years.[34] One can only surmise. They never talked about it. They were engrossed in tackling the new jobs, and almost without exception they made good at them. They became carpenters, masons, plumbers, painters, auto-mechanics, electricians, truck and tractor drivers, and blacksmiths. In these new occupations a new differentiation of skills and abilities began to appear; by mid-year, 1936, one-third of them were rated as "skilled" workers in these jobs, several rose to be "labor foremen," one became a boss painter. Their education in learning new trades should be remarked upon, also their adaptability and flexibility and capacity to learn. It was, I think, remarkable and significant.

---

[33] Of 106 married men on the project, 35 were between 40 and 50 years of age; 34 were between 30 and 40; 16 were in the 20's; 16 in their 50's; 4 between 60 and 70; 1 was over 70. There were 21 unmarried men between 18 and 25.

[34] Summary of positions held by homesteaders in the coal mines before January 1934:

Foreman or pit boss	3
Skilled jobs	21
Electrician; pillar man; fire boss; timber sawyer; trackman; cutter.	
Intermediate jobs	19
Weighman; driver; builder of brattices; lamp repairer; pumper; motorman; shooter.	
Unskilled jobs	85
Laborer (10); coal loader (60); trapper; boiler fireman; tippleman; mule driver; handy man.	

(Labor Inventory of Arthurdale Homesteaders, Jan. 1, 1934.)

Positions other than in mines held by homesteaders prior to 1934: electrical machinist; machinist's helper; auto body assembler; glass-blower; barber; cook.

They wanted to do it. They meant to succeed. They were determined that "the kids should have a better chance." About themselves they felt discouragement. "You ain't never going to make nothing of us," they said that first winter. "We're like them old apple trees out there, all gnarled and twisted." It was for the children that they made the effort and that they gave support to the School. The help the School gave them they received without much notice. *Arthurdale* helped them. Well, the School was Arthurdale.

If one seeks explanation, it was perhaps the stock they came from that gave them their physical vigor, which survived the hardships and revived with work and food and hope: Scotch-Irish, 70 percent; Pennsylvania-Dutch, 25 percent; French, 2 percent; Austrian, 1.5 percent; Czech, 0.5 percent; Scandinavian, 1 percent.

As time went on, certain needs became apparent which only the slow changes of growth and experience could meet. They arose from insecurity and fear which were too deeply ingrained to be shaken off. The occupation of mining, which is destructive work and a dangerous job, and life in mine camps, bred habits of complaint, suspicion, obedience to "the boss," and recourse to the relief of excess, and also casual and irresponsible living. If this description appears negative only, it is partly because these bad effects of their former life persisted, appeared time and time again, and were often referred to by the people themselves in explanation of their difficulties and problems.

When they first came onto the homestead, exactly these same attitudes and practices threatened to dominate. Although they had risked their fate because of a new hope and an untested belief, they expected everything and nothing, were aroused to suspicion by the slightest mischance, complained from dawn to dark. There were a few exceptions. It was clear that we had somehow to rid ourselves of this burden of mistrust and suspicion, if we could. To counteract it, the School group, whom they knew well as neighbors, soon made clear the fact that there were to be no concealments or doubledealing or political pull, that "things were to be done decent" as they hoped, and that whatever was done they were to have share in doing. And the men and women themselves possessed traits of generosity and humor and an unbroken gaiety— traits that must also have been engendered by their life and experiences as miners, and by their upbringing and racial background. But at first it was difficult, and for everyone. After the bewilderment of the first months, and the hopes of spring and summer and early fall that first year, came the days of winter with necessarily slack work on construction and frequent idleness, when the old ways swept over them. This rhythm held the second year also.[35] Gradually, however, there grew out of the new work and living and better health some new and different interests, expectation of wellbeing, and shared purpose. The changes were at once greater and less than one would expect.

At first, each person held himself apart from the others. In the camps, the mothers said, they had feared to have their children "run" and play outside the house. Many of the children had been held back from attending school because of the dangers of going there and back. However, at Arthurdale, the School which they had helped make, the interest and concern of the teachers who came and visited with them and "looked after" the children and whom they knew as neighbors, their own share in a life where "things were done decent," reassured them. They dared to relax and to trust other people and believe in their good fortune.

---

[35] See Chapter VII, pp. 356–65.

THE MEN'S AND WOMEN'S CLUBS: SOCIAL AND CIVIC INSTRUMENTALITIES

The Men's Club and Committees

The Men's Club was from the outset an entity, its nucleus the group who had lived in the Mansion barracks the first winter of 1933–34, with the memories of their life there as a bond. Some had known each other in the State Garden Clubs back in the Scott's Run days. These earlier experiences, however, contributed grievances and feuds, as well as bonds of association, which appeared during the Club's first year of activities, and reappeared at times during the second year also. A feeling—a strong feeling—for the Club was dominant, but there seemed at first to be no business to engage it. Fundamental decisions were made, probably from necessity, in Washington or by the Government's representatives. What could be done by the Club in the organization of community life was not, in the beginning, clear. Later, when the Club was faced with some pressing community problem, the men found that it could not be handled satisfactorily in the large Club meeting and decided to refer such questions to committees. These committees studied the problem and reported to the Club their findings, together with recommendations for action.

Mr. Collins, one of the School staff and himself a member of the Club, gives the account following of the work of the Fire Committee on which he served:

Fire Committee
Getting Off from a Bad Start

In the early days of Arthurdale one of the Federal construction foremen had undertaken to recruit a community fire department. There was a large turn-out for the organization meeting. Having been accustomed to fire-fighting in the coal mines, most of those who came to this meeting thought that, as in the mines, all members of the fire department would be paid for their services. When in a few weeks they discovered that no one was to be paid for this community function, interest in the fire department faded. Nevertheless, the need for adequate protection against fire had in this way been brought to everyone's attention and it was not long before the Men's Club was demanding to know why there was no fire department.

Preliminary Talk and Opinions

Everyone who had spoken of serving on the committee was invited to meet and discuss the problem the following evening. About twenty men appeared.

Some were in favor of expensive fire-fighting equipment; others advocated an inspection and clean-up of fire hazards in the houses and community buildings; others were interested in developing a first-aid team to learn how to resuscitate those overcome by smoke, and to learn the fireman's carry; others had a strong conviction that the main thing was for the fire department to have a shooting range, like the one firemen at Sabraton had. Finally, the necessities of a fire department program were catalogued, and those men who had been especially interested in each necessity formed themselves into sub-committees to work out the details of the program.

First Things to Be Done

Two men who were particularly interested in fire-prevention made up a blank form for recording the results of house-to-house inspections; the twenty firemen passed on this form, criticized it, and emended it. After it was mimeographed by the School, the two men spent two Saturdays and Sundays making the rounds of the houses, and carefully inspected each house for fire hazards. They made a digest of the conditions found, and separated their suggested remedies into two classes: repairs or alterations which should rightfully be undertaken by the Federal representative who acted as their landlord; and clean-ups and minor changes which the resident of the house could himself make. These recommendations the men took to the persons involved, and action was forthcoming immediately.

Another group decided that there were several things that each homesteader should know about fire hazards and fire-fighting in the home. They listed these items, together with a statement to their fellow-homesteaders urging carefulness and intelligence in handling furnace and stove and inflammable materials. The whole was mimeographed at the School and sent to each homestead family.

Still another sub-committee made a careful inspection of the school and community buildings, and made a list of hazards found which was presented to the Federal representative.

Learning from Others' Experiences

The entire fire committee also met with the Fire Chief of the local division of the Bethlehem Mines Corporation (located a few miles away), and learned much from him about fire protection and fire-fighting. He returned several times, and was a real stimulus to interest in the Arthurdale Fire Committee.

Checking Facts

The Fire Committee also investigated the existing fire-fighting equipment, such as the fire extinguishers which had been put up by the Federal Government in the School and community buildings. It was the Committee's judgment that these were too few in number and were not of a type suitable for fighting the kind of fire to be expected in these buildings. Recommendations were made by the Committee to the Federal representative.

The Committee also tried out the large 40-gallon extinguishers which were mounted on heavy steel wheels and which could, theoretically, be moved to the scene of the fire. When ten members of the Committee tried to pull one of these a short distance, they decided that never would the extinguisher arrive at the scene of a fire to be of use. Accordingly, they arranged to have an attachment welded onto the handle of the extinguishers, and to have a complementary attachment fixed to the rear of a Government automobile which was always parked in the Government garage, and which could be reached at night. The extinguisher was kept fastened to the car, and the combination served as a make-shift fire engine.

Arrangements and Preventive Measures

Meanwhile, the Fire Committee divided the Arthurdale area of nearly three square miles into districts, and a captain of each district was chosen, with instructions to organize a group of men who would drill and be ready for any fire which broke out in their district. To aid them, each of the three remaining large extinguishers was placed on a near-by hill, where they could—comparatively quickly—be rolled to the fire. In addition, a system of signaling the garage where the make-shift fire engine was kept, was evolved.

Results

During the first two years of Arthurdale, there was not one serious fire which required the assistance of others than the inmates of the house. The Fire Committee felt that this record justified its existence and that it had been rewarded for its efforts.

Furthermore, the Committee had not only learned much about ways and means of solving acute community problems, but had also developed in the process an *esprit de corps* which to them was very pleasing.

THE WOMEN'S CLUB

In October 1934, the women organized themselves into a Club under the title of "The Eleanor Roosevelt Farm Women's Association." For two or three months after organization, all that the women did at their Club meetings was to talk and visit together. To them it was at first enough just to get acquainted with each other and to gather together. They had no plans to suggest, and wanted only to hear reports from the School Director of what was being planned. Problems such as school lunches and layettes and help in sickness brought the first response.

The women enjoyed sewing together and sometimes quilted at each other's houses. They drew closer together just before Christmas in quilting a cover for Mrs. Roosevelt. Preparations for our Christmas festivities engaged everyone on committees. Groups gave plays and came together for singing. Visiting grew up. Club meetings went on.

As the women became acquainted with each other and used to the sociability of homestead life, the Club gatherings became less of a get-together and more of a meeting. Several committees were formed: "Speakers and Art Exhibitions" (the latter suggested by the children's paintings at School); "Fun and Movies" (that is, entertainments by Club members); "Children's Plays and School Work"; "Home Decoration"; "Sewing"; "Recipes"; "Current Events"; "Gardens." These did not really function as committees; rather, they named interests of the members. Temporary working committees, like the various Hospitality Committees to entertain visiting groups, were formed on occasion.

Toward spring, a Constitution and By-Laws were drafted. Discussion as to whether they were to be a Farm Club, or to affiliate themselves with the National Federation of Women's Clubs, ran on all year. They heard speakers from each national organization. They felt themselves to be farm women in their interests on the homestead, yet they rather coveted the information and programs of the other association. However, they decided— for that year, at least—that there was enough going on at Arthurdale to satisfy their desires.

What was important, it seems to me, about these two Clubs was not so much their organization or operation, as that they were social and civic instrumentalities. Their existence brought people together, matters of common interest were there considered, and through the Clubs the men and women made acquaintance with each other and with the needs of the community. They were the means for group community action and the channel for education in civic matters. At them and through them, we and the homesteaders slowly made out together what was our part in community affairs. Most of the women teachers and I and the wives of the men teachers usually attended the Women's Club meetings, and the men on the staff and I, as Director of the School, attended the Men's Club. On the homestead, teachers took their place as citizens; they and the other homesteaders jointly attacked their community problems.

COMMUNITY EDUCATION—LEARNING BY LIVING

What the foregoing accounts of the health work, recreation, "Night School," summer activities, early farming problems, School gardens and School lunches, the people and the Clubs, disclose is needs, and the ways in which the community school functioned in meeting them. The pattern weaves back and forth between community events and the life and work of the School. *Arthurdale—a School* is the truest statement of the facts. The accounts reveal also that, so far as community and School enterprises were successful, it was due to shared efforts to meet needs that were recognized.

It is in this matter of the recognition of a need, and in the joint endeavor to meet it, that community education lies. For no people would it have been any more difficult to face the problems of building a new community by their own efforts than for people of mine camps, and after a period of unemployment. Of course they did not expect to be well, did not know how to farm, conduct town meetings, solve civic problems. Why should they? How could they? Yet the interesting thing is that they learned quickly how to do all these things. Adult education? This education of adults was learning to live. The demands of the situation, and their efforts to meet these, taught them. Compare the genuineness and potency of such learning with usual courses in adult education.

Community education is, it seems to me, more concerned with life and people and places than is realized. It names a process, a growth. It takes account of the means at hand for the discovery and development of resources and methods and materials. The unique feature of community education is that it refers to some kind of inclusive situation in which people of all ages, in all their activities and relationships, together work for shared results. Social functioning delimits the term "education," and makes it a function of living. This changes education as we have known it. It becomes less impervious and predetermined and more penetrated by realities. Community education subserves needs. They alter its approach, condition its content. Its scope is widened, necessarily; its basic responsibilities become imperative.

No better or more challenging educational situation could possibly be found than that offered by a homestead community. There, all the social and economic forces that shape lives are clearly known and must be grappled with. There, genuine needs make responsible and authentic every effort to meet them. The situation itself prescribes action, and tests every endeavor. This is, in my judgment, the only "evaluation" intellectually valid of the social functioning of education.

How community education can and does take place, the various stages of its process, and the movement from one stage to the next, the factors involved, the obstacles and opportunities which change—and often change places—the accelerations and retardations, all these need to be described if we are to grasp exactly what community education is, not as a theory, but as a matter of fact. This chapter, and the ones that follow, attempt to give an account of this process, now from the viewpoint of the School and its work, now from that of community activities.

Co-operative working on common problems is a process whose course is slow, and often halting. A community school is not provided—it grows, by concurrence and consent. It is a function, never a system. It is a joint production, the result of living and learning, shaped and guided by many events, as well as by ideas and purposes, and by the feelings and responses of a large number of people, above all by the desires and needs of the people whose school it is.

CHAPTER III

THE SCHOOL AT ARTHURDALE

Environment and Education in Rural Areas

IN working out our program plans for this rural school, we knew from our work in Kentucky just how essential it was to familiarize ourselves with the region and the State, for the sake of understanding better the background and lives of the people with whom we had come to live and work.

Kentucky had shown us that when people shared the information they possessed, we were the gainers as well as they. For books and statistics never contain the revealing and pertinent incidents or the illuminating details that people can supply. They are able to furnish facts about the history, folklore, and culture of their region undiscoverable in other ways, that are of great significance. Memories, traditions, stories handed down from father to son, provide data that histories seldom if ever capture. Stored in barns and sheds and the old small houses are possessions of historic value—land grants, bills of sale, inventories, old flax wheels, lamps, tools, and utensils—remnants of a living past.

Children and adults in remote rural areas have, of course, few contacts with events beyond their own neighborhood, and therefore scanty information about the outside world. That is to be expected. More surprising, however, is the fact that they know—most of them—little about the region in which they live. Or, rather, it is truer to say that, although they know a great many things about it, the meaning of what they know is not clear to them. A countryman's observation of what goes on around him is acute and minute. With this knowledge, however, goes an ignorance that underlies his daily familiarities. It is not likely that he knows the source and the outlet of the river into which empties the creek that flows by his door; the other parts of the State like and unlike the part he lives in; its products and industries; the States that border it; the whole picture of the days in which his grandfathers lived, and the part they played in the development of the region and of the State. Especially he needs to comprehend his own life that passes, sunrise to sunset, in the familiar round of living. He cannot, of course, comprehend it or the lives of others in other places and times except through the experiences he has himself had, and the understandings he may have gained. The way out of his limitations, and the only way out, is through gaining the meaning of what he knows, and by fresh experiences going on to new learnings.

I cannot claim that we started to familiarize ourselves with the region and the State, and to bring others to a realization of what they knew, with awareness of just how salutary and steadying this enterprise was to be. On the principles I have been describing, we began to find out all we could about this region to which we had come: its topography, its soil, rivers, animals, trees, and plant growth. What was raised here? Where was it marketed? What industries were situated here? What was the history of the region? Who settled it, and when? As we looked into these facts together, an interesting thing happened. These people—these miners, who had as children left farms to go with their fathers into the mines—discovered their past, and this past gave them security because it linked them up with their new future. So that these studies, which yielded information to us, gave to them background for their new lives at Arthurdale, a sense of belonging here, a feeling that the land was theirs.

Mining camps and miners we had none of us known before, and a homestead project was as untried and unknown to us as to the rest of the country. So there was little danger, conscious as we were of the need of familiarizing ourselves with new conditions, that we would make the mistake of trying a Kentucky recipe on a West Virginia problem. The differences of set-up and surroundings were dramatic and obvious.

Yet certain materials and methods we had forged to meet rural conditions were serviceable here. Some of the programs we had worked out in the rural school in Kentucky we used, developing and changing them so that they served as ways of learning what we needed to know in order to live in a homestead community. *And just so far as they were basic to a better understanding of the conditions of living,* they served the needs of this different rural section. Study of farms and farming, of transportation, of the building of a village, for instance, were made markedly different by the fact that here, at Arthurdale, life itself was a matter of raising gardens, building houses, making roads, clearing land, hauling materials, and developing a community. These occupations and concerns penetrated and shaped studies at school, not only farm and village studies, but science and history and mathematics, also.[1]

Again from our work at Ballard, we had learned something of the mental furnishing of rural children, the educational background of rural schools. We knew that in all likelihood knowledge of the Three R's would be scanty and uncertain; that there might be a small amount only of general information; that aptitudes might be undeveloped; and that the children would doubtless expect little from school. In West Virginia, as in Kentucky, we found the children far behind "grade level" in the "fundamentals," owing here to irregular schooling during the period of little food and no clothes and also, as often in remote rural areas, to overcrowded schools with

---
[1] See Chapter VI, "A Rural High School."

large classes or with many grades under one teacher. The children's information was very meager. Their experiences and contacts had, of course, been quite limited. They suffered, as was indicated earlier,[2] from the effects of malnutrition and lack of medical care, and from strain and insecurity.

"Do you like this house?" a homesteader who was fixing my plumbing asked. "Yes," I said, "do you like yours?" He turned his back. "There ain't no way of my tellin' you how I feel about my house. It's a dream come true, somethin' I always wanted, somethin' I never thought to have." Suddenly he rubbed his sleeve across his eyes. "And to think we have a good school for the kids, too. I was took from school when I was nine, in the fourth grade."

"A good school for the kids"—that was the first need.

It is astonishing always to me, the ease with which schooling is initiated. How easily and naturally children learn and work and play together. How little is needed to begin. How rapidly arrangements of organization are made. We had an empty mansion, and in no time at all it was a schoolhouse filled with children. There were 167 children waiting to come. Already they had met their teachers, had been in and out and around during the days of preparation, when they had helped with the rest. Once registered and their reported grades accepted for the time being, they went off to their classes quite as a matter of course. After weeks of getting ready, School was a reality at last.

"Making Bricks without Straw"

The difficulties of starting school work without equipment or teaching materials are described in the teachers' diaries. Fletcher Collins, the director of drama and music, who for the

---
[2] See Chapter II, pp. 93–4.

THE SCHOOL AT ARTHURDALE

first eight weeks in the fall taught the combined Seventh-Eighth Grade before the arrival of the County teachers, writes:

> For the first year, the physical equipment was more meager than that of the schools the children had come from. Hastily constructed pine benches and tables served as desks; there was no library until November. There was literally nothing but the bare tables and benches. And while both teachers and students felt the strangeness of the situation, we teachers later agreed that having started so primitively had been healthy. We were building from the ground up. Though equipment could not be added as soon as it was needed, every addition was functional and contributed to an organic development. Concretely, the question was not: "Here is a blackboard on the wall, what shall we do with it?" but rather: "Do we want a blackboard, and for what?" We found out, in brief, what was essential equipment, and what was merely ritualistic.[3]

The teacher of the Fourth Grade, Elisabeth Sheffield, whose group lived up in the corner room on the second story of the old Mansion, writes in her January report:

> School opened, yes, with one broken table, four temporary benches with backs on which to write, 12 penny pencils and a filler of lined paper—all for the Fourth Grade. That and nothing more. We were even missing two panes out of the bay windows. I didn't have a chair for a month. But the children—they loved it. The Mansion itself was a big, beautiful school to them, and toilets that "flushed." I was glad, very glad, when I saw how just right it was to them that we had started so simply. Neither the desks, nor the window glass, nor the blackboard mattered to them.
>
> One day the desks came—beautiful, shining desks, with grooves for pencils. They would tilt for writing, adjust to height, a drawer of one's own; we investigated everything about them. Then a blackboard—appreciated mostly by the teacher. Still no books, no shop, no clay, no anything.
>
> I looked around for what we could use. John Masters got clay from his creek. We collected corn and ground it between rocks, went over to Stearns' on a husking bee, visited flax threshing—everything we could think of that needed no books or materials.

---

[3] Half-Year Report, January 1935.

Let me say that I never saw such eager bringing of things from home. Hatchets were loaned, pots to dye in, and sacks to "pack" things in.[4]

The experience had its amusing side as well as a stimulating effect. I remember an incident of those badly equipped days. First to arrive were office desks, large and shining; but no chairs. We did not sit down as teachers for many weeks. One night about six o'clock, I was kneeling by my big office desk writing a letter. One of the homesteaders came into the office, which had been theirs, too, earlier, and to get into line for conversation knelt on the other side.

"Miss Clapp," he said, "you and the teachers work too hard."

"I know it," I said. "What can we do about it?"

"Well," he answered, "I ain't speaking just for myself but for the other men, too. There's a bunch of us ready when you call us. When a thing's to be did, I always say, 'Let's did it.'"

I cannot express how much that offer of help, which I so gladly accepted, warmed my heart.

When equipment finally arrived—desks for the children and teachers' chairs at last, some blackboards, some folding tables, blocks, and playground equipment for the Nursery School and Primary Grades—it still left many needs unmet. In the School Shop, with tools bought before we began, the teachers and the classes and the parents made tables, bookcases, and easels. One of the Federal purchasing agents himself chose the kitchen utensils and the sleeping blankets for the Nursery School. No provision, however, at first could be found for teaching materials—for books, and wood, and paper and paints, not to mention office and school supplies. Finally, legal opinion ruled that, as a dollar-a-year member of the

---

[4] Half-Year Report, January 1935.

Government, I was entitled to paper towels and toilet paper, telephone facilities, coal, electricity, and janitor's supplies. Later a fund was privately raised to supply the teaching materials and such necessities as paper napkins, soap, paper, chalk, etc. Afterward, the Preston County Board of Education provided the School with the usual school supplies.

Educational Use of Environment

When School began on the project in September 1934, the first fifty houses had been put up and were being finished and occupied. All through our two years on the homestead, construction went forward on additional houses, barns, and the new School buildings. Roads were made, land was cleared and farmed, wells were dug and septic tanks put in. This was ideal educationally. We made the fullest possible use of this situation at the School—with children of all ages.

The First Grade in its study of farming, and the Second Grade in the building of its village, were in fact learning from the activities of their own fathers in farming, in trucking, in building construction. What they studied everyone was learning and doing. Under no other circumstances would these studies have been so literally and so fully a part of their own lives. The trips they took were to see *their* house being built, *their* corn being planted, *their* cow being milked. All of everyone's time was spent in the midst of these activities. They went on around us all day long, and absorbed everyone's interest and attention.

To these children from the mine camps, all the farm processes were new and fascinating—disking the ground, planting and plowing, threshing, husking the corn, digging potatoes, milking and churning. Equally absorbing were the trucking, the building of houses and barns, the well-digger, and, in the spring, the laying of the foundations for the new School buildings. What the children learned about these activities went directly into their lives—their new lives at Arthurdale. To them, as to their fathers and mothers, the miracle was that the house and the cow, the barn and the corn, were theirs—their very own.

FARMING ON THE HOMESTEAD: FIRST GRADE

In the First Grade [Ethel Carlisle wrote] we study farm life to the extent that is sensible with little children. As farming is such an important part of the life on the homestead, this seemed the best study for them.

This fall we saw them thresh buckwheat, disk potatoes, plow, harrow, and plant wheat. The children also saw the homesteaders' display over in the High School Shed of produce raised at Arthurdale. In the spring there will be many more opportunities. Many of the homesteaders now—in January—have cows, and more are getting them all the time. We studied about milk. We made butter and cheese and used milk in cooking. We often go to see the cows.

We follow very closely all the building that is being done, also. They can just see Arthurdale grow. We watch the trucks, steam shovels, cement mixers, electric saws, road rollers and scrapers. When the barns were being built, we watched that very closely, too. Such little children have a keen interest in all that goes on around them. In their block building they show this variety of interest vividly. They build many houses, barns, trucks, busses, trains and aeroplanes. They were also interested in locating where they had lived, or where friends lived.[5]

Excerpts from Miss Carlisle's diary make clear the class's study of the various farm processes on the homestead:

THRESHING BUCKWHEAT

September 17, 1934. We went over to see the field of buckwheat across the road. We got some of the grains and saw the white substance inside and talked about making flour out of it. I found they had little notion of when it should be planted, etc.

---

[5] Half-Year Report, January 1935.

THE SCHOOL AT ARTHURDALE

September 25, 1934. I found out from Mr. Gordon (one of the homesteaders who knows about farming) last night just where they were to be threshing today. The men were so pleased that we came down to see it. We stayed quite a while, but we could have stayed much longer. The children asked to go again tomorrow. I said we would, as they will get more the second time.

September 26, 1934. We had a long discussion about our trip yesterday. I discovered that about all they had noticed yesterday was the grain coming out. Walter was the only one who had seen down inside the threshing machine and knew what happened. Today I wanted them to notice the machinery. They did, and Ben was especially interested in the tractor.

DIGGING POTATOES

September 29, 1934. This morning we discussed the kind of potatoes grown here. They saw trucks taking bags of potatoes that had been dug, so they were eager to go to the patch. It was down at the new school site, and was the community potato patch.

Down at the potato patch, the children immediately began to pick up potatoes and put them in a bag. Fern's father was working there and he isn't at all well, so he was very grateful for their help and sat down and rested for a few minutes. There was a team of horses there, too, which pleased the children. Several of the children's fathers were there and they were eager to answer any questions.

The participation of the children in the work they went to watch, and of the fathers in giving information sought, was certainly a unique feature of the Arthurdale trips.

DISKING AND PLANTING WINTER WHEAT

October 2, 1934. This morning Bradford told me that his father was disking down on A Road. As he is getting the field ready for planting wheat, I thought it worth while going down to see it. A big truck was unloading fertilizer on the way. We saw it and talked a little about it. They all had to walk around after the tractor and disk, and watch it break up the clods.

On the way down, Mrs. Thurston came out of her house and wanted to know where we were going. The mothers are always very much interested, and they seem to think it's so fine for the children to go out and see things.

October 3, 1934. This morning we had a discussion about harrowing and plowing and disking. We also talked about wheat—winter wheat and summer wheat.

Someone noticed Mr. Spelman planting wheat just across the road. We went down and watched. He was very nice and stopped the tractor and showed us where the wheat and fertilizer went into the ground.

Husking Corn

November 9, 1934. This morning the children decided that they wanted to help the men husk corn. They planned to ask them to give us one shock to husk. When we got there, they all went up to the man who was working and started husking. Wally was quite an expert, and told the others just how to do it.

Spring Planting and Plowing

April 23, 1935. Up until today the men were plowing so far away on the project that we could not go to see them. We have talked about the plowing and preparing of the soil, planting and growing of seed. So when Wendie said they were plowing at Mills's place just down the road I thought we should go. A man was plowing there with two mules instead of the tractor.

April 24, 1935. Mr. Gordon told us this morning that they were spreading lime on his place. On the way there we saw Mr. Spelman plowing under a field of rye. We stopped and watched him. Then we went on and saw the men putting on the lime. The children were keenly interested in both processes.

Tractors

April 25, 1935. Bradford made a caterpillar tractor today and plowed for the others, in block building. We had a great many more tractors, plows, and also caterpillars. The children started having two go around together, so that the front one did the plowing and the second one the disking.

Walter and Jonathan had milk trucks again. They sold milk.

Suddenly Jonathan stopped and said he had better get his plowing done. He got a tractor and did get his plowing done, he said.

Group Story
The Caterpillar

The caterpillar pulls lots of things.
It pulls cars.
It pulls trucks.
It pulls tool boxes and sheds.
It pulls plows.
It pulls the disk.
It pulls the road scraper.
It pulls the snow plow.
It pulls the corn planter.
The caterpillar pulls the wheat planter.
It pulls logs and telephone poles.
It pulls stumps out of the ground.
It can go all kinds of places.
It goes slowly.
It pulls hard.

In Kentucky, when the First Grade studied farms, they were able to see small and large dairies, to watch the planting of vegetables on Mrs. Ballard's model farm next door; and they themselves planted a school garden of early vegetables, with the help of the farmer and gardener fathers. That was good. But at Arthurdale it was better still. Every family had a small farm-holding in which it planted vegetables, corn, and potatoes and sometimes wheat, rye, or soy beans. So the opportunities to see and learn were many and were in our midst. Subsistence farming was a part of the families' work and of the children's lives. They all helped in planting and cultivating, and the School helped them to understand what they were doing and what they saw others do. Their learning was part of the learning of the whole community.

BUILDING THE VILLAGE OF ARTHURDALE: THE SECOND GRADE

The Second Grade gained as much from the situation in their village study as did the First Grade in its study of farming. Never before had children with whom we were working studied the building of a village when this was their own fathers' occupation, and the work and interest of the whole community. Eunice Jones's Half-Year Report in January gives an account of their work:

> Living in this growing community of Arthurdale, the construction of the buildings of a village seemed the natural activity for the village study. I began a discussion with the children the second day of school about plans for the year, and they said right away that they would like to build houses. We walked around outside looking for locations. They all had very sensible ideas about the kind of location they should have—level land—and they all wanted shade! When we were looking for a location for the houses, Joseph Matthews said: "When we get our houses built we ought to call it 'Arthurdale.' " [6]

The crude buildings that grew up on the slope of the hill leading up to the old Mansion may have shocked the visitors that streamed through the project, and certainly afforded amusement to the engineers, but they completely satisfied the children and made clearer to them perhaps than anything else could what it was to build a new village. To them, and to their families, building a home to live in, living in a house of their own, sharing in the making of a community, was new and very different from the life they had known. That the Second Grade village helped the children to make the adjustment more easily and with greater understanding, even the parents recognized. As for the children, they identified their work with that of the project. A visitor asked: "Are you mak-

---

[6] Half-Year Report, January 1935.

ing little houses?" Brant answered in the midst of sawing a board: "Yes, we're homesteaders."

Miss Jones's diary shows the children's interest in construction, in the way that buildings are made. This was revealed in their keen observation and in their patient and painstaking work. The obstacles of lack of tools and materials, that first year, made little difference. The group climbed past difficulties as if they did not exist. Pieces of wood and old crates were all we could find to use. One of the children got a friend of his, one of the fathers who drove a truck, to haul these over from the scrap lumber pile for them. Only a small number of tools from the School Shop's limited supply could be spared, but tools were brought from home, and the work went on.

September 18, 1934. We began with a discussion of how it would be best to start the actual work on the village. Joseph Matthews said: "Put the floors in." Herndon Bruce said: "Lay the foundation." When I asked if there was anything that had to be done before the foundation could be laid, Irwin Barrett said: "Find the place you want your house."

Mr. Macdonald, one of the parents on the homestead, came over while we were working and said: "You know, I like the way you people have of having a school—letting the children get out and around, instead of being cooped up all the time. I think it's good."

September 19, 1934. What enthusiastic response the whole group made to the need for shovels, wagons, and string! The only two children who had wagons brought them, almost every child in the class brought pieces of string, and three brought hammers.

September 20, 1934. The interest still holds, and all available tools from home came to school today. Ridgeway said he could bring the fire shovel again, because his mother uses lump coal and just puts it in with her hands and she takes the ashes out first thing in the morning, so she is through with the shovel by the time he is ready for school.

October 5, 1934. The children discussed what buildings they should have in the village, and the outcome is that, in addition to houses and a barn, there will be a bank, a postoffice, and a store.

The Children Study Buildings under Construction

October 28, 1934. This morning we walked over to see the Regans' barn which is in process of construction. The framework had just been started, and the group was pleased to see that the men had begun their building in the same way we did. Ray Alice said: "They had to piece their boards, too." The workmen were using the level, and the children noticed that right away. Joseph Matthews and Brant wanted to see it at close range, and the workmen let them go over and watch. One of the men explained how it was used.

October 30, 1934. We went to see the barn again. The window framing impressed the children. Joseph Matthews saw one of the men using a square and called the group's attention to it. "It's just like we do," he said. Rudolf was interested in the men sawing, and pointed out the way Lance uses a saw is wrong. Joe Lipton said: "I see how the roof goes on, now. I think I'll know how to do our roof."

When the snow and the cold held the class indoors, they played village in their room and made the furnishings for their buildings. Housed in the long narrow "parlors" of the Arthur Mansion, the group lived out its interests unhampered by lack of space. By spring they were out at the village in full force on the job again.

The Village the Second Year

This group entered School [Miss Jones reports] with a desire to make a village as the Second Grade did last year. On discussing it the first day, I found that the buildings the children wanted to have in their village this year were: a hospital,[7] a store, a postoffice,

---

[7] Probably because their parents were talking about the proposed cottage hospital.

two houses, and a farm. We talked about location and found a place near the Nursery School beyond all the new School buildings, which is partly meadow and partly woods. Mr. Carlson, the Shop teacher, offered to let a group of older boys clear out the part in the woods.

September 11, 1935. We walked over to the Mansion hill to get a bird's-eye view of the lay-out of Arthurdale. They got an idea of the general planning that was done at the beginning of Arthurdale.

Susan Lee said: "They planned to have barns and chicken yards." Fulton said: "They planned to have corn to feed to the cows and chickens." "And things to feed themselves," said Susan Lee.

Walter said: "This here where Arthurdale's at was all trees once and they cut lots down, but they left some for shade like those there by the Mansion."

They talked about how the fathers and mothers took care of the food so it would last during the winter. As a result of this trip, the children brought corn, apples, onions, and beans for us to dry for winter. When we get our village laid out, they have already planned to bring beets, cabbage, and turnips to bury in the ground.

This was, of course, the group who, as first graders, had studied farms with Miss Carlisle the year before.

The second year we were able to purchase some lumber for the Second Grade village building. The children erected their buildings from the ground up, patterning their work after that of their fathers who worked on "the big houses," and did an extremely good job. They and we knew more about building the second year, and observation could be more acute and detailed.

When the group was ready to begin the construction of the houses [Miss Jones writes], there were many barns being started for the newest lot of homestead houses. We visited those nearest the School in their early stages, and also as the work progressed, so that the children might see the need for corner posts and studding. These same barns were visited later to see the ridge poles, rafters, and sheathing—how they were put together, and why they were needed to make the roofs. We went later to see shingles being put on the barns.

It is not too much to say that these second graders were beginning to learn those skills which we had felt it was desirable to teach the boys in the High School in Kentucky. While the village study at Ballard enabled the Second Grade children to gain some hand skill, and to come to know and understand the composition of a village community, the village study at Arthurdale gained a unique significance from the fact that the fathers of these children were, as a means of livelihood, building their own village and new homes for themselves and their children. The work that the children did enabled them to comprehend and share in the work of their fathers, and to realize what was involved in this building of a new community.

The New Arthurdale Store

In Kentucky, the children had taken trips to see grocery stores in the neighboring towns; in Arthurdale, the children heard from their own families about the plans for the cooperative general store, and watched it being built and stocked with goods. One of the group stories during the first week of January carried news of the new store which was opening at the Town Center:

The New Store

There is a new store in Arthurdale.
The new store is big.
The men built the store.
The store has vegetables in it.
They have groceries in it.
They have meat in the store, too.
Lots of customers come to the store.

May 20, 1935. Instead of painting today, the group voted to visit the store. In the discussion before we left, there were many questions brought up to be answered when we got there. Delia said she would like to know how they knew how much to charge for their merchandise, and how the store gets the things it sells.

The delivery man from the Kingwood bakery was bringing in the bread. Hildegarde, a High School graduate who works in the store, explained how he made his charge slip and she paid him. Fresh strawberries were on the counter, and she told us they had come from Baltimore by truck. Hadley Duke wanted to know where the overalls factory was, and Hildegarde said it was in Pittsburgh. The canned goods had come from a warehouse in Morgantown, and the meat from Wheeling. Some of the supplies, she said, had come by freight, and we talked about what that meant.

The next day Elaine brought a map to school, on which we spent much time locating the places from which the store's supplies had come.

The Stone Quarry

To the Second Grade, the stone quarry on the homestead and the use of stone for paths and for the new School walk were as interesting as they were to the Nursery School children.

April 28, 1936. This morning we went over to M Road to see the new houses being built there. The first one was being faced with stone. The next one had the stone work finished. At the house beyond, the workmen had reached the second story with the stone facing.

The children watched the spaces left and saw how the workmen measured for the stone to fill the space, chipped off pieces that protruded, and filled in the cracks with cement. The guide line that they used the children also noted, and recognized its purpose. Edwin said he was helping his father make a stone fence, and that they ran a line so the fence would be even.

April 29, 1936. We followed up today with a trip to the Stone Quarry which is just up the hill from the School. The children were very much interested in the colorations of the stone. They noticed the way the stone was cut by drilling holes at intervals, then wedging the whole row at once. Fulton remarked how different the stone looked where it had been exposed to the weather, and where it had been freshly cut.

May 21, 1936. At recess we went to watch the stone workers laying the School sidewalk. An influence of this trip was noticeable at the village. Grant made a stone stoop for the postoffice. He went through all the motions that the masons had found necessary—pounding the rock into place, wedging smaller pieces under and around it to make it level.

The houses and farms, the store, the stone walks, are but a few of the countless incidents of interactions between the life and work of the community and learning at the School. Unless we were very much mistaken, the study of farming by the First Grade and the building of the village by the Second Grade did, as a matter of fact—not theory—interpret the children's lives to them.

PIONEERS IN WEST VIRGINIA: THE FOURTH GRADE

Elisabeth Sheffield
Teacher of the Fourth Grade

At once we went out to a piece of woods not far away. I remember what impressed me most was that they had never before played in the woods, and how they absorbed the beauty of it—starved as they were. They brought me everything to admire—moss, mushrooms, pretty leaves, flowers. They were uplifted and buoyant, anyway, all that time they were in the woods. That first month or so they were just so many cramped, neglected, starved little minds awakening in sunshine (literally) and common interest and the right chance to play. I was discouraged by what I was not teaching them, but we still had no books. One thing we did have that was most precious—

BUILDING THE VILLAGE OF ARTHURDALE
The Second Grade

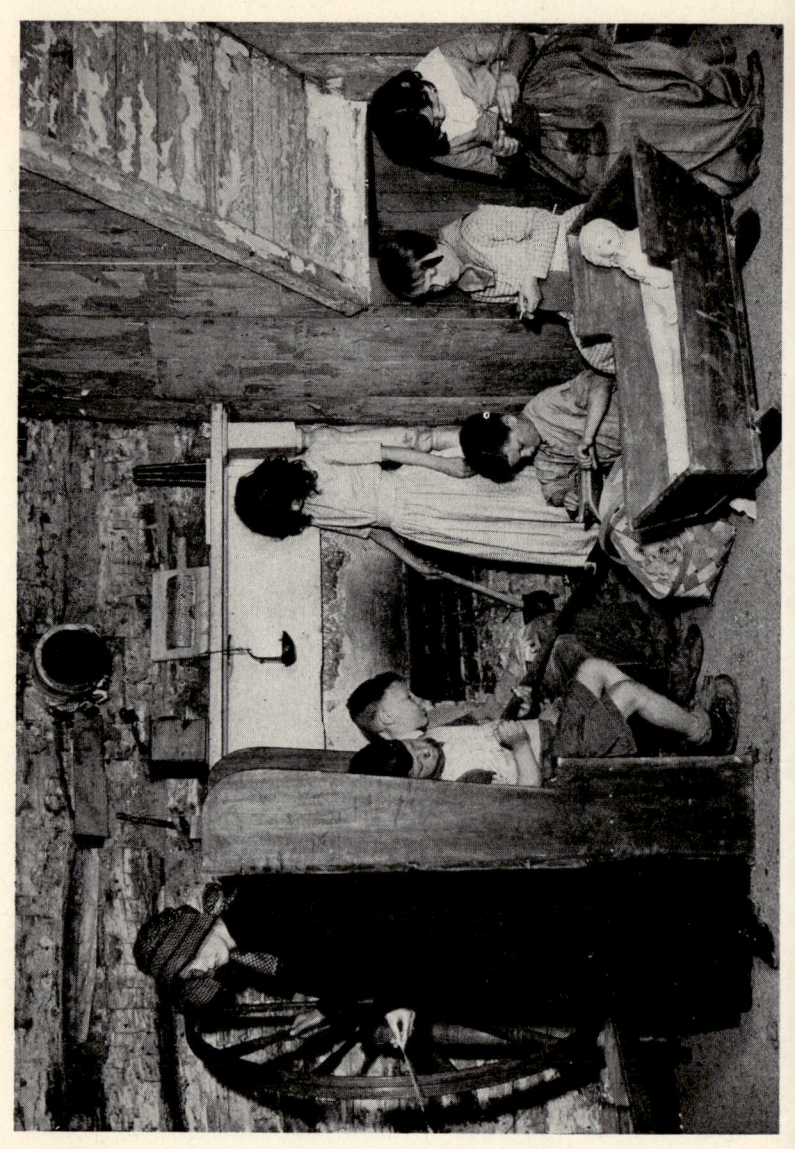

a bat and ball. They skipped and hopped and ran in utter joy in the sunshine of those warm fall days. I don't believe I will ever be lucky enough again to feel in others such happiness as they had playing baseball together.

Study of Pioneer Life

The Fourth Grade is studying pioneer life. Almost half of the class have grandparents now living in log cabins.[8] All the rest have relatives and friends living in them. Their parents tell the children tales of this life: how they cooked over open fires, wore homespun, and slept in the loft over the one main room. It is their direct heritage. Since going into the mines, money has come to mean a great deal, and they were beginning to look down upon their humble origin. Studying this pioneer life in School as an important period in the history of our country puts a value on the cabin life which these people know. Their heritage is recognized. It takes on meaning. The few pots and crude tools and furniture that have come down to them become valuable. It seems to give them a most satisfying feeling of being able to respect their origins.

Further than that, a "pioneer study" interprets present-day living to these children. They are living in a time long after the industrial revolution. They press a button for light, buy shoes or a dress—or, at least, goods—at a store. They take it all for granted. But after they have carded, spun, and woven wool, they start to understand more about materials; after they have tanned a hide, they begin to know what goes into the making of a pair of shoes; after they have cooked over an open fire, a stove has more value for them.

On the other hand, the simple lives of these country children are not so removed from pioneer living that these fourth graders cannot comprehend it. Hunting for food still goes on. The kitchen with its preparation of food is still the important

---

[8] See Chapter V, p. 253.

place in the home. Vegetables are still dried and buried, soap made, and square dancing enjoyed. With their own pattern of life not too different, the children can get many meanings from studying pioneer life that interpret present-day things.

THE OLD FAIRFAX LOG CABIN

Along with the other buildings which the Government received when it bought Arthurdale was an old log cabin probably built for Colonel John Fairfax's slave foreman, Watt.[9] No doubt it has been standing since about 1790. At the time Arthurdale became a homestead, the cabin was being used by Mr. Arthur, who had acquired the Fairfax land, for grain storage. The roof had been raised half a story, the chimney raised, and a slate roof put on. The old cabin probably would have been torn down had not the School seen its historical significance and educational possibilities. After we came in September, the grain was cleared out and the cabin, with a rotting porch in front and a leaking lean-to in back, was left standing for the School to use as it would. The Fourth Grade undertook the cabin as its special responsibility.

The first year there were hopes that the architects might be able to make fundamental changes in the restoration of the cabin, such as lowering the roof. So it was left the way it was, and its main use was as a background to the pioneer study program. There it was just outside our window when School was held in the Mansion. The children cleared it up—a heavy task—and made many, many crude wooden things to furnish it. They gave a play in the cabin in the spring, but altogether did not spend a great deal of time in it. Nor did it that first year grow to look very convincingly like a pioneer home. Nevertheless, it was the core of the Fourth Grade program.

To begin with, it welded that newly assembled class to-

---
[9] See Chapter V, pp. 251-3.

gether; at once, they felt a united effort. They were very much stimulated by the idea of fixing up the cabin, and never did one weaken a minute in his interest in doing that. But perhaps the cabin did most for that class, regardless of what we wanted, by satisfying a certain craving they had, just coming from the desolate mine camps, for possessing something of their own. Though I had wanted the point of view that the cabin was the community's and we only public servants, as it were, that was definitely not the children's point of view the first year. It was "our cabin." "Ours" versus the other children's in school. It gave them a sense of importance and security. Perhaps this does not seem a healthy attitude in general but to these children, poor, starved in every sense, it was immensely important.

Shop, Dramatic Play, and Painting

When the West Virginia teachers arrived for the third, fifth, and sixth grades, Harry Carlson was freed for Shop. And Shop was a tremendous release to the Fourth Grade. They reveled in sawing, hammering, chiseling, and sandpapering. They literally worked furiously in each Shop class. They made some furniture for the cabin: split-log benches, crude tables, a settle, a candle stand, a cradle, and a churn. Also wooden dishes and trenches, wooden spoons and bowls, knives, butter paddles and scoops, hunting guns, a plow, and flax tools. Pioneer life became real.

I started them on knitting—satisfying to both boys and girls. They dyed with native plants, fruits, and nuts; strung apples, buried turnips, and baked cornbread from hand-ground cornmeal and flour. We got a fleece, washed it, fluffed it, carded and spun the wool, dyed it with vegetable dyes, and wove it into small pieces of cloth. They collected or borrowed a candle mold, a coffee mill, and a calf skin. They planted an old-fashioned garden of herbs and flowers and a flax patch. Mrs. Haskins, one of the homestead mothers, was pleased to show us how to make the belt for our spinning wheel.

All the time in the classroom, I was feeding the class all the source material I could find about pioneers on their journey into West Virginia, and their dramatic play about the lean-to which they had built "on the trail" was becoming richer and richer in content. With this age, work and construction are inextricably mixed with their dramatic play. As the cabin was gradually furnished with the pioneer furniture and implements that the children made in Shop, the class, whenever the weather was not too cold, lived out scenes of pioneer family life in the log cabin. Each child came to have—or to be—a certain character in the family of settlers.

The renaissance, or maybe the first birth, of the mental life of the Fourth Grade came when the paints arrived. They had seen some of the pictures painted by the children in Kentucky and longed to try their hand. At once they felt competent. Again, enormous satisfaction came. They seemed to forget their public school barren copying and tracing and feel a demand from their own inside power. They suddenly seemed an imaginative, gifted group, full of ideas. I don't know how it happened; but now, instead of always empty heads, they seemed to be wondering or thinking about lots and lots of things. They are now—in January—the sort of class that is limited in accomplishment mostly by the teacher's shortcomings. Some time along here, we got some reference books with pictures and some readers. These helped in information and making mental pictures for our work. It interests me that I feel with the children that we are just too lucky to have such marvelous equipment: paints, shop tools, nice desks—instead of taking these things for granted as ordinary equipment. In a way they are necessities to the growth of the mind and spirit, shall we say. You have to go

THE SCHOOL AT ARTHURDALE

without these things for a while to realize what they do for children.[10]

THE FOURTH GRADE IN 1935–36

The next class used the cabin quite differently. As the project developed and became a definite entity with many services and organizations, the children naturally took on the idea of the cabin as a sort of institution in the community, and considered themselves its guardians. Tradition builds fast, and they had thoroughly expected to take it on this year. Further, they expected to give it up at the end of the year, whereas last year's class never were reconciled to that. Some of the older boys tore off the front porch for us and took the wooden frame off the fireplace, exposing the old stone one. Later in the year, the shed was removed from the rear. The NYA boys made a shutter and an old-fashioned door and also steps.

Though the severe winter prevented our going to the cabin from December through March, we spent a good deal of time there in the fall and spring. The class was too large for much free play or many activities in the small cabin; thirty-two children more than filled it. They did, however, compose a play and rehearsed it up there daily. The large class were all members of either the Doddridge [11] or the Dutcher families, and the "play" consisted of a scene in the cabin life of these people and the visit of some friendly Indians.

In Shop the class the second year made more, better-constructed things, and more complicated things: neatly smoothed wooden dishes, plates and cups, a tape loom, harrow hoes, rakes, candle molds, tin lanterns, and guns. This year they almost finished the wool-wheel started the year before. They also did the home industries in good form with

---
[10] Half-Year Report, January 1935.
[11] It was from a member of the Doddridge family that Mr. Arthur had purchased his farm.

better results. It was possible to do more with them on the background and technique of these industries. We got better spinning and better weaving. What they learned about the making of cloth they set down in their "wool notebooks." In the late spring, the whole class visited a woolen mill about fifteen miles away, and wrote an understanding account of this visit in their record.

The children also entered into the process of making linen cloth. They worked with the flax that the first Fourth Grade had planted in the spring, which was already so rotted by a wet summer that it did not need to be retted.

One of the outcomes of this study was a play. Its plot followed familiar lines. Act I: Working in the flax field. They stop to rest; one boy falls asleep, and the Indians capture him. Act II: Mr. Fairfax declares that he needs stouter clothes for his long journey to the faraway Indian camp, and the family set to work at once. Act III: The family mournful and anxious. Will they return? Act IV: They return with the boy. General rejoicing.

The audience moved with the children first to the sunny flax field on the hillside above the cabin; next, into the cabin where Mr. Fairfax was outfitted for the journey; then out again, to follow his journey over the hills and hollows to the Indian camp seen far down on the slope below; and, finally, back to the cabin for the celebration of their homecoming. The scenes acted outside were almost entirely pantomime, and the words in the cabin seemed merely an accompaniment of the spinning and weaving, and of the dancing and rejoicing.

One day, we were in the cabin and ready to start on the last scene of the play. Frankie needed help on tuning his fiddle. He looked out the cabin door. Way over yonder, sitting on the caterpillar tractor, was his father. Frankie was off like a shot. Mr. Spelman leaned down and "tuned her up,"

THE SCHOOL AT ARTHURDALE

and in less time than it takes to tell Frankie was back and the dance went on. The tune he played, to which the family and neighbors danced and sang, was "Weevily Wheat."

For Charley he's a nice young man,
Charley he's a dandy;
Charley likes to kiss the girls
And give them sugar candy.

Over the river to feed my sheep,
Over the river to Charley;
Over the river to feed my sheep
And bake a cake for Charley.[12]

COMMUNITY INTEREST IN THE CABIN

The work on the cabin has involved many more people than the Fourth Grade—not only the High School boys, who made shutters and a door for the cabin, and the older boys not in school, who tore out the brick from the fireplace, revealing the old stone chimney, but the fathers on the homestead. Mr. Foster, who works at the forge, is making an iron crane. Mrs. Spelman, Marion's mother, made us a nine-patch quilt and lent a sickle, candlestick, and sugar bowl. The Bostwicks gave a big copper bowl and the Kings a gridiron over one hundred years old. The following loans and gifts have been brought in by the children: rakes, sickles, hatchets, a mattock, candle molds and a candle holder, a turkey wing, coffee mill, ladder-back chair, pots and kettles, a calf skin, dyestuffs, and a rug made by a parent. Morgantown and Reedsville friends have lent and given us a spinning wheel, old-time flowers for the cabin garden, pots and kettles, and a betty lamp.

Many, many people are interested and come up and tell us what they can get when they go "up home," or what they will lend us as soon as the cabin can be made secure, or what they wish they had kept or brought along. They recall where

---

[12] "These are the stanzas," Mr. Collins reports, "which the Arthurdale Fourth Grade knew and sang from oral tradition. At Arthurdale, the dance for 'Weevily Wheat' was not known, had dropped out. In other sections of West Virginia, the melody has become a fiddle tune played for any square-dance figure.

"The song seems to be clearly connected with the Scottish Prince Charlie, who was Charles I of England. The Scots brought this song, already a century old, to America in the eighteenth-century migrations.

"The rhythm of the song, and its history in rural America, indicates that it was always a dance-song. In other words, 'Weevily Wheat' belongs with 'Skip to My Lou,' 'London Bridge,' 'Dusty Miller,' 'Strip the Willow,' and other play-party songs imported from England and Scotland in the eighteenth century."

they have seen this and that. Mr. Spelman knows a great deal of local history, and Mr. Stearns does, too.

More and more are awakening to the sense that there is appreciation of that simple home life of which their mothers told them. They themselves are glad to find respect for their forebears. In other words, the cabin is a sort of center for the interest (which every homesteader seems to have to a greater or lesser extent) in the days of their grandmothers.[13] They are proud to be able to contribute to the subject matter of School and are interested to learn further from it about something that touches them so closely.[14]

County Teachers in a Community School
Elsie Ripley Clapp

The School at Arthurdale was a public rural school of Preston County. Teachers were assigned to the School by the County Board of Education on the regular basis of average daily attendance during the last three months of the preceding year. In 1934–35, only 87 of the 167 children who entered school in September had attended Preston County schools the year previous. The School was, therefore, entitled to three teachers only. The second year its enrollment entitled it to five. Fortunately, because the School was for the first two years an experiment in community education sustained partly by private funds, it had the services of a group of trained, experienced teachers who could carry the work of the other classes. These supplementary teachers taught also the young adults and engaged in many community activities. Because they were versed in methods of active learning, in the organization of programs, and in the functioning of a community school, the School was able to carry out what had been planned as an essential part of its program: the use of the

---
[13] See Chapter VII, pp. 382–3.
[14] Report written in July 1936.

School as an educational and training center for local teachers.

This plan and purpose directed our work, to a large extent; it conditioned procedures and programs and in part prescribed the kind of equipment used. From the reactions of the many State and County teachers, principals, and superintendents who constantly visited the School, I know that they were impressed by the simplicity of equipment and interested in the School's use of environment. The inexpensive and partly home-made equipment persuaded them that it was possible to do much with little and suggested possibilities to them. The special point of their interest in the work was in what they called "activity programs," and their concern was to discover just how these were compatible with "the regular work." It was the teachers training with us, however, rather than the visitors, who realized fully the care and study necessary in planning and arranging the mutual interdependence of the active and informational sides of the work, the philosophy and psychology on which it rested, and the need for constant conference with all the people involved.

Almost all the teachers who came to us from the County showed unusual adaptability and initiative in learning and in using methods of study and teaching which were new to them. They had, each of them, industry and they approached the new materials directly and without confusion. They had all taught in County schools. Coming to teach at Arthurdale involved adjustment. From our work in teacher-training in Kentucky, we had learned to allow teachers who came from a different teaching background and different training, time to adjust slowly to new educational demands and conditions. We assured them at first that they were expected to do only what they already knew well how to do, and then gradually exposed them, by contacts with different ways of learning and with the variety of activities in the School, to new experiences. At Arthurdale they had, also, to adjust to the community-education character of the work.

THE THIRD GRADE STUDIES INDIAN LIFE

Mrs. Liston, who had the Third Grade, had been an outstanding teacher in traditional methods before she came to Arthurdale. After she had been in the School perhaps two months, she came to me and asked what was the matter with her as a teacher that she could not do the kind of work that she saw in other groups. She would like, she said, to learn pottery herself from Miss Carlisle and weaving from Miss Sheffield. When this had been done, she came again to say that she was ready now to introduce the children to these activities. For the rest of the year, she went on gradually learning herself and teaching the children the various arts and crafts indigenous to Indian life, which the class was studying. Equally ably, she addressed herself to research on the Indian tribes in West Virginia and the surrounding territory, and to a study of Indian life and customs, showing an aptitude for accurate and thorough work as a student.

By the next year, 1935–36, the Third Grade was working with her as actively as they might have worked with a teacher who had always made this approach to learning with children. She perhaps more consciously made connections between activities and learning from books, and followed recommended methods in reading, writing, and arithmetic, but her diary records an active and interested participation by the children in the processes of Indian life.

A country environment offers an ideal situation for a program of Indian life. Mrs. Liston's diary makes it clear how many materials were to be found for the looking: the fields yielded corn, the farms sheep and wool, and the stone quarry stone for a grinder. In the woods close by the School, the Third Grade built their tepee and their trading post. Bark for the tepee, sticks for the meat-drying racks and for the looms, stones for the fireplace, berries for dyes—all were at hand.

Mrs. Liston grew convinced, as we were, of the suitability for eight-year-old children of the hand skills of Indian life, of their special interest in the family tribal life of the Indians, and also of the fact that in this locality Indian life and culture is inherent in the heritage of the people. In West Virginia, as in Kentucky, stories of the Indians of the region are still local tradition, and traces of their occupancy of the land are still discovered and collected by every child who roams the countryside.

FIFTH AND SIXTH GRADE PROBLEMS OF ADJUSTMENT

The Fifth and Sixth Grades in the fall of 1934 presented a problem. The children of this group showed the effects of what they had been through in undernourishment and emotional instability. While we waited for the assignment of teachers by the County, we combined these two classes and put them, for the first seven or eight weeks, in the shared care of Harry Carlson, the Shop teacher, and Carl Saunders, the teacher of Mathematics and Athletics. There were some good features in this obviously unsatisfactory arrangement: by the time the County teachers arrived, certain expectations and routines had been worked out with the class.

These classes had so few interests and dependable workhabits at first that we felt our way in the choice of material for them. Mr. Saunders tested them in reading and arithmetical facility, and the results showed most of them to have about fourth grade ability by the standardized tests; one or two children tested lower than that. He began to tackle their arithmetical difficulties with them, and explored their knowledge of Morgantown, which was near the mine camps in Scott's Run, and of the countryside. The most positive interest they showed was in some arrowheads that Mr. Saunders himself had found and brought in. Finally, we decided to work with them on some aspects of life in West Virginia.

On December 5, the County teachers arrived. Mr. Carlson and Mr. Saunders were able to go back to their own work, and the Fifth and Sixth Grades were established with their own teachers, each in a small room on the second floor of the old Mansion. The Sixth Grade under Mrs. Kimble fell gradually into the ways of school life and work. The Fifth Grade with Miss Funk made some headway the first year in adjustments and in ways of working, but were still, the year following, an undeveloped group. By the end of the second year, however, pride in accomplishment (the lack of which was among their difficulties), knowledge of the ways of working—*how* to read and spell and "do" arithmetic—and satisfactions in activities that were within their power of accomplishment, began to tell in both groups. The second year, also, their health was improved and their emotional equilibrium with it.

Shop work that first year, in spite of handicaps, was a major release to their energies. The things they made in Shop not only gave them satisfaction but began to stimulate their interests. Although some of the boys in the two groups were, in the fall, capable of no work more demanding than the burning out of a log for a canoe, by the middle of the year Mr. Carlson was able to report progress in Shop work for the two classes:

Week of January 26 to February 1, 1935. The Fifth Grade has had a very good and profitable week in Shop.

Oscar has at last found something that he both enjoys and that fits in with his class work. The bench he is making gives him the muscular activity he needs. Tompkins is quite interested in the butter scoop he is carving out of poplar. Daniel is developing his initiative a great deal by making a mug. Its shape and the fact that the work is concerned with the tough fibers of pine, give endless opportunities to try new methods, etc.

By the first of April, the Fifth Grade had produced also a flatboat, a dug-out canoe, a fork, a churn, and looms. For the Sixth Grade, Mr. Carlson reports:

> The trencher table being built by Winchell, Dennis, and Justin has proved quite a job, although within their pooled abilities. It combines a great deal of muscular activity with quite a lot of thinking.
>
> Martin Dykstra has stuck tenaciously to the making of a candle mold, which he has made out of scraps of tin we rescued from the builders. It has brought in a good deal of arithmetic, which I shared with his teacher, Mrs. Kimble.

By April 1, the Sixth Grade had produced, in addition, a seed box, wool cards, a stool, a horn-book, a bowl, flutes, and looms—both carpet and tape looms. Not a poor achievement for children whose co-ordination and work habits were so undeveloped in the fall.

We had used a study of West Virginia with these groups in 1934–35, not as furnishing ideal subject matter, but rather as a means whereby we could extend their understanding, and enlighten them about the State they lived in, so that through it they could become acquainted with the life and ways of other people in other places. For a beginning, it seemed desirable to use material in which they had some interest, however little, as well as material with which the County teachers felt familiar.

COLONIAL STUDY: FIFTH GRADE, 1935–36

In 1935–36, the next Fifth Grade, who had the year before relived pioneer life with Miss Sheffield, studied with Mrs. Kimble, the third of the County teachers, the conditions of life in colonial times in West Virginia and, for contrast, also in New England. Mrs. Kimble had a personal interest in this period and, helped by Miss Sheffield in bibliography, in the use of materials and of local resources, she assembled many facts and many articles and, with the children, made illustrative implements and utensils, furniture, samplers, etc. The Fifth Grade found out about the people of the colonial period, their occupations, industries, commerce and trade, their travel and transportation, and the part that taverns played in colonial times.

The children dried beans, apples, pumpkins, and corn; they cooked johnny (journey) cakes, baked beans, and made apple butter. They collected silk from milkweed for candle-wicking, and oak leaves which they strung on twigs to be used as kindling for the fire. They went into the subject of schools in colonial times, which greatly interested them, and made horn-books and ink. They knitted mittens and made samplers. They contrived a dramatic fireplace in their classroom and placed around it a collection of authentic colonial articles that were lent or given them, and also many reproductions of their own making.

In the Shop, they made such things as a wooden up-and-down churn, a long-handled shovel, a split hickory broom, a crooked stick for drawing out coals from the oven, and a rush-light holder. They also made a tankard, a niddy-noddy, a pipe box, a turkey-wing broom, stools, and a corn grater; and they finished their spinning wheel and a tape loom. They made a trivet and a toaster in iron. The longest and hardest piece of work was a chest. They made several attempts before they learned how; finally, they succeeded in making a substantial chest that satisfied them and on which they carved scenes of colonial life.

One recalls Miss Sheffield's description of this class's zest for shop work the first year and her characterization of them as a gifted, imaginative class. Yet, even so, their achievement along these lines was marked. These studies proved to fit in well with their lives and interests. The countryside furnished them with materials for a number of the things they made, such as milkweed and oak leaves, fruits and vegetables, wood for the split hickory broom, and turkey-wing feathers. The skills of the colonial period are easily developed in children of pioneer background.

In geography, they located on the map where the colonists came from and where they settled, and considered the problems which the land and climate presented to them. Realization of distant lands and places proved difficult for them. At the beginning of the year, the children believed that England and New England were one and the same place—both being equally unknown and remote to them. However, they recalled that I had spent my vacation in Maine and that Miss Sheffield's mother lived in Rhode Island—connections that at least fastened New England in this country.

THE SIXTH GRADE IN 1935–36

The class that had been Fifth Grade in 1934–35 was handled the year following by a new County teacher, Mr. Blamble. To meet the needs of this group, who had come to us one and two years "below grade" in their ability to read and write and spell and "do" arithmetic, and also to make use of their teacher's experience in teaching the Three R's, the group settled down with him to gaining a competency in these skills. He and they were also interested in early Indian cultures and built a Mound Village up in the woods beyond the School and later visited Moundsville, in West Virginia. In the spring, they studied birds and made a number of bird houses of approved design, fed the birds, and studied their habits.

STUDY OF WEST VIRGINIA: COMBINED FIFTH AND SIXTH GRADES, 1935–36

To Miss Funk, who had Mr. Blamble's class the year before, we gave in 1935–36 a Fifth and Sixth Grade undivided group

THE SCHOOL AT ARTHURDALE

of new children whose families had just moved onto the homestead. We were determined not to classify these children until we had had an opportunity to test them in work and to work with them individually. Some of the children were wan and listless and seemed undernourished at first, but not as depleted as the children of this age the year before. They came from families of Preston County who had been miserably poor, but whose needs were not as desperate and whose background not as wretched as those of the first homesteaders from Scott's Run. The adjustment problems which some of the new group presented were also emotional instability and lack of sustained effort. Their difficulty, however, seemed to have to do with adjustment to work and life in school, rather than with a total social adjustment. They came, too, with more knowledge of the Three R's at least, although with meager general information.

With less pressing problems, Miss Funk was able to devote a great deal of time to each child. She reported in detail observations of each child and made frequent visits to his home and learned something of his family and the background out of which they had moved to Arthurdale. As one child became adjusted, she took up another for special help and study. It was interesting to see how well and understandingly she did this. By the end of the year, only one child had not made a good and happy adjustment. That they thrived so well was due in some measure to their large, quiet, sunny room in the new building, which in itself gave space and a sense of peace; and was due especially to Miss Funk's calm and sympathetic handling of the class. The children felt that they could rest in that and depend on it. Partly, it was due also to their interest in the work and to their pleasure and satisfaction in their progress in it.

The study of West Virginia which these newcomers to the homestead made had a different approach from that of either the Fourth Grade's pioneer activities or the Fifth Grade's colonial study. This new class, in its study of West Virginia, was interested particularly in the history of the State: from the mound builders through the later Indian life to the coming of the settlers, their explorations, their first settlements, the forts that they built, the growth of these settlements, the State's struggle to free itself from Virginia's domination, and its later growth and development. They sought facts and arranged these in the order of happening. Probably this type of work, for which their teacher was prepared, was well suited to children of that age who had come from other rural schools in the County. They had a lively interest in West Virginia of today, its products and industries and its points of interest, historical and scenic. It represented a great widening of mental horizon for them to realize the State's geographic situation and the States which bordered it. A trip to Fort Necessity in Pennsylvania, and gradual acquaintance with Maryland, which was only about twenty-five miles east of us, made at least these two bordering States real to them.

Under Miss Funk's guidance, they made topographical maps and finally a large and beautiful wall map of West Virginia, showing products and industries, for which they made a border frieze of the State's birds, flowers, fruits, and vegetables. Both the class and Miss Funk had decided art ability, and their illustrations of places of special historic and scenic interest, which they made with crayon on cloth, were unusually beautiful: the Great Mound at Moundsville; Nancy Hanks's home near Antioch, West Virginia; the home of Morgan Morgan, who established the first permanent white settlement in the State at Bunker Hill, Berkeley County, in 1726; Daniel Boone, who journeyed in the Kanawha Valley and became the first mayor of Charleston, Boone County being named after him; the iron furnaces, the first of which was built about 1790 in Hancock County; James Rumsey's steamboat, which had a trial trip in 1783 on the Potomac near Berkeley Springs; Fort

Henry, situated where Wheeling now stands. They made for themselves all kinds of charts and maps and, perhaps more than any other class, achieved a sense of the sequence and significance of the stages of the State's growth and development.

In Shop they made an excellent replica of a flatboat and of a covered wagon. With Miss Funk, who had worked with Miss Carlisle the first year in her "Night School" class in pottery and who had unusual ability in work with clay, they made many bowls and jars, using the excellent clay which was to be had for the digging from the creeks on the homestead.

Like Mrs. Liston, both Mrs. Kimble and Miss Funk made a successful adjustment to the new methods of work. In the study of colonial times, Mrs. Kimble struck a deep personal interest of her own and not only drew on the School's resources and Miss Sheffield's special knowledge of this period, but used also her knowledge of the region and acquaintance with the houses still standing from colonial days. Miss Funk's skill and interest in hand processes suggested her taking over the pioneer program the next year, and in preparation she assisted Miss Sheffield in the work and life at the log cabin during the summer.[15]

COUNTY TEACHERS BECOME INTERESTED IN COMMUNITY EDUCATION

The three County teachers who joined us in December 1934 were with us for nearly two years, and shared the experiences of the School's functioning as a community school. They came to believe in the idea that actuated us.

After they had been with us a month or two, they came to see me and inquired why I never asked them to serve on the staff committees that chaperoned the square dances on Saturday nights. I said that, since they lived several miles away, I hadn't wanted to suggest evening duties for them. "Why," they

---
[15] Chapter VII, pp. 382–3.

said, "Miss Bowie lives over in Kingwood, and Mr. Saunders too, the same as Mrs. Liston and Miss Funk. And Mrs. Kimble only lives in Reedsville." "But," I said, "we came to do just this, and I know the County engaged you only to teach school." This reason did not seem good to them either. "Isn't this a community school?" they asked. So they began to share such responsibilities with us, taking their turns chaperoning dances and often, despite distance and weather, coming to the Women's Club evening meetings and entering into whatever was going on.

In the fall of the second year, Mrs. Liston wrote:

Most towns, as we enter into them to make our home, have social and civic matters already worked out, and we just become part of their formed plans. In Arthurdale, everything was not worked out, and we had to become part of its planning. We had to take time for the studying of the problem, planning something, and then giving it a trial by putting it to use.

She instances health work, water testing, trash disposal, transportation of the school children, and recreation. She writes:

It seems to me that Arthurdale School plays a more important part in the community than any other school with which I have been connected. The Arthurdale Women's Club, by holding its meetings in the School building, gets a feeling of being more closely connected with the School. They seem to feel they are a part of the School. The School seems to be the center of all organizations, as teachers usually attend the community meetings, and teachers and parents become so much better acquainted through these associations.

Clearly, too, Mrs. Liston sees community education in terms of the Third Grade's work:

This being a rural community gives us a great opportunity for community education. The interests of the community are woven into the School, and at the same time the interests of the School are woven into the community. This is done for the Third Grade program in this way:

THE SCHOOL AT ARTHURDALE

While studying Indian food—pumpkins, beans, and corn, for instance—we looked at some of the gardens in the community and decided on one that had thrived well and got permission from its owner to visit it. We studied how this food was planted.

In the building of the Indian village, the children were eager to furnish their own tools for working, so they discussed with their parents what they were doing and what tools they would need. Their parents let them bring tools to school, and some of them helped the children repair old tools that had been discarded.

The Third Grade program takes up the study of Indian weaving and, because of the fact that the older members of the community also have an opportunity to weave, the work of the community and the School are more closely related and more interest is shown in both. The children discuss the difference in the way the Indian looms are made and the way the modern looms are made; the way in which the designs are woven into the rugs, and the needles used.

Katherine Kimble grasped readily the part the School played in the community. In October 1935, she wrote:

The School, to me, is the most important part of any community, for it is there that future citizens are molded.

In many schools, only those experiences that happen to children between the hours of nine and four are considered important. In Arthurdale, we are concerned with the whole individual, and with school as the means of finding out these things. By that I mean, we follow up outside of school leads noticed or introduced there: rebuilding of bodies wrecked by years of depression living; removal of tonsils, fitting glasses; hot lunches at school and the habit of drinking milk at home.

Any child who needs medical aid may visit the nurse in a regularly scheduled period which is part of the school day. There are also proper toilet and washroom facilities.

Here the whole health program is taken as a matter of course. The children go to the nurse for a cold, knowing a cold can develop into many things. This is so extremely different from the attitude in general in the communities and schools around us, that to me it is almost unbelievable that so much has been accomplished in such a short time.

The subjects—reading, writing, spelling, arithmetic, etc.—are taught here, but are so arranged that they are interwoven with the everyday experiences and are not some foreign thing to be drudgingly learned.

The interests the children are forming at school are being carried out at home in their leisure time. For example: two little girls went to near-by woods to gather material for dyeing over the week-end; and a little boy set up a dye-pot at home and experimented with combinations of colors. Others bring in articles that are connected with school work that have taken several hours to make at home. Our library has a direct connection with leisure time, since children take books home for themselves and their parents.

And in January 1936, Mrs. Kimble wrote as follows on the usefulness of the work at Arthurdale to other schools and communities:

Arthurdale could be studied by an average citizen as a place where all the things he has dreamed of so long for his own community have been put to work. There is much in Arthurdale that other communities could use to their satisfaction: the way the resources of the people are used; the set-up of the community.

The other communities that closely surround Arthurdale profit by the people buying at their stores. Church attendance and recreation exchanges are noticed; people coming from surrounding communities to the dances, ball games being exchanged, and music groups from other communities participating in the music festivals here.

The teachers of surrounding rural communities are eager to gain knowledge of the Arthurdale School and use it in their own schools. I know of two at present that have been especially benefited in this way. Personally, I wish every day I had had the experiences I have gained here before I taught in one community three years. There are so many things learned here that could have been used in that rural community several miles away.

A teacher could use ideas gained here in any school: the type of program, the central units of work; the systematic arrangements that make a smooth-running connection between school and home; the manner of dealing with the children. Topics of study, or work for each group; working together as we do here—is so different from teacher groups generally that I'd like for many teachers to have the experience.

Miss Funk saw the matter from a philosophical point of view:

> The changing of customs, ideas, and opinions often comes about very slowly. A few individuals are ready to accept newer points of view, but most people hug the well known and established. Society in general is indifferent to change. We must face squarely our present conditions. We must make changes that are sound and effective.
>
> Just change is not enough. The changes must be valid. They must prove beneficial to children, and not be what adults think is of benefit to children. These changes will be determined by what children actually need and thrive on in adjusting themselves to their place in the world. Even all this is impractical unless supported by actual experiences.
>
> In our social work in school at Arthurdale, we are attempting to bring the children into contact with genuine life experiences. We are supplementing book learning with real life. As often as possible, we use books as supplementary to life itself. In our School, we try to create valid impressions, appreciations, and attitudes, which contact with life outside of school may and should supply.
>
> Instead of having our School seclusive, we are making it a co-operative enterprise, which is far more human and effective.

The Three R's in Rural Schools

If, in describing the educational use of environment, I have omitted the Three R's, it is not because the School did not consider these skills socially important. Certainly life in a rural district makes inescapably clear the school's responsibility to teach the Three R's with all the science and art and psychology it can muster. We realized with great vividness in Kentucky the fact that a person has to learn how to read and write and figure if he is going to take a job above that of a day laborer, conduct his business affairs, take an active part in his community affairs, or learn through newspapers and books and magazines what the rest of the world is doing. In a certain sense, these skills determine what his life is going to hold. It is not too much to say that it was not until we worked in Kentucky that we fully grasped the economic and social, as well as the educational, advantages of these skills.

In West Virginia we also found, as we had in Kentucky, that certain of the procedures in use today in the best modern schools are especially useful to the rural teacher, who is working with people to whom symbols and their use are difficult. In the First and Second Grades particularly, impelled by the speech difficulties of many of the children, we gave special attention to speech and sounds. Aside from these difficulties, the children's learning to read was normal in rate and comprehension. While we spent much less time in the first two grades on reading than does the usual rural school, the children's progress was as rapid and their understanding much greater.

In spite of the traditional ways of teaching reading current in the locality, and the value placed on "learning to read" as a guarantee of learning, we encountered in West Virginia no special resistance in any quarter to the newer methods used. In fact, the County Superintendent sent us a girl who was about to start a school for children in one of the mine camps, to study the methods we used in teaching reading. Nor did we meet resistance to our more practical use of arithmetic and, in the younger grades, to less emphasis on number manipulations, since the children's grasp of combinations and their ability to use numbers had, in fact, increased.

The first year, we had children in the Fourth Grade, and particularly in the Third Grade, who were hampered by not knowing *how* to read or write or use numbers; children who had been taught to read without understanding, and who counted on their fingers and manipulated figures without reason; children who had somehow escaped learning to read, to write, and to handle arithmetic at all, practically; children who were already accustomed to not knowing. It must be remembered, however, that these children had attended school very irregularly during the days of destitution in the mine camps, and many of them had been unable to receive individual attention in the crowded one-room schools with six and eight grades to a teacher. In fact, with the exception, of course, of the First Grade, the entire elementary school was, when School started, from one to three years "below grade" in the techniques. By the end of the second year, however, all the groups, except the class that had entered as Third Grade in the fall of 1934, were up to grade level (not including those individuals who continued to be "special students"—not able, for various reasons, to make the usual progress in this kind of learning).

Learning to read and write and gaining ability in the use of numbers were in themselves a special source of satisfaction to these children and a reassurance to parents, not only that the children were "getting along," but that they were "getting an education." The children were delighted with all the interests that reading opened up to them, consuming avidly all the books that we could, one way or another, procure for use in the classrooms, and besieging the library for books to take home.[16]

The investigation we had made in Kentucky at the Ballard School into the functioning use of mathematics we were able to use at the Arthurdale School in the First, Second, and Fourth Grades, which were taught by the supplementary teachers who had had the benefit of this experience. The County teachers in the Third, Fifth, and Sixth Grades naturally taught Arithmetic in the more traditional manner.

Study of Language in Living and Learning

In the chapter on the Nursery School, records of the children's conversations and talk in dramatic play are given,[17] and

---
[16] See Chapter VII, pp. 366–8.
[17] See Chapter IV, pp. 201–10.

in the chapter on the High School, Mr. Beecher discusses language problems at that age level.[18]

In Kentucky, the staff had begun a study of language [19] and in West Virginia, George Beecher, himself a linguist, started with all the teachers to collect and analyze examples of language expression from two-year-olds to adults. This piece of work was barely begun when our work at Arthurdale closed. However, we went far enough with it to have grounds for the belief that such a study would result in carrying work in language far beyond our current practices.

Our approach to the problem is best told in Mr. Beecher's own words:

At Arthurdale we were fortunate in having before us the picture of language development from the two-year-old level in Nursery School through the eighteen-year level in High School, and beyond with the unschooled young adults in "Night School" or WPA–NYA work; and with adults, of course, in many activities, such as drama groups, clubs, etc. And then, too, we wanted to know the language of the people we were living with.

It was better to think always in terms of Language than to let the word "English" add to the confusion. Language is a major part of people's lives, it touches so much and lacks the comforts of a well-ordered study of English. It is the medium of action, growth, feeling, thought, reason, record, creativity. And just because it is such, it fits in perfectly with a program of constructing and developing a community life. It fitted in also with building a school for a community.

The teaching of language at Arthurdale came to be based on two assumptions: first, that the experiences of children in active processes of learning yield the best results in language for creativity and understanding, just as in drama and art; secondly, that we had to study the situation in which we were working—analytically, from the point of view of language—to see where it stood culturally, to see what were its needs in training and provision of resources, and to watch the adaptation of a growing curriculum which was to supply experiences for a rural culture. This latter

---

[18] See Chapter VI, pp. 326–30.
[19] See Chapter I, pp. 51–2.

assumption was responsible for our examining every part of the curriculum critically for its contribution to the use and knowledge of language. Language is the medium of subjects, rather than another pigeon hole in the curriculum.[20]

Teachers Learning in Community Education

The progress of the County teachers has been stressed, but community education taught all of us who participated in it. It was a searching and challenging experience, insistent in the demands it made for flexibility and knowledge, clarity of purpose and resourcefulness. The penalty for careless or unconsidered action, for shallow comprehension and inadequate information, was heavy.

Community education is, from the point of view of the people working in it, primarily education of themselves in facing new problems, in working with others on these, and in guiding work upon them. It is here that learning is not only shared, but mutual. Leadership is direction by participation. A teacher who enters community education surrenders prerogatives. His authority is the authority not of position, but of usable knowledge confirmed by action and events. Community education is not brought into being by the putting over of a plan, or by the imposing of ideas. It requires that full recognition be given to people's desires and needs, feelings and opinions, ways of doing and thinking; and that the relation of any particular enterprise to other enterprises and to the whole be currently understood. The demand on anyone directing it is to recognize opportunities when they appear—usually unlabeled—and to use the capacities of everyone—including himself—at the time and in the way that will help the enterprise and the people working in it; to discern new developments, fresh approaches to the problem, and different ways of getting past obstacles. Community education puts a

---

[20] Report written in July 1936.

premium on everything a teacher knows about learning; it requires a liking for people and a knowledge of them, and some experience in working with them. All of which is to say that community education is social education—especially of those directing it.

New Elements in Our Understanding of Environment

Experiences in West Virginia added to our understanding of environment—the influences and conditions that shape people's lives and personalities. This further element in the conception of environment was, of course, dramatically present in the process of rehabilitation which the homestead represented. In addition: we all became aware of the homestead as a *milieu*—the medium through which and in which life went on. One other realization of environment we gained, which the second year's work with High School students and young adults will illustrate: namely, the potential uses of natural resources for livelihood enterprises.[21]

Socially Functioning Studies Tested in Action

In Kentucky we had worked on ways to learn through and from the environment, and we had perforce to revamp the content of studies in our use of them. We glimpsed the possibility—the necessity—of studies functioning socially.[22] What Arthurdale gave us was the opportunity to test in genuine life-situations the usefulness of information, its applicability and meaning; together with a chance to discover how to translate information into understanding. On the homestead, "socially functioning" meant community-functioning. The use of subject matters that the situation demanded was has-

---

[21] See section on "Economic Resources of the Environment," pp. 350–5, in Chapter VII.
[22] See Chapter I, pp. 48–9.

tened by crowding events and insistent needs. Urged on by the necessity to refashion material so that it could be used and understood, at Arthurdale we really began to tackle the job of organizing subject matters for use in community education. This, however, is particularly the story of the High School.[23]

---

[23] See Chapter VI, "A Rural High School," pp. 273–332.

CHAPTER IV

THE ARTHURDALE NURSERY SCHOOL *

Section 1: The Nursery School in 1934-35

THE Nursery School at Arthurdale was, I believe, the very spring and heart of the community education. This fact will, I hope, emerge from the account which follows.

However the Nursery School might be appraised as an ideal or "good" nursery school, it was of especial interest as a center of community education on the homestead, and as a nursery school in a remote rural area. The problem of its creation demanded imagination, faith, and the ability to select essentials in equipment and procedures, and to create these out of whatever materials were at hand. This last requirement made it necessary to choose procedures and equipment not on the basis of what were "ideal" conditions or even accepted practices in a nursery school but freshly again on the basis of what would be good conditions for the lives of little children. This was done not as a self-appointed task, but in response to urgent need; we insisted unrelentingly on certain necessary conditions, and surrendered arrangements and equipment which, though desirable, were not in fact essential.

Perhaps never before has a nursery school so actively served a community as a laboratory. It was a center of all the child care in the community, with its baby clinics, health work, and parent education. It was the place where parents came for help and advice, where they really saw for themselves how

---

* Jessie Stanton, Director of the Nursery School at Arthurdale, has edited the material of this chapter.

the children throve as a result of good feeding and regular routines of eating, sleeping, and toileting. The Nursery School worked with the other agencies in solving community problems. For instance, the problem of nutrition was attacked in a fundamental way by teaching the fathers how to raise certain foods, while the mothers were learning how to cook and can in the home economics classes; but some of this work might have been wasted if the children had refused to eat the new foods, which were unpalatable to them at first. In the Nursery School the children learned to eat them, and this made easier the acceptance of these foods by the families.

The creation and development of the Nursery School was undertaken by Jessie Stanton, Director of the Harriet Johnson Nursery School in New York. Miss Stanton participated in the first planning of the building and the equipment in Washington during the summer of 1934, and on a month's visit to West Virginia in July became well acquainted with the FERA nursery schools near Morgantown which Nadia Danilevsky had created and directed, and with the nursery school teachers who worked in them. She visited Scott's Run and Arthurdale, and came to know some of the families, so that she had a realization of the needs and conditions of the people, and also the opportunities and resources that the homestead afforded.

STARTING A NURSERY SCHOOL IN A RURAL COMMUNITY

I wonder as I look back what upheld us that summer as Miss Stanton and I drove back and forth those hot weeks across the hills between Washington and Arthurdale, where no slightest evidence of school buildings or equipment appeared. In Washington we taught draftsmen the requirements for a nursery school building: in Arthurdale we showed Bill Simkin of the Mountaineer Craftsmen how nursery school furniture and materials should be constructed by means of a cot, a folding table, a chair, and blocks shipped down from the Co-operative School for Teachers in New York. We were always strengthened by Nadia's achievements in Scott's Run and Jere, and by her generous enthusiasm; but, chiefly, we were driven by the needs of the children in the dreary, dread awfulness of the mine camps.

When Miss Stanton returned in September, a place for the Nursery School had been found. All that remained was to bring it into being!

The report of Mary Elizabeth Sedman, whom Miss Stanton placed as resident head of the Nursery School, written in January of that year, perhaps gives the best account of those opening weeks:

I learned that there were eighty-one families in all who were to come to Arthurdale; that forty-nine were living in their houses on the project, and that the remaining families lived in Reedsville, Burke, Bretz, and Masontown—all neighboring villages. Then I started out, trudging over the dusty roads, and visited as many families with children supposedly of nursery school age as I could. To my surprise, all the women said that they wanted to send their children to nursery school, and when was it going to begin?

Meanwhile the Nursery School building was taking form with great rapidity. It was a one-story white frame building set on the southwest side of the Town Center, between two former supply sheds. There were four large sunny rooms and two bathrooms, one at either end. The tan-colored celotex walls and the white woodwork made a most attractive setting.

Our doors opened on a little yard ringed about with rhododendron bushes and protected from the road by a white picket fence. There were three gnarled old apple trees. The men who worked on the building, of their own accord, put in a little wooden forked walk leading from the gate to the doors. It would, they said, save us "a heap of trouble in the wet weather."

On September 12 Miss Stanton arrived and we began preparations in earnest. We brought out the stored supplies from Morgantown—sand pails, small shovels, doll babies, hammers, nails, dust pans and brooms, etc. We asked local grocery stores to save orange crates for us. We called on the local newspaper office and were given old newsprint paper to use for painting pictures. We saw a large wooden packing case in someone's front yard and persuaded him to sell it to us for a quarter. We tied it on the back of the car and got it safely to Arthurdale, a most valuable piece of equipment. Nadia loaned us a truck to bring out the dozens of orange crates and the cots she was lending us. We scrubbed the crates with soap and water and set them up in the classrooms, where they made very good shelving. The Mountaineer Craftsmen carpenters brought up chairs and tables and blocks. We put up hooks for dust pans and brooms. We cut up donated cloth for dolls' blankets, and felt that, though it was meager, we could begin with this indoor equipment.

Then we wrestled with the outdoor equipment. We used the little yard in front of the school for the two-year-olds' playground. We had saved the very long wooden box in which our New York samples of nursery school furniture had arrived. We painted it green and, filled with sand donated by the Greer Gravel Company, it made a fine sand box. We ransacked the scrap lumber pile and found some old boards. We borrowed a saw and cut these into three-foot lengths, staggered up the hill to the playground with them, and painted them. They made good climbing apparatus for the two-year-olds. The Mountaineer Craftsmen carpenters had made us saw horses and blocks, and we had two little red wagons. How the fathers, as well as the children, loved those little red wagons!

In the meadow across the road from the Nursery School we fenced off a playground for the four- and five-year-olds. There we placed our prized packing case, some blocks, and a pile of sand. Late on Saturday afternoon we felt so worried about our outdoor equipment that we consulted the Shop teacher and he helped us cut up some old boards into four-foot lengths. Hot and weary, we stood near the planing machine watching the wood particles flying into the air and felt so thankful that there was some way of getting these few boards for the children's use. So many nursery school people work in cities that they have little conception of the difficulties encountered in setting up a nursery school in a country situation.

While we were getting together the outdoor equipment, the homestead women had been polishing windows and scouring floors and finally, late Saturday, we were ready.

We started off with a staff of two West Virginia teachers, a dietitian, and 33 children between the ages of two and five. For the first two weeks we were on half-session only—from 8.00 to 11.30. Only those children came who could walk or had some way to ride. Mr. MacDonald, a homestead father, who was a strong believer in the Nursery School, brought thirteen or fourteen children every day in his old Ford car.

First Problems of Health and Adjustment

The health problems were those of malnutrition, which only a long-time program could affect; skin diseases, such as impetigo and scabies; and sores on the feet coming from small scratches or wounds which had not been cleaned the minute they happened. The records show how the nurse worked in the Nursery School to clear these up, and then how she and the teachers carried information to the mothers and encouraged them to continue the treatment until the difficulties were overcome. Miss Sedman and the teachers were working under great pressure at this time because of lack of equipment and lack of storage space, so the records do not tell in detail the children's fear of a doctor or nurse and how much work was done to break down this fear. The timid children were allowed to watch the children who were not afraid. They saw that these children did not cry when the nurse put medicine on their sores. They were very gently handled, and a record of October 10 says:

Today Helen Rose let the nurse put iodine on some scratches without crying and throwing herself on the floor.

Inspection took a long time, for many of the children had a fear of the doctor or nurse, and cried before the nurse touched them.

September 26, 1934. Clyde Bruce was examined by the nurse. He has scabies. I went to see Mrs. Bruce after school and gave her instructions that Miss Shaffer had left with me. They were that the boy should be bathed each day all over and the infected parts carefully scrubbed and afterward treated with sulphur ointment which I had bought. Mrs. Bruce was very friendly and said that she would do all those things. She said that she had never treated scabies before. Clyde is to stay at home until the condition has disappeared.

October 3, 1934. Miss Shaffer washed and treated many small cuts and scratches, dressed impetigo sores for seven of the children today. Dorothy Wilson came readily to her without the usual tears.

October 10, 1934. Mr. MacDonald talked this morning about how much good the Nursery School was doing Helen Rose and Rosalie Wilson. They are much less timid. After several days' work Helen Rose let the nurse put iodine on some scratches without crying. She even hunted for a scratch herself. The whole adjustment made by the children has been really remarkable.

How carefully it was necessary to obtain the mothers' cooperation in cases of impetigo and scabies, so prevalent among the children in the fall, is shown by Miss Sedman's notes in November:

November 5, 1934. Davey Regan was brought to school by his sister this morning, and both of them were in tears. Molly, the sister, said that Miss Shaffer was not to put any gentian violet on Davey because he had on new underwear. She said that her mother said Davey couldn't come back at all if he were sent home today, and that Davey didn't want to come to school and "he laid hisself down in the road and like to get runned over."

I kept Davey for Miss Shaffer to see and he soon stopped crying. After talking the matter over with Miss Clapp, we decided that Davey could remain in school but must be kept isolated, and that the gentian violet treatments were to be given in school and that Davey was to take off his new underwear and wear some furnished by the school.

November 7, 1934. I took Davey Regan home and explained to his mother about the treatments and the isolation. I told her about the underwear and the bathing at home, and that I knew it would be hard but that if she did her part along with the School's part, the condition would clear up soon. She was very friendly and co-operative and seemed more interested in getting to work on it than before.

November 8, 1934. Miss Shaffer said that she had to plan the medical supplies for a year today, and that it was impossible for her to treat Davey Regan this morning. I told her that I thought it would be too bad for us to fall down after we had enlisted Mrs. Regan's co-operation and interest. We then decided that I could give the treatment at the Nursery School with careful directions from Miss Shaffer. So, in the midst of a busy morning, I set up a table close by the iron stove in the store room, and bathed Davey with a weak Lysol solution and then painted him with gentian violet. I washed the table, chairs, and oilcloth with Lysol afterwards.

November 18, 1934. Davey Regan's scabies is improving very much. His mother puts clean clothes on him every night and bathes him carefully, for the purple medicine is washed off.

There is a satisfactory sequel to this. A record of May 13 notes:

Davey, who suffered so with scabies in the fall, looks as fat and is as frisky as a little squirrel.

Working Problems of Heating and Cooking

Starting a Nursery School is difficult enough under the most ideal physical conditions, but keeping everything neat when there is no storage space in the rooms, and cooking lunch when there is no kitchen, are herculean tasks. As we had started out with very little equipment, materials kept arriving from the Mountaineer Craftsmen Co-operative Association—hollow blocks, saw horses, planks, beds, etc., and one room was given up to storing them. Miss Sedman's report continues:

On October 8, when the upper School started on a full day session, the Nursery School started to serve lunches.

We cleared a corner in the store room for two rough tables. One held our two-burner electric plate, the other served as a work-

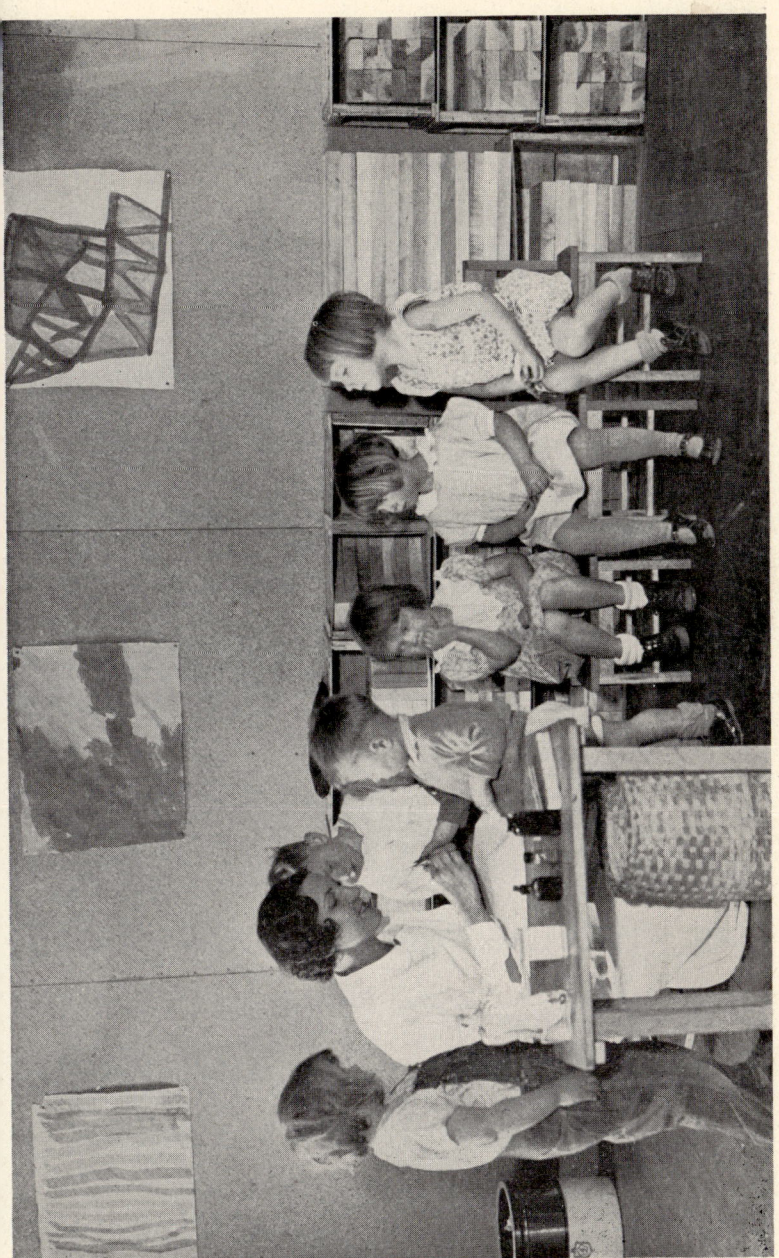

HEALTH INSPECTION AT THE NURSERY SCHOOL
with Miss Plummer, the Project Nurse

table and cupboard for dishes. Underneath the tables were big carboys of distilled water; for the water on our side of the road was not yet fit to drink. All the water to be used for cooking was carried into this room from one of the bathrooms. Miss Bayles, our dietitian, did all the cooking and dish-washing for nearly three weeks. On the first day we served 32 children. On the second day, the hot plate burned out in the midst of the preparations and we had to serve the children bread and milk, but that happened only once. We learned to boil potatoes at 8.30 for an 11.30 lunch, and to scramble eggs at 9.00.

Meanwhile, a small kitchen was being added to the Nursery School, and the Relief Office in Kingwood agreed to furnish us with a cook. The dietitian, then, not only planned the meals and helped with the cooking and serving, but also acted as an extra teacher.

During the period just described, the weather had become very cold and, as the central heating plant had not been completed, the Project Manager scoured the countryside and found us four old iron Burnside stoves. One was installed in each room, with a smokestack out the window. These worked well unless the wind was in the wrong direction, and then all the smoke blew back into the rooms.

It was interesting to see, however, that in spite of these physical difficulties, the children made progress. Miss Sedman writes on October 29:

Today was a typical Monday. The wind was in the wrong direction and the stove smoked badly. It was so cold that, after the children had been outdoors about ten minutes, they began to cry. So we had to bring them indoors. The milk was late and almost too cold to drink. Those were our liabilities.

Our assets, however, made up for them. All the children ate well today. Rosalie Wilson ate two dinners and did not cry when I said that after she had finished a second dinner she could have a second dessert. She usually pouts or cries when anyone suggests anything new, particularly in the matter of food. She even took a few bites of shredded lettuce which she refused at the beginning of the meal. That, with Rosalie, is a signal victory.

Within a few days, the central heating plant was completed, and then the Nursery School's most difficult working problems were solved. There remained the fact that none of the children had warm enough clothes, but this was remedied in December by the sending in of snow suits and galoshes. The mothers who wanted their children to have these worked for the Nursery School and received them in payment.

THE CHILDREN IN ARTHURDALE

During these first months the teachers had been watching the children closely. They could not take full records, but certain things stood out about the children. They were much calmer and less high-strung than city children, and their tempo was slower. They were very friendly and sociable, after they had become adjusted to the school situation. At first, they came in clean clothes with admonitions to be "good," but after home visits by the teachers had made the mothers realize that we welcomed overalls at school, and that it was a working place, the situation became more natural.

Children in these families were loved and cherished. We found the older children always willing and eager to take care of the little ones, especially in the case of those older children who had a younger brother or sister in the Nursery School. The security of family relationships seemed to have its effect on the children, for we found few so-called problems. There were some extremely shy children, however.

Emotions seemed to be nearer the surface, and displayed themselves quite naturally and simply in outward forms of sudden anger when occasion arose, or in a natural and impulsive display of love, affection, or sympathy, to which the children seemed to be easily moved. For instance, a child might strike another in sudden anger, and have it over with in a moment, carrying no hidden resentment, or be just as quickly moved to hug or kiss or wipe the tears of some child who was crying or had hurt himself. The children had the ability to take hard knocks without crying.

As would be expected of children from families where there are a number of little children, they could do many practical things for themselves and would work determinedly and with concentration at putting on a sock or shoe without calling for help. On the other hand, if the child had older sisters or brothers, he was as used to being waited on as the child from a well-to-do family.

THE ARTHURDALE ENVIRONMENT

Arthurdale was, of course, a fascinating place to young children. Trucks were constantly bumping and rattling by the School carrying coal, lumber, stone, pipes, window frames, etc. The whole place buzzed with activity; wells were being dug, roads were being built, houses were being constructed. The children had all moved into new houses—with new stoves, new bathrooms, new kitchen sinks in them. When the new barns had been completed, cows and chickens were purchased. Farming and gardening were everyone's interest.

Here was ideal material for use with young children. Obviously, the School's function was to provide the right kinds of materials, to be aware of what was going on in the home, to be ready to help the children to see relationships—in other words, to think.

The Nursery School in this case had a double job, as the new teachers had to be trained in how to do this with the children. Whenever Miss Stanton came down, she worked at this in staff meetings, getting the teachers to keep charts of the play activities, pointing out a subject for discussion—such as how Daddy lights the fire—showing how a group could dramatize the way Mom does the washing. When she left, she often sent down new material or a new book that would enrich the play. She suggested trips for the four- and five-year-old groups, and then discussed with the teachers on her next visit the stories the children had told about these trips.

Not alone chairs and tables and beds, but blocks and dolls and lumber and hammers and nails and crayons and paper make a nursery school child's world—things to handle and move from place to place. In Arthurdale, baby dolls to love and nurse, dishes to set tables with, were very important. The little girls had lived so closely with their mothers that they were intimately acquainted with cooking the dinner, setting the table, and washing the clothes. The boys knew all about the different kinds of trucks. They played with the blocks day after day making roads and trucks. And outdoors? No money went into expensive climbing apparatus as there were trees near by,[1] but we did have big hollow blocks, a few packing cases and ladders and saw horses. The children had never had such material, and it took them some time to see its play possibilities. But when they did, what interesting things they made! A little girl placed two saw horses side by side and hitched them up with rope to some blocks made in the form of a seat. The teacher, passing, said: "What are the names of your horses, Mathilda?" Mathilda roared in reply, pointing to one of the saw horses: "That thar one ain't a horse, that's a mule."

Some of Miss Sedman's early records follow:

October 3, 1934. The five-year-olds are hauling blocks in trucks and making radios. They co-operate very well in putting away blocks. I told a story about how Letitia's mother washed all of Letitia's clothes. There were many corrections from Letitia. Her mother washes in the bath tub and has no ironing board.

October 8, 1934. The four- and five-year-old children made automobiles, cows, and a motorcycle on the playground today. Dave Regan used a wooden saw horse as a cow, and the children talked about it. Davey said: "Her name is Tessie Cow. She gives lots of

---

[1] In the second year we were able to clear a space near the site of the new Nursery School building, for a "Playground in the Woods." See pp. 208–9.

milk. We drink it and eat it on our cornflakes. We killed the calf and made meat."

Lawrence sang, "We'll be coming 'round the mountain with four red horses."

December 2, 1934. I had an interesting discussion about hog-killing with the five-year-olds. Alice Siddon could tell the whole story, step by step.

Here is a spontaneous story told at the lunch table by Junior Matthews, who is three and a half:

> *My Daddy shot a pig. I watched them—they had a .45 gun. We had a knife and some little boards. We had a big garbage can to put it in. When they shot one of them, every one of them got scared. Yes, sir. Boy!*
>
> *When my Dad shot it, it kicked. They cut their legs off. They take the skin off. They hang it, and cut the guts out. Dad has a big ratchet he hangs it on.*

February 7, 1935. In block building today, the Fives as usual built roads, roads, and more roads, with an emphasis on mileage and telephone poles. Jerry Marshall put up a barrier at the end of his which marked, he said, "the end of the world." One truck was going to "Jane Loo," a near-by coal mine.

HOME ECONOMICS AT THE NURSERY SCHOOL WITH HIGH SCHOOL AND "NIGHT SCHOOL" STUDENTS

Like all the teachers in the Arthurdale community school, Miss Sedman participated in "Night School." She directed Home Economics, which was taught at the Nursery School. The course stressed especially preparing meals for children.

November 27, 1934. The two High School girls, Gertrude and Victoria, are splendid. They are thoroughly enjoying this work because they know we really need their help.

Even so early we used the Nursery School as a "laboratory" for the study of child care. The Gertrude here referred to was to enter the Nursery School as a student teacher in the fall of 1935, after graduation, and to become, in the summer of that year, a teacher of a group.

THE WORKMEN AND PARENTS APPRAISE THE NURSERY SCHOOL

At Arthurdale, the workmen were fathers of the children in school, or neighbors living near us. They all had a keen interest in what went on. Nothing escaped their notice. And we took pains to see that they understood what was happening and the reasons for the arrangement of equipment.

December 11, 1934. The carpenters are showing an increasing interest in the routine of the Nursery School. I brought some in to observe dinner and the rest period today. We had to have health inspection in a room in which they were working, and it was good for them to see what the nurse did and how the children responded. Mr. Payne came in when the children were taking their milk. They were all at the tables and were talking seriously and quietly together. "Well," Mr. Payne said, "it sure is wonderful."

Absorbed though we were in school with the children, we were nevertheless being tried in the balance. Notwithstanding the newness to them of this type of school, the homesteaders could and did appreciate the evident care and concern for the children and knew for a fact how untiringly their teacher-neighbors worked. "Words is passing about the Nursery School," one of them told me, "good words."

I was walking one rainy day along the road in front of the Nursery School, and met one of the workmen who came from Morgantown.

"Wait a moment," he said, "I want to talk to you." He carefully set down his plumbing tools on the fence. "I wanted to ask you. It seems you believe in having the children learn by doing." He jerked his head at the School Shop beside us filled with boys and girls. "Is that right?"

"Yes," I said. He nodded and went on.

TOY MAKING BY PARENTS FOR CHRISTMAS

It was Miss Sedman's special desire that parents of Nursery School children should have the opportunity to make simple toys for Christmas. She and the teachers made some models, we gathered together bits of wood, borrowed a few tools from the School Shop, and opened the Nursery School building several nights a week during December. The parents were delighted. Husbands and wives came and worked together. The place was crowded with workers and onlookers.

Miss Sedman, Miss Stanton, and I were at Arthurdale that first never-to-be-forgotten Christmas. Indeed it was Miss Sedman who nursed Beulah Jane Bradley, who had pneumonia, through her first crisis on Christmas Eve. It was from Miss Sedman that the child readily took her medicine when she would not take it from her mother. In this situation it was entirely natural for the teacher to help, and the relationship between the mother and the teacher was deepened because they had realized their dependence as neighbors.

THE NURSERY SCHOOL AT MID-WINTER

Miss Sedman's diary of events in the Nursery School is resumed in January:

January 14, 1935. I saw Mrs. Conners today. Her baby is a week old. We sat in the kitchen and talked about the twins. She said they had been examined for "decay of the bone" before they came to Arthurdale, and "the woman told her not to take them across water for six weeks, but it never done no good." Mrs. Conners said, however, that the babies had improved since they had come to Arthurdale.

January 15, 1935. Mrs. Conners had been up one day. The new baby is cunning and Richard was delighted when I said it looked like him. Mrs. Conners asked me to stay for supper. Supper was on the table—a big joint of meat and a bowl of macaroni and tomatoes. The table looked very nice with its green plates, with the fork and knife crossed on each one.

The heavy snow and cold made work on construction difficult, and wages were less. When illness kept the children home, they lost the gains they had begun to make at Nursery School, where, by the help of friends, we were able to serve good nourishing meals.

January 23, 1935. Rosalie Wilson returned today. She is very white, with blue circles under her eyes. She seemed chilled during lunch, so we put her to bed with a hot-water bottle and an extra blanket. She went to sleep. She eats little, very little, and refuses most foods.

January 30, 1935. Little Helen Rose Wilson came back today and looks like a tiny ghost. She has hardly strength to smile and is thinner than ever. We are going to give her extra milk in the morning.

We obtained some cod liver oil for the Nursery School.

February 13, 1935. It has been interesting to see how the different children reacted to the cod liver oil. Most of them took it as they take everything, but three or four were prepared for a vigorous fight and, when they saw that no fight was forthcoming, their resistance and hard feeling melted away.

FIRST PARENTS' MEETING

February 25, 1935. Miss Stanton came yesterday. She visited in all the rooms to gather some material for the parents' meeting in the evening.

We had a staff meeting this afternoon, and then worked hard getting the rooms ready for our first parents' meeting tonight. We were quite handicapped because Mrs. Stearns, who is janitress at the Nursery School, has a broken rib. Mrs. MacDonald, however, came and helped us out, along with Mr. Stearns and the Stearns children. We put up paintings and then set up typical block buildings from sketches in our weekly diary reports in the different classrooms.

There were about thirty people at the meeting. The entire

audience listened with concentrated attention while Miss Stanton talked about the day in the Nursery School and the importance of having little children understand as much as possible about their world. There were no questions during the meeting, but everyone stayed for nearly an hour afterward talking and looking at the rooms. Mr. Lathrop said after he had seen the buildings, etc.: "Well, this is much more interesting than I had thought." Then, after a long pause: "I never had nothin' like this and I'm just beginnin' to think it's what I should have had."

In all, five parents visited the Nursery School the next day as a result of the interest aroused by what Miss Stanton had told them of the children and their work.

"VISITIN'" ON THE HOMESTEAD

Calling on the families of the children was always "visitin' " in the country sense, whatever the errand might be:

April 25, 1935. I went to Richard's for supper and to watch churning tonight. I had a grand time. Mrs. Richard's mother, a charming old mountain woman, was there.

April 26, 1935. At the Littles', I had to see the new chickens and the fine new bull calf. Mattie Alice said: "I named that calf Mattie Alice. Ned says it's a bull calf, but it hain't."

April 29, 1935. It rained so hard at the close of school that I took Jessie Cartwright, the four Peterses, and Dave Regan home, and Mrs. Henry took four or five Dibbles. The oldest Peters girl said: "Now, Miss Sedman, you just come in and visit awhile. Ma'd be real pleased to have you." When I said I had to get right back, she said: "Well, you must come some other time."

CHILDREN'S PROGRESS IN MARCH, APRIL, AND MAY

Life in the Nursery School continued to be vivid and interesting. The children's play constantly reflected their environment. Note the square-dance orchestra, steam shovels, and the rabbit shooting in the following records. The teachers often talked with the workmen about how we were trying to help the children to understand the life about them, and the men were fine about notifying us if anything especially interesting was going to happen near the school.

March 5, 1935. I took *The Little Red Auto* in for Mrs. Henry to read to the Fives. They were delighted. Junior said: "That car's red. That's just my flavor." I explained that Miss Stanton had sent the book and that we must take good care of it, and they were much interested.

Later, "Scottie," the electrician, sent word that a telephone pole was going up, so the five-year-olds went down to watch. Mrs. Henry got a very nice story about the trip from the group afterward.

April 8, 1935. On Friday, some of the Fives improvised a square-dance orchestra during block building; violins (double units with pillars for bows), Harry and Bob Scott; drums (boxes), Jerry Marshall; horn (cylinder), Richard Conners.

April 9, 1935. Block building was a serious business in all the groups today.

The five-year-olds made steam shovels, and then had to widen their roads to fit them. Marion made a large house and carried on much dramatic play, doing elaborate housework and cooking. Suddenly Jerry Marshall grabbed up a broom, calling it his "gun," walked over to the corner of the room and, taking aim at an imaginary rabbit, fired, calling out: "Bang, bang." Then he brought the "rabbit" home, skinned it, and cooked it for dinner.

So, at the discussion period, we talked about how rabbits are prepared for eating and how they are cooked.

April 12, 1935. The four-year-old group grows more interesting every day. They are doing excellent block building, and even Mathilda works with purpose and concentration. Sally built a house with three rooms. She was the mother, Junior Matthews the dad. Junior said: "Don't you know every woman has to have a dad?" Before lunch they all built a train of chairs and went to "grandma's." Rosalie passed a pan of cubes, which she called "cakes."

This is the first group dramatic play of any sustained type done by the Fours.

In late spring the progress in the children was noticeable.

April 28, 1935. Mrs. Loy, the teacher of the two-year-olds, notices a great improvement in Johnny, and said he seemed so much less fussy and had a happier expression. I saw his father at the Square Dance and Mr. Marshall said that he noticed a change in Johnny at home, and that Johnny went to sleep by himself now.

May 10, 1935. Eating is going very well. All the two-year-olds, except Johnny Marshall, eat carrots now. Johnny consistently refuses to eat most vegetables, but he is gradually learning to taste and like fruit and other desserts. He is used to the regulation local diet of fresh pork, fried potatoes, and green beans cooked with bacon, and buckwheat cakes. I believe it will be only a matter of time until he will eat everything.

May 15, 1935. Jerry Marshall ate all his dinner. Ernest fed Johnny a spoonful of green beans which Johnny usually scorns. He ate them from Ernest's hand.

FIRST "WELL BABY CLINIC," MAY 1935

In May we were able to reap the benefit of the medical services of the doctor and nurse and of the child care of the Nursery School in a "Well Baby Clinic." Just eight months earlier, it was held that no one "had the doctor" unless he was near death, and that babies should grow up as they could. The eyes of the homesteaders had been opened by really excellent and interested medical and nursing care to the fact that health was possible and within their grasp. And the Nursery School's concern with the welfare of little children and its example in physical routines, coupled with the good results for the children, which all the parents noted, began to convince them of the fact that the right food and habits of toilet, proper eating and sleeping, and fresh air and sun would make babies well and strong.

Miss Sedman's diary describes the Clinic:

May 21, 1935. I went to call on four families to ask about bringing the tiny babies to the Well Baby Clinic on Thursday. Mrs. Bradley said she would bring George. Mrs. Brooks didn't think she would bring her children. Mr. Brooks was listening from the kitchen and said he thought this clinic was the "best thing they've done yet."

May 23, 1935. We had our first Baby Clinic today, and Dr. Timbres seemed very much pleased with the way it went off. There were 23 babies, out of a possible 30, present. Dr. Timbres examined the children, and Miss Plummer showed the mothers how to wash the buttocks and put on a diaper. There were sample packets containing nose swabs, cotton, zinc oxide ointment, and talcum powder, for sale for five cents. Most of the mothers bought them.

It was, of course, the fact that the first Well Baby Clinic had been held, and that it was well attended and helpful to those who came, that made it possible for other clinics to follow more easily and, within the space of a year, to come as an expected and welcome event.[2]

VISITORS: THE NURSERY SCHOOL USED AS AN OBSERVATION CENTER

Visitors to the project numbered several hundred a week all through 1934 and 1935. The School in its first months was fortunately somewhat protected from an influx of visitors, because it was not then generally known to be at Arthurdale, and because there were as yet no school buildings to announce the fact. However, we did have many guests. Happily, they were the people who were really interested in the School. Some excerpts from Miss Sedman's diary will give an idea of their variety and suggest that already the School had begun to serve as a teaching center for other teachers and students.

---

[2] See Chapter VII, pp. 372-4; and this chapter, pp. 212-4.

October 25, 1934. Today we had our first visitors during school hours. Miss Bonar, State Supervisor of nursery schools, brought twelve teachers from an institute in Morgantown. While the children were outdoors, Miss Barrett and Mrs. Rider, a supervisor and a principal from Morgantown, Monongalia County, came. Then five women from Morgantown came over with the School secretary.

December 7, 1934. Today was visitors' day indeed. First, eight teachers from the Emergency Nursery School in Morgantown came to visit. Next Miss Barrett and Miss Lyons, also from Morgantown, came. Then Miss Clapp with eight or ten principals from the Morgantown schools.

January 23, 1935. Dr. Boudreau, from Geneva, visited the Nursery School. He was interested in the construction of the building and in the appearance of the children.

May 13, 1935. Miss Stanton was here with Miss Bonar (the State Supervisor of nursery schools). Miss Bonar was delighted with the way the children knew routines and carried them out with a minimum of supervision.

Workers in adult education, high school students, and university students were other visitors, and teachers from other schools came. Two things seemed to impress most visitors: first, how children respond to patience and kindness from a teacher, and second, how children's play reflects the life going on around them.

I think that perhaps the most interesting guest experience happened in the fall. A Conference of Friends was held at Arthurdale. I spoke as Director of the School. Afterward, of course, many of the audience came up to ask me questions. Mr. Stearns, one of the fathers, whose wife was janitress of the Nursery School building, and who as "boss painter" had been working there a good deal too, came to the rescue.

"Are these folks asking what good the Nursery School is to the families?" he said. "Just leave them to me." And he took them off to explain and to show the School to them.

In the spring, when thirty student teachers arrived from

the Co-operative School for Student Teachers in New York, a group of homestead women acted as hostesses on the project. They felt already acquainted with these students, of course, through Miss Stanton, whom they knew so well.

The summer of 1935 we used as an exploratory period. The County schools regularly close at the end of May. Farming, planting and cultivating their gardens, absorbed the families, even to the young children. We debated, Miss Stanton and I, about keeping the Nursery School open, but finally decided to concentrate our energies that summer[3] on health work and on farming activities.

Section 2: The New Nursery School in 1935–36

THE NEW NURSERY SCHOOL BUILDING

When the Nursery School opened again in September, it was in its new building, which, like that of the "Big School," represented the third of the building plans we had made. The experiences of the first year had induced us to enlarge the space for the Nursery School, now that we were aware of the large number of little children in these families. In 1935–36, with 115 families out of the 165 (and a possible 200) who were to come on the project, the enrollment rose from 47 to 82, so we decided to plan for 120 children.

The Nursery School was a long, low one-story frame building. It was lined with celotex inside and, because of its fine proportions and high ceilings in the classrooms, was really quite beautiful.

There were six large sunny classrooms. Each one had its own toilet facilities and a separate entrance to its own play-

---

[3] The second year the Nursery School continued through July and reopened September 10, after a month's interval.

ground. The physical conditions were very carefully planned so that one teacher could handle a good-sized group of children. Moving a group of two- and three-year-olds is a difficult performance—they cannot walk in a line, they wander and straggle, so that a direct entrance to one's own playground is a great asset.

For children of these ages, sleeping quarters, where cots can be left set up, are desirable. For the youngest groups there were three sleeping porches. Closet space for storing blankets was provided, and the burden of preparing for the nap hour was greatly lessened. The older children, who could put down the cots themselves, slept in their own classrooms.

The sleeping porches proved valuable for other uses. On rainy days and on bitterly cold winter days, the teachers brought up big blocks, boards, and saw horses from the playgrounds, and the children put on their coats and played out on the porches. As the Nursery School was built on a slope, these porches extended out over the playgrounds and provided a shady play space on very sunny days and a refuge when a light shower of rain came up during the morning.

One-way observation screens were placed in several classrooms and saved the children from the distraction of the coming and going of the many visitors. These screens proved extremely useful, too, as the mothers could see their children without the children's being upset by their presence.

Other rooms were a kitchen with a separate outside entrance, a small director's office, a nurse's office, and an isolation room with a shower for use in hot weather.

The classrooms had closets for storing cots, but no cabinets or cupboards or shelves of any kind. All the materials were put away in orange crates, the ones we had collected in grocery stores in Morgantown and painted ourselves. It was really amazing how well the classrooms looked furnished with orange crates! The way they were placed in relation to the wall space in the room, the color they were painted, and the way the materials were put away in them, determined both the appearance of the rooms and their usefulness.

We felt it important to keep this provision for storage of materials simple, to show our State and County visitors how easily and inexpensively they could duplicate it.

CHILDREN'S IMPROVEMENT IN THE FALL

Miss Sedman's diary of the opening weeks in the fall of 1935 records improvement in the children and the problems of living in the Nursery School in the midst of workmen in the still unfinished building:

September 9, 1935. Most of the Threes acted as if they had had no summer vacation at all. They all looked well, especially Helen Rose Wilson. She is so active and so happy and tall and well-nourished that it is hard to believe that she was so weak and thin just a year ago.

Carpenters hung doors most of the day, and there were no toilets in the Threes' room.

September 10, 1934. I took Betty Spear and Grace Carter to the nurse because of sores on their feet. It was interesting to see how well Betty behaved, although Miss Plummer hurt her. Last year she wouldn't let the doctor even touch an infection on her leg.

September 11, 1935. Miss Stanton let the five-year-olds tell a story about this new building, and in the afternoon Mrs. Morris took them on a tour of the rooms. The workmen in the building are fine. They seem to know just what to say to the children, and the children love talking to them.

The sleeping porches are now arranged so that the beds do not have to be put down. I hadn't realized just what a difference that would make. Each day we all realize a little more just how fine this new building is.

September 17, 1935. Carpenters are still here in full force. The bathrooms are not yet completed and the four-year-olds have to go in and out between plumbers, carpenters, and litter when they want to wash. Fortunately, that group is used to Nursery School and does not seem to mind. Nor do the various outside distractions seem to make them forget their old habits; they go through the day with very little prompting.

The eating situation is interesting in these first days. I was disappointed when we found that our food allowance had been cut and that we would be unable to give the children the regular lunches they had last year. The lunch of sandwiches, milk, potatoes, and a vegetable did not seem quite right for them. To my great surprise, the children eat everything quickly and happily with absolutely no discussion. They all eat large quantities and every plate is cleared without any urging from the teachers. Our feeding problems of last year seem to have vanished. Johnny Marshall eats his vegetables and Rosalie Wilson eats everything without any of her former shyness. The atmosphere at tables in each room is quiet and very happy. We have had little difficulty, either, in getting the children to rest or sleep.

This report of the steadiness and vigor of the children at this time in the early fall is very interesting. The year previous, it was April before they reached this point. Evidently, they had not lost but gained over the summer.

September 24, 1935. The toy horses, cows, and garden tools Miss Stanton sent were put in the Fives' room today, and quite naturally their interest turned to barns, pastures, etc. They all know a lot about cows. They milked, shoveled manure, carried feed and water, etc. Dave Regan made a toilet for his cows! Mrs. Morris took the group to see the cement mixer.

October 8, 1935. Mrs. Morris took the Fives on a trip to the Elementary School building. Dave Regan could tell a lot about it. (His father works there.) The group went on, at Dave's request, to see the cement mixer. They brought home boards and nails for their bench work.

October 15, 1935. The Fives did very interesting block building today. Alice Siddon made the Mansion, and Dave Dibble made the road that goes from the Mansion to Masontown. Elsie Richards made a barn with windows and manger, not unlike the barn on their place in Reedsville. She put cows and horses inside.

A carpenter was fixing something in the bathroom and gave boards with nails to Dave Dibble and Dave Regan, who were working at the bench. He showed them how to use another board with the hammer to pry nails loose. Davie Dibble had the patience to learn this new way, but Dave Regan had not. They are interested now in folding their own blankets. It seems often that these children now are at the point the other Fives had reached in June.

October 31, 1935. The Fives played "Cow Daisy" today and then made an automobile of saw horses, boards, and hollow blocks. Justin was daddy and then they started to drive to Morgantown. Justin made noises and motions for driving the car and said once: "Now I don't have to make noise. I turned the key off and let her coast." They stopped several times for gasoline. Once the motor broke, so Justin crawled under the car, called for the children to give him the screw driver, lay on his back, and fixed the motor. He said: "I have to get my tools, it's sure broke down." Soon it was fixed and the family climbed in and started on with the baby crying.

In January of the second year, Miss Sedman had to leave, much to our regret. Fortunately, through Miss Stanton, we were able to persuade Ethel Wadsworth, who had charge of one of the FERA nursery schools in New York, to join us at short notice. Miss Stanton and Miss Wadsworth had several conferences in New York before the latter left for Arthurdale, and Mrs. Henry, our senior West Virginia teacher, gave Miss Wadsworth her wholehearted support, so that school was soon running smoothly. Miss Stanton continued her usual visits every month.

At the end of the year, Miss Wadsworth wrote the account of the Nursery School work from January through July which follows.

THE NURSERY SCHOOL FROM JANUARY THROUGH JULY 1936

Ethel Wadsworth
Head of the Nursery School

Parents' Visits to Nursery School

At Arthurdale, the parents were free to come to the Nursery School at any time—to observe the children and to talk with the teachers when they were not occupied with the children. Many of them did drop in—mothers and fathers alike—to watch the children and to ask questions about the things they had observed. Many of the mothers used to stop in regularly after cooking in the School lunchroom. Sometimes they came to talk to a teacher about their child in her group; sometimes to ask for help with some problem in training the child at home; or just to see the children sleeping. It was the policy of the Nursery School to have time to give the parents the help which they needed.

Visits to Families

The Nursery School teachers also kept a close contact with the families in the homes. Frequent visits were made to the homes for establishing a friendly contact with the families, for gaining a better understanding of the child in Nursery School through a knowledge of the home situation, and in order to be ready to be of service in case parents wanted help on any particular problem in their home.

January 29, 1936. Visited the Dibble family after school. Mrs. Dibble was out feeding the pigs when I came, as no one else in the family, she thinks, seems to do it just right. Her home is clean and neat, considering the size of the family—twelve in all. She showed me all over the house, and I was quite impressed with her arrangement of sleeping quarters for all the twelve children. Mrs.

Dibble took great pride in showing me the bathroom, and said how much she enjoyed having it.

February 14, 1936. Mrs. Lincoln has not been sending Jean Alice and Patience to school, as she said she could not manage to get them ready for school while she was in bed. She promised to send them back in a few days.

While I was there, Jean Alice amused herself with a few simple toys, and a great deal of imaginative play. She needs no attention or help from adults to keep amused. She seems to be getting intelligent training at home. She has been provided with a place of her own to keep her toys—and gets them out and puts them away when finished with them, by herself.

March 1, 1936. Made a long visit at the Carrolls' this afternoon. We talked about fixing up a room which they are not using as a playroom for the children, who are in the habit of being held and rocked on every occasion. Mrs. Carroll said the children just wouldn't sleep in the afternoon at home. The only way she could get them to sleep was to rock them.

Mr. Carroll thinks the children have all gained and look much better since they have been going to school and getting cod liver oil.

I had a nice talk with Mr. Carroll. He told me of his work, and how he came to Arthurdale. He said he wished there were some night classes at School for the adults, as he would like to get some more education. He thought many of the other homesteaders would like to go to school, too.

Use of the Environment

TRIPS

Many of the same activities that engaged the community during the first year on the project were, of course, going on also in this second year of the Nursery School. The following account shows how the teachers helped the children of the four- and five-year-old groups to see relationships by taking them on trips, and how they told about these experiences and played them out with the school materials.

The first trips to be taken with the children were in the immediate environment of the Nursery School—to the kitchen to see the dinner being prepared and cooked; to the storeroom, where the canned goods were kept; to the furnace room to see the coal being put on the fire, the coal bin, and the little stove for heating water, with its pipes to carry the hot water up to the kitchen and bathrooms; outside, to see the ashes being hoisted up from the furnace room and carried away in a truck. Trucks that brought supplies to the Nursery School were seen and recognized—the milk man, the bread man.

Gradually, interest began to be extended outside the Nursery School building. Trips were made to the various School buildings along the road. The children were soon able to point out and name all the School buildings, and know what was inside each one, joyfully shouting and pointing out the classrooms of their older brothers and sisters. Several visits were made to the School Center building: they saw the lunchroom, where their older brothers and sisters came for their lunch; the kitchen, where their mothers came to help cook the school lunches; and, upstairs, the medical rooms and offices of the doctor and nurse, where they came to be weighed.

As the children became oriented in this school environment, reflections of these trips began to appear in block building, particularly with the Fives, where the School buildings were reproduced in blocks and placed in relationship to one another—a simple and rudimentary form of map-making. The gymnasium was realistically reproduced several times in blocks—with rows of seats, and standpatter dolls for people.

Many trips were made to the Community Center—to the postoffice there, the Co-operative Store, the Mountaineer Craftsmen's shops, the barber shop before and after completion, the Co-operative's gasoline station, and the garage where trucks and the School bus were kept at night. The children were able to pick out and name the buildings that the Nursery

School had used the year before—now housing the Arthurdale Store's stockroom, the weaving room—the project's Government offices, and the tea room. In this way they were becoming oriented in their environment, and gaining a simple understanding of some of the things necessary in the life of a community.

The houses under construction were always a source of educational experience. Trips were made to see the houses in various stages of construction—some with just the foundation, some with only the framework, and others in more advanced stages, showing the pipes, electric wiring, etc. Even in the elementary stages, the children were able to name the various rooms of the house—the kitchen, furnace room, storage room, living room, bedrooms, and bathroom—from observation of their own homes built on a similar pattern. Interest in the workers was always keen, and seeing their own fathers or neighbors working on the houses lent an added personal interest.

A group of houses under construction within easy walking distance of the Nursery School was visited regularly at two-week intervals, so that the progress of the work could be noted. In this way, the children began to understand some of the things that go into the making of a house and the people involved in the building of it—the carpenters, the masons, plasterers, electricians, etc.

When some of the children came in to tell of the new stone houses that were being built near their homes, a trip in the School bus was made to see them. They watched the stone being cut and put into place on the sides of the houses. This was followed by a trip to the stone quarry, to see the native stone being taken out of the hills and cut into various sizes. Later, when trips were made to watch the laying of the stone walk connecting the School buildings, the children recognized the stone from the quarry.

The children saw the building supplies when they came into the station at Reedsville and were loaded on the big project trucks, the lumber yard, and the piles of supplies at the Community Center. A trip was made to the Mountaineer Craftsmen's shop, where they saw window frames being made, and the kitchen cabinets and cupboards which were to go into the new houses. Here they also saw furniture—beds, chairs, tables—which they recognized as the same as those in their own houses.

TRUCKS

In all the groups, trucks-and-road play is of paramount interest. Networks of roads with many turns and hills are built, covering the entire floor. Cars and trucks, which have been built of blocks, or may be just plain unit blocks or irons, are pushed over them. The cars and trucks fall off the road, get "tore up," and there are many "wrecks." Owing to the many recent experiences of the School bus and cars and trucks being stuck in the snow when the roads were so impassable, much of the road play has centered upon trucks and cars getting "hung up" in the snow, and having to be hauled out by the "caterpillar" tractor. The caterpillar is usually an iron, which is tied to the unfortunate car. Sometimes an iron is the "wrecking car."

Truck Play—Junior Matthews—Four-Year Group

(Junior knew all about trucks, as his father was in the trucking business. Every day Junior made a different kind of truck, with characteristic details of construction. His truck today was called a "standard-bed" truck.)

Junior (singing): "Get me some more standards." [Standards—pillars.] "Go get me two more standards. Oh—do you see my standard-bed truck?"
Teacher: "What do you haul?"
Junior: "Lumber—and a lot of pieces of blocks."
Teacher: "You wouldn't be hauling cinders, would you?"

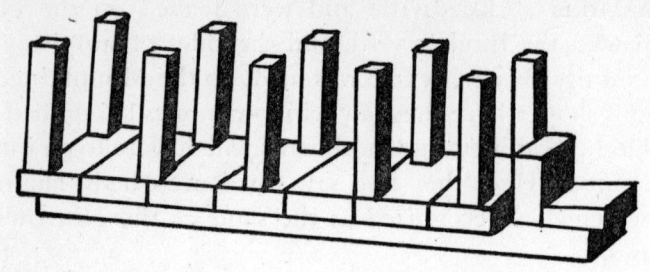

STANDARD BED TRUCK

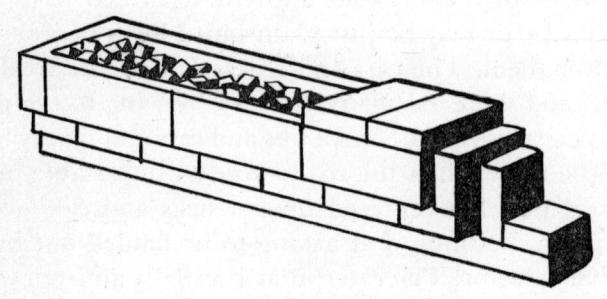

TRUCKLOAD OF CINDERS
(COLORED CUBES)

Junior: "No—'cause it would fall off the sides. You could haul the big lumps of rock—or 'red-dog'—or coal—just the big lumps of coal."

Teacher: "You couldn't haul the regular coal, could you?"

Junior: "No—them would fall out the back."

(Junior began building road beside his truck.)

"I'm gonna make a long road. Is this a good place for the road? You have to make turns in your road, don't you?" (Adding curves.)

THE NEW NURSERY SCHOOL BUILDING, 1935–36
Sleeping Porches Provide Play Space Underneath for Rainy Weather

"THE SCHOOL WAS, IN EFFECT, A LITTLE VILLAGE IN ITSELF"

(After road was built, Junior tried to figure out how to get his truck up on the road.)

"Wish I could get this truck—standard-bed truck—up on the road. Help me!"

THE SCHOOL BUS

The School bus, which transported all the Nursery School children to and from school, played a most important part in their lives. Their fathers had rebuilt this bus—thus solving the serious problem of getting these little children to school. It was "their own bus" more truly than any ordinary school bus. All the groups often dramatized coming to school in it.

The three-year-olds joined in making a "school bus" out on the playground. They laid planks across saw horses and then made seats on this flooring with outdoor blocks. When they had finished the bus, they carried on the following dramatic play:

Bessie: "I'm going to be the school teacher. This is for your feets, ain't it? We'll come back after it, Bobbie.

"Honey—see—you can make your seat back this way. I'm gitting up on the bus now."
Mary: "That's my seat."
Bobbie: "You ain't the driver, Laura."
Bessie: "I'm the teacher—that ain't your seat! Hey, Barbara—there's your seat. Oh, honey, git out of Martha's seat."
Everett (getting on the bus beside Bessie): "I'm the schoo' bus driver."
Bessie: "Honey—you git on this 'un." (Held Everett on her lap.) "You're my little brother."
(Barbara came out of her house, carrying Mary. She waved frantically to "teacher" on the bus.)
Barbara: "Hey, hey! The baby's coming. Help the baby up.
"She's mine.
"Honey, let her sit here.
"Help her up, 'cause she's going to school today.
"Scoot over and let me sit in this place."

The four-year-olds often built the school bus with the indoor blocks and took the dolls to school. Two sketches follow:

SCHOOL BUS

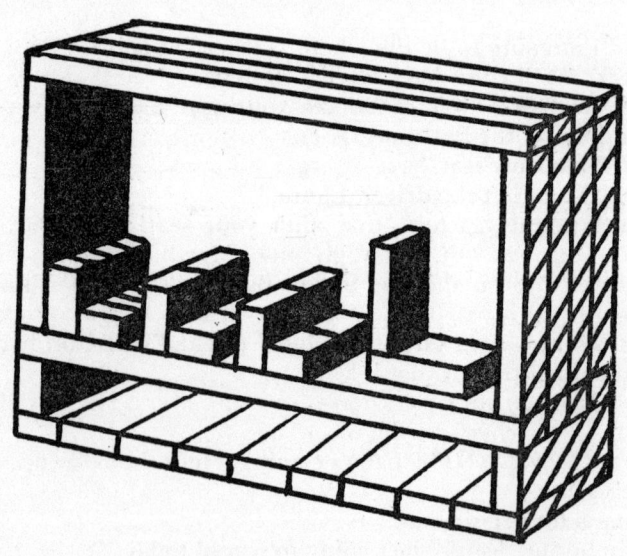

ANOTHER VERSION OF THE
SCHOOL BUS

The teacher gave the children an opportunity to tell about the bus at the story-telling period. She wrote it down as they told it. The story follows:

I look for it out of the window. You can see it. It blows its horn. Beep! Beep! Ouga! Ouga! Sometimes he forgets to blow the horn. We have to watch the clock, then.

The wheels go round. When you turn the steering wheel, the wheels turn. He doesn't go fast, only down hills. He drives easy, so he won't wreck. The roads are bumpy.

The bus goes along— Chug—chug—chug! Four wheels in back, and two in front. Two wheels right together in back.

He stops. He puts up the brake. He doesn't have to blow the horn to stop. We get on. Mr. Jenkins and all the kids are on the bus. He starts the bus. He gets all the kids. He stops everywhere the kids are to get on. He goes to school. He stops and lets us out.

SPRING GARDENS AND ANIMALS

In the spring and summer months the children saw all the processes involved in farming, clearing the land, cutting down trees, pulling stumps with the tractor, plowing the land, disking, spreading lime, sowing seeds, and cultivating. As all of the families were planting gardens, the children came in with much to tell, and the teachers gave them the opportunity for group discussion and individual stories about farming. Some of the children brought in seeds from home, made flower boxes and planted their seeds, taking care of them during the summer months. Farming, in all its phases, was reproduced in the outdoor play activities of all the groups.

Spring meant the advent of many baby animals: pigs, new calves, and baby chickens, or "peepies," as they were commonly called by the children. A group story follows:

Group Discussion: Five- and Six-Year-Olds

Elsie R.: We have little peepies. One is white, one is black, one is yellow, and one is brown. We feed them cornmeal."

Bonnie: "We're getting one hundred peepies from Mr. Pharr. He's the farm man."

John Atwell: "He's the pig doctor. Our little peepies can fly up over their box."

Bryant H.: "We got one yesterday, and one last night."

Elsie: "About tomorrow my little 'banty hen' will have some peepies."

John Atwell: "We got our little peepies from eggs. The settin' hen set on them."

Bonnie: "Our chickens climb up and go to bed. They stick their heads under their wings."

James Bradley: "Our chickens stand up when they go to sleep. They eat shells."

Farm children recognize that chickens are raised for food. The four-year-olds tell how their fathers and mothers get them ready for eating.

GROUP DISCUSSION: FOUR-YEAR-OLDS

Betty: "Daddy killed a chicken Saturday."

Justin: "My Daddy kills chickens, too. He cuts off their heads with a butcher knife."

Terry: "Mine uses a hatchet."

Adult: "What do you do next?"

Betty: "You clean them. You pick all the feathers off with your hands."

Terry: "First you put them in a pan of hot water and let them stand for a while, then pick off the feathers."

Justin: "Take it in the house and put water on it, and then cut it up."

Terry: "Mommy doesn't cut it up. She puts it in a pan and puts it on the stove. Hot water's in the pan. After it's done boiling, take it out and cut it up. Put it on a plate and then set it on the table."

Betty: "Then eat it."

Terry: "Yes—eat it after a while."

Betty: "When you clean it, you take out hearts and liver. They're good to eat."

Bruce: "The chicken flops all around when you cut its head off."

DISCUSSION ON GARDENS

Four-Year-Olds

(Teacher started discussion by asking what you have to do first when you make gardens.)

Terry: "First you get the plow and plow. It has handles and——"
Jonas (interrupting Terry): "No—you get the tractor to plow."
Terry: "You got to have a plow. Tractors can't make those ditches through the ground."
Elaine: "Horses plowed our garden. We borrowed them. We don't have any horses."
Terry (to Jonas, continuing argument): "You have to have a plow —to make rows. Down at the old house we had to spade the garden."

(The teacher told Jonas that Terry was right, you had to have a plow, and that the tractor was used to pull the plow, or that you could use horses instead to pull the plow. Then she asked what you did next when the garden was plowed or spaded.)

Jonas: "Put lime on it."
Elaine: "We put fertilizer on ours and mixed it up—so our beans would come up."
Terry: "We didn't use any on ours and our beans came up."
Jonas: "You have to put it on so they grow."
Terry: "We didn't."

(The teacher tried to explain to Terry that things grew faster with fertilizer. Mentioned rich dirt, but this seemed confusing. Terry shook his head in a skeptical manner and accepted Jonas's suggestion of fertilizer to help plants grow.)

Jonas: "Then the garden is ready to plant. You put them in rows—the seeds."
Terry: "Not close together or they won't grow."
James: "Our potatoes came up—they were grew."
Jonas: "Black, huh?"
Terry: "No, when you roast them, they're black."

(The teacher brought the discussion back to gardens by asking what kinds of seeds were planted.)

James: "Every kind."
Elaine: "Beans, corn, lettuce, and onions. Before we lived here we had radishes."

Terry: "We planted cucumbers, some at the house and some down in that garden."
Jonas: "You put fertilizer on the seeds."
James: "Cover up the seeds with dirt. The rain makes them grow. You have to water them."
Dorothy: "Some people have jars in their gardens."
Elizabeth: "We have jars on our tomatoes."
Dorothy: "What are the jars for?"

(No one knew so the teacher explained that they were to keep the new, young plants from being killed by frost or hot sunshine.)

Jonas: "Our beans were that high" (measured several inches) "when the frost eat them up. We had to plant some more."

THE PLAYGROUND IN THE WOODS

Although the children took many walks in the woods, it was not until late spring that we were able to move to a real playground there. We found a delightful spot where a huge tree had fallen across a little brook. We roped off a level space in front of it and included a steep wooded hillside the other side of the brook.

There was much to be done on the new playground before it could be used by the children. The help of some of the High School boys was enlisted in clearing away a mass of tangled thorny bushes and cutting down dead limbs. We tried to keep the setting as natural as possible, only eliminating those things which would be of danger to the children, many of whom we knew would play there barefoot.

After the playground was ready for use, a spell of rainy weather prevented its use for a week or so, but the first day finally arrived.

The children ran up and down the hillside, climbed up and down the old tree, with excited shouts greeting each new discovery. At Bryant's suggestion, they made a bridge of planks across the stream, using saw horses on either side for railings. Then they decided it would be easier if there were steps to climb up. They dug holes in the steep bank and laid flat stones for steps.

As the days went on, the children discovered new bugs and insects, caterpillars and worms of all sizes and descriptions, crayfish, land snails, a snake or two, new forms of plant life, and last year's acorns hidden among the leaves, to be retrieved and sailed as "boats" in the little brook.

One day the group went out to see an owl perched on the grapevine, and the next day told about it:

The little owl was on the grapevine. He was sleeping there. He was brown and white. He blinked and he winked his eye. He leaned his whole head over when he heard us. The wind blowed his feathers. It made the brown and white stripes crooked.

His feet were right around the grapevine. We got some bread from the kitchen. We put some pieces on the ground under the grapevine. We put one piece up in the tree.

This morning the little owl was gone, he must have gone home.

It is difficult to put into words a picture of how a group of children learn together—the vivid play that fills the morning hours, the delightful conversations that go on at luncheon. One can only say that the Arthurdale children seized upon their experiences and lived with vim and gusto.

EARLIER LIFE IN THE MINES REFLECTED IN DRAMATIC PLAY

An amazing bit of play, reminiscent of their lives before Arthurdale, brings out the determination of the male members of the families.

Five-Year-Old Play
March 5, 1936

(Mathilda King and Jack Benton built a house of blocks and carried on domestic play, with Mathilda as "Mother" and Jack as "Daddy.")

Mathilda: "Baby! Baby! Where's the baby at?"
(She found baby doll, wrapped it up in a blanket, and went off with it.)
"Daddy—you take care of these kids. Ah'll be back pretty soon. You have something put on the table when Ah get back."
(Came back in a few minutes.)
"Ah told you to have the dishes on the table when Ah got back!"
Jack (leaving house): "Hey, kids—have my dinner ready when I get back!"
(Mathilda packed lunch for "Daddy"—gathering cups and dishes, and hoes and rakes for eating utensils. Took them over to where Jack was "working.")
Mathilda: "Here's your lunch, Dad."
Jack: "I'm working now."
Mathilda: "Where ya working at now, Daddy?"
Jack: "I'm working in the mines."
Mathilda (very dramatically): "You better not work in those mines, Dad. You died there once. You better not do that no more. Better get out of those mines, Dad."
Jack: "It's a lot of work running that machine. If I keep on working in the mines, I'll have a lot of money."
(Kept piling blocks on interlocking block train as he talked.)
Mathilda: "You better not work in those mines. All some men got killed there. Better stay at home, Dad."
Jack: "I'm not gonna quit, anyway."
(Pushed off trainload of "coal," while Mathilda stood by, watching.)
Mathilda: "Daddy—you be sure and bring those dishes back."

Relations with the Community

As a teacher living on the homestead I found that a much closer contact could be made with the families than it would have been possible to have otherwise. In the first place, you were living more or less as a homesteader, not set apart, but as one of the families on the project—living in the same kind of house, on the same type of land, and meeting some of the same problems which they had to meet. In this way, you felt that you could come to a closer understanding of the people and their way of living, and the problems which confronted them.

Walking back and forth to school, by direct and sometimes by devious routes, I found to be a valuable way of getting to know the people in their everyday life. You were always sure to meet one or two or more of the Nursery School parents en route and stop to chat, or to give the latest news of their child's adjustment to Nursery School, to gather some bits of information, to inquire about their garden or the new calf, or just to pass the time of day. In this way, it was possible to develop an acquaintance built upon an understanding of the problems with which they had to deal. This type of everyday neighborly contact soon developed into a confidence not to be gained in any other way. Many were the "roadside conferences" which were held along the way, when you were stopped, or called into the home and asked for some bit of advice or help in regard to some problem with a child at home or in school. Thus parent education came about in a very simple, natural way.

Living on the homestead also made it very easy to drop in and visit families, either as an informal social call, or as a planned visit with some definite purpose in mind. Getting to know the family as a whole, and seeing the Nursery School child in the home situation, made it possible to come to a better understanding of the child in school. It was also possible to gather up such information as the routine habits of the child at home—what time he got to bed, what he was given to eat, etc.—information quite necessary to the successful handling of the child in school.

Living on the homestead was also a valuable means of keeping in close touch with everyday occurrences in and around the homes, and getting to know some of the things the families were doing on the homestead. You knew what each family were doing in their garden—how they were fixing up their land. You knew when the new calf was born, or when the "settin'-hen" hatched out the first batch of "peepies," or how many pigs the family owned, or who milked the family cow. With this knowledge, you could enter wholeheartedly into the stories told you at school, even in the most rudimentary language of the youngest twos, about their experiences at home. It was a means of contact with the child in school, through an active interest and knowledge of his life at home.

I found the people very friendly and sociable. They always seemed pleased to have you call, urging you to "set and talk awhile—you don't need to be in a hurry," whenever you attempted to leave. Usually you were invited to stay for a meal, and on one occasion I was asked to stay for the night and listen to the radio during the evening.

Baby Clinics in 1936

Through the Baby Clinics, the Nursery School extended further out into the community, by reaching families which had no children in Nursery School. Many of the mothers who brought babies to the Clinic visited the Nursery School for the first time; they became acquainted with the set-up and were told something about the Nursery School work. As they were future Nursery School parents, it was a valuable means of building up an understanding of the Nursery School.

The following account reveals clearly all that was involved in holding a successful Baby Clinic on the homestead: the planning of the Clinics; the home visits to interest the mothers; the co-operation of the homestead women's Medical Committee with the teachers, doctor, nurse, Nursery School dietitian, and Home Economics director; and the technique of running it off smoothly. The spring of 1935 saw the first "Well Baby Clinic." [4] By the summer of 1936, Baby Clinics had, slowly, become an established fact, accepted and valued by many of the mothers on the project.

---

[4] See this chapter, pp. 189–90.

THE ARTHURDALE NURSERY SCHOOL

April 28, 1936. I stopped at the School Center the first thing this morning to get a list of the babies from the nurse, Miss Plummer. There are 15 babies for the younger babies' Clinic, and 19 for the Clinic for the babies of twelve to twenty-four months.

April 30, 1936. Saw the President of the Women's Club, Mrs. Simkin, about the meeting of the Medical Committee on Tuesday. Also saw Mrs. George Beecher and asked her to serve on the Committee. She will be glad to do so.

May 3, 1936. In the evening, visited Mrs. Douglas to make sure she wanted to serve on the Medical Committee, and acquainted her with the plans for the baby Clinics to be held this summer.

May 5, 1936. The Medical Committee met this afternoon, and Dr. Wills told of the plans for the Clinics throughout the summer.

Plans were made for the Clinic on Thursday. The Committee members took it upon themselves to notify the mothers of the babies and to tell them the time that transportation would be arranged for them. Each member volunteered to see those living on her road.

THE YOUNGER BABIES' CLINIC, MAY 7

The Baby Clinic ran smoothly this afternoon. Transportation was supplied for all the mothers and babies by the teachers of both the big School and the Nursery School. Fourteen babies were examined. Two could not come on account of illness, and one parent wasn't convinced about bringing a *well* baby to a clinic. (This was a family lately moved onto the homestead.) The mothers seemed most interested and anxious to have their babies come regularly to the Clinics. Theresa Nash, as part of her Practical Nursing Course,[5] assisted Miss Plummer in the Clinic with the babies. She worked hard and did a good job in handling, dressing and undressing, and soothing the babies.

THE OLDER BABIES' CLINIC, MAY 21

In spite of the small number of babies at the Clinic this time—12 in all—it seemed successful. Dr. Wills was able to spend more time talking with the mothers, and Helen Cawley, the director

---
[5] See Chapter VII, pp. 370–1.

of Home Economics, and Mildred Bayles, the Nursery School dietitian, were there to follow up his recommendations. (This Clinic for the older babies stressed especially feeding problems.) After the babies were examined, the mothers came back to the Threes' room, where they sat and talked in a group. Three members of the Medical Committee served as hostesses. None of the mothers seemed anxious to leave; they talked together for over an hour while the babies, who have all learned to walk, played with the equipment around the room.

Physical Examinations

As the Nursery School children had received no physical examination on entrance to Nursery School, other than the examination given the families when they were first admitted on the project, we felt that a thorough physical examination should be given in order to check up on the children physically. At the end of the second school year we began arranging for examinations of the children, with the mother present. Two or three children were examined in an afternoon, allowing plenty of time for the mother to talk with the doctor or nurse. Those children especially needing physical check-ups, or showing marked physical defects, were taken first. These examinations were valuable as a means of showing the mother what could be, and should be, done by her to promote the child's health. Before each examination, the doctor was acquainted with the special health problems observed by the teachers, and with the child's behavior in the Nursery School. Recommendations to be carried out by the parent in the home, and recommendations for the Nursery School, were both given by the doctor.

This whole enterprise of a thorough physical examination for each child, which was to be carried out with the older children as well as the Nursery School children, marked a long step forward in the health restoration and health education of families from the stage some twenty-four months before when the mothers fatalistically accepted disease and ill-health for their children as inevitable.

THE NURSERY SCHOOL A SOURCE OF COMMUNITY EDUCATION AT ARTHURDALE
Elsie Ripley Clapp

I understand there is some debate regarding the need and value of nursery schools in rural areas. To us, after seven years' work in country districts, there is no question about it. In Kentucky, where no school provision for children is made by the State until they are six years old, and where our daily contacts with the families made us aware of the urgent need of teaching child care, we had offered nursery school classes to the County Board of Education the first year we were there—an offer which they did not see their way clear to accept; and the next year we encouraged one of our parents to start a private nursery school. This school, although its charges were very moderate, did not of course meet the needs of the country children from the underprivileged homes. For them, we saw our chance, just before we left, to start a health group and clinic, which would have been substantially a small nursery school group; but we did not stay to execute the plan. We went to Arthurdale, however, determined above all things to have a nursery school in this other rural situation. Fortunately, we found in West Virginia, owing in large part to the work of Nadia Danilevsky in the FERA nursery schools in and around Morgantown, a predisposition to regard them as helpful and essential. And the Arthurdale Nursery School, which was Jessie Stanton's creation, more than fulfilled our hopes and expectations.

The improvement in the little children physically, mentally, emotionally, and socially through their life and care in a nursery school was so marked at Arthurdale as to strain credulity. At the end of the first eight months, it was hard to recognize the children who had come to us in September. At the end of the two years, their improvement had become their permanent wellbeing. The need at Arthurdale for the child care which a nursery school especially can give was obvious; the value of such care to the children and their families was proclaimed by every soul on the homestead. The results of what the Nursery School did for the children were things which the mothers and fathers understood very well indeed. In fact, the Nursery School and the High School—each in its own field—made clear to the people on the project the purposes and procedures of work with children throughout the School. In an emphatic and pervasive sense, the Nursery School was the heart and spring of community education at Arthurdale.

CHAPTER V

CULTURAL RESOURCES AND OPPORTUNITIES

The School the Center of Culture in Rural Areas

IN rural communities it is the school that introduces what is called culture. It brings the child into contact with facts and ideas which he would never know without its aid—literature, history, science, and world events. Except for the school such interests would never come into the lives of children in remote rural areas at all.

The school is, moreover, potentially a cultural center of its region. Recognition of the cultural heritage of a region, which is to be found in the people and their folk ways, their arts, and their historical tradition, is one of the services a rural school may render its community. Often this heritage, although operative, is overlooked or derogated. Yet in it lie the group's basic culture and their opportunities for expression and enjoyment. Furthermore, this indigenous culture provides the natural and sound means of understanding the culture and heritage of other regions and other people, present or past.

Awakened to these facts by our experiences in Kentucky, and conscious of the responsibilities and opportunities they entailed, the school at Arthurdale sought to discover the cultural background of the people on the homestead and the cultural resources of the region, to recognize these and to encourage their expression and development. The following account of its efforts was written by Fletcher Collins, who directed music and drama at the School and in the community:

Cultural Resources at Arthurdale
THE SCOTCH-IRISH TRADITIONAL CULTURE

Fletcher Collins
Director of Drama and Music

In attempting to advance the cultural status of the community, the School was early aware of the cultural and racial history of the families living at Arthurdale and in the surrounding area. Although most of these people had come from coal camps in which the population was polyglot, the homesteaders were preponderantly (70 percent) Scotch-Irish in ancestry, with a fair admixture (25 percent) of Pennsylvania-German, and about one percent each of French, Austrian, Czech, and Scandinavian.

The Scotch-Irish, or old American, element immigrated to America in the eighteenth and early nineteenth century; the Pennsylvania-German arrived in this country at about the same time. These two racial strains converged in West Virginia, the Scotch-Irish coming north and west from Kentucky and Virginia, the Pennsylvania-German spreading to the south and west. In culture the homesteaders were even more homogeneous than their ancestry indicates, for the Pennsylvania-German strain, being for generations a minority and having mingled through marriage with the Scotch-Irish, had completely shed its peculiar culture and had been absorbed in the Scotch-Irish traditional culture. It is this culture that is so widespread in rural areas of the United States; evidences of it are everywhere from Maine to Texas.

CULTURAL RESOURCES AND OPPORTUNITIES

The School was, therefore, faced by homesteaders with a fairly homogeneous culture and one which represented a vast rural culture. Anything, then, that could be done to advance this culture would have an extensive significance.

The traditional culture of the homesteaders certainly was in need of assistance. While still basic to them, and very much "in their blood," it came to Arthurdale layered over by coal dust; their experience in the mine camps, brief though it had been, had obscured to them their cultural heritage; and being in the shadow of urban Morgantown, they had also been disturbed by the radio, the movies, and by bourgeois cultural standards. If the homesteaders' sojourn in the mines had been much longer, there might have been at Arthurdale no basis for culture; but since they had grown up on farms, and had in Arthurdale come back to the land, their cultural roots were hardy and were beginning to find again a non-sulphuric and fostering soil.

Expressions of this culture were present at Arthurdale from the beginning in the traditional arts and crafts. Even before the School began to function or the teachers to arrive, there was square-dancing on Saturday nights, with its concomitants of fiddle-playing, guitar-picking, and mouth-harping. There were also secluded ballad-singing, and nursery songs, and jigs. On Sundays there were sometimes gospel-songs and white spirituals. Some of the men were making reproductions of early American furniture in the Mountaineer Craftsmen's Workshop at Arthurdale. The women were beginning to think again of making quilts with the traditional patterns handed down from early times. And there was also in solution much traditional lore of various kinds.

How the School used this cultural heritage as the basis of its work on community education in culture can most clearly be described by relating in some detail the history of its contact with, and sponsorship of, each of these arts and crafts.

SQUARE-DANCING

Square dances were held in the Assembly Hall at the Town Center.[1] For a time, the dances seemed to do fairly well; the attendance and, consequently, the cash receipts were good enough to pay for the hiring of a square-dance orchestra, and still leave a tidy little net profit for the Men's Club. In time, however, there came about the gradual substitution of a volunteer dance orchestra for the overly expensive hired band of musicians. Led by two of the teachers, who tried manfully to play the difficult square-dance music on fiddle and guitar, a small group of homesteaders practiced until they had a repertory of tunes sufficient for a night of square-dancing, and then took the place of the professionals. There were, of course, some complaints from hypercritical dancers that the music "warn't fit to dance to." Slowly, though, the orchestra improved in technique; the Men's Club and the School together subscribed forty dollars for the purchase of fiddles, guitars, and banjos, so that the orchestra might expand its membership and do more practicing. By spring, 1935, the orchestra was putting forth fairly good square-dance music, and the number of players was almost double the number of instruments, so that no player was worn out by the end of the evening. A really excellent fiddler, in the person of a young man from the neighboring hamlet of Dogtown, wandered into the orchestra one Saturday night, and was its constant fiddler ever after.

Square-dancing is one of those rare art forms which combine a social expression with an artistic expression. Most arts and crafts are ruggedly individual; square-dancing is impossible without at least four couples, a Caller who shouts out the "calls" for the figures of the dance, and three or four musicians —all performing together with synchronous, rhythmic artistry. Square-dancing has, characteristically, few in the audience,

---

[1] See Chapter II, pp. 100–1.

and many in action. It is the most social of the traditional American arts. It is at once for everyone from high school age to ninety, with no discrimination in favor of either youth or age. At Arthurdale, square-dancing had also the added social value of bringing the homesteaders into easy, natural contact with the people of the region through the sharing of a cultural expression which was inherent in both groups.

One serious obstacle to the furtherance of square-dancing at Arthurdale—or anywhere, for that matter—was that there has not yet been any serious research into the nature of the American square dance, no thorough investigation of its historical antecedents in Scotland and England, and no collected or printed repertory of square-dance figures. In some traditional arts and crafts, like balladry and quilting, there is a firmer basis for accurate progression in repertory and artistry. At Arthurdale, there was on the premises a fairly large repertory of dances, however, and I came across a Caller in Morgantown who claimed to know four hundred and fifty different square dances. Some of the ones most danced at Arthurdale were: "Chase the Squirrel," "Bounce 'Round Your Partner," "The Ladies' Dos-ee-dos" (from the French *dos-à-dos*), "Cast Off Six," "Grapevine Twist," and "Lead Your Lady through the Hall." The calls for these figures were rich and racy, as, for instance:

> *Dress your partner, re-address;*
> *Sixteen hands and circle to the left.*
> *Half-way 'round, chase 'em back,*
> *Lady in front, and gent to her back.*
>
> *Pat your honey on the head;*
> *If she don't like biscuits give her cornbread.*
>
> *Chaw your tebaccer and spit agin the wall,*
> *Meet that girl and promenade the hall.*
>
> *First couple out and chase the squirrel,*
> *Boy 'round the boy, and girl 'round the girl,*
> *And a right back*

And on the back track,
Girl 'round the boy, and the boy 'round the girl.

While the West Virginia Callers have lost the chantlike melodies to which these calls were formerly sung, the Arthurdale Callers, in shouting out these homespun verses, contrived an irresistible rhythm and inflection.

FIDDLING

The rural American art of fiddling "hoe-down," "breakdown" fiddle tunes is as ancient as square-dancing. Fiddling was so taken at Arthurdale, and the School's efforts were chiefly on behalf of developing more and better fiddlers among the homesteaders, young and old. No rural community is complete without one good fiddler. At Arthurdale, there was a homesteader who had not done much fiddling for a number of years, and who made a gallant come-back for his own enjoyment and for the benefit of the square-dance orchestra. He was the only homesteader who had enough facility to be able to *lead* the music; one other homesteader could manage a second, but could not lead. The young man from Dogtown was therefore very welcome; he had more technique than these fiddlers, and they had more of a repertory of the kind of fiddle-tunes requested by the callers, "quick and devilish." Their favorite tune—it was almost the Arthurdale anthem—was "The Lop-Eared Mule," with "Mississippi Sawyer" and "Soldier's Joy" close seconds in popularity.

I quote "Soldier's Joy" in its Arthurdale form, as an admirable specimen of American fiddle music.[2]

---

[2] "Soldier's Joy" is one of the widest-spread and best-loved of all American fiddle tunes. I have personally heard versions of it from Texas, California, Tennessee, North Carolina, West Virginia, Pennsylvania, and Connecticut; and it is known to exist in many other States.
Like most of the contemporary fiddle-tunes, the words which were formerly sung to this tune have nearly disappeared. The only words known to me are those given by Carl Sandburg in *The American Songbag* (page 140) under the title: "Love Somebody, Yes I Do." Generally, these fiddle-tunes are derived from traditional Scotch-Irish folk-songs; if used solely for fiddle-music the words naturally atrophy and disappear in a few generations.—F.C.

Soldier's Joy

FIDDLE-MAKING

At the Saturday night dances those High School boys who did not dance every *sett* would come up to the orchestra and watch the flashing bow and fingers of the fiddlers. It was clear to see that these boys were dreaming of themselves as fiddlers. The young man from Dogtown had something to do with their desire, too. Accordingly, the music teacher groped for ways in which these cultural ambitions might be realized. His first step was to locate and make friends with an old fiddler who lived in the back-country seven miles from Arthurdale. This man was more of a fiddle-maker than a fiddler, and in the former capacity was invited to come to Arthurdale for a day in the spring of 1935. Before he came, some of the ambitious boys had set out in their Shop work to "make them a fiddle." The old fiddle-maker was a great incentive to these boys, and he taught them a number of useful tricks of the traditional craft of fiddle-making. If this craft had not been traditional in the Scotch-Irish culture, the boys would probably not have undertaken so boldly to make fiddles, nor would the School have felt that a project with such technical difficulties was feasible.

There were a good many heartbreaks before the fiddles finally emerged in the spring of 1936. Experimenting with the ordinary wood from the lumber mills, the boys found that such wood was not very desirable for fiddles; they also found that the gouge chisel used in hollowing out the top and back of the fiddle had a disheartening way of plunging through the thin wood just when the piece was almost finished, and that measurements of dimensions had to be accurate within a sixteenth of an inch on curved surfaces. The only thing that kept the boys going was the example of the old fiddle-maker, who had made many a fiddle with no other tools than a broken saw, a penknife, and a piece of window glass; if he could accomplish the making of a fiddle with such materials, surely they with their professional violin-maker's tools (invested in by the School) could do as well, though they were seldom boastful about their ability. After the old fiddle-maker, with wood secured for the purpose by the School, had made a fiddle which, because of its well-seasoned spruce and maple woods, far surpassed any of his earlier productions, and after the boys had learned how to measure accurately and to gouge precisely, the School in January of 1936 agreed to buy for three boys, as a loan to be paid back in installments, woods such as the old fiddle-maker had found superior. With the music teacher and the Shop teacher co-operating in the direction of the boys' work, the boys forged ahead, and the speediest boy completed his instrument and drew a bow across its strings in late April. The tone and craftsmanship were judged by competent authorities to be those of a twenty-five-dollar violin. And the boy for weeks thereafter was never seen without his fiddle clutched tightly and proudly or tucked under his chin. The other two boys completed their instruments shortly after this, and all three fiddles were exhibited at the annual Music Festival in June.

The varnish on the fiddles was hardly dry before the boys clamored for the music teacher to give them lessons, as he had offered to do for anyone who made an instrument. Such was their intense earnestness that in the latter part of July the boys were already playing in good square-dance time the easier fiddle-tunes—"Skip to My Lou," "Little Brown Jug," and "Buffalo Gal"—and were on the way to playing in the square-dance orchestra by fall. It was the fiddle-tunes which the boys wished to learn to play, and which in themselves offered a nicely graduated series of exercises in technique. These boys were thus already established in a culture in which they could function socially and enjoyably.

Throughout the development of the fiddle-making, the old fiddle-maker was important not only as an encouragement to the boys but also as an advance guard in discovering the best craft methods and materials. He was on relief, and was very happy to be subsidized by the School to the extent of ten dollars for materials and a few violin-maker's tools. He and the music teacher found that the use of well-seasoned woods, in place of the green scrap maple and pine woods, more than doubled the value of the product. He learned also the technique of varnishing, and greatly improved the appearance of his instruments. The independent experiments of the Shop teacher in varnishing his own violin were also of great service. The old fiddler dreamed of setting himself up in a small craft shop on his own plot of ground; and he knew two younger men in his neighborhood who also were fiddle-makers and who were keen to join him in the operation of the small shop.

When the three boys began to make violins, there was also a demand from other High School boys and girls to make guitars and mandolins, which instruments were functional not only at square-dances but also at more private moments when one felt a song or ballad coming over him, and at your best girl's house as an implement of courtship, and at picnics and junkets. The making of guitars was temporarily shelved as beyond the immediate abilities of the boys and girls, but the entire Ninth Grade undertook the making of simplified mandolins, one for each member of the class. The best of these, made by a girl whose father was a skilled cabinet-maker, was exhibited at the Music Festival.

In the process of constructing these mandolins there was involved the same necessity for accurate measurement and careful planning that the fiddle-making boys had encountered. In addition, the mandolin-makers found that in order to place the frets accurately in the fingerboards, the teacher of mathematics had to be called in; he and the music teacher had foreseen this moment, and a fair amount of functional mathematics and physics of sound was learned by the class. Instruction in playing the mandolins was offered as it had been in the case of the fiddle-makers.

BALLADRY

It was through the School children that we first were made aware of the extent of the homesteaders' repertory of traditional ballads. Early in the fall of 1934, a girl in the Sixth Grade sang to the class one day the old English or Scottish ballad of Barbara Allen.[3] It went like this:

> *In Scarlet Town where I was born,*
> *There was a fair maid dwelling,*
> *Made every youth cry "Well-away,"*
> *Her name was Barbara Allen.*

---

[3] "Barbara Allen" was the most common of the old Child ballads known at Arthurdale, and is probably the most prevalent Child ballad in the United States. In *Traditional Ballads of Virginia*, A. K. Davis, Jr., presents no less than ninety-two Virginia versions and fragments of "Barbara Allen." Samuel Pepys in the seventeenth century knew this ballad as the "Scotch song of 'Barbary Allen.'" Dates are impossible to determine for the older ballads and songs, but one would hazard a guess that "Barbara Allen" is at least five hundred years old in oral tradition.

BARBARA ALLEN

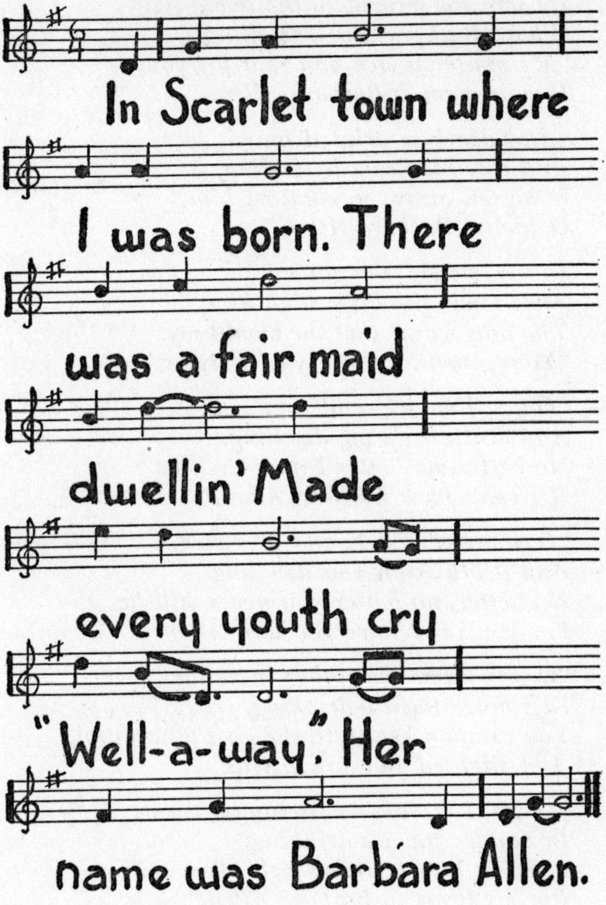

In Scarlet town where I was born. There was a fair maid dwellin' Made every youth cry "Well-a-way." Her name was Barbara Allen.

All in the merry month of May
When all things were a-budding,
Sweet William came from the western states
And courted Barbara Allen.

All in the merry month of June
When all things were a-blooming,

Sweet William on his death-bed lay
For the love of Barbara Allen.

He sent his servant to the town
Where Barbara was a-dwelling:
"My master is sick and sent for you,
If your name is Barbara Allen.

"And death is printed on his face,
And o'er his heart is stealing,
O hasten away, go comfort him,
O loving Barbara Allen."

Slowly, slowly, she got up,
And slowly she drew nigh him;
The only words that she would say,
"Young man, I think you're dying."

"O yes, I'm sick, and very sick,
And death is on me dwelling.
No better, no better I never will be
If I can't have Barbara Allen."

"O yes, you're sick, and very sick,
And death is on you dwelling.
No better, no better you never will be,
For you can't have Barbara Allen.

"O don't you remember in yonder town,
In yonder town a-drinking,
You drank a health to the girls all around,
And slighted Barbara Allen?"

"O yes, I remember in yonder town,
In yonder town a-drinking,
I gave a health to the girls all round,
But my heart to Barbara Allen."

As she was on her highway home
She heard the birds a-singing;
They sang so clear they seemed to say,
"Hard-hearted Barbara Allen."

She looked to the east, she looked to the west,
Till she saw the corpse a-coming.

*"Lay down, lay down that corpse of clay
That I may look upon him."*

*The more she looked, the more she mourned,
Till she fell to the ground a-crying,
Saying, "Take me up, and carry me home,
For now I am a-dying.*

*"O mother, O mother, go make my bed,
Go make it long and narrow;
Sweet William died for me today,
And I will die tomorrow.*

*"O father, O father, go dig my grave,
Go dig it long and narrow;
Sweet William died for pure, pure love,
And I will die of sorrow."*

*They buried him in the old churchyard,
And she was buried nigh him,
On William's grave there grew a red rose,
On Barbara's grew a green brier.*

*They grew and they grew to the old church tower,
Till they couldn't grow no higher.
They lipped and they lopped to a true lover's knot,
The red rose and the green brier.*

From the music teacher's experience he knew that her version of that ballad was unusually complete and clear. He asked her where she had learned that song, and she replied that her aunt used to sing it a lot.

At nearly the same time two boys in the Fifth Grade volunteered to the music teacher as a good song a ballad called "Scotty's Last Flight," a vivid narrative of an airplane disaster which in content and spirit was closely parallel to the ancient ballad of "Sir Patrick Spens"; others in the class added that they had seen the disaster happen near Morgantown, a few years before, and that everybody had known Scotty. And shortly thereafter, the Seventh and Eighth Grades spent more than an hour of what was properly called "English" in singing and recalling a small storehouse of ballads about "The Jealous Lover of Lone Green Valley" and "Fair Charlotte," and many another ancient or more recent hero or heroine of balladry. The children were in almost every instance singing from the oral tradition of ballad-narrative, which has always been a prominent feature of the Scotch-Irish rural culture. Likewise in the Seventh and Eighth Grades there was much ballad-singing, and an opportunity to clarify a little their cultural history through the discovery that many of the ballads they were singing were called in the poetry books "Old English or Scottish." From this time on, music in the Elementary and High School was very often a group recital of a traditional ballad already known by many.

The music teacher also made the acquaintance of the successor to J. H. Cox at the University of West Virginia, Louis W. Chappell, and from his vast store of ballads and ballad-lore in West Virginia obtained a comprehensive and accurate picture of the local situation in ballad-singing and ballad-scholarship. As a means of checking up on the validity and direction of what he was teaching at Arthurdale, the contact with Professor Chappell was invaluable.

The adult homesteaders were not so immediately ready as the children to share their knowledge of ballads with the music teacher. Not until they knew him pretty well, did they begin to say: "That's a real good song, that story about Pearl Bryan. Did you ever hear it?" And it was mid-winter when one evening the music teacher thrust his head into the boiler room where old "Dad" Matthews was night watchman, and Dad peered through the shadows at him, and began to sing:

> *Young Collins rode out in the fields one day*
> *When the trees and the flowers were in bloom,*
> *And there he spied his own fair Ellen*
> *A-washing a white marble stone. . . .*

a song which any ballad-scholar is delighted to identify as a Child ballad, and which had only once before been reported in West Virginia. Dad stopped after a few stanzas—he couldn't rightly remember the rest of it. "Why," he said, "it's been thirty—no, forty—years since I've thought of that one. You coming in that way just made me think of it, you know." He also knew a ballad of the old railroad camps, "The Rock Island Line."

The homesteaders' knowledge of ballads was, on the whole, decidedly rusty, smeared with coal dust. To recall ballads they had not sung for many a day—either to give the children to take to School, or when the music teacher knew them well enough to break down the excuses of a cracked voice or a bad memory—resulted in the restoration to them of one of their finest cultural resources. Husbands and wives began to sing ballads together in the evenings after the dishes were washed and the shades pulled. Mrs. Hogan played the accordion while her husband sang "Old Ninety-Seven" and "The Jealous Lover," and Mr. Carter borrowed the homestead guitar during the week and accompanied his wife's rendition of "Down in the Valley" and "Fair Charlotte."[4] At School the children sometimes told of lively disputes between father and mother over the proper words to a ballad which had a dozen versions, and which they had been singing more or less together. Such incidents were evidence that what was happening could be called a cultural awakening. Of course they had not yet developed much discrimination between an artistic ballad and a modern fake like "Nobody's Darling." They sang both with equal ardor, though one noticed that the older ballads were

---

[4] The ballad of "Fair Charlotte," sometimes titled "The Frozen Girl," is obviously less ancient than "Barbara Allen." Mr. Phillips Barry has presented evidence that it was written by one William Lorenzo Carter in Vermont before 1833. Certainly the atmosphere is of northern New England, but the ballad has for a hundred years been sung by rural Americans in many States. The ballad was highly appropriate to an Arthurdale winter, and was known by many homesteaders.

perennial, while the very recent ones faded in less than a year and were succeeded by other sentimental ones. Perhaps that is the only kind of discrimination that the folk ever exercises—a weeding out of the unfit through generations of ballad-production. One has to listen to "Nobody's Darling" if one wishes to hear "Barbara Allen." And the School never adopted an antiquarian approach to such expression as ballads. There was always a belief that new ballads could be good ballads, and that such people as the homesteaders, rather than the radio "cowboys," were the most likely creators of artistic new ballads.[5] Rural culture will not remain static. For a time in the coal camps it was disintegrating in the lives of the homesteaders; at Arthurdale through the impetus of the School it was on the way to expansion and growth.

CHILDREN'S SONGS

In rural areas in which traditional culture is waning, much of traditional song has become the property of old people and children. At Arthurdale, it was the children who first unloosed upon the community a repertory of traditional songs, and the parents approved even before they themselves would admit that the old songs and ballads were pretty good singing for grown-ups. In fact, the School's experience in nearly every field of activity showed that the children learned first, and prepared their parents for a later learning, even sometimes themselves educating the parents. Thus adult education in music and poetry properly began with the discovery of traditional song in the grades.

The music teacher met with each grade in the School at least once a week for singing. At these hours during the first months of the School, the teacher taught no songs which the group did not already know—mainly from oral tradition.

---

[5] See Chapter VI on the High School, pp. 288–9.

CULTURAL RESOURCES AND OPPORTUNITIES 233

When he first asked these groups what they wished to sing, he was not sure whether the children would come forth with the songs which are the usual song-diet in public schools and Sunday schools, or would prefer from generations of experience the traditional folk-songs. In all the grades, only one song of public school origin was recalled and asked for by one child, while everywhere there was a storm of demands for such lovely songs as "Mister Frog Went A-Courting"[6] and "A Paper of Pins." This is the way they preferred to sing those songs:

[6] A volume could be written about the history of "Mister Frog Went A-Courting." It is today as widespread a children's song as "Barbara Allen" is a ballad. In Elizabethan England, it was a political pasquinade on the courtship of Queen Elizabeth by Philip of Spain. But it was already then an old song; Mr. L. W. Payne, in *Texas Folklore Society Publications, No. 5*, shows that the song had been "in continuous use for four hundred years." Its origins seem to lie in the timeless delight in animal fables, old in Aesop's day.

He rode up to Miss Mousie's door . . .
He gave a loud knock and he gave a loud roar. . . .

He said, "Miss Mousie, may I come in?" . . .
"O do come in and watch me spin." . . .

He took Miss Mousie upon his knee . . .
He said, "Miss Mousie, will you marry me?" . . .

Miss Mousie blushed and hung her head . . .
"You'll have to ask Uncle Rat," she said. . . .

Uncle Rat he went to town . . .
To buy his niece a wedding gown. . . .

Where shall the wedding supper be? . . .
Way down yonder in the hollow tree. . . .

What shall the wedding supper be? . . .
Two green beans and a black-eyed pea. . . .

The first guest there was a bumble bee . . .
He took his fiddle upon his knee. . . .

The second guest there was a little old fly . . .
He ate up all the wedding pie. . . .

The third guest there was an old blacksnake . . .
He ate up all the wedding cake. . . .

And when they all sat down to sup . . .
An old gray goose came and gobbled them up. . . .

And that was the end of one, two, three . . .
The Rat, and the Mouse, and the little Froggie. . . .

A PAPER OF PINS[7]

I'll give to you a paper of pins, And that's the way our love begins, If you will marry, marry, marry, If you will marry me.

> I'll not accept your paper of pins,
> If that's the way our love begins,
> And I'll not marry, marry, marry,
> And I'll not marry you.
>
> I'll give to you a dress of green,
> That you may look just like a queen,
> If you will marry, marry, marry,
> If you will marry me.

---

[7] In England this song is usually called "The Keys of Heaven." It is as old as its theme, and invariably contains as much poetic imagery as stock humor. With children, a part of the appeal of the song is the semi-dramatic nature of the dialogue, usually sung at Arthurdale antiphonally by boys and girls in a singing group.

*I'll not accept your dress of green,
That I may look just like a queen,
And I'll not marry, marry, marry,
And I'll not marry you.*

*I'll give to you a dress of red
All bound round with a golden thread . . .*

*I'll give to you a coach and four
That you may ride from door to door . . .*

*I'll give to you a coach and six
With every horse as black as pitch . . .*

*I'll give to you my hand and heart
That we may marry and never part . . .*

*I'll give to you the keys to my chest,
That you may have money at your request . . .*

*I will accept the keys to your chest,
That I may have money at my request,
And I will marry, marry, marry,
And I will marry you.*

*Now all you people can plainly see
She wants my money but she doesn't want me,
So I'll not marry, marry, marry,
So I'll not marry you.*

The children seemed amazed that a music teacher was not supercilious about such songs, even welcomed them. No song books were needed, and indeed none which contain such songs in any quantity are available for school use. There was naturally a differentiation by age in the choice of songs they wished to sing, as well as much overlapping. The First and Second Grade were strong for songs, the words (and unfortunately never the music) of which are to be found in the pages of *Mother Goose;* the Third Grade thought some of the *Mother Goose* songs were a bit childish. The Fourth Grade liked the play-party songs ("Skip to My Lou" and "Weevily

CULTURAL RESOURCES AND OPPORTUNITIES

Wheat,"[8] for instance), and the Fifth and Sixth Grades went in for such pieces as "A Paper of Pins" and "Billy Boy." Yet the First Grade enjoyed "Skip to My Lou," and the Fourth Grade liked "Mister Frog Went A-Courting." A complete list of the traditional songs these children knew and loved would be the table of contents for an excellent book of American folk-songs. Both music and words were so exactly in the idiom of their environment—many of the songs deal with farm animals and birds and insects—and at the same time had poetic and lyric significance.

When the repertory of these songs began to be exhausted, and there was a demand from the children for more songs like the ones they had been singing, the music teacher culled additional pieces from Cecil Sharp's collection of Appalachian folk-songs,[9] and from the Sandburg and Lomax collections. Some of these new-old songs were considerably adapted by the children, and often added to. An instance of this practice of theirs is the song called "The Crazy Horse," which the music teacher extracted from Sandburg's *American Songbag* and sang to the children of the First and Second Grades. Compare Sandburg's text (p. 145) with this, which the Arthurdale children made, many shouting out suggested words that were accepted or rejected by the group:

THE CRAZY HORSE

I used to have an old grey horse,
He weighed ten thousand pounds,
And every tooth he had in his head
Was eighteen inches around.

Refrain:
  I'm a-goin' down to town,
  I'm a-goin' down to town,

---

[8] See Chapter III, pp. 148–9.
[9] *Nursery Songs from the Appalachian Mountains* (1st series), arranged with pianoforte accompaniment by Cecil J. Sharp, London, Novello & Co., Ltd.

> *I'm a-goin' down to Morgantown*
> *For to take my potatoes down.*
>
> *I used to have an old grey horse,*
> *His eyes were as big as the moon,*
> *And every hair he had in his tail*
> *Was a hundred inches long.*
>
> *I used to have an old grey horse,*
> *His feet were as big as the sun,*
> *And every time he started to run*
> *He stepped right on his tail.*
>
> *I used to have an old grey horse,*
> *His ears were a hundred inches long,*
> *And every time he took a step*
> *He knocked himself right down.*
>
> *I used to have an old grey horse,*
> *He stood as high as a tree,*
> *And every time you wanted to ride*
> *You had to climb a tree.*

The first stanza is practically identical with Sandburg's. The refrain is adapted by the children to more local conditions, Preston County potatoes being a famous crop in the Arthurdale area, and Morgantown being the market center for such produce. Ballad-scholars find this practice of adapting ballads to a local situation very common. The succeeding stanzas are a spontaneous creation by the children, who found the stanzas from Sandburg awkward to sing. Of this practice there were in all the grades frequent instances, sometimes less extremely variant from the text introduced to them, but nearly always adapted or supplemented. The creation was, furthermore, concerned not only with the words but also with the music, particularly in songs from the Sandburg and Lomax collections, in which the notation only roughly approximated what the folk actually sang. I append the variant melody of "The Crazy Horse" as the Arthurdale children shaped it through singing.

THE CRAZY HORSE

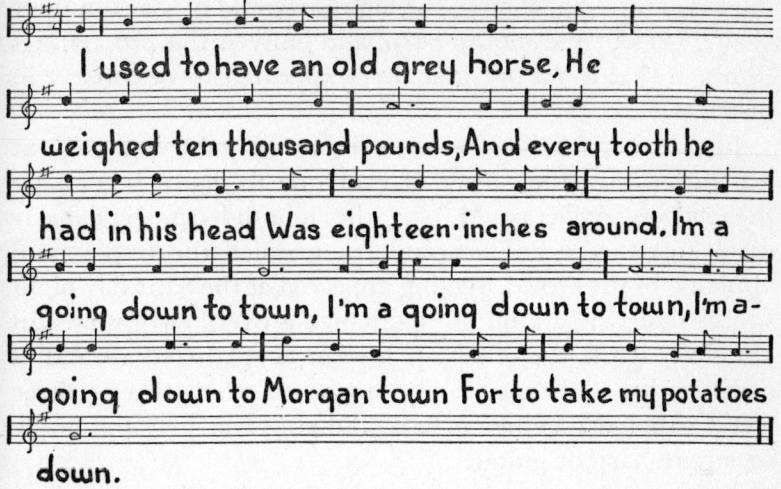

I used to have an old grey horse, He weighed ten thousand pounds, And every tooth he had in his head Was eighteen inches around. I'm a-going down to town, I'm a going down to town, I'm a-going down to Morgan town For to take my potatoes down.

In the arts of poetry and music, then, the Arthurdale School children were creating, not out of a heterogeneous cultural grab-bag of European and American art-songs, but out of their own ancestral culture.

MOUTH-HARPING AND JIG-DANCING

There were many facets of rural culture that were not susceptible to direct stimulation by the agency of the School. Mouth-harping and jig-dancing were of this sort. Boys on Sunday afternoon walks would take along a mouth-harp (also known as a mouth-organ), and play it as they strolled up the road or across the fields, each boy taking a turn at playing such tunes as "Old Joe Clark," "Chinese Breakdown," or "Too Young to Get Married." The men would come to the square-dances with a mouth-organ in their pockets, and when they were not dancing would "help out" the orchestra by furiously blowing on it until they were purple in the face and quite breathless. And sometimes when the women folk were ironing the clothes, the men of the families would tip back in their chairs, get out the mouth-harp, and enliven the proceedings so much that to an outsider there appeared to be a party in progress.

Jig-dancing was of the same informal nature, though it was not within the power of everyone to dance a good jig the way everyone could play the mouth-harp. Jig-dancers dwelt apart, like fiddlers, and commanded the respect and applause of the crowd. Jigging appeared at the Saturday night square dances as a kind of "spontaneous overflow of powerful emotion" while the other square-dancers gathered around as a discerning audience. It also appeared when two or three were gathered together to talk and sing and play the fiddle or mouth-harp or guitar.

There was nothing much for the School to do about these traditional expressions. They needed no stimulus, and could hardly be taught by anyone who was not himself born to such expressions. Some research did disclose, however, that the mouth-harping was related to the old Scottish bagpipe music, and that the jigging was a lineal descendant of the very ancient English and Irish jigs. At least two styles of jigging were present at Arthurdale: one fluid and *con moto,* and the other a wild whirlwind; and there were confusions of style within these.

GOSPEL SONGS AND WHITE SPIRITUALS

A large amount of the group singing which the homesteaders had done before they came to Arthurdale was gospel songs and white spirituals. Many of the homesteaders had in earlier years participated in the "singing schools" which were common in rural areas until recently, and which had as their practical purpose the training of choirs for the rural churches. In these singing schools, which met under the instruction of a peripatetic "singing master," rural people learned to read the shaped-note, or "buckwheat" notation, of the evangelical hymn books. They sang in four-part harmony and with a steady *fortissimo*.

When the music teacher arrived at Arthurdale he found that group singing was already under way—and under the auspices of a minister from a neighboring village. The music teacher was at first invited to join the singing group "to sing base"—the choir needed more basses. After a night or two, some of the singers suggested that the music teacher lead them in the next song. At the next meeting of the Men's Club it was voted that the music teacher be appointed singing master of the homestead singers.

The music teacher then proceeded to make two mistakes. First he convinced himself and the singers that all of them should learn to read musical notation as soon as possible, so that their repertory and consequent enjoyment would be increased and they could become musically literate. For a few weeks they listened to his painstaking explanations of the mysteries of notation, and sang over and over with unfading relish the comparatively few songs they all admitted to knowing. Then something began to go wrong; the size and interest of the group, which had at first been immense, began to diminish. Finally, after a month of this sort of blundering, the music teacher realized that the group had no concentrated desire to learn to read music; that what they did want to do was to sing with all their might and main. They wanted an emotional release, and he was urging an intellectual approach. Without the emotional motivation of singing for church, they did not care to undergo the discipline of notation.

His second mistake was to persuade the group that it should be composed of both men and women; the women wanted to sing with the men, and the men were too polite at first to say bluntly that they wanted to sing without the women. When the music teacher discovered this state of affairs, the

Christmas season was approaching, and everyone did wish to sing the well-known Christmas carols together. The combined groups' most successful singing came a few days before Christmas when more than ninety of them crowded into the Assembly Hall for a last Christmas sing. After Christmas, the necessary reorganization of the group took place. Two groups, male and female, met on separate nights. They sang nearly the same songs, but the men at least continued to sing; the women, discouraged by the prospect of a long walk through wintry weather, sang together less often, and from time to time made overtures to join the men's group. That situation never was solved more equitably, and the women did very little singing in groups unless weather and household conditions were nearly ideal, except in their Club meetings in the second year.

The men's singing group met once a week all winter. They sang gospel songs, and they sang from oral tradition, not from notation. And they had a grand time "letting go" with every musical thing in them. Some of the men began to recall the white spirituals which their parents and grandparents had sung, and the group leaned into these songs with immense gusto. There was also organized at the men's request a men's quartet, which represented the cream of the larger group and was steady enough in attendance to gain some proficiency. The quartet was invited to sing on this or that occasion at Arthurdale or Reedsville, and sang together all through the two years.

MUSIC FESTIVALS, SUMMERS OF 1935 AND 1936

It seemed highly desirable that a way be found for this cultural heritage in music and dancing to be expressed regionally, and actively shared by homesteaders and their neighbors. It also seemed desirable to make Arthurdale a focal point for the cultural development of the region; the basic musical culture, while encouraged by the School, was in need of the further encouragement conferred on it by public attention.

An obvious and satisfactory answer to these needs was the staging at Arthurdale of a regional Music Festival, with events in the various forms of musical expression: fiddling, balladry, mouth-harping, and jig-dancing. There were other convocations in the region which were called music festivals, but they were not drawing out the traditional music of the region. They drew large crowds, but mainly tourist and city people, and their directors had little understanding of rural culture.

The method of organizing the Arthurdale Music Festival may be explained in some detail, for it was the method that produced a genuine rural music festival. Participation in the Festival was to be limited to amateurs, who were of course the overwhelming majority of the carriers of rural music and dancing. These people were to be stimulated to enter the festival by the announcement of contests in the various fields of music and dance expression. The prizes were to be blue, red, and white ribbons for places in each contest. No cash prizes were offered. The Festival was talked up as an opportunity to get together with one's neighbors, have some fun, and see who could sing the best ballad or dance the best jig. The festival was, furthermore, not publicized through newspapers or by fliers or hand bills of any kind.

The approach to these rural people living within a twenty-five-mile radius of Arthurdale was by actually finding them out in person, making friends with them and inviting them to the Festival. The music teacher, who directed the Festival, relied mainly upon the wide acquaintance of a homesteader, Charles Stearns, to discover the "right people" in the County. The two men together, Stearns as an enthusiastic partner in the enterprise of the Festival, drove in the teacher's automobile a great many miles over back-country roads about a month before the Festival was scheduled to take place. Stearns introduced the music teacher as a friend to enough men and women in the back-country so that they and the other musicians and dancers they mentioned made up a pretty complete roster of the rural musicians and dancers of the region. The music teacher and Stearns tried to see all of these "leads," and to encourage them to come to the Festival; in one case a group of good but penniless musicians was supplied with gas and oil for transportation to and from Arthurdale. Stearns was chosen from a number of possible assistants because of his larger number of old friendships in the region, in which he had lived before his coal-mining days.

They did not neglect the musicians and dancers in the immediate vicinity of Arthurdale. Particularly did the music teacher endeavor to attract participants from the near-by village of Reedsville. Still other participants were drawn from the homesteaders' friends or relatives in the mining region where most of them had lived before coming to Arthurdale. These participants were among the finest at the Festival. One remembers particularly Mr. Harry Rich, and his two sons, of Laurel Point on the Monongahela River. Mr. Rich was a real artist at the fiddle, with exquisite rhythmic flow and balance, and fine tone quality. He was bringing up his sons, still in their 'teens, in the same fiddling tradition—to the delight of the boys.

In planning for the Festival night, a number of subtle technical points connected with the management of the contests had to be well understood in advance by the director and the participants; such questions as: "Shall the Caller be judged with his square, or separately? And is he allowed to be a dancer in the square, or must he 'call' from a position outside the square?" These questions could not be answered arbitrarily without creating injustice and dissatisfactions, and the director accordingly consulted and was guided by the wisdom of Owen Peters and a few other homesteaders, who, as Callers

CULTURAL RESOURCES AND OPPORTUNITIES 245

at homestead square dances, were recognized authorities on that subject. In order to give credence to the contests, three judges were appointed in advance. They were the cashier of the Reedsville bank, who was interested in such things and eminently fair-minded; a piano-tuner from Kingwood, who was well known and liked in the County; and a grand old patriarch and former "singing master" from back in the country near the Cheat River. Several alternate judges were arranged for, in case one or more judges should fail to appear.

The First Music Festival

The first Music Festival opened at eight in the evening of July 7, 1935. The small Assembly Hall was packed with homesteaders and their neighbors, and space was reserved for a group of guests from Washington, including Mrs. Roosevelt, who awarded the ribbons to the winners of each contest. The music was so excellent that none of the participants or homesteaders was self-conscious in the presence of so many distinguished Washingtonians, and the ribbons, so awarded, instantly became of greater value than gold or silver. A description of each event follows, though it cannot hope to recall the ecstatic hush that fell over the audience.

Fiddlers' Contest: There were twelve contestants, each of whom played two fiddle-tunes of his own choosing in quick succession. The names of the tunes each fiddler played were announced by the director when each contestant was introduced. They were "Devil's Dream," "Leather Breeches," "Mississippi Sawyer," "City Quick Step," "Too Young to Get Married," "Phoebe Ice," "Soldier's Joy," "Chinese Breakdown," "Money Musk," "Arkansaw Traveler," "Irish Washerwoman," "Haste to the Wedding," "The Lop-Eared Mule," "Pop Goes the Weasel," "The Girl I Left behind Me," and half a dozen other pieces.

Jig-Dancing: There were four dancers in this contest, three men and a boy. The boy appeared out of the audience in response to the announcer's invitation for anyone to come up front and try a jig; this technique in announcing was followed throughout the Festivals. Two of the contestants, homesteaders, were known to have practiced several hours for the performance.

Ballad-Singing: This event was open to individuals, accompanied or solo, and to groups—ballad-singing being authentic in all three instances. A group of boys and girls from the Arthurdale High School won this event with "Fair Charlotte." The event was particularly open to women entrants.

Immediately after this event had been run off, the announcer called forward his friend, Professor L. W. Chappell, of the University of West Virginia, who made a scholarly speech about balladry in West Virginia.

Mouth-Harping: There were no advance entries in this event, for mouth-harping was known to be almost universal among the audience. After one player was persuaded to "go first," the others followed him, and the contest could have proceeded for at least an hour. It was cut short after five had played, in order not to make the program as a whole too long.

Square-Dance Contest: This was the "big" event of the evening. Each square, dancing only one figure, took about fifteen minutes to dance it out. Four squares appeared, two from Arthurdale. The winning figure was danced by a group of the oldest homesteader boys and girls (ages nineteen to twenty-two), who danced "The Ladies' Dos-ee-dos" with considerable grace and skill. Second place was taken by a group from the hamlet of Rohr, who were winners from the point of view of gusto and the Caller's "calling." The original intention was to have each group bring its own orchestra. This plan fortunately broke down toward the end of the preparations, for there were present many more instrumentalists than could be accommodated in the other events (guitar and banjo-pickers particularly), and these players, in ensembles, played for those squares which had not brought their own orchestras. The playing of these orchestras was judged separately, and ribbons were awarded to each member of the placing orchestra.

With the square-dance competition the Festival ended. The whole program lasted about two hours and a half. Everyone seemed to have had a grand evening, and there was talk about it for days thereafter, by the men as they worked and by the women as they chatted with their next-door neighbors. One homesteader came to the music teacher as late as the following September and said that the Festival was the finest thing there had ever been at Arthurdale, and he hoped there would be another very soon.

Educationally, the Festival accomplished what it set out to do: the musical culture latent in the people of Arthurdale and the region was encouraged and dignified by the emphasis of the Festival. The music and dancing were the people's own, and they knew it.

The Second Music Festival

The second Festival, held the year following, in 1936, was very much like the first, with a few additions which improved the quality of the program. Because the success of the first Festival had been bruited throughout the region, there was a huge list of available performers, and one new event; consequently, it was decided to hold the Festival for two nights—the first night devoted to all events except the square-dancing, the second exclusively to the square-dance competition. On both nights, the large new Recreation Building was crowded with more than a thousand people, yet there was the same ecstatic hush as had come upon the comparatively small audience of the year before.

Before and after the Festival, there was an exhibit in the hall of musical instruments made by the three Arthurdale fiddle-makers, the old fiddle-maker from the back-country and his two shy associates. A mandolin made by an Arthurdale High School girl was also exhibited.

Ever since the music teacher had lived in Arthurdale he had heard of Professor Ira Groves, the renowned "singing master" of that region, who had taught singing school, according to his count, in no less than 167 villages in more than fifty years. Groves was itinerant, and consequently on the move from one "singing school" to the next, so that the music teacher did not catch up with him until the spring of 1936. The upshot of their congenial conversation was that Groves promised to, and did, bring to the second Music Festival two of his current "singing schools" from Mount Zion and Dellslow, two villages in the region. The homesteaders knew Groves—he had taught some of them years before when they were young men and women on the farms—and his appearance at the Festival was the occasion of much rejoicing. Expecting these singing schools, the music teacher had added to the plans for the Festival another event called, for want of a better name, Gospel-Singing. Groves's choirs were so good in the eyes of the audience that they were the whole event, and the scheduled competitors from Arthurdale decided to waive their turns in favor of more selections by Groves's choirs. The ribbons for all three places were distributed among them.

QUILT-MAKING

A traditional craft which is strongly integrated in the rural culture of the Scotch-Irish is the making of quilts by the women. This is a seasonal occupation, worked at only in the winter months when the duties of farming and canning are over. There were several women at Arthurdale who were recognized by the community as expert quilters. All the women knew how to quilt. Traditional patterns were well known to the quilt-makers, varying—like the fiddle-tunes—from the comparatively simple and easily executed to the very intricate and difficult; from the "Nine-Patch" to the "Mississippi Daisy," "Wheel of Fortune," and the "Wedding Ring." The degeneration in quilt-making in that region was chiefly in the materials used, although the less expert quilters were not above trying patterns that came out in the daily newspapers. The practice had sprung up there, as everywhere in hard times, of using whatever scraps of material they had left over from clothes, and as a result the patches were often poor in design and the quilt pattern had no strong or regular arrangement of colors.

Partly because the School wished to advance this phase of the homesteaders' traditional culture, and partly because quilt-making seemed like a likely economic enterprise, with possible sales in metropolitan areas, the School decided to subsidize a small amount of quilt-making in the community on a business basis. This decision could not be intelligently executed until one of the teachers had made a careful study of traditional quilt patterns and colors; this investigation was being completed in the summer of 1936, and the quilt-making enterprise was to begin as soon as the women had finished their fall canning. The adult-education implications of this enterprise need no commentary.

FURNITURE-MAKING

While it was not under the auspices of the School, the School was much interested in the furniture-making shop which had been established at the Town Center by the Mountaineer Craftsmen Co-operative Association. This enterprise had been started before Arthurdale came into existence, in the mining camps near Morgantown, with the idea of giving restorative occupation to the stranded miners and providing their shanties, stripped of all but the heap of rags that was a bed, with seats and tables, and prompted also by the hope that it might furnish some of the people in the camps a positive source of income. The enterprise was sustained in the beginning by relief funds and, as skill increased, by the production and sales of handmade copies of old American furniture. Its shop, situated first in Morgantown, moved—first in part and then later wholly—to Arthurdale. Some of the men who, as relief workers, had been trained in furniture-making, moved onto the homestead and the enterprise later became a part of the Arthurdale Co-operative Association.

The Mountaineer Craftsmen furnished beds, tables, and chairs for the homestead houses and thus had an important cultural influence on the daily lives of the homesteaders. Gradually, small groups of homestead men were taught how to make the additional pieces of furniture they needed—cribs, and more tables and chairs.

Here and there throughout the region were men who had skill in wood and cabinet work; one met an occasional clockmaker and a number of men who were skilled in the making of corner-cupboards. There were also the old fiddle-maker and the group of younger men who worked with him. Woodworking is a familiar, if not a general, skill in rural areas.

The Craftsmen also operated at Arthurdale a metal forge, which supplied the lighting fixtures for the houses, and in which fine craft-work in copper, pewter, tin, and wrought iron was produced; two or three of the homesteaders had definite artistic skill in this work. Groups of women, working under the auspices of the Craftsmen's Co-operative and with encouragement from the School, also learned to do simple weaving of rugs and curtains for their homes. Several of them exhibited unusual taste and ability.

HISTORICAL TRADITION
Elsie Ripley Clapp

One of the resources in rural culture, to the School's way of thinking, was the historical tradition current in the region in which Arthurdale lay; yet it, too, needed fostering and reviving. The homestead was itself an historic spot, and the older people of the neighborhood were full of stories and memories of the "old days."

The region around the project known as "The Glades" was bought about 1790 by Colonel John Fairfax on the advice of his friend, George Washington. The land next to Fairfax's was settled perhaps by 1800. By 1772, Zackquill Morgan had settled in "Morgantown." These facts clearly linked us on the homestead with the early history of the region; in fact, Arthurdale as the home of Colonel Fairfax was part of the history of northern West Virginia.

Miss Sheffield, the teacher of the Fourth Grade, who were studying pioneer life and who had charge of the old log cabin built by Colonel Fairfax, which was still standing on the homestead,[10] writes:

We are trying to piece together the specific history of Arthurdale so that the village will be conscious and proud of its past, as any good town ought to be. People in Reedsville have been invaluable in this attempt. They have recalled much information about the early days here, and they can connect us with sources. We have taken trips to spots they recommended as historically interesting and have visited the Fairfax sisters, descendants of the original family of Colonel John Fairfax.

This year (1935-36), the cabin with its own history played an important role in our work. From last year's work on it local interest was aroused, and we collected all the stories about the place which we could find. From the history of the cabin itself, we branched out into the history of the Fairfaxes and their farm—

---

[10] See Chapter III, pp. 144-5; also Chapter VII, pp. 382-3.

that is, Arthurdale. The children recorded this information in their history notebooks:

History of Arthurdale

Monongalia Glades

This is the way Arthurdale looked back in the old days. It was all woods, except there was just a little cleared space where the cabin was. The cabin was a big one for those days. It was two stories high and had two rooms downstairs. These two rooms were divided by a dog-run. Out back was their well with a sweep. Today you may see the old well right in front of Stearns' house. The garden must have been in a cleared space near the cabin. They raised corn, flax, and vegetables in it.

The name, "Monongalia Glades," came from the fact that it was swampy with trees growing in water down along where Decker's Creek is now.

When George Washington Was Young

When George Washington was a young man, he came through this part of West Virginia to survey. He noticed a lovely place called Monongalia Glades. This place is now called Arthurdale. Washington later told his friend, Colonel John Fairfax, about The Glades and advised him to buy it. So Fairfax bought this good land from a man named Doddridge and had a house built on it.

Colonel John Fairfax built some little cabins for his slaves to live in. These were built in a half circle back of his own cabin. The only one that is now standing is Watt's cabin. He was the boss slave.

What We Have Heard about the Log Cabin

Colonel John Fairfax had his sons build a big house for him over where H Road is now. It was just one and a half stories high then. As soon as the house was finished, the two Fairfax sons moved into it. Then the Fairfax slave, Watt, and his family moved into the cabin. Old Watt worked faithfully for the Fairfax family for many years. He is buried up in the old graveyard.

Log Cabins

The children branched out also into stories of other log cabins, especially those of their families:

My Grandfather's Log Cabin

> My grandfather and my grandmother are living in a log cabin that my grandfather made. He got logs from an old tumbled down log cabin and carted them to his farm and put them into place. It is a two-story house. It is about like the cabin we have here.
>
> Annie's mother told her her grandmother lived in a log cabin, but she doesn't know where it was. Luke's grandfather and Albert's grandmother each lived in cabins, too. They are both real old people. Ada Nell and Flora Grace's Dad was born in a log cabin and lived there until he was two years old. Their mother lived in one, too, when she was four years old.

Many log cabins still remain in our region: the Fairfax cabin, two cabins near Brown's Mills, and one on the road to Morgantown. The earliest houses were undoubtedly log cabins. Some sod or thatched roofs may have been used. The earliest cabins were one-room and one-story; then came those with two rooms divided by a dog-run, and one-and-a-half stories. The cabin on the Zinn farm in our neighborhood, for instance, was of hewn logs, two stories. Stone houses came very early. The earliest house in Morgantown was of stone, as was Colonel John Fairfax's second house, built from quarries around here.

It was clear, then, that the region was rich in historical material. The School, we felt, should add its appreciation of the historical significance of these evidences of a living past.

ART AND PAINTING

Elsie Ripley Clapp

The homesteaders, like most rural people, had a keen appreciation of beauty in nature. They noticed and spoke of the colors of a sunset or sunrise, of a bird's wing, of moss and flowers, and of the fields and foliage in spring and fall. Their enjoyment of beauty was something quite apart from the "art lessons" they had had in school, something that was part of their living and their work in gardens. Coming from the stark squalor of the mine camps, Arthurdale seemed to them very beautiful—as it was—and they never tired talking about it. The older people admired the few among them who could "draw or paint most anything," but they themselves never thought of painting. Yet in pottery, in weaving, and in the block-printing class the women showed ability in design and in form, and they all had a lively interest in home decoration and in rock gardens and an intense love of flowers.

When the paints finally arrived, the children, like all children everywhere, painted naturally, without any constraint. There is frequent mention in the teachers' diaries of the children's joy in painting. The schools from which they had come had had "art" only to the extent of drawing lessons of the old-time school variety, exercises in perspective, or making paper cut-outs—mainly copies of those paper flowers, chickens, and rabbits one may see pasted in windows of public schools. Yet, furnished with paints and paper, and encouraged to paint unhampered by "instruction," the children at Arthurdale painted happily and freely. "Only two days now till painting," a second grader said. The Fourth Grade, painting in a sunny attic room of the old Mansion, sang at its work.

It is of unceasing interest to educators that the paintings of children of entirely different backgrounds and surroundings are, at each age level, so similar in subject and treatment. Painting is for children, evidently, a kind of expression with typical forms. The paintings of the children at Arthurdale all showed freedom, enjoyment of color, and were direct in statement. They were much more free and fearless when they began than the children had been at first in Kentucky, although at Ballard they came to use this form of expression later with unusual ease and had a rare sense of beauty. By the end of the first year in Arthurdale the children had begun to express enjoyment of the world around them. In another year or so, they would probably have unconsciously revealed reactions interpretive of their life and surroundings. This happened only occasionally in the first year, occupied mainly with adjustment to new conditions and to the country, although certain features of the landscape that appeared in their paintings—like the fields covered with the dead stumps of trees—were directly a reflection of the environment they had known.

Several people in the High School had art ability, and the oldest group the first year were interested in art and enjoyed drawing, but in general the painting of the older boys and girls was, as might have been expected, less free and somewhat influenced, too, by impressions of poor magazine and calendar art. The High School boys, unaccustomed to this kind of expression, on the whole rejected it, although they admired the paintings of classmates. Drama and music were easier forms of expression for them. Yet they always noticed with appreciation the paintings of the younger children that were hung in the School lunchroom, and commented on them with discrimination. Some of the High School girls especially enjoyed painting and had art ability. They were spontaneously sensitive to form and color and, sketching on the homestead, unerringly chose landscape compositions of subtle and unobvious beauty.

In costuming plays—which is, of course, especially an art experience—the High School girls' sense of design and feeling for color were unusually developed. The boys, too, understood and appreciated these same elements in their costumes; and in painting scenery for the Christmas play, where for some reason they felt freer, the boys had good color and design sense. This quality of art appreciation came out in the acting of the High School boys and girls in plays—in feeling a scene, in tempo, and in a sense of contrast.

DRAMA

Fletcher Collins

In addition to sponsoring traditional arts and crafts of the homesteaders' rural culture, the School also attempted to graft upon their traditional culture an art which in a creative way has very seldom been known in rural American areas— the art of Drama.

Drama was already being used by some of the homesteaders and children, but in a wholly imitative way, so that there was almost a necessity for doing something positive and functional with it. The profound psychological healthiness possible in a vital expression in this art was quite imperative to foster, particularly at such times as the homesteaders were in a despondent or griping frame of mind, which it was possible to heal particularly through the drama.

The Arthurdale people were limited in their dramatic horizons to minstrel shows, black-face comedies in the minstrel style, and the cheap uncopyrighted plays that one "sent away for" and produced at a church sociable or at Christmas. Beyond these vehicles, they had no idea of drama except for an occasional movie in Morgantown during the boom days of the mining camps. There was no visible connection between the people's idea of drama and their traditional culture as expressed in their other arts. The School's approach to this situation was to attempt very slowly to liberate the natural dramatic spirit of these people by directing them to the use of the materials of their rural culture, the method being the composition by the group of the plays produced. How this approach functioned may be seen through a description of the birth and life of plays produced by the children[11] and by the adults of the community.

High School Drama Group, 1934–35

When the School opened in September of 1934, the High School boys and girls found that one of their courses was to be dramatics. They were interested in the idea of putting on plays, and the first meeting of the class was full of eagerness, generated by girls who pictured themselves in the leading roles of some high romance. The boys were silent and skeptical of the course; they certainly did not intend to memorize dull lines and speak them letter-perfect before an audience that would snicker at their awkwardness. But the entire class united in dismay and distrust when the teacher said that he thought they had better not send away for a printed play, as they were about to suggest, but that they would find much more satisfaction in a play composed and produced by themselves. He shortly afterward discovered that most of the class thought the teacher had made such suggestions because he did not know any printed plays. One of the girls, who became a highly gifted imaginative actress and playwright, told him several months after School began that she certainly had not been in favor of the group's making up its own plays, but she was now ready to admit the superior fun and quality of the plays they composed themselves.

The teacher, sensing that nothing would happen if he did not start the ball rolling, suggested that the first play be one of two scenes: *Arthurdale, 1934,* and *Scott's Run, 1933*. He gave no other indications as to plot and dialogue. The group came back the next day with some fairly dramatic ideas for the play. A certain amount of plot developed from the discussion that followed, and one girl returned the next day with some dialogue written out for the characters to speak. These

---

[11] See Chapter IV, pp. 201–10, for descriptions of dramatic play.

lines were very much in the style of the local plays they knew. The teacher asked the class if they thought the characters in their play talked that way, and suggested that the class begin immediately to act out the plot they had contrived, and just let the dialogue come to them as they acted. Some in the group began with enough confidence to carry off their everyday and extempore lines. They were, however, like most country children, extremely laconic. One of the boys, who was cast as a labor leader in the Scott's Run scene, was faced with a tense moment in the play, when hot words were clearly called for. He said not a word, and when the teacher said: "Jasper, what would you as the labor leader say here?" Jasper replied: "I wouldn't say nothin'." Thus invention of the dialogue proceeded slowly, while they loosened their tongues and shook off their self-consciousness. However, they had sufficient pleasure from the more or less pantomimed action of the play to carry them over the period when speech was slow in coming; with no ponderous lines to remember in the middle of a physical action on the stage, they began to romp through the plot, and the boys had to be shown how to give a semblance of landing a right to another actor's jaw without actually knocking him out.

Along with the composition of the play, there came the necessity of contriving some kind of stage for rehearsals and for the final performance. A small stage was constructed by the boys and girls from scrap lumber, and a curtain of unbleached muslin was stretched across its front. In those early days, there were no footlights, no constructed stage-sets, in fact no other backdrop than the French gray plaster finish of the Assembly Hall in which the stage was placed.

This first play by the High School was performed the night before Thanksgiving Day, and was an astonishing revelation to the audience. "Those kids made up that play? Why, I never knew my kids could act. They never was much good in them Sunday school plays down the Run." And even those who were shocked that the play was not one that was "sent away for," and who felt that somehow the proprieties had been offended, said: "Well, it wasn't half bad, considering that the kids made it up."

With confidence begotten of a play seen through to production, and with the commendation of the audience, the group was ready to plunge immediately into the composition of another play. They realized that there would be just about enough time to evolve a Christmas play before Christmas was upon them. Steered somewhat by the teacher, they hit upon the idea of acting out a group of six well-known Christmas carols, which in sequence made up a fairly complete narrative of the Christmas story. The group chose the carols, and so really determined the plot and shape of the play. The action was completely pantomimic, with no words spoken by the actors; they merely acted as the words and spirit of the carols instructed them.

The words of the carols were sung by a group of High School boys and girls not in the play, one of the homestead fathers accompanying them on his guitar. Somehow they caught and gave to the onlookers the very mood and spirit of the shepherds watching on the hills, the proud kings on their way, the glory and ineffable tenderness of Mary and the Christ Child. This, in spite of a stage that invited no imaginings and before an audience moved and shy to the point of near scoffing. The homesteaders, religious at heart, were deeply moved by it and entranced, too, by its splendors. One of the men came up and said: "You know, I ain't never seen a play like that. I saw a movie oncet, and I liked it so much I saw it twicet."

After Christmas, the Drama class plunged eagerly into the composition of still other plays. The content and spirit of these next two plays were rural and traditional. The teacher had held no particular brief for a rural play with the groups, and they had come upon such conceptions mainly because they had been sufficiently enfreed to choose instinctively from their own cultural environment.

There was no square-dancing or ballad-singing in the idyllic romance which they produced early in the first winter; instead, they caught and appropriated to the dramatic form the same spirit that a ballad or a square-dance figure has. The group called the play *Memory of a Bygone Time*. It was a flash-back romance, with elderly Uncle Dick recollecting his courtship of many years before. The main scene was in Aunt Hattie's garden (represented symbolically by a branch of the community Christmas tree, which had been kept green under the bushes surrounding the Square), and concerned the successful efforts of Dick to decoy Aunt Hattie out of the garden in order to leave it to him and Hattie's niece. The idyllic quality came from the setting, the induction, the slow, full speech of the actors, from their bearing and gestures, from Dick's coonskin cap which he twirled as he casually meditated Hattie's exit. Instinctively the actors had selected the perfect materials, and only those girls and boys who had composed the play could have acted it with such utterly graceful comprehension.

The other of those first after-Christmas plays was called *An Old-Fashioned School*. It pictured the interior of an old one-room schoolhouse, the educational background of the Arthurdale parents and some children. The atmosphere was again thoroughly and naturally rural, and the humor was of the *Tom Sawyer* variety.

For a time during the winter the boys of the drama group were needed elsewhere, and the girls straightway set out to make up a play for girls to act. They hit upon the precocious idea of satirizing a *Ladies' Aid Society Convention*. The "ladies" convene in a grove, and are immediately split into warring factions representing the countrywomen and the militant urban crusaders for "women's rights"; after both sides have been resoundingly thumped by the playwrights' barbed wit, the convention is shattered by one of the city women's seeing a big red ant and crying havoc. The actors "took off" the city women and the racy, snuff-taking women from Pokey Hollow with equal and devastating aplomb; where the actresses got such understanding of the city clubwomen one does not know, but the characterization was consistently clear and incisive. At the final performance of this hilarious play, two of the actresses "ad libbed" a particularly comic moment for six minutes. And there was unerring taste in the gesture with which one girl, as a delegate from Pokey Hollow, scooped snuff from a tin with her thumb.

By this time, there was promise of spring, and thoughts turned to the discovery of a spot for an outdoor theater. The spot was found a few hundred yards back of the site of the new School buildings—a grassy glade surrounded by dogwood and tall beeches, and giving way on three sides upon ferny hillocks.

The drama group had been studying American history, particularly the Westward Movement, and had been shown therein possibilities for a play about the Forty-Niners; the actors understood those people, and were themselves pioneers of a sort. They looked up all available historical material, and they transformed their English class, which was no longer needed for tongue liberation, into one in which they read Forty-Niner stories by Bret Harte and Jack London's *All Gold Canyon*. But even more important to the spirit and content of the resulting play, the music teacher found for them and they sang "On the Banks of the Sacramento," "Joe Bowers," "What Was Your Name in the States?" and "Sweet Betsy from

Pike"—all traditional songs and ballads of the Forty-Niners. The spirit of the play was set by such stanzas as these from "Sweet Betsy":

> *They reached the wide desert where Betsy gave out,*
> *And down in the sand she lay rolling about,*
> *While Ike in great terror looked on in surprise,*
> *Saying, "Betsy, get up, you'll get sand in your eyes."*
>
> *The Shanghai ran off and the cattle all died;*
> *The last piece of bacon that morning was fried.*
> *Poor Ike got discouraged, and Betsy got mad,*
> *And the dog wagged his tail and looked wonderful sad.*

In fact, one of the chief characters in the play was called Betsy, and she did fry the last piece of bacon. Joe Bowers and his girl also figured in the plot. And one of the most stirring scenes in the play was when the fight in All Gold Canyon was enacted on one of the hillsides, and the two placer-miners rolled over and over down the slope to the center of the stage.

The scenery for the Forty-Niner play, *The Gold Rush*, represented some skillful engineering on the part of the actors. Under the direction of the Shop teacher, they brought down to the outdoor stage discarded strips of lumber from an abandoned sawmill near by and fashioned these boards, the bark still on them, into a Forty-Niner hotel-dance-hall and a general store. The play opened back home in West Virginia with the announcement of the discovery of gold in California, and only the last long scene was in Hangtown. The actors so contrived the false-fronts of the two buildings for this scene that they could be erected from the ground up *during* the scene. As a result, the mushroom growth of the Forty-Niner towns was strikingly recapitulated, and the background for the action of the scene was one of ringing hammers and snatches of song.

This play represented an expansion of the basis for play-productions at Arthurdale. While the spirit and theme were drawn from the songs and ballads which were of the rural traditional culture, the action and characterizations were enriched by contact with the kindred historical and literary source material of Bret Harte, Jack London, and a bit of Fenimore Cooper. These materials did not clash with the more immediate cultural materials, but rather supplemented them and opened up new and vital sources for plays.

High School Drama in 1935–36

The next fall the original Drama group, which wished to continue its productions for another year, augmented by several new girls and six or seven boys, proceeded to make up a play for acting in the Outdoor Theater. The play dealt with a harvest supper, and had an effective background of cornshucks and pumpkins borrowed from the fields of some of the homesteaders. But the play itself was less shapely and satisfying to the actors than the earlier plays had been, owing in part to the presence of the new and yet unassimilated members of the drama group.

When in the first year the English teacher had exposed the class to the Wessex stories and novels of Thomas Hardy, he found that this author had an appeal for these rather Wessex-like Arthurdale people, and the story of *The Three Strangers* had that year been mentioned by the group as "good for a play." After the *Harvest Supper* play was performed, and the Outdoor Theater grew too frosty for use, and the new Recreation Building stage gave promise of soon being ready for productions, the attention of the group turned again to *The Three Strangers;* and a free dramatization, with additions and omissions conditioned by the cultural environment of West Virginia, was created through rehearsals.

There were two Christmas plays the second year. On Christmas Eve, the High School boys and girls gave an expanded repetition of the carol play, for which there was a strong demand on the part of the community, this time with more carols and some older ones like "The Cherry Tree Carol," which is traditional in the Appalachians.

The other play was a venture which, at first glance, might have appeared thoroughly out of key with the cultural environment, and an exotic suggestion: it was the production at the School just before Christmas of the Ben Greet synthesis of the Coventry and Towneley Craft-cycle Plays—*The Second Shepherds' Play* and *The Adoration of the Magi*. The Ninth Grade, augmented by children from the younger classes, produced the play with gusto and understanding.[12] The secret of their success with this fourteenth-century English folk-play was precisely that it was their ancestors, culturally speaking, who had composed and acted the original craft-cycle plays. Actually, their fourteenth-century ancestors had proceeded in play composition in a way quite similar to that which the Arthurdale boys and girls had found so fruitful, the chief difference being that the medieval craft-cycle playwrights had a long tradition of liturgical plays behind them, while the Arthurdale group had no immediate contact with a living dramatic tradition. In a sense they were discovering their nearest tradition in drama.

After the Senior High School group had produced *The Three Strangers*, there was a period in which the group cast about in literature for suggestions for another play. From a broad selection by the teacher, which emphasized mainly good stories and situations which had elements of the dramatic in them, the group read variously for more than a week, consulting with each other as to the dramatic possibilities of the stories they were reading. At the end of this period they had

---

[12] The Arthurdale boys and girls enjoyed producing the play and climbed past difficulties with the old English words and phrases—just as the children in Kentucky had done—because the play was close to the way they thought and felt, and expressed something of their own reverence and their sense of humor. The parents came to see it and liked it so well themselves that they wanted to have it as the community Christmas play the next year.—E.R.C.

chosen for dramatization and production a part or all of Poe's "Masque of the Red Death," Benét's *John Brown's Body,* and Shakespeare's *Love's Labor's Lost* by way of *Lamb's Tales from Shakespeare.*

The play which derived from *John Brown's Body* was called *Spade,* and was a portrayal in chiaroscuro of the fortunes and misfortunes of the Negro Spade, who left his home and journeyed through thick woods and deep rivers in search of freedom, to find in Northern industry much the same slaveries that he had escaped from in the South. The group enjoyed the disillusioning end, for they were in their own lives beginning to see that there are no fancy escapes from the realities of everyday living. The "escape" of Spade was conceived and executed by the group with an intensity that was reminiscent of O'Neill's *Emperor Jones,* and was acted by a strapping Arthurdale boy with entire self-forgetfulness and an emotional breadth and sweep that carried the audience with him. Off-stage singing of Negro and white spirituals by those of the group not acting in the play added to its effectiveness and lent to it color which counterbalanced the black and white stage setting.

With this play, the group really came of age dramatically. They had their own director—a boy who had contributed a majority of the ideas for this play—and the teacher did nothing but consult with the director when something during rehearsals would not turn out the way he and they wanted it to.

Adult Drama Group, 1934–36

The School's ambitions for the adults in the dramatic art were the same as for the children. But the process of inducting the older people was necessarily quite different. The grownups were more deeply mired in the existing tradition of minstrel and church plays; their bodies and their tongues were in need of more limbering than even the High School students had been; and the amount of energy they had to spare for play production was never great. For all these reasons, they proceeded much more slowly than did the High School groups.

They began in the winter of 1934–35 with the simultaneous production of two plays—so large was the number of adults who wanted to be in a play. They wanted to "send away" for plays, just as the children had; and the teachers knew that these older people could not be thrust immediately into the composition and production of original plays, as the children had been. The compromise was to get from the University Library a few volumes of contemporary one-act plays, from which the players selected two which they thought would be good to produce: one called *The Mad Breakfast* and Lady Gregory's *Spreading the News*. The latter play caught a gossiping situation squarely on the chin, and was mightily cheered. *The Mad Breakfast* was rough and tumble enough to keep the actors' and the audience's interest. Through these experiences enthusiasm for play-producing was engendered. The actors were chiefly impressed by how comic they had been and resolved to be even funnier in their next plays. That resolve threw them back into the idea of minstrel and black-face comedies; and so there followed *The Battle of Rolling Bones,* a black-face comedy of Negro soldiers at the front. The actors sent away for this one.

Then they got *A Mock Trial,* which was an attempt of some hack dramatist to burlesque the usual court proceedings. The High School group produced the *Ladies' Aid Society Convention* on the same evening, and the comparison helped to bury the already mortifying *Mock Trial*. At a post-mortem on this play the acting group, which had boiled down to about twenty men and women, declared for no more *Mock Trials,* and were open to suggestions from the directing teachers about the next play. The teachers completed their search for a skeletonized version of a play which would start the adult group moving toward their cultural resources.

That play was called *The Jealous Lover of Lone Green Valley*, and while it had nothing in its plot to connect it with the ballad-narrative of that title, the temper and mood of the play were set by recurrent off-stage singing of that ballad and other traditional ones. The plot was simplified and adapted from a Broadway play of a few years before—*Green Grow the Lilacs*. The action was almost entirely pantomime, so that the adults were able for the first time to move freely and abundantly about the stage and really to act; as a consequence, the heroine and hero at one point in the play did a square-dance step back and forth as they flirtatiously sang "A Paper of Pins." Before the actors had finished rehearsing this play, which was from the beginning their creation except for the plot, they had changed even the plot so drastically that none of the few urban visitors in the audience who had seen or read the Broadway play could see more than the vaguest similarities. The actors, once they got going on this kind of play and acting, really enjoyed it, and the audience approved also. The actors were so taken with it that they wanted to tour the country with the play, and as late as the following winter they referred to *The Jealous Lover* as "the best play we ever done," and wished to revive it.

Their next play was a satire on themselves. There had been a wave or epidemic of newspaper reporters at Arthurdale, apparently sent by their metropolitan editors to snoop at subsistence-homesteading. The homesteaders had had their fingers burned by some of these reporters, notably by one pair who impersonated Federal officials of the newly created Resettlement Administration and got the homesteaders to tell all their troubles so that they, the bogus officials, could set things right. Out of such incidents the adult drama group built a comedy which castigated reporters and homesteaders alike. In this play the adults truly created their own vehicle of expression. The language was immensely racy and witty, being the free product of the actors' imagination placed in an essentially humorous situation. *The Jealous Lover* was rural melodrama; *The Newspaper Spy* was comic satire. The School felt that a community which could laugh at itself was a healthy community. The homesteaders did not worry about newspaper reporters after that.

This chapter on Cultural Resources would not be complete if it did not include not only the arts, indigenous to the Scotch-Irish rural culture, of balladry, fiddling, square-dancing, and the like; the acquired art of the drama; the crafts of fiddle-making and quilting and furniture-making; and the fostering of historical tradition in the region; but also the work of the School in opening up channels of communication through the creation and publication of a community newspaper printed at the High School.

COMMUNICATION

"The News" and School-Community Life

One of the chief lacks in the traditional culture of American rural people has been that of adequate means of communication in their locality and with the nation. Oral means of communication have, so far, in the country regions been practically the only means and, while they have been active, they have at the same time, when applied to contemporary events, been lacking in factual content and decidedly "rumorish."

By the time Arthurdale had a population of five hundred, the homesteaders really did not know what was happening in their own community, and amazing stories were freely circulated and believed. Many of the homesteaders read the Morgantown daily newspaper, but they read mainly the murder and sports articles. They also saw local journals and news-

CULTURAL RESOURCES AND OPPORTUNITIES

papers from other towns and cities. Outside news about Arthurdale was liable to be as inaccurate as the orally circulated news on the homestead. The inaccuracies affected more than the minds of the homesteaders; they were the basis of fears and feelings of distrust of one's neighbors and of the homestead and the School. The grapevine line spread depression and mistrust and dissension.

As a therapeutic measure, the establishment of a local newspaper was highly desirable at Arthurdale. There was another need which the establishment of a local newspaper would also meet. In the early days, the bulletin board at the Center, plus personal contacts, sufficed for spreading the news of this or that meeting or coming event, or notice to the community about typhoid inoculations, etc. But as the community grew in size, not everyone passed the bulletin board every day, and local announcements were no longer adequately circulated by this simple means. While there never was any substitute for personal contact among the homesteaders, and between them and the teachers—the printed word does not establish the essential, intimate understanding of one's neighbors and community—there was clearly needed a means of communicating dates and times of meetings and events. For this reason, some of the earliest sheets from the School press were community calendars of meetings and events for the following week. It was what a newspaper could do for the community psychologically, however, that especially interested the School.

By the fall of 1935, it was apparent that the time had come to launch the newspaper. There were, of course, a number of technical matters to get straight first. With limited funds the School had to invest in a press, in type, and in paper; and some group of Arthurdale people had to be trained in the craft of typesetting and printing, there being no background of such experience in any of the homesteaders' lives. A second-hand, and very temperamental, hand press was found and purchased in a neighboring town for ten dollars, and a small amount of type was thrown in. More type was purchased in small amounts each month, and a supply of paper was stocked.

The most tedious part of preparing to publish a newspaper was the training of a group in printing and in news-writing. The group chosen to undertake this enterprise was the Eleventh and Twelfth Grades of the High School. They worked at this enterprise as a part of their daily High School schedule. They began, not by attempting to write and print a newspaper—even one page would have been impossible for them —but with kinds of job printing in which the time requirements are adjustable to the slowly developing skill of typesetting; such items as Fire Directions, Class Schedules, entertainment programs, and, finally, Christmas carols. By the time the group had finished a sheaf of Christmas carols, they were ready, as far as typesetting and printing ability were concerned, to attempt a one-page newspaper. While the training in mechanical skill was progressing, it was paralleled by training in news-gathering and news-writing. The group was anxious to try a School newspaper as soon as possible; yet it knew fairly well the amount of skill required to produce one page of original material every week. The children wrote trial news articles for several weeks, while the carols were being printed; and when the first of the year arrived, they had developed enough understanding and facility in news-gathering and news-writing to be able to undertake the publication of a small school paper.

Modestly, then, the High School children embarked on the publication of a weekly one-page newspaper. There was established a regular schedule for news-gathering, news-writing, typesetting, proofreading, and final printing; this schedule spanned the week. At first every member of the group tried his hand at both writing and printing, but there soon began to appear differences in ability and preferences for the editorial or printing sides of the newspaper work and, while the division of labor was never very strict or compulsory, some spent most of their time in the editorial room and some in the printing room. They found the publication of their first issue of the newspaper a tremendous effort. Not before had they realized how dominating a factor time could be, nor how much care and thought had to go quickly into the composition of timely news and articles. Viewed objectively, that first issue was a puny little thing, hardly worthy to be circulated even in the High School, but it was at least a start, and the publication of the paper continued from then on without interruption.

By the time the group had published five weekly issues, there was a noticeable improvement in the format and prose style of the paper. There was also enough increase in facility to allow the group to venture to expand the paper to two pages. With the sixth issue, community news began to creep into it— inevitably, for there was no valid distinction between school and community interests and activities. Gradually the community news increased and crowded out mere High School chatter. The newspaper's function had from the start been seen as a bearer of *news,* not of poor jokes and idle, semi-literary writing; and the paper expanded in the direction of more and more inclusive news items about the community. In another month, the paper was increased to three pages an issue. A few adults were by this time interested in the enterprise, and were encouraged to send in news articles about doings in which they were engaged. Editorials also began to appear. By the end of the regular school year in June 1936, *The News* was an out-and-out community newspaper, appearing in three pages every Friday and circulating through a fairly large subscription list.

The News issues gave a fairly full picture of both community and school activities, and contained notices and news items on topics such as the following:

Matters of local history, like the history of the old Mansion recounted at the time that the building was torn down; announcements and descriptions of plays given by the School drama group, and by the adult group; of the raising and sale of cabbage and tomato plants in the School's greenhouse; news about the Co-operative General Store, the forming of the Arthurdale Co-operative Association and its project of poultry-raising and the proposed restaurant; notes of the activities of the Men's and Women's Clubs, of work on construction, and of NYA projects; notices of the School's savings deposit "bank," of the baby clinics, of the benefit supper and other entertainments for the Medical Fund; announcements of concerts and of the Music Festival; news about the Log Cabin and the other enterprises of the Fourth Grade, and the activities of the various School classes; and, in almost every number—an item of both community and school interest—notices and reports of basketball and baseball games.

Not only did the paper announce events, and correct misunderstandings by accurately reporting news, but it also made everyone aware, from the facts reported in its pages, that the community and School were live and going institutions with many interests and enterprises—a fact in itself most reassuring and calculated to encourage and invigorate the most despondent and skeptical. The fact that accurate and full news was to be had each week in their own community newspaper was also understood, as was also the conclusion that the events thus reported, with care and accuracy, were really news—better even than the grapevine gossip. The problems and techniques of news-reporting became entirely clear to the High School staff of the paper, and to all the adults who contributed articles. The newspaper did, in fact, supply what is so frequently a chief lack in rural culture—an adequate means of communication.

CHAPTER VI

A RURAL HIGH SCHOOL

George Beecher
Principal of the Arthurdale High School

Section 1: An Account of the Beginnings of the Arthurdale High School, 1934-35

THE only account of the Arthurdale High School which I can give is one of growth. The word "experiment" in social affairs has conflicting connotations. The School was a step forward in our experience rather than an experiment. The new school, conceived while we were still in a Kentucky school, was an experiment only to the extent that we had developed a practice for studying environment and for developing the relations between school and the life of a community and were willing to test this practice in a new community.

WHERE WE MUST BEGIN

Making a beginning is one of the most unimpressive pieces of work that I know—at least in a school. If one could be sure that the school could do no wrong, it would be possible to begin with fanfare, but in our case not even the physical equipment was in existence two days before the date of opening school. We felt that this was pioneering, but more confusing than in pioneer times. We had the semblance of buildings, and there were tools, shops, foremen, and workmen. It was a matter of reconstructing two capacious sheds, painted white on the outside, but obviously barns on the inside—rough-timbered and unfloored. They were supply sheds for the homestead project, that is, until the week before school, when we looked them over and designated the places where windows should be cut and electric wiring installed. Floors, a sink, and lavatories practically completed the work. The inner walls were lined with celotex, which turned out to be more admirable for thumbtacking exhibits than to shut out winter winds at the points where barn timbers and walls did not fit snugly.

We could wait until late November before a heating system was put into operation. There was a Burnside stove in one end of the room which fairly warmed its corner on frosty days. On days when a wild wind poured down our mountains, the smoke puffed from the doors of the stove like grandpap in the corner with his pipe, and then we had to open windows to let the smoke out. After steam heat was installed, the buildings were liable to be insufferably hot unless the outdoor temperature was near zero.

I can remember sitting in one of the buildings at an anomalous smooth-topped office desk. Invariably when one or two people moved across the loft floor above me, hayseed would trickle down. I would give my hair a flick and blow off the smooth top of the desk. Then I would ponder on the fact that everyone liked those sheds and patiently felt that some good could come of them. Everyone, boys and girls alike and adults, seemed both relaxed and absorbed, actually grateful for this working environment. It bore small resemblance to a school.

The school work began in much the same way. We had no books, no laboratory equipment, in fact no accessories of any kind. In the other shed, which was used as the School Shop for the whole School, there was one cabinet and a number of saws, hammers, etc., which the High School could use. There were two teachers, to round out our stock in trade. Perhaps I should mention as an asset the brand-new environment of a West Virginia mountain glade, being reclaimed for the life of a community, itself in the formative period. The newness of the environment and the possibility of growth in the social life are to be emphasized. They are the prerequisites in interpreting our building of the school. The first is an essential only in the sense that you must look at an environment with new eyes, and the latter in the sense that you recognize growth as a possibility, or even a necessity. I am only repeating that the school-social-change relation in our case was clearer from the start than it might have been in an old established community.

SCHOOL OPENS

A group of about twenty boys and girls came on Monday morning, September 10, to begin High School with the two teachers who sat at a small table in the Assembly Hall. This Hall with the very high ceiling was commonly the meeting place for the Men's Club or community gatherings or for square dances.

We began our orientation with a good many questions: What sort of school had the boys and girls attended? What work were they anticipating in the School? What were their interests outside of school? What resources did they have, such as radio, or newspapers, or books?

In the days preceding the opening of School we had met more of the adults than the young people, but had begun to get an inkling of the situation. The families came from various mine camps. Often they knew several of the other families, but there was a more usual feeling that the community was new in neighbors as well as in pursuits. The young people had a certain unity in past school experiences. That fact provided both our point of departure and a preconception that was difficult to drop.

On our beginning day we were dealing with regular students, and a few irregular ones. Girls were in the majority and on the whole more satisfied with their concept of what a school was. The boys, with a few exceptions, were dubious to the point of apathy. We were to find later that the exceptions were the ones who were regular and who could stick. The rest were to be erratic friends who reached perhaps their peak of achievement when hired for a few months as laborers' helpers in the project construction work. In the following year they were in and out of school again, partially satisfied with NYA and WPA work, tentatively joining shop groups, drama groups, classes. They were to be a constant reminder of our problem,[1] almost an index to the life of the community. Two or three in the group were either married or soon to be, and without much prospect of homes and employment. Some had dropped out of school during the past five or six years in the mines. Some had continued school in the scattered two- and three-room elementary schools or in the consolidated schools in Morgantown and had definite ambitions to finish High School. Some of the boys were going to have to take every odd job that came along, even making special arrangements for carrying along school work, in order to buy their clothes for school. We had grown used to this sort of thing in Kentucky, but just the sight of a wholesome-looking group of boys and girls does not suggest that food, clothing, and shelter and social adjustment are problems for a school to face. What has a curriculum and patterns of regular attendance and tests, etc., to do with these?

POINT OF DEPARTURE

Our groping amid confusions was not illuminated greatly by the answers to our questionings. Here are the subjects of study which were given as having been "taken" previously by the group:

---

[1] See Chapter II, pp. 103–7; also Chapter VII, pp. 343–7.

Arithmetic
Reading
Spelling
History
Art
Home Economics
Music
Hygiene
English
Agriculture
Mathematics (including Geometry)
Science (meaning General Science)
Physical Education
Social Science
Business Training
Geography
Biology
Chemistry
Salesmanship
Economics
Commerce

This seems to be a fairly complete catalogue of the usual High School curriculum. The list of subjects which the boys and girls wished to carry on was a little smaller:

> Mathematics
> Social Studies
> English
> Home Economics
> Art
> Dramatics and Music
> Business
> Science (including Agriculture)
> Library Work
> Physical Education

The outside interests, as near as we could draw them out, included reading, sports, dancing, music, working away from home, working at home, and a few single expressions of interests, which made a meager list of interests indeed.

Reactions such as the following seemed to indicate that education in the lives of these young people thus far had held out a hope to them for a better economic future:

"Want a business course in order to leave Arthurdale and get a job."

"Not financially able to go far in school, so want preparation for a job."

"No interest in science. Want business course—or home economics, if business opportunity fails."

"Prefer business course for bookkeeper or librarian. Not interested in science or agriculture. Home economics would also prepare for a job."

These are responses conditioned by a city school, of course, where there is a basis for the hope of becoming a stenographer. We were all to come closer to the reality later and to recognize typing and bookkeeping as desirabilities but certainly less as "business training" and more as preparation for opportunities as they appeared in our own environment. In the following year we were to see both girls and boys using their knowledge of typing and bookkeeping in very real offices or on farm and household accounts.

The reactions to English were also fairly stereotyped:

> "Grammar, because it is necessary."
> "Reading and Literature."
> "Speeches."
> "Letters, invitations."
> "Study and pronunciation of words."

These are very definitely the studies in English which go on year in and year out in school. Our reaction to them was to omit them all. There were clear needs even in the first few days—others became apparent in a few weeks. First, there was the need for a collection of books, the start of a library, the beginning of reading as reading and as a resource in study. Then, there was the need to begin thinking along the lines we planned to study, to gain the use of words by using them for the problems of this new environment. There was scarcely a member of the group who was not language-starved.

BEGINNING AFRESH

If there is little of the remarkable in making a slow start, perhaps that is the remarkable fact. In our second year we were to have definite expectations, but even these were conditioned by several new factors: there were new buildings to use, new families had moved into the community, and the economic problem of existence was to move up into a position of startling importance.

One thing that interests me now is to compare our community with other communities. One environment is similar to any other in that it presents advantages and disadvantages for living, community and eccentricity of social feeling, and cultural and uncultural patterns of activity. Inconsiderate as it may sound, one has here in Arthurdale to rule out the ordinary factors which determine the practice in schools: the traditional, compartmentalized curriculum which seems to "cover everything"; the layout of the High School; the concentration of so many students that there has to be a system for handling them; the textbook limitation. These are all apparently fixed conditions. We were free from all four at our start, so of course it is unfair to compare this school with others which are solving their problems in their own way. I hope only to bring out by comparison the value of beginning afresh.

ORGANIZATION OF WORK IN THE HIGH SCHOOL

HIGH SCHOOL GROUPINGS

September 10, 1934 (diary notes). The tests for the High School show pretty fair results, except those in Algebra, I hear from Mr. Ipcar [the other High School teacher]. There are so many different age groups in the High School and these are variously divided over the four classes (freshmen, etc.), that the testing so far gives only general information.

The grouping into two or three main courses of study, rather than into four standard classes by age, seems to be working out all right.

The two main groupings that we have made base themselves on two main interests that were discovered:

One, Science and Mathematics as applied to everyday life, with such practical additions as Home Economics, Shop work, and reading and spelling.

The other, Economics as it applies to everyday life and industry, History, Arithmetic and practical calculations, and reading—especially about modern events. In this second group are those who have studied typing, shorthand, etc.

In both groups, the understanding is clear that no special training is offered—such as agriculture or straight business training, though at some time the need for specialties may come.

September 21, 1934. In the main, the temporary schedule has functioned well and very few students have raised objections. Some have asked very polite and reasonable questions about their standings and the possibilities of electing new work as the school day lengthens and more teachers are available. The group is fairly conscientious and quiet and steady working.

Any definite vocational needs seem to me to be more a division of adult education, where each individual follows one or more lines of work under special supervision from members of the staff, or from County and other official workers (such as Mr. Grimes, the agricultural adviser).

The older pupils of High School age who need to go into some line of vocational work, such as stenography, woodworking, accounting and bookkeeping for the Farm Co-operative, marketing, agriculture, Nursery School work, etc., could better work under the adults than with the more liberal High School groups. The difference in emphasis would be more easily brought out and the two uses for the School buildings and equipment kept apart.

The third grouping which is just getting under way has definitely more mature leanings towards the arts and Literature, Library work and Music—even teaching has cropped up.

Within a month the whole High School was settling down to definite pieces of work, and an hour here and an hour there were found free for introducing courses which could not be considered at the start. Foreshadowing of future developments is seen in the record from week to week:

October 8, 1934. The High School was able to begin its permanent schedule (omitting Home Economics).

Fletcher Collins took two combined groups into a class in

Literature. Carl Saunders took one group in applied principles of Mathematics, working in close contact with Harry Carlson's Shop studies in Electricity, metals, etc. There has been renewed interest in all the classes, owing to this expansion and variety, and the work in all lines is done enthusiastically.[2]

The group which has been working mainly with Adolph Ipcar has been going along steadily in the economic field, with practical Arithmetic and keeping of accounts, English and typing. It has Social-Economic History and Shop work, which goes under the name of "industrial laboratory"—meaning that manufacturing processes, power, etc., are both studied and experimented with in Shop. Next week this group will also have contacts with Fletcher Collins in Music.

The oldest group in High School, which has shown greatest interest in the arts, Home Economics, Library and reading, can now have a fuller schedule, too. Home Economics will include considerable work in the Nursery School and at the School lunch. The drawings which the group has been doing have developed into work which is both free and enfreeing. This group, too, not only has Literature with Fletcher Collins in the morning, but will also join the Music-Drama work with him in the afternoon.

Two other valuable class groupings for the afternoons are: typing with Alice Bowie, the School executive secretary, or discussion group with Adolph Ipcar.

December 14, 1934. Considerable thought and discussion have gone into planning out a fairly complete High School course to meet the needs of the community.[3]

The needs are also apparent: an extension in English and Literature, in History and Social Studies, Industrial Arts—sewing, etc., for the girls.

The present year seems fairly well provided for otherwise.

The English Literature (and American) and the Music-Drama are extremely important here, because so much of the program

---

[2] This evolution of developing interests in a group whose conventionally expressed expectations displayed only formal and vague ambitions and practically no real desires has been described because it represented a skillful handling of a situation that was at the outset anything but promising for "educational" development. The grouping of students in the beginning not by high-school grades, or by age, but by lines of endeavor was an experiment undertaken because it seemed more likely than any other plan to organize—or reorganize—high-school work along fruitful lines. It succeeded.—E.R.C.

[3] See Appendix III.

is scientific (or historical or practical), with studies in Mathematics. Science and Shop.

The plans for future Seventh and Eighth Grade work can easily be appended to plans for the upper classes of the High School.

Mobilization of Interests in the Seventh and Eighth Grades

The Seventh and Eighth Grades, because of space requirements, were housed the first year in the old Mansion on the hill with the Grade School, since certainly no more than the thirty-odd students of the four upper High School years could be accommodated in their two-story shed and one room over at the Town Center. Because of teacher shortage, these two grades were grouped together. They were under Fletcher Collins's direction for part of the year and, later, when Mr. Collins's work became too heavy and the need for his services elsewhere too pressing, they were supervised by a young teacher, Henry Esterley, who joined the staff as an assistant teacher for a few months. In 1935-36, when the full six-year High School entered its own building, this combined group was organized into separate Eighth and Ninth Grades.

In 1934-35, the Seventh-Eighth Grade group was a lively, enthusiastic class with many able and several emotionally unstable members. Mr. Collins reports in January 1935:

This group was composed of children whose previous education was acquired in the public school system of this and surrounding Counties. A number had been in the schools of Scott's Run and Star City; others had been exposed to one- or two-teacher schools in more agricultural areas. The parents were not much impressed by the quality of education previously received by their children and, consequently, were hopeful of a "better" school at Arthurdale.

Yet while the parents looked forward to a better school for the children, they naturally retained the old idea of a school as a place where youngsters were "learned" the Three R's and where corporeal punishment was the chief instrument of control. Mr.

Conners, in introducing his eleven-year-old boy to me, said: "He's a bit contrary, and you'll have to look out for him playing hooky. If he runs away, or doesn't get his lessons good, I want you just to whip him good—just give him a good whipping." Confirmation of this point of view toward the educative process was apparent in the Seventh–Eighth Grade in the first weeks. They had stories of blood and thunder in last year's classrooms. But they felt no sense of the inhumanity of such treatment; in fact, they rather relished the drama of these experiences, and were genuinely surprised at the lack of switchings and knuckle-rappings in the repertory of their new teacher.

On the other hand, having no great faith in traditional education and hoping mightily for a "better" school, the parents were surprisingly quick to appreciate the nature of the Arthurdale School. Mr. MacDonald approached me after school had been running for about two weeks and said: "Mr. Collins, I like the way this here school's been doing things. 'Course, it may be slower in getting the kids educated, but it's sure. These kids will know what they know." Thus, the initial set-up was distinctly one favorable to the operation of the School.

The Seventh–Eighth group was not a unit when it first appeared on Monday morning, September 10. The children had been on the homestead property only two or three months, or less, and were not well acquainted with each other or with the property. The group was unified first by the enterprise of making a five-by-ten-foot map of Arthurdale. In considerable detail and with some scientific precision, the group crayoned in a map of the homestead in autumn colors. The map-making involved all thirteen members of the original group for about two months, at the end of which time they had produced not only a magnificent map but also an *esprit de corps*. While the Seventh–Eighth Grade program was much developed in the succeeding three months, the map-making enterprise was the spiritual basis of all the later three-dimensional study of mountains (geology, resources) and mountaineers.

The following notes from Mr. Collins's diary during the time that he lived with these boys and girls give a picture of a group finding itself:

September 7, 1934. In addition to the central map project, I have insinuated a beginning on the matter of good English. Asked about the properness of the word "ain't," one of the group volunteered that "ain't is all right, but 'hain't' ain't much account."

A start has also been made on reading; some of the reading coming from my own library, some from their mathematics textbooks. The reading list corroborated my impression of their backwardness in this field, and I intend to work them hard for development.

As a group, the boys and girls seem a sturdy, enthusiastic, earnest lot. In a few instances I am trying to check up on physical difficulties, which at times make these students seem inefficient or unco-operative. Health records will help.

At recess, the girls enjoy baseball as much as the boys, and all play hard. No tendency for girls and boys to oppose each other or to feel much differentiation. The only separate work for Grades Seven and Eight has been in Mathematics. In that subject, one group studies while the other works with me. Elsewhere, results seem superior when all sixteen are working together.

Week of September 24, 1934. Shop work centered this week on designing play equipment for the Nursery School. After a committee from the class visited the Nursery School and talked with Miss Sedman, the class designed and sketched sand shovels, wheel barrows, and saw horses for see-saws. The Seventh and Eighth graders thought up the idea of helping the Nursery School themselves, and they have been pretty intelligent about figuring out dimensions for two- to five-year-olds. Mathematics has entered functionally into this work.

On Wednesday I sensed that the group needed a sudden change of activity and that they would like to compose "poetry." We were all very quiet and scribbled furiously about anything we felt very much. The result was some original and spontaneous poems —some sad, some whimsical, some fantastically funny. A few good ones about the Arthurdale landscape and spirit. On Thursday, just to see the other side of their poetry, I asked them to bring in and speak for us their favorite poem, but not one they had had to say in school last year. What they brought in was inferior (by any canon) to their own productions the day before. Some of the speakers insisted on sing-songing and pronouncing "the" as "thee," and "a" as "ay." But we made some headway in speaking poetry as if it were a tune, and naturally.

Week ending October 19, 1934. A new enterprise began this week —a logical outcome of the Arthurdale map. The general subject is Mountains and Mountaineers, using the immediate Appalachian region as the focus, and investigating its geology (historical and economic—i.e., coal), the life of highlanders, their music, climate, etc. We have been finding out about the Carboniferous Period when coal was formed; this includes some drawing of dinosaurs and other prehistoric and entrancing monsters, study of fossils, also study of rocks. This enterprise ought to expand all year.

Week ending November 9, 1934. The Mountaineer enterprise is now focused on the collection and study of rocks. There is enough interest in limestone so that we expect to construct a small lime plant as Shop and Mathematics work, and investigate thoroughly the handling and uses of lime and limestone.

Week ending November 15, 1934. The limestone business has begun, with scientific search for a quarry site (of small proportions). We have located one down near the site of the new School buildings, and the stone is easily accessible. Aiding our search was a mound, from which were first gleaned a couple of small limestone rocks. Examination showed that something had burned those rocks. More excavating of the mound disclosed the whole process of a lime kiln, and gave specimens of limestone in each stage, from hard gray rock to powdery near-lime chunks.

Week ending January 12, 1935. The high point of their week was hearing the President's speech by radio January 4. They took notes, wrote them up, and compared the original as it was given in next day's New York *Times*. One sentence-idea, in particular, seemed relevant to their own investigations: ". . . the security of a livelihood through the better use of the national resources of the land in which we live." We intend to use this idea in our overhauling of the Valley District. We are very ready to use the "Report of the Monongahela Valley," when it is out.

Week ending January 31, 1935. Continuing their related study of climate and weather (specifically at Arthurdale), we walked down to the United States Weather Bureau Station in Mr. Gordon's back yard, and examined the instruments for measuring the maximum and minimum temperatures and precipitation. Mr. Gordon explained his daily routine in recording these facts, and the youngsters asked some good questions. They returned to the schoolroom with new understanding of how weather records are kept, and with renewed enthusiasm for their own crude weather station in the classroom. We have a brilliantly colored graph on the wall which shows the daily outdoor temperature at the School, four feet square, and stretching from December to February. Several of the children are now planning with George Beecher in Science a crude measurer of wind-velocity, to be executed by them in Shop.[4]

A renaissance of interest in writing poetry. I begin to regret that I allowed their scientific and pictorial activities to eclipse this kind of expression. They do some simple lovely work in words —almost wholly without my pedagogic motivating. Just now they are planning an anthology of their literary efforts. My old blunderbuss of a Remington typewriter has been loaned to them, and they redouble their literary productions in order to have the privilege of painfully picking these out on the machine.

ENGLISH

Within a few weeks, Fletcher Collins was free one period a day to take the whole High School as one group. There is no name on any curriculum for what they did. They did some reading of poetry to see what sort of picture it gave of rural life. Soon they were a chorus arranging a poem of Shelley or Lindsay for oral presentation. Many in the group had never opened their voices before. Fletcher Collins kept saying that there was no use trying to teach a person English until that basic experience was known. He remembers one boy, who had his eyes on past studies of spelling, sentences, and punctuation, saying when he came into the room where Lindsay's "Congo" was being worked out: "Is this supposed to be English?"

In the meantime, the group had with difficulty caught the

---

[4] In 1935–36, the next Seventh Grade made a study of weather followed by an introductory study of Geology, an account of which is to be found in this chapter, p. 309.

idea of composing its own drama as a group.[5] Soon it wasn't necessary to touch pencil to paper. Language was being used in experience and out of experience. And the members of the group knew how to spell, read, and write. Speech was the initial problem for individuals and also the primary medium for group activity. It was an easy step to group singing of poetry, especially that kind which is familiar to West Virginians—the mountain ballads. The story of the discovery of both language and music with this group is a story by itself.[6] It was the discovery and use of a very real local culture. The group held together for two years as the starting point and nucleus for drama, music, and square-dancing as creative developments in the community. There is no story in the High School of greater interest than this.[7]

Mr. Collins's diary records the steps in this process:

RURAL POETRY

October 2, 1934. Signalized by the beginning of my work with the High School. We are studying what we call rural poetry, what scholars call "the Romantics" (Cowper, Gray, Collins, Coleridge, Wordsworth, Shelley, Keats, Emerson, Whitman). Purpose: to discover in this kind of poetry possible new understandings of the rural environment of Arthurdale—a poetic (seeing) understanding to supplement the scientific. Fits in well with this group's present work in Botany, for instance. Also gives a functional approach to the nature of poetry as something vital in their lives.

I find their present acquaintance with poetry extremely slight and mostly of the jingle-rhyme sort. In fact, on Thursday they realized for the first time that rhyme is not the only earmark of verse. I plan to use their increased awareness of their environment to stimulate their own compositions, in prose or verse. After sessions with the poets, we shall probably go on to the prose of some American naturalists, chiefly Thoreau and Burroughs.

---

[5] See Chapter V, pp. 257–8.
[6] *Ibid.*, pp. 223–30.
[7] *Ibid.*, pp. 258–65.

Week ending October 25, 1934. I am pleased with their quick improvement in handling the English language, both in matters of pronunciation and enunciation and in written work. We have read nothing but poetry, and I think they are beginning to get the feel and tang of rich language, and to enjoy words and speaking them musically.

Week ending November 1, 1934. The ability of this group to handle language (as written by rural poets) is steadily growing. Whitman has been for them a great solvent of conventional attitudes to, and performances of, poetry. And they care more for Wordsworth's verse than any group I've ever seen—as I hoped they, rural people, would. They understand Wordsworth as no city-dwelling critic or academician possibly could, and they have an uncanny way of choosing some of Wordsworth's lesser-known poems and making these pieces seem suddenly valuable and lovely.

We are beginning now an attempt at choral speaking of poetry —blending male and female voices, and working out a group orchestration of Shelley's "Hymn of Pan." Such work is the best sort for this rather heterogeneous group.

Choral Speaking

Week ending November 9, 1934. Most of the week spent on choral reading by the whole group. Much enthusiasm and pretty decent results. Such group rhythmic work is very good for these people. They reinforce each other, and discover rhythmic possibilities otherwise ignored or repressed.

Week ending November 16, 1934. Verse speaking (chorally) continued, with discovery of Vachel Lindsay's "Congo" as decidedly down their alley. Such gusto for language these people are getting! Even the phlegmatic members leave the meeting at the end weak from sheer physical exercise and as pleased as if they had been playing football. I think I have, in this kind of work, found a good approach for them to literature and language, and I intend to continue it as means of some good education fitted to their needs.

Week ending January 12, 1935. The group has been enlarged to seventeen by the revised schedule and meets daily. Work on ballads continued.

It was not many weeks (Mr. Collins wrote) before the class tried some ballads of their own creation. The results were ballads which were very definitely in the tradition.

THE BEGINNING OF A LIBRARY

In the first blueprints for the School there had, of course, been a large library. We could think of few things more important for a rural community than to have a library which could grow out of both the uses of the School and the uses of the adults in the community. There were several steps in its growth which are really incidental to the concept. From the first days of School, when two girls had wished to do library work and we had started with scarcely a dozen books for either pleasure or reference, we were working on the inevitability of a library.[8]

September 17, 1934. Found some publications of the School of Agriculture, West Virginia University, which were to be constantly useful: *West Virginia Trees, West Virginia Weeds*. Took from my own collection of books Gray's *Manual of Botany* and the bulky *Encyclopedia of American Horticulture,* of Bailey.

October 26, 1934. With considerable luck, I found a copy of Britton and Brown, *Illustrated Flora of the Northern United States,* at the University Library, and the plant study of the Botany class is proceeding with a great deal more precision and interest—owing to the successful identification of difficult species.

We used the three volumes strenuously for months the first year and in the following year until late in the spring when the School was finally able to buy them. How the University Library bore with us! But it was a real resource in Science, and History, when our bibliographical lists for purchases remained unfulfilled. It helped us find the kind of materials we needed, while we made our purchases cautiously.

---

[8] For an account of the development of the Library, see Chapter VII, pp. 366-8.

October 19, 1934. In regard to other furnishings—the boys have completed an excellent bookcase for use in holding the High School library and reference books. All classes are in great need of good books for study and reference. Already quite an interest has been aroused in the fiction department, which is just barely large enough to be a beginning. A great deal of the teaching has to be word of mouth, or using the New York *Times*—which is very valuable in both History and Literature, and quite valuable for Science, too.

November 16, 1934. There may be no immediate problem of book storage and library facilities, but we would like to begin some plans for shelves and to have reading space to use as a temporary library until the School is built. Already there is a considerable stock of materials, including a large number of agricultural pamphlets and contributed magazines.

November 23, 1934. The School library has permission to use a room on the third floor of the Mansion.[9]

December 11, 1934. We move to the library quarters with books, magazines, and cards.

December 13, 1934. The library list is expanding at a good pace and is shaping up into its first form. Suggestions for books keep coming in.

December 14, 1934. Another lot of books was contributed last night by the Appletons (one of the homestead families). When our visitors send in the books they promised, the bookshelves which were constructed—six separate cases—will soon be overcrowded.

---

[9] At the top of the old Mansion, under the eaves of the house, in a room where the plaster was falling, with books contributed by teachers and parents, the School Library started.—E.R.C.

A community with no library! [Miss Sheffield writes]. There was a terrible lack. So we put yellow oil cloth on three tables, the "Night School" Shop made some shelves, and the School bought a lamp, and the Library began. As for books, at first our collection was pitiful—those gathered from teachers and homesteaders and those I had purchased from the five-and-ten-cent store. But the children came in droves, especially while they waited for the School bus. We gave out twenty to thirty books a day.

It is a very humble, meager little library, but there is something attractive about it. Felix said when he saw the room fixed up: "It looks like a Park Avenue apartment!" It is a nice-shaped room, and the books we have are cherished.

A RURAL HIGH SCHOOL

The books grew in number,[10] partly by their own power of attraction. Guests as well as parents caught the idea and gave books. The County Superintendent looked at the collection and lent us fifty books.

SCIENCE

In Science the first reactions were varied:

"Living things, tools."
"Shop work, machines; animals, reptiles, world and stars."
"Chemical things, mechanical work."
"Shop work, study of wild life: bird, animal, tree."
"Plant life, flowers and their care."
"Flowers and animals, name and care and use."

WORK IN BOTANY

September 21, 1934. The Science work has been botanical so far. Many fine specimens have been collected and mounted. The Science group has amassed quite a collection of plant and tree specimens and done considerable work in identification and observation.

With just a little more equipment nothing can beat a big shed like this for a Science room. The Science room in the new School building ought not to be elaborately plastered, fixtured, and blackboarded, because experiments thrive best in a plastic atmosphere. But a great deal of care can be lavished on the equipment room and special laboratory storeroom, which is the heart of good Science work.

The use of our shed room for the Farm Products Exhibit has upset the work for two days, but it was a very fitting kind of exhibit for a botany room. Advantage of the imposition was taken to go on a long hike for collection of new specimens.

October 5, 1934. The Botany class is working on the increasingly difficult task of identifying the many plant families that have

---

[10] Three hundred books in June 1935 to twelve hundred a year later. But the point to emphasize is this beginning—the end is not possible without it—and the fact that anything—an attic room, some paint and oilcloth, shelves and tables, and whatever books each can spare, as in our case—is a sufficient start.—E.R.C.

been collected and mounted. If the main family groupings can be learned, then there will be harder work on genera and species. The study of classification is made only as a way of introducing subjects of similarities of plants, or differences, dispersion, structures, uses, and—eventually—laboratory work with the microscope, or plant experiments in hot bed and greenhouse.

Next spring the whole subject opens itself again, with such matters as spring wild flowers, garden and field plantings, and perhaps specialties—such as an experiment to carry over the summer.

It will be helpful to carry the experiment of scientific study over into a study of animals, too, and perhaps have a full piece of work in Biology, but that is not inevitable.

At least, if plans have to be made for equipment and materials to last all year, it will be well to take into account all the needs for Biology, rather than just Botany. The sciences which possibly could be needed most seem to be—Geology and soils, and food and soil Chemistry. The materials for these can be easily included with the orders for Biology.

October 19, 1939. The Botany class this week took one more field trip to see what was the nature of the forests after heavy frosts. Many new species were discovered which previously had been hidden by foliage, or overlooked. Some of the evergreen plants were found which had not been noticed before. Thus our collection of specimens grows.

Sometimes progress was made at strange times and places. On Hallowe'en there was a big evening party in the Assembly Hall—square-dancing, gingerbread, and cider. The Government project manager was there. It was a good moment after meeting him to ask for a large piece of wooded land on the slope of a hill between an old sawmill and the future site of the School. The High School wanted land for outdoor study of plants, care of woodland, and any other uses that might come up.

We did not foresee then that the next spring one group would survey this woodland, and that another would build the outdoor theater on it and spend almost whole days up there in forests of dogwood. Here was inspiration for a long time to come, which gave the community desires to enjoy park lands, and gave the School thoughts about possible economic resources—in the coming age of cellulose. Perhaps the land could be a source of seeds and seedlings for sale. In our first summer we kept the subject of woodlands alive; in the second summer we prepared ground for a plant and shrub nursery.[11]

November 9, 1934. The Botany class, owing to the good fortune of finding Britton's *Illustrated Flora,* has developed considerable skill and ingenuity in identifying the plants of our collection. Up until this week the work has been collecting and hit-or-miss identifying, because our books were so scanty and the subject is really a hard one; but now everyone has a good system of working for identifying new species.

The mounted specimens are now being regrouped on the walls in strict family classifications, and within a week or so our whole collection will be known and classified correctly.

The result should be good scientific training, however, probably better than a course in which all the material is already arranged in a predetermined manner.

December 7, 1934. The class is beginning to prepare for some laboratory work after Christmas by making the equipment which will be needed to carry out experiments with plant growth, and to study the relations of soil and animal life to plant growth.

Even to perform simple experiments, we shall need some more lumber in small amounts; some glass and some flower pots, jars, bottles, pieces of wire screen and cheese cloth, a set of weights for a homemade scale, etc. The class will get more out of the experiments if they have to make their own set-ups, but there are some materials that need to be supplied.

December 14, 1934. The Science room is now also to be used as a reading room for the men who want to study out from problems under Mr. Grimes and me.

It looks as though the Science work should center on plant and animal growth and care, and on organic Chemistry, rather than on abstract Chemistry, Physics, and Biology.

---

[11] See Chapter VII, p. 351.

Plant study was our first enterprise partly because of the interest the students expressed, partly because materials—if not equipment—were available, and partly because the planned agricultural development as a resource for the community naturally demanded our assistance.

We always had less intention to teach Agriculture than to give meaning to it in a rural community. And it influenced us as we expanded into other scientific interests. Chemistry would become the study of materials in the soil and the use of elements within the plant in making sugar or storing starch. Geology would consist of the effects of weather and the formation of the mountain soils; Biology would be concerned with the plant cell, the chemical life cycles, bacteria in soil and in milk and water, or the purity in breeds of animals. It would be impossible to avoid the reality of Science if we began with problems at hand.

DEVELOPMENT OF WORK AND OF INTERESTS

January 11, 1935. The High School has begun using its full-time schedule, with additional groups working in American History and in Home Economics in the Nursery School. The schedule is fuller, and there is a greater division into older and younger groups. Everyone has started in work again after the holidays with considerable concentration and apparently more satisfaction in the distinctions between beginning and advanced work.

The Botany class is beginning experimental work on the cultivation of plants. This work is to be carried right along to the point of outdoor planting and is to be the laboratory work accompanying a more biological study of plant growth. We have already collected some soils, and many different forms of apparatus or equipment are being made in which to experiment, or raise plants.

Each person is going to follow through the whole life-history and science of raising one vegetable, flower, or vine. Some very interesting plants were chosen. All the boys and girls are raising something which will be for home use, such as sweet potato vines, grapes, tomatoes. Research in books and bulletins is accompanying each experiment.

There is a great need for a greenhouse in this sort of work, and it could function for the whole community if there was a class such as this to take care of it. We could build a pretty fair greenhouse 18 x 10 feet, but there would be some expense in glass. It ought to be down where the School is going to be—so probably we had better get along with a hot bed, etc., this year.[12]

January 25, 1935. In Science, the class is making strides with our new equipment in developing a real garden study, coupled as closely as possible with the biology of plant growth and the chemistry of soil and growth. There have been some successful starts in raising seedlings of cabbage, etc., indoors, and in experimenting with local soils. Mr. Grimes said today that the School ought to be the custodian of the hot-bed up beside the Arthur Mansion and study how it can be made useful in stocking the School garden flower beds, and perhaps other gardens, with early plants or seedlings which could be furnished at cost prices.

The classes have been functioning very smoothly and doing a great deal of work. The last Assembly showed that they had their own resources to draw on with very little coaching from teachers for the occasion. The Electricity class had a sound understanding of its telephone system. Others had developed a playlet with singing and pantomime. And, for the main number, the High School English class revived its choral interpretation of Lindsay's "Congo." The High School committee took charge of the program-making and of the Assembly, with almost no help.

There are many different kinds of people in the High School, but they are fairly similar in their receptivity and knack of finding some personal interest in every subject that is offered. This quality constantly fascinates me.

---

[12] The frequent mention of equipment was called out, not only by our needs and lacks, but also by the fact that during these first months of 1934-35 the second plans for the School buildings were being drafted, and the staff was constantly being asked to clarify its needs and desires. Fortunately this demand for a second formulation of school functions came when we were in the midst of working, and the effect was to keep us very plain and definite in our planning. It did not prove possible at this time to purchase the lumber—and especially the glass—needed for the greenhouse which Mr. Beecher and his class wished to build, so they constructed instead window-greenhouses, and used the old hot-bed frames alongside of the Mansion. In the new School buildings, the greenhouse was attached to the Science room.—E.R.C.

February 22, 1935. Many of the boys are opening themselves up to new interests, some of whom were quite passive at the beginning of the year. The Shop work has taken hold of boys and girls, and the painting over here apparently is the greatest source of pleasure. On the whole, the High School can develop and find new interests and expressions in Drama, writing, painting, handwork, and Science because they have few prejudices or negative habits of mind.[13]

April 26, 1935. The High School play—*The Gold Rush*[14]—is the major interest right now, and the class is giving to it so much effort that it should be a perfect ending for History study that has been mainly class study or discussion. The combination of History-Drama-Shop-and-English forces ought to produce a valuable piece of work.

Parks have been started with both the play group, which is clearing ground for a stage, and with the Science group. After these groups—along with the Seventh and Eighth Grades—lead the way, the older people or older workers will have to help with the heavy clearing and building of rustic tables, etc. We have been able to carry the work far enough so that parks will be marked, paths made, and small areas cleared for picnics. If several acres are to be cleared and all dead wood stacked, older people will have to help. Perhaps a beginning is enough to get the idea across this summer, and the heavy clearing will be a late fall and winter job when agriculture is at rest.

May 17, 1935. There seems to be less and less to say about the High School as the History play progresses and makes itself the most prominent activity in the last lap of school.

Some days the High School takes to the woods with lunch, books, paints, and tools for a two-hour piece of work. Not that the gardening and botanical study, or Mathematics and other classes, have ceased, but they are much overshadowed just now by the outdoor theater.

---

[13] This observation of Mr. Beecher's is interesting, if one remembers the negativism of the adults during the first months of adjustment on the homestead. The teachers of the younger children, however, frequently remarked in their diaries on their sweetness of disposition and their kindness toward each other. Life it was, and disastrous experiences, that had unsettled and embittered the grown men. Yet they also, as has been noted, had an imperishable gaiety and capacity for enjoyment, and were unfailingly generous in time of need.—E.R.C.

[14] See Chapter V, pp. 261–3.

A RURAL HIGH SCHOOL

The Science class has a short period in the morning for study of Botany and two afternoons, alternating with games, for outside work on the hot bed for School flower gardens. The boys have used the surveying instruments they made in Mathematics to lay out the flower beds.

TEACHERS AND CURRICULUM

As a staff we had worked together in Kentucky, or learned to work together in the new environment, in such a way that in spite of many inadequacies we felt we supplemented each other sufficiently well to discover by combined effort all the kinds of work which would be useful and desirable in a community.

At Arthurdale, as in Kentucky, the many lacks in personnel perforce drew from each of us whatever gift or ability we possessed, and exercised it to the full. This fact and the variety of demands upon us stretched and enriched our capacities as teachers, and as people.

March 29, 1935. School here is very much real life, at least from a teacher's point of view. The School is just one phase among many spheres of activity.

At the beginning of the week, there were seed orders of the Farm Co-operative to complete, and the organization of thirty people into a play. Then there was the need to revise the Constitution and By-Laws for the Men's Club immediately, so that they could be mimeographed. Then, because of certain confusion in the parts for the people in the play, there had to be immediate revisions so that the players could meet on Thursday for a rehearsal. Wednesday night was devoted to the Men's Club meeting. Thursday turned out to be a fairly calm day, and some thought could be given to planning for the High School in view of the changes in the season and the possibility of changes in the schedule if a school bus begins to operate for this school only.

It looks as though—intentionally or not—we are building up quite a Science department. The addition of Esterley [the young teacher who joined us for a few months as an assistant teacher], whose interest is chiefly Physics, fills a big gap. With him for Physics, Harry Carlson for Electricity, Mechanics, and Chemistry,

Carl Saunders for Mathematics, and me for Biology and Geology—we are covering at least quite a few subjects.

We now need to develop a demand for continuous scientific study throughout the School and "Night School," and to build up a scientific approach to agriculture and animal husbandry.

To balance the scientific side, we have already under way the Music-Drama-Poetry and History study and discussion, and the beginnings of Home Economics in helping out at the Nursery School.

This is the tenor of the record. It reveals here and there among a multitude of daily details how our plans and practice and observation of the physical and social environment were fusing into a single desire for a school. From my angle, I saw three sides of the growing organism: the importance of Science in studying our environment; the formation of a Library as the building of a school-community relation, in which the High School took an active part; and the relation of the functioning of a higher school in its community to the design for a building which adolescents and adults could use. Though all of us had gone to our new surroundings with some of our ideas for layout fairly thought through, I know that the course of the first year gave us the check-up which led the way to a usable building. It suggested and aided functioning, because functioning designed it.

Section 2: The School as the Center of Resources and of Understandings

THE NEW SCHOOL BUILDINGS

Elsie Ripley Clapp

BUILDING THE SCHOOL

The High School, with the other parts of the School, moved into its new quarters in the fall of the second year. Ground had been broken for the School buildings in the late spring. The laying of the foundations of the High School and Recreation Buildings—the first to get under way—had been watched with intense interest. The work absorbed most of the homestead labor and, until mid-summer, used also the older boys. Since, as Mr. Beecher said, "the plan for the High School Building must be seen in its relation to the rest of the School, as it should be evident that the High School story is inseparable from the story of the whole School and from the community," it seems desirable to describe here the layout of the new School buildings and the process of their conception.

Plans for the buildings for the "new school" at Arthurdale were first conceived in February 1934, when Eric Gugler, the first architect of the project, generously scrapped his tentative plans and tackled the job of designing functional buildings for use in community education; and when the West Virginia School Committee in its Plan[15] for the school expressed its desire for buildings "not the traditional type, but rather simple buildings of two or three units which will be homelike in character and allow the maximum amount of sun and air." Work on the planning of these school buildings went forward all through the summer of 1934. However, these plans were not executed, and the School was opened in September in the old Arthur Mansion and in a room and the two supply sheds at the Town Center.

In the fall, a new start was made—this time with another architect—Mr. Steward Wagner (Mr. Gugler having been called away on another piece of work). The question of the site of the School was reviewed and a second set of plans was drafted. By the time we had lived through the opening months of the work at the school and all the community activities had got under way—the health program, the canning and the cooking of school lunches, the Men's and Women's Clubs, the

---

[15] See Chapter II, Section 1, pp. 72–5.

recreational program of plays and singing groups, square dances and the dance orchestra, entertainments and athletics —we felt we knew clearly just what kind of accommodations in the way of buildings for a community school were needed. Interestingly enough, however, the only significant changes we made in the first plan were in the placing of units in a different relation to each other, owing to the configuration of the land, and in the assigning of certain activities to one building unit rather than to another. Our work and living did not alter, but rather confirmed, the plans that were first made from what we had learned of community school needs in Kentucky, and from our first observation of the needs at Arthurdale.

The second set of plans was not executed, either. It had been decided in Washington that the buildings for the School must come within a certain figure. With this amount, which was less than one-third of the original estimate, and perhaps half the sum a town expends upon one high school building, we had to meet the needs of a nursery school, and a primary, an elementary, and a high school designed for six hundred children, together with the medical, social, educational, and recreational needs of the community. Only Mr. Wagner's sound knowledge, expert resourcefulness, and generosity made it possible to do this on so small an allowance. It was an assistance, too, to have come to know what was needed so completely and exactly that there were no hesitations and confusions between necessities and desirabilities. By Mr. Wagner's ingenuity, all the necessities were met, even within the reduced figure. This third set of plans was approved, the buildings were erected during the summer, and we moved in for the opening of School in September 1935, although work on two of the buildings and on details of construction continued through the first half of the year.[16]

---

[16] See *Progressive Education*, April 1938, pp. 304–15, for a parallel account of the School buildings. (Footnote refers to this book.)

The School Itself a Village

The School site was a long, sunny meadow under the lee of the Mansion hill and across the road from the Town Center. The first year spent on the hill top in the old Arthur Mansion taught us the value at that altitude and in that climate of protection from the high winds of winter. All day the sun lay in the meadow and the Mansion hill sheltered the School. In accordance with modern practice, a unit building plan was followed which would allow additions over the years, and which gave the greatest amount of sun and air—the last item important especially in a community where health rehabilitation was a primary object.

The Recreation Building, as the building whose games and entertainments would be most attended by the public, was placed nearest the County Road and adjoined the athletic fields which fronted on it. This building consisted of a combination auditorium and gymnasium with a full-sized basketball floor, showers and dressing rooms, a stage for plays and concerts, with space in the wings for work on scenery and properties and costumes, and an orchestra practice room above. The High School, which used the Recreation Building the most, was placed next to it.

The "School Center Building" was situated between the High School and the Elementary School Building. In it were located the School cafeteria and kitchen, the Home Economics rooms and the community canning kitchen, the doctor's offices, the School "bank" and bookstore and its business and typing rooms, as well as the Director's office.

Beyond the Elementary School Building, still farther from the public road, was the Primary Building; and, more secluded still, at the end of the meadow, the Nursery School and its playgrounds.[17]

The School was, in effect, a little village in itself.

---

[17] See Chapter IV, pp. 192-4.

The buildings were functionally planned in every detail, the only consideration being the use to which they were to be put. The dimensions and arrangements of each classroom, and its situation in relation to all the other rooms in the building, were determined by the educational needs of the children at each age level. The teachers and I, working in constant collaboration with Mr. Wagner, planned the dimensions and arrangements of the rooms, their ventilation and lighting and their equipment. Miss Jessie Stanton, who was the Director of the Nursery School, planned that building and equipment.[18]

The Primary and Elementary Buildings

The Primary and Elementary Buildings were identical in plan. Each was designed to accommodate ultimately 150 children, when all the families should have moved onto the project. Each was a long, low one-story building, open to the sun and air on all sides, containing five [19] large classrooms, so that there could—at need—be a division of two of the three grades. The two end-rooms, which had the largest floor space, were for the two younger classes in both the Primary and Elementary groups. The three rooms in between had high windows on the inside wall that opened onto a sunny corridor, whose front was entirely of glass. Each room had an alcove workroom opening off the larger room, for bench work or for a separate reading or study group. Each room also had a sink, so that the lavatories were relieved of children washing up for lunch, and the problem of cleaning up after painting or cooking or bench work was made easier. The ceilings were high, so that each room had a sense of space and peace. The walls were lined with celotex, with wood stripping. For fire protection each building had three entrances—or exits.

---

[18] See Chapter IV, pp. 173–4, 182, 209.
[19] In rural areas, registration is heaviest in primary and in elementary grades.

HIGH SCHOOL QUARTERS IN 1934-35
Supply Shed next to Nursery School Building

ASSEMBLY HALL AT THE TOWN CENTER AND DISPLAY ROOM
of the Mountaineer Craftsmen Co-operative Association
Used by the High School the First Year

NEW HIGH SCHOOL BUILDING, 1911.

The High School Building

The High School Building was planned to accommodate the six upper grades. The classrooms on the first floor of the building housed the Ninth, Tenth, Eleventh, and Twelfth Grades, each separately, and served also as rooms for Mathematics, History, Social Science studies, and English. The Seventh and Eighth Grades each had a separate room also on this ground floor. The School Shop, which was located in this building, was dropped below the first-floor level to save the expense of a reinforced or concrete floor. A lumber room and an electrical room opened from it. A big barn door at the end of the Shop permitted the unloading of lumber and the entry of farm wagons for repair.

The Science room, at the other end of the building, was—as Mr. Beecher desired—a big "shed" room that provided space for varied activities, with windows on three sides and a greenhouse opening from it at one end. It was not arranged or furnished like the usual laboratory or Science classroom, but equipped with long work tables, work benches, and shelves. A smaller room opening from it was designed for science equipment that needed to be protected from the free uses of the larger room. For the first year, it housed not only the School's precious microscope and supply of chemicals, beakers, etc., but also cages for snakes, a beehive, and aquaria.

Upstairs, a half-story accommodated the School and Community Library, a printing room where the community newspaper was issued, a bindery and editorial room, a pottery room, and a large art room shared by all the High School classes.

BUILDING FOR OLDER STUDENTS AND ADULTS

On the architect's plans the High School Building was labeled "Building for Older Students and Adults," which expressed the right idea, but in truth every building was for their use and used by them: notably the Nursery School, where the Well Baby Clinics were held, and where the mothers—and fathers—came and went all day; the Recreation Building, with its basketball floor—"the best in the State," the homesteaders declared—its stage for plays and concerts used by adult groups, and its orchestra practice room where the square-dance orchestra rehearsed; the School Center, in whose kitchen and lunchroom the mothers prepared the School lunches, and which contained the doctor's offices, the savings "Bank" that carried community accounts, and the Home Economics rooms—canning kitchen, sewing room, and food demonstration room—used by the women in the afternoons and evenings; as well as the High School Building itself, whose Science room and greenhouse, and whose School and Community Library, were frequented by the older men and women.

While the Town Center across the way, with the Craftsmen's workshops, forge and weaving rooms, and Co-operative General Store and Postoffice, as well as the houses—theirs and ours—were the scene of learning and teaching as much as the group of buildings called "The School," the School buildings helped forward all the learning activities. It was as if the idea that was embodied in the design of the School buildings was also expressed in the structure of our lives, the pattern of our living; or as if the School buildings, to the extent to which they were geared to the ongoing activities and interests of the homestead, gave impetus and meaning to the community practice of "living and learning."

We made the discovery on moving into the new School buildings that a provision for enterprises, no matter how simple, actually furthers them. For instance, the window boxes, which the Science class constructed outside their windows in the Supply Shed that housed the High School the first year, made sensible and understandable the greenhouse which opened out of the Science room in the new High School Building; but it was the greenhouse, by its adequate provision for plant growth, that helped develop the study of that growth, expanded and deepened it. So, the High School Building itself increased the vitality and individuality of the community High School. Similarly, we realized with each group in the School the way a building may shape and expand the character of the life and work that goes on in it. The importance of functional buildings in the operation and understanding of community education cannot be exaggerated.

The High School in 1935-36
George Beecher

THE PROBLEM OF THE OLDER BOYS AND GIRLS

At an early date, our development was complicated by the group of irregularly schooled boys and girls who were just as deserving of attention as the steady ones, and harder to deal with. Set standards and prescribed practices are just the sort of barriers which shut out these young people from the advantages of constructive work. They were not "school material." They were CCC and WPA material. But we were determined to find where the School was at fault if it could not take on their problem.[20]

The conditions of the moment had strong influence on our dealing with them. In the first year it seemed that the boys could get their feet on the ground best if they learned construction, working on or in the new environment while also attending a few evening classes in "Night School." [21] In the second year, the NYA–WPA made it possible to direct work that centered at the School. Recognizing the economic and social needs of this group of young people made us grasp at chances of work for them, and at chances of making the higher

---

[20] See Chapter VII, pp. 343-7.
[21] Chapter II, Section 2, pp. 103-7.

school as much a home base for them as for those who were both younger and more regularly schooled.[22] The High School Building could be for them, too. It could and would be for adults, although each new expansion added to our work.

WORK AT THE HIGH SCHOOL IN 1935–36

Attendance was considerably larger this year, and included Grades Seven to Twelve. And more varied perhaps, because the irregularly schooled boys and girls came in larger numbers, now that jobs for them had been discontinued, and also because new families had moved into the community all during the year.

Beginning somewhat as in the first year, with the need of creating equipment and resources, we took up what tools and books we had, walked the countryside, talked, wrote, calculated, and prepared to work along lines we had thought of or started the year before.[23]

There was the Library, a steadily growing number of books, and a small library fund which made it possible for the classes to secure some particularly necessary book and for us to see new stories appear among the well-worn books on the shelves. Then there was the study of communication—electrical, visual record, and printing—which symbolized to us both Language and History and a serious community problem. In the previous winter we had seen how hard it was to communicate—no telephone, biased or inaccurate newspapers from the outside, rumor rampant, expression at a low ebb, misinformation common. The School would have had to be blind if it had to stumble on the subject of communication to discover it. Previously, as in many schools, we had valued the subject of communication because of its instructional and cultural significance, and

---

[22] Chapter VII, pp. 347–9.
[23] See "Curriculum, 1935–36" and "Curriculum, 1934–35," Appendix III.

had tested it in that light, but now its social significance was becoming apparent.[24]

It would be possible to continue thus with each piece of work which thrust itself upon a school that is looking for its functions in a community. Where canning and the preparation of home-grown foods and the making and repair of clothes are perhaps half the subsistence of families, Home Economics is too obviously needed to talk about, though its special applications to each locality may be worth study. Similarly, carpentry, construction, farming, and mechanics present unmistakable opportunities for work. But it is not always easy to see how a subject, however common its name, can both touch the reality of living and be a field of a cultural experience. If I describe two less "obvious" subjects it will, perhaps, explain how a reality may be a cultural experience and at the same time will suggest the kind of use we made of the tool Shop.

The two subjects are Music and Science. The beginnings of our work in Science were related earlier.[25] Music was mentioned as consisting of singing. Its growth was phenomenal in the summer as a result of the efforts and interest put into the first Music Festival.[26] Not the mere existence of Music and Science, but the intensification of their meaning in our special environment, is the theme of the second year.

Music: Instrument-Making

The summer had provided more than just a stimulus to singing and fiddling. Several boys and girls, who had begun to express their interest in music and their desire for it by studying the problems of instrument-making, spent long hot hours gouging out fiddle backs and other parts of instruments.

---

[24] See Chapter V, pp. 268–72.
[25] See above, this chapter, pp. 291–7.
[26] Chapter V, pp. 242–8.

But it would take better wood and finer tools to produce instruments that would play.[27]

In the fall, the interest went right on. There was now a good prospect of securing the wood and the tools. Did anyone foresee how long it would take to make an instrument? Or what effect it would have on the individuals who made instruments or on our feeling for the music and musical-instrument craft of that region? Everything was to be worked out and interpreted.

The group which had begun the work were now the Ninth Grade, but it is easier to think of them as the instrument-makers, for to that work flowed much of their attention and energy from History, Mathematics, and Shop. They had a share in Science, of course, and read and wrote and played games. But their achievement in Music was the embodiment of what the people of that region felt about it. Here were genuine fiddles; here was the very basis of stringed instruments, singing, and dancing.

This work on instruments was not on the order of an extra-curricular hobby. It took hold of Mathematics and thrashed out the relationship between notes on the scale and the positions of frets on the neck of a mandolin. It was fractions, decimals, ratio, and proportion. It supplanted History and gave its own interpretation to the Middle Ages. Shop periods were increased in number and given over entirely to instruments.

Lest anyone think that too much time was given to Music, I will mention the record of this same group in Science. There never was a clearer instance of how people's capacity for work increases as their interest increases. The group (part of the Seventh-Eighth Grade described in the first section of this chapter),[28] which was far from being of high rank scholastically or free from quirks and humors, began to be characterized by

---

[27] Chapter V, pp. 222-6.
[28] See pp. 282-6.

the ability to get work done, to move about with considerable freedom, and to absorb itself in a variety of interests. In Science, this group was the one selected to carry on the investigation of plant life which had been started by the corresponding class the year before.[29] But the whole subject of the Sciences in the second year needs to be described before I go into the discussion of the details of one branch of them.

SCIENCE IN STUDY OF THE ENVIRONMENT

In the fall of the second year, the Sciences in the different High School groups were studied separately. This is inevitable unless one can foresee how they will fit together. Not that one cannot map out a completely articulated program ahead of time, but then the relationships are most likely not to be real, but only projected upon the scene by the instructor. If one's environment were an open book there would be little opportunity for Science. As in the preceding fall, we could begin on new problems at hand besides plant life, but we assumed no fixed attitude toward their relationships until we thought we had discovered them.

The youngest High School group—the Seventh Grade—began with a different feature of the environment: the weather. Its importance for the School, after the weather station had been constructed in Shop and barometers made in Science class, was that a study of the environment was being made which was to be Geology: the formation of the soil, of the physical features of the land, of the pottery clay, of the pure glass sand, of the environments for plant life, of the coal which everyone knew or could see not many feet below ground, of the limestone, of soil acidity, of the minerals and raw materials used in chemistry. We did not make these studies in two years. We did not even go very deep into weather and the forces that transform the face of the earth. But we were begin-

---

[29] See pp. 291–4.

ning to interpret the direction in which this group was moving, and what Chemistry, plant and animal study, living on the soil, or working in industry would mean for it as it moved on through new experiences.

The next High School group—the Eighth Grade—began with electricity and communication. History, Science, Shop—and we may as well say everything, because Language, Mathematics, even Drama, contributed—all became either a background for, or a direct illumination of, the work.

The group itself was interested in hydro-electric power, for it knew something about it from seeing or hearing of two near-by stations. That is a good interest because it involves information about the physics of water and turbines, as well as about the generation of electricity and its economic aspect; but it was somewhat difficult to demonstrate—particularly in the region near the School, where the problem of drainage was so much more serious than that of water storage. Nevertheless, that interest kept alive the whole year, and trips to both a steam generating plant and a hydro-electric plant were tremendous stimuli.

Good History, or "Social Science," if you want to call it that, is to be found in the study of Electricity, its applications, and its use in communication. What is Social Science if not to work with experiences of learning such as these? What is a Shop for if not to design and work materials into a telephone? What is Mathematics for if not to measure and calculate? When the class had to lay out on sheet metal the pattern for a telephone mouthpiece, they gained a real respect for Mathematics, since it provided a permanent way of stating the relationship between circumferences of circles. These are not details you can predict, though they are the sort you expect. You could predict them for the next year, but if you did so without the hope of discovering equally valuable new details or applications, you would be slipping into the rut which does not characterize either learning or the practice of science.

The growth of the curriculum is something abstruse, unless you analyze the details of how it takes place. It is both the arrangement of studies to meet current needs each year and also the understanding of the status of a whole community's thought. The class is an agent doing a job which won't need to be done in the same way again. There will be a new meaning to work for, a slightly different view of the environment.

If that is not easy to perceive in regard to the subject of electricity, I will mention a few of the problems which faced the community. The homesteaders, who paid a rather high electric rate, and were eager to make use of electrical appliances in the home as well as in tool shop and recreational buildings, had to know the measurement of electricity, the costs, and the factors in production. This field for learning and investigation was practically untouched. And if one group did ever so little in figuring the costs of home lighting and in understanding the principles of the telephone, the next group working in Electricity would see the stage reached by the preceding group and also something of what remained undone. That is the basis of the growth. It is also the only significant test of a school.

The subject of Biology was divided between two groups: the Ninth Grade, which was doing the plant study; and the next older group, Grade Ten, which was doing something quite different. It is almost unnecessary to apologize for using the word "biology" because of its lofty connotation. Biologists would be the first to hold the term to the study of living things, whether in the field or in the laboratory, whether with elaborate classifications or with simple ones. Schools can hardly avoid being amateurish, but they do not need to bury their heads in the presence of the life that is going on around them.

If what I am saying seems to be away from my previous remark that the problem of economic security of the community gave great impetus to the work of the School in just this matter of research, I am returning to it through the discussion of Sciences with the older groups. This fact worked retroactively in our interpretation of all the Sciences and gave them an intensification of cultural, social, and economic meaning that has only partly been developed.

In the Plant Study we knew where to begin in the collection of specimens, mounting them, and studying their relations, structures, uses. But two new major problems confronted us: one was the 18-foot greenhouse off the Science room; the other was that there was no good record for the plant life of that locality. People somewhere knew about greenhouses and about the flora of West Virginia, but right there and then there was neither knowledge of these nor even recognition that something was lacking. Here could be work, usefulness, learning. Again, the conditions and events had much to do with the selection of which problems to take up. The presence of an agriculturalist on the project led us to see in him the demonstrator of greenhouse technique. The purchase of a small hand printing press for the School paved the way for concentrating full attention on the production of the record of plant life.

This was the piece of work which the Ninth Grade found time to establish: to collect the specimens and the facts about them, to write them up and set them in type and print copies for everyone in the class and for the School Library, and then to draw and color the illustrations and arrange the mountings of specimens on each sheet, which was large for just this purpose. Even if only some fifty species were completed, or in the process of completion, here was a record which it would take many classes to finish, and which would expand to take in new interests. The subject of plant experimentation and growth was yet to be studied after we had watched the handling of the greenhouse in its first year's attempt to produce plants for local gardens.

There was some analogy, of course, in doing with a study of animals and animal life what had been done with plant life. It was fairly certain that at least domestic animals and insects were important in the rural setting, if not the fauna in general. It was not long, that fall, before opportunities appeared. Another class had been wandering along a marshy stream and found the water teeming with wrigglers. They collected a jarful and brought them into the laboratory. Many individuals, including adults who heard about our interest in local fauna, sent in mud-puppies, snakes, spiders, water beetles, etc. It was difficult to house them all; we had to work upon pens, cages, and aquaria. This was the beginning of an enthusiasm, which lasted into the following summer and infected the Fourth Grade, who built an outdoor aquarium, and a summer group, who took up the study of insects with eagerness.[30] We had foreseen that the Sciences among the older groups should logically extend themselves down through the whole School (as well as into adult life), and were now finding that the younger children were showing as much initiative in the matter as we.

The wrigglers lived actively before the eyes of the class and metamorphosed and one by one flew up to the gauze that covered them as full-fledged mosquitoes. Malaria was of little importance in that region, but water and drainage were, and so was insect life, in the menace of bean beetles if nothing else.

The discovery of a bee tree one night by some boys in the class turned attention to the more constructive efforts of insects. Men had cut the tree down and taken most of the honey, but the bees were still there cleaning up. The boys

---

[30] See Chapter VII, pp. 381–2.

gathered them and brought them in. Here was something out of the wild to study; here, too, was a suggestion that perhaps the enterprise of keeping bees could be built up for some of the local families. Bees cannot, of course, be made an economic asset without considerable effort and skill, but neither can they without a beginning being made and without investigation.

Within a few weeks the matter of the economic future of the community was the problem uppermost in everyone's mind. It seemed to boil up in December when winter intensifies its inevitable challenge: if you get through this winter how about the next and then the next? None of us could help feeling that any investigating we did would be to the good.[31] It was an opportunity for learning, but even more a responsibility. Where were resources? What do you do with materials, even if you find them? What are the markets, the costs? These were questions which invaded or pervaded the Sciences, Mathematics, the discussions in the Social Sciences, the contacts with the older boys and girls, the guidance of the NYA activities,[32] and our thinking about the use of the buildings and grounds.

In a book where there was information about mosquitoes there was another chapter about bacteria in milk. Would it be too hard to study milk, to get ready for the day when milk production was to be a source of income for the community?[33] The oldest Science group was studying a basis for Inorganic Chemistry. Let them investigate the chemistry of glass-making and other industrial processes which could take their raw materials from our very ground, or near at hand. Are such fields exhausted? That is something to find out. It is the pressure of such stimuli that intensifies work and helps bring out relationships in the course of action, and

---

[31] Chapter VII, pp. 348–55.
[32] *Ibid.*, pp. 343–8.
[33] *Ibid.*, pp. 352, 383–4.

A RURAL HIGH SCHOOL 315

tests them. If the first problem had been to distribute the Sciences among groups, it was now the second problem to see in what ways Chemistry was implicit in the geology of soils, in electricity, in living plants, in the use of plants for food or for humus or for industry, in animal life, in promoting health, in industrial processes. Obviously Chemistry is not a matter of a year's study. We would build up a knowledge of it through many years, just as we would with a knowledge of living things, and a knowledge of economics. Here was an undertaking to which could be coupled our work with young adults, our interest in seeing the community secure, and our intention that the School produce graduates who would take a place in the community as agents of the School to keep alive its lines of growth in community life.

UNDERSTANDING AND RESEARCHES

In the course of the second year we were able to watch the Sciences rise to a major position among subjects because of their relationships with economics, with the investigation of resources, health, dairying, the water supply, soil, farming, and with the understanding of history and the use of mathematics. A change in the curriculum to this extent was likely to produce other changes which we would need to watch. Other lines of work, such as American History and the study of the present social and cultural environment, were developing investigations and understandings from different points of view. Communication, since our acquisition of the handpress, was ready to enter the field of printing for the community.[34]

In this description of the work of the High School in its second year I would like to give some instances of research and to show how it affected the work and the direction of

[34] See Chapter V, pp. 268–72.

SCIENCE SURVEY

Community	Geology	Botany	Biology	Chemistry	Physics Mechanics & Electricity	Mathematics
Shrubs as economic resource Book record of local plant life Bees	Weather instruments & phenomena	Local plant life collection & study Methods of preservation arrangement and relating	Natural history of this region—materials to study & classify as method of study of animal life & environment—bees in the wild & under domestication	Basis of inorganic materials & properties of elements & compounds	Practical knowledge of electricity	Economics of plant produce and mineral resources
Glass—natural resources & as industry	Effects on earth, soil, environment, of natural forces	Research and record of local botany printing & writing Laboratory drawing	What is place of biology in community? Life history of mosquito as biological basis of study of environment; disease, parasitism, life process of animal organism Water supply & bacteria	Chemistry & craft of glass making	Wiring of home and measure of electric fuel	Metric system Measures weights and calculation
Natural resources and soil tests	Earth's crust Fundamentals needed as basis for soils and local resources		Milk and bacteria Useful and harmful sterilizing	Research & experiment in a science and craft and industry	Water power and electricity	
Greenhouse and garden plant production	Visual and plastic studies in strata and erosion	Watching greenhouse operated professionally and scientifically	Cultures and incubation growth, & environment & chemical actions of living organisms, as seen in bacteriology	Acid-proof finish Mirrors Etching	Electric communication, transmission of signals, voice, etc.	See Mathematics Chart (Appendix V)

Community	Geology	Botany	Biology	Chemistry	Physics Mechanics & Electricity	Mathematics
						See Mathematics Chart (Appendix V)
Bacteria & disease Water supply Milk supply & products Chickens Agricultural-economics	Drainage Sewerage disposal Seepage	Write-up of use of greenhouse and its possibilities	Chicken incubation for study in another life history & community livelihood	Laboratory work in composition of glass, furnaces, science in life of community	Mechanics of simple machine, such as pulley, wheel principle, and gasoline motor levers, etc.	
Local strata	Magnetism in earth? Deep well-log, coal, lime, etc. iron		Analyzing the factors in biological study as science: metric system enzymes food making & use in plant-animal chemistry particularly sugars and cellulose in agricultural community			
Construction and possibilities for industry & plant products	Quarrying Clay deposits Tests for acid soil, etc.				Screw press	
Plant food Animal food & growth in agricultural-economics						
Physiology of animal life—human and domestic			Practical laboratory analysis of wells and local drainage & milk supplies			

Sequence of course and revisions in curriculum extending through High School—older boys—adults.

work. By research here I mean the "active research" of living in a community, observing how a school can function in its life, and then slowly altering the course of the school tradition until it approaches the desired function. The instance I wish to use illustrates particularly growth of the individual in the discovery of environment. It is a sample of the work done in investigating the glass industry and its possibilities as a source of income. The study was one in Chemistry, in History, and in a craft or branch of industry. It required books that were both scarce and high-priced, contacts with the Department of Chemistry at the University of West Virginia, drawing in men among the parents who had been glass-blowers, and even digging in one man's basement for the best kind of clay for molds that the region afforded. It was easier to make trips to near-by glass factories, and they were helpful in presenting the class with blow pipes or giving information about the sources of raw materials.

It would be easy to quote essays which were written by the group on the materials of glass-making or aspects of its history. These all show that factual writing and even analysis of processes are by-products of a group's work. The following piece of writing is more on the side of understanding which I mentioned. It turned up, not as you might expect, in our observations on the sciences, but in our research on language. In studying the uses and the development in language it was necessary to look first to see what was going on that was material for expression, to see what uses people made of language through the experiences of learning. It happened that one field of expression was the Science work. This was just one piece of evidence that language ability was improving simultaneously with intense interest in a science.

The following report of the glass investigation under Carson V. Ryan, a member of the High School staff, was written by one of the students at my request several months after the work had ended:

Experimenting with Glass

During the second half of the 1935–36 school year the Eleventh and Twelfth Grades spent half their entire time in the making and studying about glass.

When glass was first introduced to the above mentioned grades, every member of the Chemistry class knew very little about the inside facts of the manufacture of glass.

The first step was to know a little about the ancient glass-makers and how they obtained the raw materials for the small batches they made up in the manufacture of glass. This type of information was a little difficult to find and books had to be borrowed from the West Virginia Library of Morgantown, which contained only a few copies of the books required for the study of glass.

After finding all the valuable information that could be found from a few good books, the students thought that it would be more interesting to make a trip to a local glass factory and really watch the step-by-step process in making glass. The trip to the glass factory was new to many of the students and they had no idea on how glass was manufactured before they entered the factory. Many of the students really picked up some fine pointers when visiting the factory, while others went as "passengers" just to enjoy a pleasure trip, and when the work was started it was unclear for the ones that paid no attention to the employees while visiting the factory.

The most complicated job was to erect a glass furnace that would produce enough heat to melt the glass compound. Some suggested using carbons from a dry cell battery and making an arc-furnace, which would act as a heating element to produce the required heat in order to melt the compound. Now it was up to the entire class to make plans and make simple drawings as to how the arc-furnace would be made. After a few days a simple plan was adopted by the class and the following pieces listed below were required to make the furnace.

1. Two old carbons from a dry cell battery that would be approximately 10 or more inches long and ½ or more inches in diameter.

2. A crucible that would stand very, very high temperature.

3. A box-like form composed of cement and fire brick. This form was about 18 inches square and 8 inches high.

4. Sand to be filled around the crucible and within the above mentioned form.

5. A resister that would control the voltage, transformer and also a self-adjusting screw, which adjusted the carbons.

6. Other minor things needed in the construction of the arc-furnace were as follows: clips for the end of each carbon; electric wires; pieces of pipe, approximately 3/4 inches or less in diameter; tin; nails; screws; and wood.

Four boys of the Chemistry class worked constantly on the arc-furnace and within two weeks time it was completed. Now everything was set to try out the arc-furnace one morning. The previous day a few girls mixed a cheap compound for glass, then the compound was poured into the crucible with small bits of glass. The electricity was turned on, the carbons began to hum. After waiting patiently for a few minutes the lid was removed from the crucible and we found that heat wasn't produced sufficiently to melt the bits of glass and the glass compound. The arc-furnace was tried over and over until a definite study was made on the amount of heat required to act on the mixture.

Now something else had to be tried, and a few knew gas or coal would supply enough heat in making glass. The question was, "How would it be possible to maintain a suitable coal furnace without running into large expense?" The next problem was, "How could gas be obtained when there isn't any local company that could supply gas for this locality?" We were in a position that would be given up by many schools and other individuals, but we found that compressed gas known as "Thermoline" was the most economical and best source of fuel for making glass in small quantities. Now we were getting down to "brass tacks," as some people would call it. An air-compressor was installed in a suitable place, two tanks of Thermoline brought in, pipes were put in, a gas furnace was borrowed by the instructor, more chemicals were given to the Chemistry class, a regular blow pipe and a mold were borrowed, and many other little things that are needed in making glass were bought, borrowed, or given by other individuals. The installation of the above mentioned equipment was done by the boys of the chemistry class, and in the mean time the girls made up some simple compounds for making glass. Various color schemes were tried, and many were interested in different colors that occurred when the glass compound was being melted.

After everything was ready for a first test, many of the students really believed that this type of furnace would also fail, but after seeing how the bits of glass were melted into a liquid form they really were becoming more interested and excited and couldn't wait to see what would happen when a mass of this melted glass would be picked up on a blow pipe. A great deal of time was spent on blowing glass. Perhaps some one may think that large fancy glasses were made by the group and that they possessed the skill of a good skillful glass worker, but this is not true. The glass making by the group was just an example to show each and every individual of the class how glass is really made. We didn't have time, annealing ovens, grinders, and so forth. It took time for the glass to form because we didn't have high glass making furnaces, and only small quantities could be made up at one time.

In order to make it clear to a person who had no experience with glass, I would like to describe the simple method we used in making glass.

> The first step is to mix a glass compound and add bits of glass to it. Then the compound and the bits of glass were poured into a crucible. Now heat was applied and it took several hours until the compound was melted into a liquid form; here the glass is now ready to be blown.

Every student of the group found it a great deal of fun to blow glass into simple and queer shapes. The blowing of the glass gave us an idea as to how glass is blown, but I will not say that every one of us possessed ability in blowing glass. I am quite sure that we all learned more by working with the materials directly than we would if it was read from a book.

I started to etch glass and with the aid of two helpers we accomplished a lot during the few remaining weeks of school. Etching is very simple to understand and if the directions are followed closely the result will be a success. Etching was done on bottles containing chemicals such as: Sodium hydroxide, hydrochloric acid, alcohol, sulphuric acid, and various other acids.

Some of the girls experimented with mirrors. Time after time a little error was made and the entire work was simply wasted, but after doing it a few times they were more successful and the result was good.

As a summary of what was accomplished by the group I would say that if one was willing to learn about making of glass and other steps following the process, he or she really had the opportunity to do so. Surely every one will have some idea on how glass is made, or how etching is done and the problems of making a good mirror by following the directions very closely. As a matter of fact I learned a great deal and I hope that the rest of the class did the same.

My comment to James after he had batted this out on a hot July afternoon was that it was a pretty good account. He answered: "Yes, it's a pretty good article." He was a regular contributor to *The News,* during its swaddling days as well as later in its summer community issues. Every Thursday evening he came to the *News* editoral room upstairs in the High School Building next to the Library and wrote up the athletics for the past week. He was a good typesetter, too. He was well on the way to overcoming the handicaps to style in language caused by the use of Czecho-Slovakian or broken English by his parents.

The above sample will do for Science. It was a step in one branch of the subject, one piece of the expression of it. We had no doubts about the immense amount that remained to be done in the development of Science. Glass sand, which was common in West Virginia, was just one lead into the geology of the area. On our shelves in the Science room we had the "log" of the deep well just being drilled more than 700 feet into the earth, a sample of each stratum in the descent. Each house in the community had a well and its own sewage disposal system. The geosyncline on which we were located was a factor favorable in drilling the wells, but the need for artificial drainage of the Glade and several unfavorable tests of the drinking water suggested that here was a problem in science and public health that would require long study.

A combination of factors—interest of the County Board of Health (through the collector of water samples) and of the project engineer of water and drainage, and the project manager, who worried over the possibility of unsafe drinking water, and our own growing activity in community health, whether through the doctor or through the laboratory in the School—was sufficient to cause a concentration of effort on the School laboratory. Equipment and help was to come through all the above-mentioned interested agencies. It was along the same line that we had tried to further through the study of Biology, our handling and testing of milk, and our investigation of bacteria and community health. A laboratory was set up, equipment was ordered, and a subject of study was prepared for the following year that would influence our work with Geology, Chemistry, and Biology.

MATHEMATICS DISCUSSED

If it was possible the second year to bowl along in the Sciences, there were some rough spots in Mathematics. We brought the hard-going on ourselves by opening up the subject to discussion.

The record of our investigation of the uses of mathematics was prepared by Carl Saunders on a large sheet of paper to which all the teachers contributed their experiences of the needs and practices of mathematics in class and shop and laboratory, or kitchen and bookstore and bank.[35] This was preliminary to discussing what we would need to plan. We needed full descriptions of the occasions for the use of mathematics and of the principles involved, and we needed an ac-

---

[35] See Second Draft of Mathematics Chart, Appendix V.

count of the beginning of the learning of mathematics from the youngest grades up to the High School.

It was clear that in Shop everyone did a great deal of measuring in situations that were not the same as those in a Mathematics class. Where really does a person learn to measure? By the seventh and eighth grade, the Arithmetic studies had made fractions a commonplace, yet in the Shop boys and girls of those ages were seen neglecting the quarters of an inch in measuring wood for sawing. This is the kind of fault in the School that will gradually disappear as the children in the younger grades move higher up in regular sequence. Experiences in Nursery School and in the First Grade with unit and fractional blocks, with triangles, cylinders, arcs, and cones, and experiences in all the younger classes in measuring, computing, using money, and building with tools, were preparing groups who had had experiences both in learning mathematical principles in the Arithmetic class and in using these in practical situations. But even so, what is the responsibility of a rural High School?

Our chart showed that much use of mathematics was made in many parts of the curriculum. Mathematics in common use was penetrating, or implicit in, nearly every subject. It was the mathematics that was needed, if you grant that the occasions were valid for learning. What, then, of courses in Mathematics? What of Algebra, Geometry, and Trigonometry? In the previous year we had found these needed for the mathematics used in surveying. But in their unadulterated and complete forms these subjects take time which is outside of experience.

HISTORY

It was our previous work in history and records and drama and economic surveying of the environment in Kentucky that gave us a groundwork to begin on in West Virginia. American

History for West Virginia was also that of the expansion of a people over a continent, their solution of the problems of food and shelter, and their constant amazement at the vicissitudes of a growing national economy. A great deal of our time was given in the whole School, as well as in the High School, in the first year, to the American scene and the American economy.

The study of American History in the High School had not at first definitely turned to a study of the environment and resources and the interactions of people using them. In the first year, there had to be considerable effort put into mere reading and comprehension of what was read. By the spring of the year, the History groups had sufficient grasp of an approach to history for the High School Drama group to produce *The Gold Rush* play in the outdoor theater.[36] In the second year, the westward expansion was better material for the large and irregular Seventh Grade. The older groups were divided between American industrial and social life in the nineteenth century, and European expansion and cultural growth. The same group that was studying the Industrial Revolution and some of its reflections in social life was also working at Economics and School Banking, group Drama, the community newspaper, and the investigation of the glass industry. The trend was to let History and Science and Language study and our interests in the community move along at least within reach of each other.

In the second year, we were confident about the place American History was to hold and were able to proceed in other types of experiences in history which would be relevant to individual development and to the life of the community. In the Ninth Grade the History study centered in the medieval period —which might seem strange for an American rural community. But the subject which led us into that period was a study of the development of written symbols and records. A

---

[36] See Chapter V, pp. 261-3.

gift of the Old English style of type made possible some printing materials which were next to inaccessible, at the same time that it showed the state of writing and records in late medieval times. The study of records soon showed us that there were aspects of medieval life of even greater concern to our modern community than was a study of communication and recording language. In fact we found that the life at Arthurdale had suggestions of problems and cultural resources common to medieval communities: division and use of land, industrial and labor organization, and community control of marketing and consumption; folk-drama[37] and music[38] and musical instruments, and hand-printing and illumination. The class was quick to discover similarities, and the medieval and modern periods could interact, broadening the boys' and girls' understanding of their families' immediate economic problems and cultural standing.

RESEARCH IN LANGUAGE

Language in Experience and in Learning

The research in language came to be an index to almost everything that was going on. The activity and the learning that were taking place in the classes were the material for expression and the most important factor qualifying the kind of expression. To study the record in language was to penetrate into every activity that was going on in the School. It was to find why we laid so little emphasis on Language classes and so much more on the creations of the Drama group, the printed records of the Botany class, the writing in classes in the Sciences or the studies in History, and the making of a community newspaper out of one group's modest attempts at writing and printing.

The first steps were to line up all the spheres of action in the

---

[37] See Chapter V, pp. 256–68.
[38] *Ibid.*, pp. 220–48.

School and where it played into the community life, to discover what part language played in each, and then to observe not only the High School but also, from the age of two up to adult years, the language and expression that were the mental environment and the record of action and learning. To complete the study meant to watch the relations and growth of the curriculum, to study the gaps in Language teaching, to examine the growth of all the groups from the two-year-olds in the Nursery School through the students in High School.[39]

The charting of the spheres of activity was, of course, a study of curriculum which may be omitted here except for a few remarks. The subjects of study, while bearing familiar names —such as History, Shop, English, etc.—do not look out of place in a study or survey of Language, because they all make definite contributions to the learning of language, even beyond the opportunities they offer for thinking. For example: the main currents flowing through History in the upper six grades were: expansion, whether geographic or cultural, communication, transportation, and industry, with their related social effects. And, being currents, they were not to be localized under the name of a subject or within a period of each day.

Printing, Electricity, or Mechanics might turn up as History, Shop, Science, Language, or Mathematics—some now one, now another, now several at once. Printing appeared in European history at a time of geographic and cultural expansion, but it also was one solution for our community problem of news and communication; finally, it was useful in teaching good writing. But we did not have what you would call a class in printing. One group in a study of recording and the materials used therein came to the subject of printing through its need for a distributable and permanent medium in their plant study. They printed the Botany record. Another group, in studying European discovery and expansion, concentrated for some time on the history of printing. Another group con-

---

[39] See Chapter III, pp. 167–9.

verted their study of Language directly into the writing of news when our second-hand press was found.

Then, aside from the applications to life of History thus studied, there were many books to read, reams to write, sidelights to discover—as when medieval life touches not only records and the materials of writing but also the stringed instruments then being made in the Shop and the ballads sung and studied in the English class.[40] The discussions, the stories, the drama and music, the digging for facts in the Library, the development of vocabulary in class or Shop, the Music and singing, make up the language expression and learning in a way which backs our English classes off the map. These show up when one examines the developing curriculum for its uses in language and thinking. The same can be done in examining mathematics or the sciences for their contributions.

Charting of Materials and Processes

A charting of materials and processes was literally our beginning in the study of Language. This revealed many processes which are a part of language, though not commonly considered so in school tradition.

One might be called the Manipulating of Materials. In Botany, for instance, there is the collecting, arranging, and classifying; or, in the history of industry in the nineteenth century, there is the beginning of a sequence, facts, effects, changes of living conditions, new facts, new interpretations, comparisons or transfers to the analysis of modern living conditions, etc. More clearly linguistic is the process which could be called Analysis of Sounds and Symbols. The matter of analysis is closely related to the age of individuals and also to the uses of language in the complete activity of the School. Analysis can begin best when a basis in experience has been made for it,

---

[40] See Chapter V, pp. 226–32.

which perhaps, first of all, means opening up to recognition the processes in the use of language and in thinking. Another form of analysis which is one of the processes in language might be called the Communication of Meanings and Understandings. Finally, there is the process of the Critical Construction of Forms or Records, the difficulty and the glory of which is that it thrives in creative development more than in conscious direction.

Language Problems

A few illustrations will show that the planning for Language in the High School took account of both school experiences and direct study of language in classes to meet the special needs of our situation.

A direct attack on language problems was necessary for several reasons: dialectal pronunciations and confused conceptions of word sounds; long neglect of any care in speech, whether in regard to articulateness of sounds or to control of tones of voice; strongly entrenched habits of using dialectal verb forms and pronoun usages (such as "come" for "came," and "yurn" for "yours"), and finally the vocabularies of reference books which were used daily in many varieties of work, but only by skipping the technical or learned words.

Instead of attempting a sweeping reform in everyday speech habits, we thought the best way to approach the problem was to draw attention to differences between local usage and so-called standard English. In vocabulary it was easy for the class to see that they were used to many regional idioms which they would probably try to iron out, and many pronunciations and verb or pronoun forms which they would change for standard forms. They were aware of differences in manners of speaking in different sections of the country and were interested to compare as many as they could think of. During the course of the year members of the class came to the point of demanding to have the language problems cleared up. There was the beginning of rapid progress in consciousness of the peculiarities of speech. The group could now supplement the speech training which it had been receiving unconsciously in the English-Drama work with a conscious analysis of language.

One special vocabulary which turned up in the discussion of words was a list for mining, which was a subject familiar to some of the boys because of actual experience in mining, or to others through their fathers and a life spent in the mining regions:

square up	*checkweighman*
undercut	*tipple boss*
faces, pillars, ribs	*jumper*
stumps, heading, butts	*slate dump*
fire boss	*gob pile*
pit boss	*scrip* (used in company stores)
super	*slate bar*
toe holes	*spike hammer*
cross cuts	*draft mine* [Error (Drift)]
bug dust	*shaft mine*
bone pile	*cutters*
buttermilk coal	*trackman*
yellow dog	*pickers*
red neck	*brakeman*
mine guard	*pumper*
grease monkey	*slate loader*
spraggers	*coal loader*
run-of-mine coal	*machine coal*
slope, section	*mine props*
graveyard shift	*coal damp*
slate pickin' table	

Almost every class in the School was troubled with the same difficulty of vocabulary and the same difficulties of dialect. Beginnings were made on the problem in a variety of ways. Only toward the end of the second year could a general survey be begun of the language situation, and the matter of dialect be taken down to the level of Nursery School.

BRINGING THE COMMUNITY INTO THE WORK OF THE SCHOOL

The detail of research carries far—and there is little danger of exhausting the resources. One educator who visited the School remarked that he thought work was humming, but what would happen when the novelty of the approach wore off? It may not be wise to give a final answer, but at the end of the second year, it was less a novelty than a practice.

It was not only desirable, but became apparently necessary, to use the summers to make investigations into fields which could hardly be touched in the winters. I mentioned that it happened that the biological laboratory became more and more a place for the testing of milk and the analysis of drinking water in the community. We had reached that stage in our work just as summer was coming on. Here was obviously time for that sort of work. A school day leaves small margin for going about, setting up a special laboratory, interesting people to work in it.

This matter of bringing the community into the work of the School was of as much importance as the directing of the work of the School into the life of the community. The two at times were interacting, but in few cases did we find that we could deal only with young people to reach the community. Just such a matter as testing milk needed the interest of the owner of the cow even more than that of his children. And the interest was such that a few men came in or sent in samples of milk before we could get the equipment assembled. The study of the community with the children could turn rapidly into study with the adults. And since the sciences and the whole physical and cultural development of community life were at stake, it would be a long time before we would find research boring.

The community itself was the field of Social Science. Could

we answer what that was? And just what was Adult Education? We could see these fields inside and outside of School, and yet we could not say in so many words that we had worked them out. They seemed to be in the formative stage, but their growth would perhaps never be so rapid in any succeeding stage. We knew that they were going to take their place and were going to influence everything the School was to plan.

CHAPTER VII

COMMUNITY AND SCHOOL LIFE, 1935-36

Adult Education

THE fact I would like to emphasize is that community education envisages the whole community and is concerned equally with the development of individuals of all ages, from babies to grandparents, with their groupings in families and their social relationships as friends and neighbors, in work and play, in clubs, in social gatherings, and in the give-and-take of daily existence.

We were often startled by visitors' asking "if we had social sciences"—when that was our whole engagement—and "if we did adult education"—when it was our daily and nightly preoccupation. What prompted these questions probably, especially the latter question, was the fact that these people were familiar with the conventional approach to, and standardized items of, "adult education" and failed to identify as such the pervasive and informal procedures we used, which sprang from our educational point of view and our approach to the whole situation, and which were prompted by the nature and the needs of the people with whom we lived and worked.

Considering the fairly limited and prescribed character of what is usually called "adult education," it seems perhaps worth while to try to describe the procedures that we found to be appropriate and effective in a rural area. Mr. Collins,

Mr. Beecher, and I have each had a hand in this endeavor in the pages following.

From the beginning [Mr. Collins writes], the School believed that by adult education was meant much more than leisure-time activities, intellectual or physical. Rather did we think of adult education as involving *all-time,* as touching nearly every phase of adult homestead experience. We consequently launched or fostered such diverse programs in adult education as health, child care, recreation, athletics, industrial arts, cultural activities, and vocational development. If community education was to mean anything, we were convinced that it had to consider the education of all individuals, old and young, as of equal importance to the full functioning of the community, even though the particular import of adult and child was, of course, quite different.

The procedures in adult education were naturally unlike those used with the children in the Elementary School and the High School. The children came to School daily for a specific number of hours, during which they followed a definite curriculum, however functional in character, of studies and activities. The adults, on the other hand, could not, because of the demands of their everyday work in house, farm, and construction, be expected to follow any such formal scheme of education. Indeed, at some seasons, when the women were canning or the men were plowing or harvesting, the physical exhaustion of the adults by evening precluded the possibility of much additional effort. Furthermore, because most of the adults had only had a few years of formal education, they were by no means ready for evening classes and lectures, such as are successfully carried on in urban and some rural areas.

New and functional procedures had to be evolved to meet the needs of our situation. They were discovered in the free exchange which was implicit in homestead life. Through the fact that the teachers and Director of the School were everyday citizens of the community, they were able to find contact with the homesteaders at many points. As neighbors, they found possible a mutually helpful intimacy with the homesteaders who lived nearest to them; active citizens of the village, they served on a variety of committees [1] in the adult clubs. A third, and very important kind of con-

---

[1] See Chapter II, pp. 118–22 for description of work on Club committees. Also this chapter, pp. 373–6.

ELEMENTARY SCHOOL BUILDING

SCHOOL CENTER BUILDING
Housing School Lunchroom, Community Canning Kitchens,
Doctor's Offices, School and Community Savings "Bank," School Offices, etc.

SCHOOL AND COMMUNITY RECREATION BUILDING

tact sprang up in the parents' interest in "what was going on" at the School, and in what the children shared with their parents. From these manifold and human contacts was derived a dynamic pattern for adult education at Arthurdale.

Educational influences, as deep as they were informal, resulted from these man-to-man contacts. The homesteaders called this sort of thing "neighboring," an ancient back-country term. One example of neighboring will serve to make clear the type of thing which happened sometimes.

Joseph Wilcox, sixty-five and with a weak heart, stepped on a loose board while working on building construction, fell and broke a rib, and was in the hospital for more than a week. For a long time after that, he was unable to do any heavy work, like gardening. He had no sons living with him, and his elderly wife attempted to plant the garden for him; she knew how vitally necessary it was to have that garden planted. So did his neighbors. One of them got two of Joseph's closest neighbors and two of the men teachers who lived down the road. The group worked several evenings on Joseph's garden, and left it planted for the season. The group called itself the P.T.W.A.—Parent Teachers Working Association.

While they worked on Joseph's garden they talked, and their talk centered around the ancient practice of neighboring in the farming country where they had grown up. The teachers realized that co-operation had been a reality long before it had been used as a slogan, and the homesteaders realized that "neighboring" was a rather immortal element of human beings like themselves. They were not smug or self-righteous about this action of theirs; they kidded Joseph, who was directing operations from the sidelines; they made him, who had a community reputation for oratory, make a speech to them as they worked. In September, when Joseph's buckwheat was ready to be cut and shocked, the P.T.W.A. swung into action again, and harvested the whole crop one blistering afternoon and evening after work hours. There was some talk this time about collective farming, and one guessed that many more such occasions would probably produce at Arthurdale a substantial development of that kind of farming. There was more than mere charity in this helping of a neighbor; there was a grounding in community organization of society and economics.

Other examples could be multiplied readily. When one of the men took an electrical job in the Supply Shed—which job necessitated the learning of more arithmetic than he knew—he went to his teacher-neighbor, and the latter tutored him in what he needed to know. This sort of thing, rather than formal classes in business arithmetic, or accounting, was the effective method.

The teachers chatted with the homesteaders daily about all sorts of things; they chatted as friends, not as teacher and pupil, and yet the teachers felt that some of their best adult teaching had been accomplished in these conversations on the corner, while walking down the road, or while riding home together.

Mr. Beecher, the head of the High School, who was active in so many community activities, discusses the function of a community school in adult education:

The School had been planned *with* the adults of the community, and it had been planned with the specific purpose of functioning for every member of the community. Only when you separate grade schools and secondary schools from adult education does the latter come to seem an after-thought.

Mention has been made of the way adults came into the School to use the Library, or to work with one of us in the laboratory, or to show a class the blowing of glass, for instance. These are incidentals in making a school usable by and for young people and adults, but they are none the less essential. They are, in effect, introductions of the uses of the school to adults. If the school consciously has the desire to make itself a resource for the entire community, there are many ways in which adults can come to an understanding of the aim of the school.

We saw our work as "building" an environment for health and opportunity: *building an environment for health* in the sense of physical as well as social and cultural wellbeing, and *opportunity* in the sense of understanding one's environment for its economic resources, and the ways of utilizing those available, or of evaluating them.

The story of the medical-health program, which was one of the major interests in which adults wished to share, is an illustration.[2] We did not see any division between the work of the doctor or nurse, and the direction of athletics on the field or in the Recreation Building; or any division between the visits of the Home Economics teacher to homes in the community to talk about

---

[2] See Chapter II, pp. 89–99, and this chapter, pp. 368–76.

canning or home meals, and the teaching of Biology and the examination of the local water supply.

Although adult education at Arthurdale did go on informally all through the day, and into the night, still it is possible, for the sake of clearness, to name and group the specific kinds of learning and teaching. A summary of the activities and agencies through which adult education took place is, on the face of it, a devitalized topic list, but it may serve to recall enterprises described elsewhere in these pages.

AGENCIES OF ADULT EDUCATION USED AT ARTHURDALE

Shared Living and Working

"Neighboring," described by Mr. Collins on preceding pages.
Shared work in homestead activities, such as athletic dinners, benefit suppers and entertainments; holiday celebrations at Hallowe'en, Thanksgiving, and Christmas—by men and women, homesteaders and teachers.
Joint membership in the Men's and Women's Clubs by homesteaders and teachers.
Shared work on committees: The Fire Committee,[3] Athletic Committee, etc., of the Men's Club; the Executive Committee, the Weaving Committee, the Hospitality and Refreshment Committees of the Women's Club; the Medical Committee,[4] the Store Committee,[5] the School Committee[6] of both Clubs.

Health Program [7]

Visits, treatment, and bedside nursing of doctor and nurse; prenatal, delivery, and postnatal care of mothers and babies.
Thorough physical examination of children by doctor, with mother present.[8]

---
[3] See Chapter II, pp. 118–21.
[4] See this chapter, pp. 373–4.
[5] *Ibid.*, pp. 374–5.
[6] See below, pp. 358–62.
[7] See Chapter II, pp. 89–99, and this chapter, pp. 368–76.
[8] See Chapter IV, p. 214.

Baby Clinics,[9] under supervision of doctor and nurse, assisted by student-nurse in training. Nursery School head, dietitian, and Home Economics teacher present for conference with mothers. Run by women members of the Medical Committee. Committee members assisting in receiving mothers and babies; teachers providing transportation. Clinic preceded by meeting of the Committee to go over plans for notifying the mothers, and points to be taken up at the Clinic.

Observation and conferences at the Nursery School by mothers and fathers on care of children, food preparation, eating habits, toilet and sleeping routines, handling of emotional upsets, provision for play indoors and outdoors.

Home visits and conferences with parents by Nursery School teachers.

Home conferences with the teacher of Home Economics on supper, luncheon, and breakfast menus and foods, and on problems of housekeeping.

> Follow-up with mothers of diets recommended at Baby Clinics by the doctor. Advising with mothers on preparation of food for babies.

Cooking classes for mothers and older girls.

> Study of food values and preparation of meals; budgets; buying.
>
> Tests of various brands of canned goods carried by the Arthurdale Co-operative Store.
>
> Suppers given to husbands and invited guests at end of Cooking class courses.
>
> Studying methods and techniques of canning. Canning School garden vegetables.

Superintendence by Home Economics teacher of five voluntary groups of mothers cooking lunch daily for children at School.

Talks by doctor at Women's Club on treatment of "summer complaint," the keeping of food in hot weather without an ice box, constipation, colds, inoculations; and at the Men's Club on matters of community sanitation and inoculations.

Superintendence by doctor of stock of drugs purchased and carried by the Arthurdale Co-operative General Store.

Shared work on early problems in the organization and running of the first Farm Co-operative by members of the High School

---

[9] See Chapter II, pp. 96–8; Chapter IV, pp. 189–90 and also 212–4; and this chapter, pp. 372–3.

COMMUNITY AND SCHOOL LIFE

staff and homestead officials of the Co-operative, in the spring of 1935.

Shared work on the School Gardens during summer of 1935 by homesteaders and men teachers.

Farm study groups for men and boys with the project agriculturalist, Mr. Pharr, winter and spring, 1935–36. Advising with him by homesteaders on farming and on the purchase of seeds and fertilizer for the 1936 gardens.

Classes for women on gardens and the raising of chickens with Mr. Pharr; group work with women on flower gardens with Mrs. Pharr, 1935–36.

Raising of cabbage and tomato plants in High School greenhouse by older boys, under joint supervision of Mr. Pharr and Mr. Beecher.

Training under WPA auspices of the older girls (married and unmarried) in courses in:

Practical Nursing [10]

With the doctor, in Physiology.

With the nurse, in bedside nursing.

With the Nursery School dietitian and Home Economics teacher, in invalid and infant diets, and in preparation of foods.

With the head of the Nursery School in child care.

Housekeeping [11]

With a WPA supervisor in cleaning, washing, ironing, sewing, cooking, and serving of meals.

With the head of the Nursery School in child care.

Recreation

MUSIC

Singing groups: male quartet; male chorus; women's chorus; mixed chorus. Mr. Collins.

Orchestra practice. Older boys and men. Mr. Collins.

Playing for square-dances.[12] Homesteaders with Mr. Collins and Mr. Beecher.

---

[10] See this chapter, pp. 370–1.
[11] *Ibid.*, pp. 371–2.
[12] See Chapter V, pp. 230–2, 240–2.

Making fiddles and mandolins.[13] Older boys and girls. Mr. Collins; Mr. Carlson, Shop teacher; Mr. Ipcar, teacher of Mathematics.

Lessons in playing instruments. Older boys and girls. Mr. Collins.

DRAMA

Adult Drama group.[14] Men and women. Mr. Collins, Mr. Beecher assisting.

High School Drama group.[15] High School group and older boys. Mr. Collins.

ATHLETICS [16]

Basketball and baseball teams. Older boys, High School boys, also men of Arthurdale and from the neighborhood. Mr. Saunders, Director of Athletics, in collaboration with the Athletic Committee of the Men's Club.

Mushball, volley ball. Older boys and men, and High School boys. Mr. Saunders.

Outdoor games: horseshoe-pitching, tennis. Men, boys, women, girls. Mr. Saunders.

"GOOD TIMES"

Square-dances every week. Homesteader men and women, boys and girls, and teachers.

Holiday festivities. Everybody.

Informal birthday parties, picnics, and house dances.

OTHER CLASSES IN INSTRUCTION

Trade instruction of men and older boys on the construction job in: carpentry, electrical and mason work, painting and plumbing, work on septic tanks, etc. Head workmen and engineers under supervision of Government representatives.

Work in School Shop on woodwork and electrical studies. Older boys. Mr. Carlson, Shop teacher.

---

[13] See Chapter V, pp. 223–6; Chapter VI, pp. 307–9.
[14] Chapter V, pp. 265–8.
[15] *Ibid.*, pp. 257–65; also Chapter VI, p. 296.
[16] See Chapter II, pp. 108–10, and below, pp. 378–81.

Instruction in cabinet work and furniture-making. Men.
Small groups of homesteader men taught to make tables, baby cribs, and chairs for their homes. Later open to boys and women. Dan Houghton and Bill Simkin, heads of the Mountaineer Craftsmen Co-operative Association.
Weaving of rag rugs and curtains on the Craftsmen's looms by homestead women, with occasional instruction by experts.
Help in accounting, reading blueprints, details of carpentry work for men. Members of the High School staff.
Pottery classes given by Miss Carlisle, First Grade teacher, for women, in the summer of 1936; for older girls and women in "Night School," 1934–35.
Block-printing class given for women by Miss Wadsworth, head of the Nursery School, 1936.
Quilting, a native art encouraged by the School, done by women singly or in groups.[17]
Lectures and illustrated talks before Women's Club, 1935–36, on gardening and home decoration by guest speakers. Movies shown by Dr. White (taken in Philippines).

At the High School

Work on *The News*, the community newspaper, issued by High School students with adult participation in writing news articles.[18]
Use of School and Community Library by men and women, girls and boys.[19] Daily circulation, 40–50 books. Open every evening during Summer School, 1936. Open for Women's Club meetings twice a month throughout the year.
WPA Project in Library Training. Older boys and girls. Traveling library project: books and magazines taken to mothers on the homestead kept at home by babies and young children.[20]
Shared work and interests in the Science laboratory in:
    Collecting of plants, animals, insects, etc.
    Experiments with incubator. Incubator lent to individuals for home use.
    Milk and water testing.
    Help in constructing of laboratory tables, cabinets, etc.

---

[17] Chapter V, pp. 248–9; also see below, pp. 352–3.
[18] See Chapter V, pp. 268–72; also Chapter VII, pp. 377–8.
[19] See this chapter, pp. 366–7.
[20] *Ibid.*, pp. 367–8.

Listing these "agencies," I am reminded that on the homestead "adults" included both the older grown people and the young adults—boys and girls, a number of whom were married, between sixteen and twenty-five years of age (not in High School). Also that the line of demarcation between the adults and the young adults and the students still in High School is one hard to preserve in listing "adult" activities, so shared were all these enterprises.

As I write down these activities and classes I am teased by the difficulty of capturing in words the daily sharing of work and interests that opened up to the adults new fields of knowledge and experience, and that provided channels through which the studies and work at the School—not only with the High School enterprises, but activities of the younger groups also—were shared by the older people. It is literally true that the older people learned *with* their children and from them. Their teacher-neighbors shared their interests with them, too, and the adults entered into everything that was going on at School.

Education of Young Adults
INDUSTRIAL ARTS AT ARTHURDALE

Among the opportunities of a rural school must be listed those in industrial arts—to use a term familiar to all school people but naming activities at once more practical and perhaps more fundamental than those usually designated. I am referring to those processes and skills through which natural resources are utilized to meet human needs. This use of the term is, I realize, stretching its usual connotations and associations.

To make the point in terms of the history of the two community schools in Kentucky and West Virginia: our earlier knowledge of industrial arts and their use in education needed to be expanded and to become functional for community education in rural areas. In Kentucky, our practices widened to include not only school and home building repairs,[21] but also the planting of gardens; the raising of chickens, pigeons, turkeys, sheep, and pigs; and an annual School Country Fair.[22] At Arthurdale, industrial arts included masonry, painting, plumbing, electricity, etc., as well as quilting, pottery, and block printing; the killing of hogs and curing of beef, the raising and canning of fruits and vegetables, as well as the processes of making linen and woolen cloth, dyeing, spinning, and weaving; carpentry as well as woodworking; farming as well as flower gardens, etc. On the homestead, arts of industry, work processes, were essential for living and for livelihood. Our conception of "industrial arts" deepened and widened. Room was made within it both for work—the mean between natural resources and human needs—and for art.

There were other industrial arts—the arts of livelihood—whose development, as Mr. Collins relates in the following pages,[23] had but barely begun when our work at Arthurdale closed. It was, I think, true that the problem of livelihood engaged our most concentrated and continuous attention throughout the two years and a half of our work on the homestead.

PROBLEMS OF THE OLDER BOYS

The "Night School" in the winter of 1934–35 had barely scratched the surface of the problems of the older boys.[24] What that work did was to steady the boys somewhat and put them again in the way of working, to rouse in them interests that had atrophied, and to build them up a little physically.[25] With

---
[21] See Chapter I, p. 58.
[22] *Ibid.*, pp. 42–3.
[23] See pp. 350–5 below.
[24] See Chapter II, pp. 103–7; also Chapter VI, pp. 305–6.
[25] See Chapter II, pp. 93–4.

the ending of the school term in May, the "Night School" courses ended also. Work on construction for a time continued. All through June, July, and part of August, FERA labor not being available, the work on the project needed the boys, both for grubbing land that was not yet cleared and for construction work on the School buildings, which was being rushed for the opening of School in September. The boys enjoyed this full work, thrived on it physically, and were proud of their part in it and their achievement. They were not skilled, but worked willingly, and the foreman found most of them useful. Unfortunately, the Government rule of employing only one person in a family cut them off from this employment in the middle of August, and threw them back again into the old idleness. Although steps were immediately taken to arrange WPA–NYA work for them, it was January before the WPA projects could actually start. Meanwhile the boys were discouraged and at loose ends, waiting along from day to day, hoping for a break either through the School's efforts in their behalf or at some job that might turn up. The older and more enterprising of the boys left the project in search of some elusive job, only to return in a few days or weeks. Others tried fitfully to dig up some business on the homestead and went into partnership chopping wood, tending furnaces, and washing cars for the teachers, or hunting rabbits and selling them to the homesteaders at 25 cents each. Several of the boys, whose former schooling had carried them to the eighth or ninth grade, tried to re-enter High School, as special students. One of them acted for a time as a student assistant to Carl Saunders in Mathematics classes and on the playfields.

The boys who entered High School had great difficulty in adjusting themselves to the regular demands and discipline of school work after their free years. It took nerve to enter school, for they felt at a loss and inferior, yet older and more experienced. In discussions they could take part and did well, but preparation and study irked them. One of them, Basil

Appleton, dropped into my office one day. "It ain't no use. I can't do it. I can't come to school every day. It just ain't no use." On any and every pretext, the boys would slip off to talk to the workmen around the School or to smoke in the boiler room with the janitor. Mr. Beecher met them half-way, boiled down to their actual classes the time they needed to be in school, and let them substitute work in the late afternoons with the WPA group for some of the school study periods. Even so, their attendance was fitful, their tardiness frequent. Partly they were held to it by their parents' determination, partly by interest in the School's athletic teams. I have the impression, which would be difficult to substantiate, that, in spite of themselves, they got something out of the School contact—something possibly less tangible but more far-reaching than they had had from their enforced attendance at "Night School" the winter before. They were bright and quick-minded, and took satisfaction in the active work of the Biology classes, building cages for the animals studied and bringing in specimens. They hung around the Science room and enjoyed their work in Shop. Looking on and lending a hand here and there was more in their line. This state of affairs was predictable, and quite inevitable considering their background of years of no work and hanging around the mine camps.

With the starting of the WPA projects at mid-winter, the activities of the group became fairly regular. When these projects became a reality and the group was called upon to express its choices among the activities offered, they had some dislikes to register but few, if any, choices. The projects for the boys included: manual activities; cleaning, painting, out-of-door repairs; shop, construction (hauling, carpentry); improving and beautifying the grounds; aiding in agriculture. For boys and girls both, there were, besides, projects of clerical work and library service and training. The WPA projects were, it proved, workable only if supervision could be provided gratis; they were effective in an individual's development only if this supervision was educationally administered. Again the staff did double duty: a full school day, followed by superintendence of WPA and NYA projects in the late afternoons. The evenings were kept free for community activities and gatherings—many of which included the older boys.

In the early spring, the Arthurdale Co-operative Association had started its poultry farm, and spring plowing was beginning. Temporary jobs were offered the boys, who wished immediately to leave the WPA projects for "a real job." Each boy was made to face the possibility that this employment would not last for many weeks, and that, once withdrawn from the WPA lists, they could probably not be reinstated. "I rather think it's a-goin' to last all summer," Edgar said. "And anyhow I want to quit. I'd rather have a job—for two weeks, at real money. First you have a job, and then you don't. It's like that. I'm a-goin' to go." The WPA ranks were reduced by half.

After the chicken houses were made, and plowing was over, the boys were again at loose ends. A few came back to be reinstated, if possible—regardless, just trying for whatever there might be. A few turned up temporary jobs in the mines, or worked for varying lengths of time as messenger boys in Morgantown, in restaurants here, there, and the other place, or at trucking and hauling coal. The Co-operative could use only a very small number regularly.

The work on WPA projects and the jobs—for a few—with the Co-operative did not adequately meet the older boys' needs, either of employment or of education. Again, they got out of it something—continuation of activity, regular while it lasted, with whatever training and experience it held for them. But their problem, and the problem of those among unemployed youth who, defeated in the search for work, have been without employment over a long period and have drifted—the years of their outreaching and teachable youth wasted—are difficult of solution. Had we been free to work on it exclusively, we possibly would have accomplished more, but could not have solved it. For the problem is not vested in the boys alone; it is rooted deep in today's economic situation, an index of maladjustments for which no remedy has yet been found.

HIGH SCHOOL AND POST-HIGH SCHOOL WORK

The situation of the older boys brought to us with sickening vividness the urgency of the need to discover, by any means whatsoever, ways of providing a different situation for the boys and girls leaving the High School. As we worked upon this problem, we came out with an altered idea of the purposes and content of High School work. It affected our thinking on the curriculum and on the function of the High School in community education. The High School at Arthurdale must, we saw, take part in the problem of livelihood. Almost immediately, plans overran the usual length of the high school course. We began to talk of "high school and post-high school work," and of their continuity and development.

We had in 1935–36 to deal with both an older group who had missed High School training, and students still in High School, not yet exposed to the experience of seeking a living, but bound to meet this on graduation. Without waiting for the graduating of this latter group, we felt that we must find for the older boys—untrained as they were—some immediate livelihood possibilities. The High School might, we felt, furnish the kind of training it uniquely could offer as a basis for livelihood enterprises, and these could be carried on outside its classes, although under its supervision. Continued study of the environment and its varied resources, used and potentially useful, yielded a long list of suggestions to be investigated further.

By mid-year Mr. Beecher had formulated for consideration an analysis of the chief local problems, and had listed some lines of work which could develop with the young adults. He first described a suggested sequence of studies and activities in High School[26] and then indicated the possibility of graduates' continuing in various lines of work developed in School. We discussed this plan for several weeks, and finally decided to take the part of his outline called "Proposed Studies of Chief Local Problems" as data in our search for work and occupation for the post-High School boys and girls. It is quoted below:

PROPOSED STUDIES OF CHIEF LOCAL PROBLEMS

Economics:
    Production, marketing, calculating costs, buying
    Essentials of business management
    Accounting and bookkeeping
Chemistry:
    Glass and minerals
    Fertilizer, soils, disinfectants
    Clay
    Plant and animal metabolism, nutrition
    Food, feeds, dairy products, substitutes
    Fuels, preservatives, consumer research
    By-products, distillation, wastes
Biology:
    Dairy health and dairy products
    Selection in cows, chickens, etc.
    Water tests, certification of milk
    Insect pests, diseases
    Bees
    Helpful bacteria, yeasts, molds in soil, industry, animal bodies
    Selection in plants, grafting

---

[26] See Appendix IV, "A Plan for a Rural High School (Grades 7 to 12) at Arthurdale."

Rural Produce—Foods:
  Butter, cheese
  Preserves
  Greenhouse flowers, vegetables, seedlings
  Honey
  Poultry, eggs
  Seed varieties for this climate
  Canned specialties
Communications:
  Newspapers
  Technical, economic, and craft bulletins
  School materials for recording and distributing literature for children and adults
  Means of expression for members of community and means of closer contacts
Recreation:
  Athletics
  Drama
  Music—singing, orchestra, folk music
  Dancing
  Library—literature, periodicals, reference books
  Arts—painting, modeling
  Crafts—pottery, woodcutting
Shop and Craft Lines Which Could Be Developed with Adults:
  Wood tools
  Glass-blowing
  Pottery-firing
  Beehive equipment
  Typesetting, printing, woodcutting
  Mechanics, design and construction
  Sewing, quilting
  Bookbinding
  Advertising

To attack the problems listed above is doing primary research on what a rural High School can be, how rural students are to be fitted to their environment and how the School may develop economic and cultural resources on which to base healthy economic life.

STUDY OF ECONOMIC RESOURCES OF THE ENVIRONMENT

Fletcher Collins

We began with a quick survey of the economic resources and potentialities of the Arthurdale property and inhabitants. Intentionally, the investigation considered the property and homesteaders both, for many an economic enterprise could be projected on paper that would be impossible to operate successfully with the experience, quality, and quantity of homestead workers available. No one seemed to know fully the extent of resources—exactly what geologic wealth was available under the land, or what kind of crops the land could produce (the Agricultural Department of the State University had done some investigating along this latter line at the start of the project). A few members of the School staff studied the geology of the region, investigated the used and potential livelihood enterprises of the area, and found out more about the latent and past vocational skills of the adult homesteaders. By November 1935, they made as a step in their study a list of possible economic enterprises. Each of these possibilities was studied experimentally, with the results—to the end of July 1936, when our work closed on the project—noted below:

LIST OF POSSIBLE LIVELIHOOD ENTERPRISES

1. Chickens, eggs, and broilers.

This enterprise was, in the spring of 1936, established on a large scale (14,000 chicks) by the Resettlement Administration as a branch of the Arthurdale Co-operative Association.

2. Bees, clover, and buckwheat honey.

Several homesteaders had kept bees and understood something of the technique of bee-keeping. The High School students studied bees as part of their work in Biology. The A & P. stores in the vicinity bought honey locally, and there was a possibility that it could be sold in the larger market centers. Later investigation disclosed, however, that this enterprise was not likely to be profitable unless a large amount of capital and skill was initially available.

3. *Berries—all kinds.*

The University of West Virginia's Agricultural Department had at the outset of the project conducted an experiment station on the homestead to determine the usability of the soil for berry raising. Strawberries did well in a short season, it was found, and could be profitably—if efficiently—marketed. Shrub berries thrived in the Arthurdale soil. The School in the spring of 1936 invested in about 80 red and black raspberries, and also currants and gooseberry plants, and induced a number of the older boys under the supervision of a High School teacher to undertake the care of these shrubs as a potentially profitable business.

4. *Herbs—wintergreen, spearmint, pennyroyal, ginseng, hops, lycopodium (ground pine), juniper, etc.*

These herbs grew wild in that region, and a market for them was possible of development. Further investigation of this market was still pending when we left.

5. *Garden Nursery—plants, trees, and shrubs.*

In the 1935 season the homesteaders had bought their tomato, cabbage, and pepper plants at random and usually, tempted by cheapness, bought a mediocre or poor assortment. With the School greenhouse, these plants could be raised at Arthurdale to be marketed at the Co-operative Store—a potential source of income for the post-High School boys. This enterprise was financed by the Arthurdale Co-operative Association, and was supervised by the Federal agricultural adviser on the project. The plants were sold at the store to homesteaders in the spring of 1936. There was, of course, a possibility of developing a regional market for such farm produce.

The School contemplated the development, in the fall of 1936, of a nursery of shrubs and small trees suitable for landscape gardening. There was a large market for such products in the suburbs of Pittsburgh.

6. *Tobacco.*

One of the homesteaders who had worked for thirty years in the tobacco fields of southern Ohio tried the raising of Burley tobacco on his homestead land, and had had fair results for his own use and that of other homesteaders. In spite of the short season, tobacco could be grown for sale at tobacco markets. Lack of capital was still holding back this enterprise in 1936.

7. *Buckwheat flour.*

Buckwheat is a staple crop in northern West Virginia and flourishes in that soil and climate. The School envisaged the sale of buckwheat flour, milled and packed in 5- and 10-pound bags, to urban people as an Arthurdale specialty.

8. *Dairy products.*

Dairy herds were feasible on the Arthurdale land. The sale of raw milk, in the experience of farmers in the region, did not yield much profit, but cream could be marketed well at the large creameries. The Resettlement Administration, through the Arthurdale Co-operative Association, was considering plans for the erection and operation of a large dairy.[27] It did not, however, contemplate the making of cheese.

In the summer of 1936 a group of girls in the High School laboratory learned how to test and pasteurize raw surplus milk, and took the first steps in cheese-making (an experience that would fit them to hold positions in a dairy products enterprise if and when it developed).

9. *Clay products.*

One of the neglected resources at Arthurdale was the deposits of white clay over a large part of the homestead area. The extraction and processing of clay for pottery and modeling use was a likely enterprise. Investigation of the quality and quantity of the clay available was made with the assistance of the geologist at the State University, and in the summer of 1936 a potter's wheel was operated experimentally by homesteaders at the High School. Classes in pottery had been held for older girls in 1934–35, and for women in the summer of 1936. Equipment for processing the clay was not yet sufficient for commercialization.

10. *Quilt-making.*[28]

The homestead women had inherited this art and practiced the making of quilts, some with special skill. It was a

---

[27] The dairy is now in operation.
[28] See Chapter V, pp. 248–9.

type of work that could be carried on at home with young children and household duties. As soon as authenticated patterns and good materials were available, it was planned to develop a reliable market for these quilts. Quilt-making seemed likely to succeed as an economic enterprise.

11. Stone Quarry.

A survey of the geology of the Arthurdale area revealed that most of the land was composed of strata of yellow sandstone at the top, and limestone beneath. Here and there was an outcropping of coal, and far underneath was iron ore. But only the sandstone was available for quarrying. There was a possibility that after the sandstone had been quarried, the limestone deposits would become available. The sandstone, furthermore, was of a quality suitable for glass-making, and there were men with glass-making experience among the homesteaders. The High School students who investigated glass-making in their Chemistry class used the experience of these men in their experiments.

12. Printing.

The High School launched a rural newspaper which, by the end of the summer of 1936, was practically self-sustaining. Started as part of the School's program of expression, and to meet the needs on the homestead for communication and for exchange of valid news, it grew from a school news sheet to a four-page community newspaper for the neighborhood.[29]

The School also saw in the Arthurdale region an unexplored need for various kinds of job printing, as well as for the publication of bulletins and pamphlets on agricultural and cultural subjects which could have regional interest and importance. The work which the High School had done with job printing, the issuing of bulletins, and the publication of the newspaper were a direct preparation for this business enterprise. The work had used a number of students, had already produced one reliable and capable printer, and had drawn in a number of the older people as contributors of news articles.

13. Canning.

The Arthurdale Co-operative Association owned some good canning equipment. The homestead women in the summer of

---

[29] See Chapter V, pp. 268–72.

1936, when they were engaged in canning vegetables for School lunches, learned scientific methods of canning. There seemed to be a likely specialty market in the cities for unusually good soups and preserves. The materials could be raised at Arthurdale and efficient production for such an enterprise be at least begun, since it was within the experience and ability of the women, under the Home Economics teacher's direction. Provided that a market could be discovered and developed, it seemed likely that commercial production could be launched.

These enterprises were by no means "sure-fire." Nor is the above list exhaustive, but suggestive only. The School's point of view was that, in all probability, two or three of these, at least, would in time come to employ, and increasingly to support, some of the older boys and men.

A start was made on the raising of berries; the garden-nursery plants, shrubs and trees; and printing. Also herbs, cheese, clay, and quilting were, in the summer of 1936, in process of development. As part preparation for such enterprises, some of the older High School Mathematics classes turned their attention in 1935–36 to bookkeeping. The accounts of the newspaper and cheese-making groups were kept by members of these groups. The Economics classes interested themselves in the computation of costs, and the investigation of costs of transportation, marketing, etc.

Two important factors have not been sufficiently mentioned. One was capital for launching these businesses. Some needed little for a start, as, for instance, the newspaper and job printing, the shrubs and berries, quilting and clay products. The policy was to use these enterprises in the work of the High School and to develop them slowly and carefully, without an initial large or expensive outlay. To the School, however, the obtaining of capital did not seem the difficult matter. The training of homesteaders to carry on an infant industry and to nurture its development through the early stages seemed the slow human factor which could not be hurried and which required time and the training of experience—a factor which a community school was perhaps able to handle as well as any other agency.

The other element which I have understressed is that of locating and developing markets for the products of these enterprises. A study of marketing possibilities was well under way in 1936; was, in fact, carried as far as it could be until the enterprises should begin to produce. Boys and girls in the High School studied distribution and marketing as applied to the region, used State and Government surveys of production and market centers for West Virginia and western Pennsylvania, and saw clearly how and why certain products from Arthurdale would be best marketed at certain centers. No one believed that marketing was simple or easy, but it was held that with intelligence and care and hard work the trick could be turned, as indeed it is currently. So the School addressed itself to developing in its work these qualities among the adults and particularly among the young people.

The Community in 1935–36
Elsie Ripley Clapp

The year 1935–36 and its developments have been partly anticipated in the description of the outcomes of the activities and events of the first year on the project. In recounting the growth of community activities in the second year, reference will be made to their beginnings.[30] The important thing in this record is to reveal the course and turns of their development; to show what factors entered into these, and which factors helped and which hindered. Above all, it seems to me, the record should make clear that in community education one is never dealing with a fixed plan, a formula, or a ready-made organization, but with needs as they are revealed—

---

[30] See Chapter II, pp. 66–124.

needs and aspirations of people with all their potentialities and prejudices, their ambitions and handicaps, their ways of thinking and feeling, their patterns of behavior, their relationships and social environment, their cultural and racial background, as well as their physical surroundings.

The surprising fact is that a social environment, even when new and radically different, is compounded of features of the old life and the new in unpredictable combinations; and that the new social environment builds so fast and so quickly takes on forms and meanings.

THE SECOND YEAR A TRANSITIONAL PHASE

In the second year, the project had entered upon a phase of its development transitional between the earlier stage of moving away from idleness and destitution in a stranded mine camp area into new houses on farm land in a new community, and the later stage of established village life. The homesteaders who had at first gone about in a daze of happy gratitude for relief from bleak and hopeless poverty, awoke some months later to find themselves in the same old world; or faced, at least, after idleness and the haphazard existence of their unemployed days, with the pressures of working for a living, and of living within the wages they made and sustaining the obligations which their new life of work and opportunities presented. It was harder, possibly, for ex-miners of the boom days than for some other group to make smaller wages cover accumulated needs.

Back of the period of unemployment—a period of three to seven years—was the life of the mine camps alternating with brief pick-up jobs or meager farming. The mine camp habits of living on a credit basis; of extravagances bred of the desire to compensate for dangerous work underground and fixed by the practice of lavish expenditure of the high wages as skilled workers at the peak of the coal industry; of careless living in rented company houses; of inbred camp living—the gossip, grievances, and lethargy of company towns at their worst—these habits still held and operated in the new set-up, which was planned for careful, considered living, co-operative working, self-denial, and constructive and continuing effort. That the homesteaders were able under new conditions to throw off these habits to the extent they did was the surprising fact. Small wonder that the habits reappeared at times, especially when something stirred their latent fears and deep-rooted sense of insecurity.

Now that they had emerged from the "bad days," they found themselves on awakening from convalescent cheerfulness living in homes that satisfied their ambition for a clean, decent place of their own, living as people whom they had admired and envied. Some of them—the ambitious group—took on as many of the attitudes and ways of these people as they knew. Others remained lethargic, but distressed. Still others continued to rejoice and tried hard to cope with all the demands this new life laid upon them. They were, most of them, thrown by any hardship—as if, nervously, they could not stand any more—back into the practices that belonged not to their new life, but their old. It was hard for them to find their footing. Emotionally unstable still, they unconsciously sought relief in dramatizing small grievances—really expressing the unabated and fundamental sense of insecurity which they had not yet shaken off. Improvement in conditions could not happen too fast. Life, even in the rapid changes of a growing community, moved too slowly for them.

In the fall, the homesteaders were somewhat depressed by a summer of fairly light work on construction and the laying off of the boys from occasional employment. It was, however, a busy time: the men after work-hours toiled late into the evening harvesting; the women were busy canning, first their own vegetables and fruit and then vegetables for school lunches. It was well into October before the harvesting and canning were finished.

By mid-November the winter set in, a long bitterly cold period that year, followed with heavy snow which prevented much outside work on construction. Work was slack and wages slight in consequence. In this enforced idleness, the old fears swept over the homesteaders, and old and new resentments arose. Expressed discontents and doubts circulated as rumors, every mischance became a misfortune. Complaints were concrete enough, but fears were vague and inclusive. The cold and snow held them indoors and gave endless time for talk and gossip. The winter was full of emotion.

A disturbance of fear and doubt of the School, which they had helped to make and of which they had been so proud, swept over the homestead suddenly in January. The High School in its second year was preparing to apply to the State for ranking as an accredited high school. This necessitated meeting State requirements in equipment and would, when granted, enable the School's graduates to enter without examination the State University. The panic, whose source one can only conjecture, centered in this matter. Fear ran rampant that if the School could not "give credits" it was " no good." Deep in their being was the feeling, I am sure, that it would be just their luck to have a school like this.

The Arthurdale School Committee

To meet this unexpected problem, I asked the Men's and the Women's Clubs each to appoint ten men and ten women, respectively, on a School Committee to go over the problem of accrediting with the School staff, and to make better known to the community the work of the School.

The twenty Committee members and the teachers met at the High School in January, and together went over in detail the list of requirements which the High School must fulfill for accredited ranking. Several men on the Committee offered assistance; they worked with the High School teachers making additional laboratory tables and brought in as contributions to the science equipment whatever useful things they had, such as tin-snips, etc. The School ordered the necessary laboratory supplies and equipment.

The Committee inspected also the rest of the High School —the Library, classrooms, and Shop—and became acquainted with the work that was going on. It proved to be an extremely enlightening experience to them. They were greatly impressed by the students' work and by the kind of reference books used, and were overjoyed when anything they saw touched their own knowledge. One woman, looking with me at a chart made by a class studying the products and industries of various States, said, her face lighting up: "Why, that's what I used to study in school!" The first meeting accomplished its purpose of enlisting their help in the effort to complete the requirements that accredited ranking demanded, but the Committee felt that they had gained so much more understanding of the work at the School that they wanted to continue meeting. We all had in mind that this Committee might be the nucleus—or, at least the forerunner—of a parent-teacher organization which would undoubtedly follow.

At the next meeting, the Committee examined with equal care the classrooms and work of the "Grade School," and visited the Nursery School. In preparation for the meeting, the teachers had put out illustrations of the work in reading, writing, and Arithmetic, thinking that perhaps the parents were concerned about these subjects, and they were on hand to explain the work. But almost invariably the Committee ignored these pieces of work in the Three R's and flocked around the pieces of weaving and pottery and shop work that were in the rooms. They needed our explanations not at all, and explained to each other what they knew about the work from the children, or from visits to the School. They were enormously interested, and eager to tell others who had not visited and to bring them to see for themselves.

They and we both followed up this lead, and systematic efforts were made by each teacher to have every one of the parents of the children in her room visit while classes were going on. A great many did come in the weeks following. They were especially impressed by the great number of books studied and by the record of books read by the children which was posted in the classrooms. Later, in the summer, one of the men on the project—not a Committee member—who had been one of those most fearful about the School's qualifications, explained to *me* the advantages of having so many books of reference in every classroom for each child to use, as over against the old practice of parents' buying for a child a large and expensive number of the same texts. It was a matter of interest to us that, in spite of the way that fathers and mothers both had been in and around the School all day as workmen and as visitors, and the constant intimate knowledge of "all the doings" at School, there had been so little known about what was taught in classes and what the children were "getting." We thought the experience very salutary for us as teachers.

A few weeks later the School Committee, at my suggestion, entertained the original West Virginia Advisory School Committee which had in the beginning drafted the plan[31] for the "new school." Several members of the Arthurdale School Committee definitely prepared themselves for this visit by coming to School while classes were going on and familiarizing themselves with any facts they did not know. Many members of the West Virginia Committee were quite familiar with the work of the School, especially those who were members of the Department of Education at the University and who had repeatedly brought out their classes to visit the School, as

---

[31] See Chapter II, pp. 71–5. For a list of the members of this Committee, see below, p. 387, footnote 51.

were also the Superintendent and Assistant Superintendent of Preston County, who, of course, had known the School's work currently. Mr. Cox, Chairman of the Committee, who was Superintendent of Schools in Monongalia County, made a special trip out to Arthurdale to examine the School in preparation for the joint meeting.

When the West Virginia Committee arrived, they were taken in charge by the men and women of the Arthurdale Committee, who showed them over the whole School and explained the work to them with such grasp and understanding that, as the Dean of the Department of Education said later to them, he "could not distinguish parents from teachers." At the end of the trip through all the buildings, the two committees sat down together. The West Virginia Committee were asked to tell us frankly how far they felt that the School, now in its second year, had carried out the plans they had made for it in the beginning, and what suggestions they had for us. They unanimously and with enthusiasm expressed the opinion that the School had more than fulfilled their dreams. Several said that they wished their own children could go to such a school.

To the homesteaders the evaluation of the West Virginia Committee was especially reassuring, coming as it did from members of the Department of Education at the University, many of whom they knew, and to whom some of the homesteaders had "gone to school." The panic subsided, and disapproval boiled down to the few objectors who exist everywhere. The equipment was completed, and the application for ranking as an accredited high school sent in. The majority of the people really had no objections or complaints, it turned out, against the School at all. Rumors and talk about the High School's ranking had touched off their fear and, always expecting the worst, they had become excited about whether the children on graduation would enter the University (without examination). As none of the three students to be graduated in June was planning to go to the University, it was not, as a matter of fact, a present issue at all. Rather they coveted the privilege, should they wish to use it. The whole incident was interesting because it voiced the new ambitions to be like and do as other successful people.

Activities of the Winter and Early Spring

The new Recreation Building, so long anticipated, was christened almost before it was finished on Christmas Eve with the dramatization of the carols and the tree. From the date when it was formally opened to the public, January 10, with a double-header basketball game, at which there were speeches made by the President of the Men's Club and the director of athletics, and to which some 400 people came from the project, Reedsville, and the surrounding towns, the gymnasium floor, which the homesteaders proudly declared "one of the best in the State," was never free. It was the scene five nights a week of games, with neighboring teams playing the Junior and Senior Arthurdale High School teams, and also the Independent Men's Team made up of boys and men on the project and from Reedsville; it was used in the mornings by all the older grades for recess games during the winter, and in the afternoon by teams of High School students—boys and girls—and by the older boys on the project. The dance orchestra met for practice there, and on the big stage square-dance setts were rehearsed, concerts were given, and the drama groups put on their plays.

Every effort was made to fill the long dark evenings of the winter with activities and interests. The Calendar of Events published each month listed the basketball games, meetings of the Men's and Women's Clubs, committee meetings, choir rehearsals, the cooking classes for women which met twice a week at the School Center Building, singing groups, drama groups and orchestra practice, as well as the square dances that were held in spite of snow and storm and cold every Saturday night all through the winter. No matter how bad the night, some of the homesteaders and *all* the boys and girls came down to the Center for the dance.

By March, with the moderation of winter weather, and the picking up again of work on construction, and better pay envelopes, more food, and less anxiety, the temper of the project sweetened. At the time of the floods in Wheeling and Pittsburgh, the homesteaders forgot their own troubles in efforts to help the victims of the disaster, whose sufferings they could so well understand, gave generously out of their own wages and clothes and food supplies, and the first week in April put on a benefit performance of music and one of the plays of the adult group for the flood victims.

Spurred on by enjoyment of the Cooking Class Invitation Suppers, when members of the class entertained their husbands and invited guests at a supper they had prepared, the women decided to give an "Oyster Supper" for the benefit of the Medical Fund. It was a great success. They served about 300 people in the large lunch room at the School Center, and to their great pleasure the Reedsville people came, and also friends from Morgantown. It was a source of real satisfaction to them to know that they could now give parties to which these people wanted to come. They felt that at last they had left behind the time when they had—as they felt—been "looked down upon."

Although snowstorms held until mid-April, the roads were more open now and more people could get out. The recognition accorded the musicians and square-dancers, who, with the High School drama group, had put on a "Big Show" as a flood benefit, by an invitation to entertain the war veterans in Washington, and the extraordinary pleasure of this trip, gave not only the performers but all the homesteaders great happiness. The project was very proud of the honor.

When spring finally came, everyone plunged into farming,

and in plowing and planting forgot the hardships of the winter. We went to sleep at night and wakened at daybreak to the sound of tractors in the fields. The older boys obtained temporary employment in plowing and in the building of chicken houses for the Co-operative's new poultry farm, and hopefulness and content revived.

It was helpful to the School to have lived on the homestead during its first year when the many unanswered needs impelled the School to function in varied and widely different activities in the community, for these experiences brought it an understanding of the possibilities for education in every phase of the life and work on the project, and a comprehension of the people, their background, and psychology. So it was possible for it to pass through this more difficult second period of delayed adjustment, with its instabilities and upsets, objectively, and to view the problem as a sociological-educational problem of the restoration of people. The second winter was a period of assimilation and adjustment. Enterprises and activities became more organized, and now the homesteaders themselves took the initiative in entertainments, in arrangements for farming, and in committees. As the village became what is called more "normal," it might not have been possible for the School, without the informing experience of that first year, to realize all the possibilities of the situation educationally.

It is crystal-clear that, if schools enter into community affairs, they are in the midst of life as it is, unprotected by isolation and the rights of assumed authority. They have to take as well as give and lay hold of conditions as they find them.

The great steadying influence of this transitional second year on the project seems, as I look back upon it, to have been the School proper—the School which taught the boys and girls and children. Day in and day out, life and work in the School buildings went on and brimmed over into the life and interests of the community. It was really the work that the boys and girls and children were doing that pulled the School Committee members and the rest of the homesteaders out of their anxieties and doubts.

In this chapter of experience belong the development of the Nursery School as Miss Wadsworth described it,[32] the second year of the First Grade's study of farm processes and the Second Grade's "village in the woods," [33] the Third Grade's Indian life activities and the Fifth Grade's study of colonial life, as well as the Fifth-Sixth Grade's competent investigation of West Virginia.[34] This year also saw the growth in understanding of community education by the West Virginia teachers.[35] In it is to be included the rise of interest in historical tradition springing from the Fourth Grade's study of pioneer days and from their furnishing, with the help of the people on the homestead and in the neighborhood, of the old Fairfax log cabin.[36] This is the year that the High School developed its work in its new building and its study of community resources, which Mr. Beecher recorded.[37] Drama and music groups continued and we had the second Music Festival, which were described by Mr. Collins.[38] The sharing of all this work and interests probably had a greater vitalizing and normalizing effect than was realized at the time. Moreover, the new School buildings made possible provision for the diversity of interests the homesteaders craved, and allowed many events to happen simultaneously. One of the resources was the development and operation of the School and Community Library.

---

[32] See Chapter IV, pp. 197–215.
[33] See Chapter III, pp. 138–42.
[34] *Ibid.*, pp. 158–61.
[35] *Ibid.*, pp. 161–5.
[36] See Chapter III, pp. 144–51; also Chapter V, pp. 251–3, and this chapter, pp. 382–3.
[37] See Chapter VI, "A Rural High School," pp. 273–332.
[38] See Chapter V, pp. 247–8.

GROWTH AND DEVELOPMENT OF THE SCHOOL AND COMMUNITY LIBRARY

From a room with falling plaster in the attic of the old Mansion, lighted only by a casement window, to the large sunny School and Community Library, was a long distance.[39] The first year, there was no one in special charge of the Library; the High School girls working with Mr. Beecher listed the books and managed a catalogue of a sort, and Miss Sheffield and Mrs. Kimble voluntarily took turns helping the children find books to take home. The Library leaped into new life and importance, however, when it moved into its new quarters and came under the care of Kittie Ryan, the wife of Carson V. Ryan, one of the High School teachers, who was herself a trained librarian and a member of the supplementary teaching staff.

Mrs. Ryan started at once to catalogue the books and to indicate content for reference. Circulation the first week ran around 25 books daily, and touched 36 the second, totaling 392 books for the twenty days in September. By November, the average daily record of books taken out was 56. Impressed by the way the children tended to read and reread the same books, Mrs. Ryan tempted them also with stories of adventure, biographies, sea stories, and tales of exploration. For the Women's Club meetings, which were held in the Library, she set out books on hooked rugs and sewing, especially books on home decoration and any books on gardens and rock gardens, which were very popular, as were the current magazines. The Library was not only the place to go to read and to get books, but was used also by the doctor for his Physiology courses and by Mr. Collins for some of his singing groups.

The older students at first were somewhat at a loss in the Library, but soon discovered its interests. By the middle of

---

[39] See Chapter VI, pp. 289-91.

the month, the classes began to be able to locate reference material themselves. In November, some of the High School students started work planned by Mr. Beecher and Mrs. Ryan on bibliographies, and did some mending and binding of books and pamphlets. They soon served as librarians themselves for the younger children. As the year went on, the Drama class and Economics groups came to the Library to hunt up material; the Fifth and Sixth Grades and all the High School students used it increasingly in all their study periods. The Fourth Grade, who lived their own life mainly in their own classroom and the log cabin, were nevertheless enthusiastic users of the Library—the "readingest" class in the School, Mrs. Ryan called them. Soon they started a lending library in their own room.

Mrs. Ryan was instrumental in interesting friends of the School to send books, and their gifts materially increased our resources. Visitors sent back subscriptions to magazines, and the University of West Virginia Library in Morgantown generously allowed us to get many volumes currently from their collection. At Christmas time came gift boxes from other schools. At great deal of valuable material was sent to us by the Department of Agriculture.[40] The Library expanded in several directions. We used our own small fund available for books for High School Science, for stories for the older boys and girls and adults, and for books for the teachers in training.

In January we had started a WPA course in library work for boys and girls. They learned cataloguing, the charging and discharging of books, the making of bibliographies; they clipped and organized newspaper and magazine material, and repaired books worn out in use. As a preparation for a Rural Library Service to women shut in by snow and bad weather or housed with babies and very young children, they set out to familiarize themselves with what the Library had to offer.

---

[40] Mr. Beecher speaks of this in the record of the High School, Chapter VI, p. 289.

At first they took to the houses books they thought might interest the women, but later they "filled orders" and exchanged old books for new. The women's greatest interest was in magazine and adventure stories, boarding school tales and love stories.

The circulation stayed at 40 to 50 books a day, increased by the house deliveries during the winter months. Not only were books taken out by the children for themselves and for their parents, but by the women after their Club meetings and when they stopped in on their way home after serving School lunches, and by the men on the project—both homesteaders and outside workmen. Another year would have extended the library service beyond the project. Such community services tend to widen—as they should.

We found it convenient to keep in classrooms reference books which were constantly consulted; botany books, geology and biology books, for instance, we placed in the Science room and certain histories in the Eleventh Grade classroom, where the students could have them at hand to consult without waiting for a chance to get to the Library. Books on a particular subject were lent to a group during their study of that topic. Mrs. Ryan kept in close touch with the classes and their teachers. She and her library students were most helpful in getting together pictures and periodicals and gathering reference materials and additional bibliographies. This was, of course, not only excellent library training for the students and helpful to them in their own reference work, but of great assistance to the classes.

HEALTH WORK IN 1935–36

The medical program, established amid difficulties the first year,[41] was in the next twelve months widened and intensified. 1935–36 saw the continuation of the School inspection of chil-

---

[41] See Chapter II, pp. 89–99.

dren, started the year before, in adequate clinic rooms at the School Center and in a nurse's office at the Nursery School, which provided an isolation room and a shower. Classes in Physiology were given by the doctor at the High School, and courses in Biology and Bacteriology by Mr. Beecher. The doctor kept and developed his cultures at the High School laboratory. This work at the High School contributed essential knowledge to the boys and girls and through them to their parents, who learned with and through the children. Posted notices that "Water must be boiled" whenever the Health Office reported the water of a well as "doubtful" were not very effective, but when the boys and girls brought home the information they had obtained in their studies in bacteriology, their parents began to boil water and to keep away from polluted streams.

A far-reaching element in health is, of course, the kind of vegetables and animals raised and the kind of food purchased. Agricultural advice and Home Economics instruction were available the second year on the project. The first year few, if any, cows were kept on the homestead; by January 1936, there were 40 cows, 22 of which had had the tuberculin test. In the spring of 1936 a vigorous 4H Project was started with over 70 members, under the direction of the wife of the agriculturalist, Mrs. Pharr; and projects for raising chickens and pigs, caring for cows and gardens for the boys, and baking, sewing, and cooking for the girls, were started. Under the direction of the Home Economics teacher, Helen Cawley, classes were given in cooking for mothers and for the older girls; also advice in home conferences. In the summer of 1936, work in the testing of milk and water and in making cheese was carried on at the High School with Mr. Beecher.

New Plan for School Gardens

Everyone agreed in the fall of 1936 that the best way to meet the problem of raising food for School lunches had not yet been found. Helen Cawley, who joined the staff in January 1936, as director of Home Economics, and who as one of her many duties supervised the preparation of School lunches by voluntary groups of mothers, was the one to devise a new plan. She had not lived through the trials of the previous summer,[42] but was impressed by the shortage of food for lunches and the spoilage which curtailed it further. The plan she suggested was for each family to raise at home a proportionate amount of vegetables for lunches at School. The Men's Club heartily endorsed the plan, and Mr. Pharr, the agricultural adviser, assisted in its execution. The canning equipment belonging to the Mountaineer Craftsmen Co-operative was borrowed and, with the help of the men, it was set up in the canning kitchen at the School Center ready for the first garden returns. Miss Cawley supervised volunteer groups of women, who during the summer canned the produce for School lunches as it was sent in by the families.

WPA Course in Practical Nursing

A course in Practical Nursing was given in 1935–36 under WPA auspices. During the first year we had met the demand for such work both on the project and in the surrounding region. The course was given under the direct supervision of the doctor and nurse, assisted by the head of the Nursery School and a WPA supervisor of Home Economics. Plans for each part of the training and for their interrelation were carefully made in conference with all the instructors. The nurse, Miss Plummer, gave a full course in bedside nursing which combined actual practice-nursing with instruction and demonstration. The doctor gave supplementary lectures on the digestive, excretory, respiratory, and circulatory systems, and their care in disease. As the course aimed to fit its pupils to go into homes of illness and not only take care of the sick person but

---

[42] See Chapter II, pp. 111–3.

also shoulder household duties, it included cooking, emphasizing especially the preparation of diets for invalids and the relation of food to health. Such work in the country usually covers the care and supervision of the children in a household, so arrangements were made for the student-nurses to observe in the Nursery School the preparation of food and eating procedures used, sleeping and toilet habits, and play supervision and materials. Miss Wadsworth, the head of the Nursery School, discussed their observations with the students. Several of the older girls on the project enrolled for this course and two completed it. Under Miss Plummer's direction, the student-nurses assisted at the Baby Clinics, nursed a post-operative case on the homestead, and took post-delivery care of several of the women. This course not only fitted the older girls to take positions as practical nurses, who were in frequent demand in the region, but also was of great assistance to them in their current home duties.

Training of Girls as Housekeepers

A WPA course for training of girls as housekeepers, to fit them to go into families and do general housework—a need that existed both in the countryside and, at times, on the project—was also given in 1935–36. This course also, of course, bore directly on health education. With Mrs. Sowers, the WPA supervisor who worked with Miss Cawley, the director of Home Economics, the girls learned laundering, ironing, cleaning, planning and preparing menus, and serving meals. With Miss Wadsworth they also studied child care at the Nursery School. As with the practice-nurses, their work included work in the community. To quote from Mrs. Sowers's diary:

> The main problem this week in my housekeeping class has been to put into practice the work they have learned to do in their classes.
> The girls have taken turn about in going out to Mrs. Rollin-

son's. A new child has just come to their family, making nine children. The oldest girl, who is fourteen, should be in High School, but her mother thought it was necessary for her to stay at home. The girls were in hopes that if they could help Mrs. Rollinson, perhaps Martha could go back to school. They were able to take over the problems of the household and to do them as they had been taught.

This practice work included cleaning of the School lunchroom, food storage closets, and Home Economics rooms; serving milk at School lunches, and helping the mothers to prepare and serve them. Cleaning the doctor's quarters and the Baby Clinic room introduced both the student-nurses and the student-housekeepers to a high standard of cleanliness.

Well Baby Clinics in 1936

The Well Baby Clinics, which started in the spring of 1935,[43] were continued through the next year. By the spring of 1936 the Baby Clinics were held twice a month: one fortnight for infants of 1 to 12 months, the next for babies of 12 to 24 months.[44] Each clinic was carefully prepared for, and each represented a wide co-operative effort. They were held at the Nursery School. The doctor and nurse officiated, assisted by the student-nurses. The record was taken by the wife of one of the teachers. The Nursery School teachers assisted the women of the homestead Medical Committee to receive and care for the mothers and babies, and the teachers of the "Big School" used their cars to take the mothers and babies back and forth. Miss Wadsworth, the head of the Nursery School, in her report on Baby Clinics at the end of July, says:

The Clinics have been well attended—averaging about 14 babies at each Clinic. Six Clinics have been held since May 7.
Special emphasis at these Clinics was placed on nutrition, the

---

[43] See Chapter IV, pp. 189–90, 212–3; also Chapter II, pp. 93, 96–8.
[44] See Chapter IV, pp. 213–4.

doctor stressing with each mother the value of giving green vegetables, fruit juices, and cod-liver oil. The Nursery School dietitian, Mildred Bayles, and the director of Home Economics, Helen Cawley, attended each Clinic and talked with the mothers, helping them to make use of the advice given by the doctor and nurse. Follow-up visits to the home were made by Helen Cawley, who also did special nutrition work with some of the mothers who especially needed help.

It has been most gratifying to see the improvement which has been made by all the babies, and to find that almost all of the mothers—even those hardest to convince at first—have been following the doctor's instructions and have been adding the things essential to a young baby's diet.

At several of the Clinics the doctor talked to the mothers about the use of Heinz strained baby foods. A display of these were on hand at the Nursery School, and they were placed on sale at the Arthurdale Co-operative Store. Many of the mothers have been buying these, and those who could not afford them have been shown how vegetables can be purée'd for young children.

The women of the homestead Medical Committee have been of great assistance in planning for and helping at the Clinics.[45] A meeting of the Medical Committee is held before each Clinic, and each member has taken responsibility for notifying the mothers on her road of the day and hour of the Clinic. Three Committee members are present at each Clinic to assist the doctor and nurse in the dressing and undressing of the babies, and to act as hostesses.

The women on the Medical Committee helped also with the thorough physical examination of children which went forward during the summer.[46] With the consent of the parents, more immunization against diphtheria, smallpox, and typhoid was also given. Remedial care and treatment and, when necessary, operations and hospital care were made available for the new families that came onto the homestead the second year. Measures to gain and maintain health were slowly established and gradually became accepted routines.

---

[45] The work of this Medical Committee, and the Baby Clinics represent phases of the adult education program.
[46] See Chapter IV, pp. 214-5.

In August 1936, the doctor could report the health of the community as "exceptionally good."

THE HOMESTEAD HEALTH COMMITTEE

A joint committee of men and women appointed by the Men's and Women's Clubs to serve as a Health Committee began to meet early in the fall of 1935. This Committee wrestled with the difficult problem of ways and means to meet the cost of hospital care, X-rays and operations, and special treatment. One result of their deliberations was the consideration of a health co-operative, and the drawing up of a tentative form of contract to be signed by every homestead family. This was sent to every family, and the Committee reported that many of the families were willing to sign it. However, at that time, mid-winter, construction work was slack, so that the Committee did not feel justified in pushing the matter then, although there was no intention of dropping it;[47] the Committee and many members of the community recognized both the difficulty and the urgency of the problem.

THE ARTHURDALE STORE COMMITTEE

Heretofore purchase of staples and general supplies had been made in Reedsville and near-by towns, largely on credit, the old habit of charging purchases holding over from mine camp days. The homesteaders themselves wished they could get away from this habit although they found it difficult, not only psychologically, but because it was hard to make the money they earned after so long a period of destitution cover both accumulated and current wants. It was felt that a store of their own where cash was paid for all purchases would be more satisfactory and, in the end, more economical. A joint committee of men and women was appointed by the Men's Club and the Women's Club to formulate plans for an Arthur-

---

[47] A Health Association has since been formed.

dale general store. Several of the members of the Committee had at one time or another served in grocery stores; one had been a cook; one was a competent housekeeper. Each member made out a list of foods and goods which such a store might carry. These lists were checked one against the other, and a composite list, mimeographed by the School, was sent to each family on the homestead, asking them to check which of the foods and articles they, as a family, would be likely to buy. Almost every article listed was checked by someone, which seemed to indicate that the list had covered pretty well the needs of the community. The list was then given to a wholesaler, who supplied many of the local grocery stores, to add names of brands and prices. Based on these figures and the construction unit's estimates of the cost of remodeling the old School Shop shed and of equipment, an application for a grant was made out and sent to Washington. Shortly after this, the Arthurdale Co-operative Association was formed and the Store became the first one of its enterprises. This is the Store which has been mentioned so often in the preceding chapters and which from the time it opened in January played such an active part in the life of the homestead. The excellent work of the Store Committee was largely instrumental in bringing it about.

To recapitulate the items in the second year program of health: continuation of school inspection of children; classes in Physiology, Biology, and Bacteriology at the High School; the acquisition of cows, instruction in farming, the raising of pigs and chickens and gardens; the starting of a 4H project for the boys and girls; classes in cooking for mothers and older girls; laboratory work with High School students in the testing of milk and water; vegetables for School lunches raised at home by each family and canned by the women under the direction of the Home Economics teacher. To these community and School enterprises must be added the courses in

Practical Nursing and Housekeeping given by the School under WPA auspices. The Well Baby Clinics increased and became the responsibility of the women of the homestead Health Committee. The group of men and women constituting the Health Committee began consideration of a health cooperative to meet the health needs of the community. All the foregoing items are, perhaps, more easily recognized as part of a health program than the work of the Store Committee, yet the Store also played an important part in the health program, furnishing as it did fresh fruit, and canned goods, which were tested by the Home Economics classes, milk, and medicines ordered on the advice of the doctor. It is clear that in the second year the health program began to deal with some of the *sources of health* as well as with the clinical and remedial work which was so urgent and so occupying the first year on the project.

SUMMER ACTIVITIES IN 1936

"Winter School," as they called it, closed the twenty-ninth of May, and "Summer School" activities began the second of June and ran through June and July. We had profited by the experience of the summer before, and this year allowed no time to elapse between the two sessions. This second year we also planned for summer activities at hours adjusted to housework and work in the gardens. The Nursery School was continued and ran without a break through July; and we planned some activities for the younger children.

PROGRAM OF EVENTS FOR OLDER BOYS AND GIRLS AND ADULTS

We had come to realize the summer before that people were free and the boys and girls and older children at loose ends and restless after supper—which, on the project, was eaten anywhere between three and five o'clock. So in 1936 we scheduled various activities at the School Center for the older children after supper in the "evening." Miss Cawley, the Home Economics teacher, held cooking classes for the girls, and Dan Houghton, of the Mountaineer Craftsmen Co-operative, opened his woodworking class to boys and girls and any women who wished to come. Work was done on the community newspaper and on job printing up in the printing room at the High School. Miss Wadsworth continued her block-printing class, and Miss Carlisle had a women's pottery class. Fletcher Collins's High School drama group met at their outdoor theater in the woods, and when it grew dark repaired to the stage in the Recreation Building. He met also with the singing groups, the male quartet, and the square-dance-orchestra group. We held the second Music Festival early in July.

The School Center and the High School and Recreation Buildings were lighted every night and, although some homesteaders were too tired, after a long day of work on construction and in their gardens, to come out in the evening, others welcomed the change of activity and were glad for "some place to go at night." The Women's Club and the Men's Club met alternate weeks, and square dances were held once a week as usual. The Library was open every evening for a magazine, newspaper, and fiction reading hour.

Mrs. Ryan's report at the end of July states:

Knowing what books were read would be read for relaxation after a hard day's work, we replenished the fiction shelves with some new books—primarily Western stories. Last fall it bothered me to have to spend money on such books—when money was so scarce—but I have begun to realize that if the Library can offer to the people here books of the type they enjoy—which, at the present, are for most of them "Westerns"—they will come in more often and develop the "library habit." In time they will go from Western stories to other types of books.

One example of this is Drake Peters, one of the older post-High School boys, who came regularly to the Library several times a week. After he had exhausted our supply of Zane Grey and Curwood, he happened to take out one of Joseph Lincoln's books. We had acquired several of these as gifts. Since then he has read all of Lincoln that we have. He has spent several evenings in the Library telling me how much a certain character reminded him of "Uncle Bill."

"Of course, I've never seen New England," Drake said the other night, "but after you read these here books, it just shows how much like people I know these people are. Captain Eza is just like a barber I used to know real well." And he launched into a detailed description of the things the barber used to say and do.

Some of our regular customers are reading the fiction shelf from one end to the other, starting with the A's and reading every book to the W's. Winifred has not skipped a single book.

We have acquired some new readers among the men who are coming to the Library quite regularly. Mr. Creighton (who works in the blacksmith's shop and in the Craftsmen's forge) came in one evening early in the summer to find illustrations of metal lamps, and since then has become a "regular." He is interested in historical novels and in history and travel books.

The garden books have been very popular among the women. Mrs. Bostwick got all the plans and suggestions for her rock garden from the book on rock gardens. Magazines have been more popular this summer than they were during the winter, especially the home-making and gardening numbers. And the men seem to like *Popular Mechanics*.

The WPA library workers had several requests from homesteaders for Government pamphlets on chicken-raising, bee-keeping, and cattle-feeding, and we were able to supply these.

ATHLETICS

The second summer,[48] the playing fields were in better shape and were used through the long light twilight. After dark, the boys and girls played on the gymnasium floor of the Recreation Building—a resource we had lacked the first summer.

The report of Carl Saunders, the director of athletics, of the summer athletic activities follows:

---

[48] See Chapter II, pp. 108–10, for an account of athletics the first summer.

As was the policy last year, there were athletics for all groups —young and old, large and small.

The boys of 12 to 17 were provided with an opportunity to play organized baseball by the fact that the American Legion of Preston County sponsored a six-team league. Despite the fact that the boys had little equipment, they enjoyed the chance to play and borrowed gloves from their opponents, lending them three or four gloves in return. By their travels to their opponents' home diamonds they had an opportunity to learn many facts about their County, which was a new experience to many of the boys. It also gave them contacts with boys of their own age, which they would not otherwise have had. A team of younger players was formed which played games with near-by communities as well as with the Arthurdale American Legion Junior Team.

The men and older boys wanted to continue with the mushball, or softball, league that was so successful last year in providing the men and older boys an opportunity to enjoy the spirit of play and a chance to "do something at night." Then the American League Junior Team wanted to be represented, and they came into the mushball league with one or two adults on their team. After the first quarter of the season was over, the neighboring town of Reedsville wished to come in. This made the fifth team in the league. Some of the best players in the league from all the teams would band together and play surrounding community teams.

When the girls and women came out, they would play softball, newcome, and volley ball. Unlike last summer, not many women came out for games, probably because of the fact that there were other activities for them this summer that interested them more. The pottery, block-printing, and carpentry classes took the place of athletics for them.

The evening games in the Recreation Building proved very popular and were usually well attended. As originally scheduled, they were for children of the Fourth to Ninth Grade. But all came. There were little tots and boys in High School and beyond. Because of lack of space for so many groups, it was finally cut down to two groups: a group of small boys and the girls, who usually played newcome and volley ball at one end of the floor, and a group of boys who played basketball at the other end. A group of four or five boys of High School age and older came in and helped supervise the games. About ten minutes before the hour was up, the younger boys would go off for their shower and the older boys would have an informal game of basketball among themselves. All the children as well as the whole community are enthusiastic, to put it mildly, about the game of basketball.

The Men's Club sponsored an Independent Baseball Team, composed in the main of players from Arthurdale and Reedsville with one or two from other communities. This team played part of its home games at Reedsville and part at Arthurdale, usually on Sunday. It provided the people of the communities an opportunity to get out on Sunday afternoon and see some of their own people perform. It was run by an Athletic Committee of three selected by the Men's Club.

James Myers, Jr., who had assisted Mr. Saunders the first summer on a visit to the project, returned the second year to take charge in Mr. Saunders's absence when he left for work at summer school. Barbara Myers, who was again visiting the project, assisted. James Myers reported at the end of July:

The athletic activities this summer showed quite a marked advance over those of last summer. Last year, the whole program was in the embryo stage; the people were not really conscious of its existence and possibilities. The main problem was to get them to come out and form their leagues, teams, and classes. Evidently during the winter, with the Recreation Building as a center, a spirit of organized athletics was born, for when I arrived the first of July the homesteaders were wholeheartedly supporting their different teams and leagues—quite a different picture.

Last year we discussed the idea of overnight camping trips, but never got around to it. This summer we located a fine place on the edge of a brook over near Albright and took two groups out Saturday nights. The first group was made up of five of the older fellows. They had had a little previous camping experience, and fell into the spirit of the trip well.

The second group was made up of five of the younger boys about nine or ten years old. One of the mothers told me that her boy had come home the night I asked him if he could go with us and said to her: "I have something very important to ask you. It's just about the most important thing I ever had to ask you. Can I go on a camping trip on Saturday?"

These accounts make clear the progress in the athletics recreation program. By the end of the second summer, games and sports had really become the people's own interest and recreational resource. This could not have happened, we felt sure, without the start of the first year, discouraging as that was. The athletic program succeeded finally because it answered a need and gave the people, when they became acquainted with it, enjoyment.

Activities with the Younger Children

Miss Carlisle met with the primary children twice a day: in the early evening "after supper" for a story hour, and in the morning for gardening. The morning group not only planted the flower bed in front of the Nursery School, but also reclaimed a piece of ground between the Nursery School building and the woods for a vegetable garden. There they planted lettuce, beets, carrots and spinach, peas and lima beans, and tomato plants. The children later added green beans and Swiss chard. They worked in the garden every day, weeding and tending it. We satisfied our own ambition of teaching the younger children how to plant and raise green vegetables. The Second Grade had, by request, left their woods-village buildings for the summer group to use, and the children played in them and tended the village gardens also.

Outdoor Science with the Older Children

Carson V. Ryan, who taught science in the High School, and Elisabeth Sheffield together worked with a group of children of nine to twelve years old. They continued the outdoor aquarium started by the Fourth Grade in the spring, made a rock garden around the pool, and collected insects, mounting about 40 specimens. In this work the School was both directing activities natural to the summer time and exploring possibilities for use the following year in Science with the younger children.

We were able [Mr. Ryan wrote] to complete a small pool which held water quite well. The boys liked the work with concrete and were quite expert in handling a trowel. In the pool we had salamanders, lizards, crayfish, frogs, a water lily, and several grasses. Around the pool were various plants which we located in the woods and on a trip back by Dogtown. Some of the plants were: royal fern, Christmas fern, two varieties of sedum, bedstraw, several varieties of milkweed, including *Asclepias quadrifolia,* false and real Solomon's seal, two cypripediums—pink and yellow—columbine, *Clintonia borealis,* May apples, rattlesnake plantain, wild roses, Jack-in-the-pulpit, pitcher plants (one of the insect-catching plants), several violets, hepatica (tubular and others)—all of which were native, with the exception of the pitcher plant and the lily.

The boys and girls built a rustic bridge, stone paths, a snake cage, etc., and, in other words, developed the pool and its surroundings. The group was small, but remained constant all summer.

Summer Living in the Log Cabin

A large group of these children centered their interests and activities in the log cabin under Miss Sheffield's guidance. In this work Miss Funk assisted in order to enable her to undertake the direction of the pioneer program in Miss Sheffield's place the following winter.

It has been this summer [Miss Sheffield reports] that the cabin has really become a pioneer home. We had one of the homesteaders who was a carpenter really fix the doors and window shutters. The Fourth Grade boys put in corner shelves, which look fine with wooden trenchers set up on them, made more gun racks, and fixed the bed better. The girls made a quilt for it. The children started a hominy block and put their flax tools outside the cabin. We bought a sheep and an old iron kettle, and borrowed a copper kettle for use outdoors. We hoed and cultivated flax and corn, developed a flourishing herb garden, and grew a promising gourd crop. We built an outside fireplace and a soap hopper. And costumes on, the children have seemed like real pioneers—carding, cooking, molding bullets, and dipping candles.

On the Fourth of July, we opened the cabin to the public for the first time. It was quite a success. Several homesteaders and teachers and their entire families came, and all seemed intensely interested. On Sunday afternoons, when it has been open to the public, we have had streams of visitors, both local people and strangers. At times, there have been twenty or more in the cabin at once. Last Sunday we went about Reedsville inviting the people who have helped us especially with local history. They all came, bringing their children.

Practically all our country visitors have themselves seen carding, spinning, etc., done in their own homes. Many have worn homespun. This is good for the children to hear about; but isn't it surprising that the day of hand processes is so close at hand here in West Virginia?

Science Work with the Older Girls and Boys

In the spring when the homestead School Committee members were helping to complete the Science laboratory equipment, several of the men expressed the desire to do work in science. They hung about the Science room a good deal anyway, watching the experiments with the incubator, keeping an eye on the greenhouse plants, looking in on work of the Chemistry and Biology classes, bringing in plants and insects. "The men," Carson Ryan wrote, "took quite an interest and brought all kinds of bugs to me. In fact, if I wasn't there, they would put them in glass bottles and jars and leave them for me." In the "Summer School" we offered experimentally a class in chemistry of soils and water, but the men felt that they could not give the time away from their gardens to do it.

The milk-testing which had been started in the spring was continued, many of the men on the project bringing in samples of milk to be tested. The High School girls learned to test and to pasteurize raw surplus milk, and to make cottage cheese. With Mr. Beecher, a group of High School students investigated milk and milk products as a possible livelihood venture.[49]

Some of the older boys with Carson Ryan started raising berries on the slope of the hill across the way from the High School—another likely economic enterprise.[50]

We felt that the summer activities of 1936 were much better adjusted to meet the needs and interests of all the different ages—the adults and the little children as well as the younger and older boys and girls. Such a program, however, needs time for full development and repetition to become a recurrent expectation in people's minds. A community school should, without question, be used twelve months of the year, and its work and activities should be adjusted to seasonal occupations and interests. A year-round program is, we found, instrumental in promoting understanding of community education in the community. Nothing, for instance, impressed the homesteaders more than the fact that the teachers spent their "vacations" on the homestead. They were sure then that it was their home, too.

SCHOOL AND COMMUNITY LIVING

Arthurdale Not "An Island Community"

1935–36 was characterized by still more contacts with people and places outside the project, although these had obtained from the beginning. Visitors and other commentators on the Arthurdale scene often expressed a fear lest it be "an island community"—a fear arising, probably, from the fact that it was a homestead. Those of us who lived there did not find this to be true; on the contrary, we had more than the usual number of contacts and connections with the people and places of the region, the State, and the County. Without minimizing

---

[49] See this chapter, p. 352.
[50] *Ibid.*, p. 351.

the ways in which Arthurdale may have differed from other villages, I can say, as one of its residents, that living went on there very much as it does everywhere. The distinguishing features of the life at Arthurdale were consciousness of the purpose and plan of the project and of the bearing of all events and actions upon that, and a desire on the part of the people for the project's success, which was held to be identical with success for individuals. The fact that the interests and learning of the people centered in the project and the community School gave them a fund of common experience. They all had part, one way and another, in plans and activities. So shared effort and a community of interests were also outstanding characteristics of the life there. Another noticeable fact, I think, was the amount and variety of work going on all day and every day, as well as the zest and enjoyment of the activities, square dances, and good times generally.

The teachers, whose life on the homestead was an intrinsic part of their educational work, lived there naturally as they would anywhere, their contacts with others intimate as they usually are in rural communities. We were constantly, all of us, involved in what went on. We sought help from our friends and neighbors, and gave ours when it was needed. The community was essentially friendly and hard-working. It grew much more rapidly than most villages, and each day brought changes and developments.

Relations with Other Towns and Cities

With other towns and cities of the region and the surrounding countryside Arthurdale from the beginning had many contacts.

With Reedsville, a village a mile down the road, the homestead had especially close connections. The Arthurdale people used the Reedsville bank, its stores, its church, and—for a time at least—its postoffice and barber shop. A good many of the

Government representatives and many visitors to the project stayed there. Several of the teachers the first year boarded there. Reedsville found in Arthurdale, its homesteaders, visitors, and the people who worked there many customers. To Reedsville, Arthurdale brought also new life and interests. The Reedsville people shared in the square dances. Their boys played on the Arthurdale teams. They came to the basketball games, suppers, and concerts, and were more or less caught up in the life and activities of the project.

What was true of Reedsville was true also of Masontown, four miles beyond Reedsville. Additional business came to its stores and garage. Masontown people also came to the dances, games, and entertainments. Three of the teacher families lived there the first year. The Masontown High School in 1934–35 kindly allowed us to use its gymnasium for basketball games.

Kingwood, eight miles to the east of us, is the County Seat of Preston County. The County Board of Health, which worked so co-operatively with us, was located there; also the offices of the Preston County Board of Education under which the Arthurdale School operated as a County school. Mr. Paul Watson, the County Superintendent of Schools, and Mr. Kenneth Shaffer, the Assistant-Superintendent, knew the School well and worked most helpfully with us. Two members of the School staff lived in Kingwood the first year.

Our connections with Dogtown, Gladesville, and other settlements to the west and northwest of the project and with the farms around about us were largely through individuals and families, many of whom we came to know. The two Bethlehem Steel mines, not working while we were there, which lay off the road between Reedsville and Masontown, we knew chiefly because of the fact that a number of the homestead families had lived there until the houses they were to occupy on the homestead were finished, the fathers working on the project, the children in school with us, and the families sharing in community activities at Arthurdale.

Morgantown was bound to the project by many ties. It had been headquarters for the feeding program for the children of the coal fields of the Monongahela Valley established through the agency of the Friends Service Committee; and many of its social agencies and people co-operated in the first work of the restoration of the people of the mine camps, from which, in very fact, the plan and purpose of Arthurdale was born. Scott's Run, the gulch containing the abandoned mine camps, from which many of the first group of homesteaders came, is situated a few miles outside this city. The Relief Office, headed by Alice Davis, was in Morgantown; the workshops of the Mountaineer Craftsmen Co-operative Association were situated there before they moved out to the project.

Morgantown is the site of the University of West Virginia, and members of its staff in many departments had been interested in the homestead from its inception and continued to give it all possible assistance in a great variety of ways. Several members of the West Virginia Advisory School Committee were members of the Department of Education, notably Dean Hudelson, Mr. Justus Deahl, Dr. Hill, Dr. Allen, and Mr. Colebank, Principal of the University High School.[51] They had been instrumental with others in drawing up the original Plan for a school at Arthurdale,[52] and continued to give aid and encouragement to the School.[53] Some of the members of the Department of Education used the Arthurdale School as a demonstration center and frequently brought their classes out to observe.

---

[51] The members of the Committee were: the Honorable W. W. Trent, State Superintendent of Schools in West Virginia, Mr. Deahl, Superintendent of Schools in Preston County (succeeded by Mr. Paul Watson); Mr. Kenneth Shaffer, Assistant-Superintendent; Mr. Walter Riddle, Assistant-Superintendent of Schools in Monongalia County (succeeded by Dr. Robert Clark); Miss Mary Jo Barrett, Supervising Teacher (succeeded by Mrs. Edith Glenn, Principal); Dean Hudelson, Dr. L. B. Hill, Dr. H. B. Allen, of the Department of Education, University of West Virginia; Mr. George H. Colebank, Principal of the University High School; Miss Alice Davis, Relief Administrator. Floyd B. Cox, Superintendent of Schools in Monongalia County, was Chairman.
[52] See Chapter II, pp. 71–5.
[53] See this chapter, pp. 360–2.

In spite of the seventeen miles between Morgantown and Arthurdale, we relied upon the clincs and hospitals of this nearest large city. The homesteaders who had come from Scott's Run thought of Morgantown as their city. To all the people on the project, it was a trading and shopping center. Morgantown is the County Seat of Monongalia County. Mr. Floyd B. Cox, the County Superintendent of Schools, who was Chairman of the West Virginia Advisory School Committee, co-operated with the School in many ways.

With the city and all these surrounding towns, then, we were constantly and closely connected. Our connections reached out beyond Morgantown to Fairmont, the site of the State Teachers College and State Hospital; and, in the other direction, to Terra Alta, eight miles beyond Kingwood, whose high school we knew well, and to Hopemont, where the State Tuberculosis Sanitarium is situated on the outskirts of Terra Alta. It is, I think, not too much to say that from the outset Arthurdale had not only the usual connections of any village with its adjoining towns and countryside, but unusually close and active connections with them.

ARTHURDALE A PRESTON COUNTY SCHOOL

The School saw itself always as a Preston County school with a special service to render to the County and the State because of its situation and because of the educational work being carried on there.

The Arthurdale School was extensively used, as the teachers' diaries reveal, by teachers of the State and County who came to observe and to visit classes. Some weeks we had 25 to 50, other weeks 150 to 200, school visitors. They came individually, in small groups, in larger classes, from other schools in Preston or Monongalia Counties or from other parts of the State, from the State University and the State Normal School.

Frequently, teachers of near-by high schools brought their students over to visit classes. Gradually we developed a technique for handling this influx of guests: members of the School staff in their free periods, the Director of the School and the secretaries, and Mrs. James Moreland, who had been identified with the work of the Friends Service Committee in Morgantown and in the Run, and who was the official hostess on the project, shared these duties. We arranged and labeled the work that was up in the classrooms so that it would be easier for the large groups of guests to understand what was going on with the least disturbance to the children. It seemed to us that this sharing was a part of the School's job, since one of the purposes of the experiment in community education which was carried on during the first two years at the School was to serve teachers in other rural areas. A large number of educators from other States, also, visited the School, drawn likewise by interest in the project.

The Arthurdale School, as a Preston County school, received maintenance from State funds for basic salaries, with supplementary salary allotments from the County for teachers assigned the School under the State regulations based on pupils' average daily attendance for the last three months of the previous year. Since only 87 of the 167 children who entered the Arthurdale School in September 1934 had attended Preston County schools the previous year, only three teachers were assigned the School the first year. The next year, five teachers were assigned the School. As the enrollment the first year was 246 in Grades 1 to 12 (including the Nursery School) and 317 the second year, there was a shortage of teachers for the classes. By the terms of the agreement with the State and Preston County Board of Education, teachers were to be appointed by the Board, but to the Director of the School was given the privilege of selection among the candidates and also of submitting names for their approval.

For the first two years the experiment in community education was sustained by funds privately donated by a few interested people. These funds supplied to the School the services of a director and a group of supplementary teachers who carried the work of the classes not provided with County teachers, taught the young adults, and engaged in many community activities. These funds also supplemented the work of the Nursery School (maintained by WPA funds), and provided teaching materials and the expenses of running the School. The School buildings were erected by the Government as part of the construction of the houses and community buildings on the project.

At the end of the second year, the donor of the largest amount of money that sustained the educational experiment decided, together with the Director of the School and those interested in the experiment, that the time had come to transfer the School to the direction of the State and County school authorities. This decision was discussed with the West Virginia Advisory School Committee, and plans were made for carrying on the School. The Committee voted unanimously to continue the School as a community school, and to carry on the work already begun as far as possible. The donors of the fund for the educational experiment continued for the following year to give the amount necessary to sustain the health program, to supplement the work at the Nursery School, and to provide additional teachers to supplement the number that could be allotted by the County Board of Education.

PURPOSE OF THIS REPORT

It was hoped in establishing the School that its work might be suggestive to other rural communities and might reveal the possibilities of community education through the agency of a school. This record, which has been kept as concrete and literal as possible, is made with the same ends in view. If it in any measure makes clear what a community school is and does, and discloses the point of view from which a socially functioning school operates, perhaps the hope of serviceableness to community education may be realized.

APPENDICES

INDEX

APPENDIX I

STAFF

BALLARD MEMORIAL SCHOOL

ELSIE RIPLEY CLAPP, *Head*

1929–1930

Primary and Elementary Grades
Abbie Phillips, Grade 1
Ethel Carlisle, Grade 2
Mary Evans, Grade 3
Elisabeth Sheffield, Grade 4
Homer Howard, Grade 5
Eleanor McArdle, Grade 6

High School
George Beecher
Carleton Saunders
Roberta Whitehead

Louisa Lawton, Shop Teacher
Mrs. A. B. Sawyer, Home Economics

Student Teachers
Alexina Robinson
Mary Norris Burge

1930–1931

Primary and Elementary Grades
Abbie Phillips, Grade 1
Ethel Carlisle, Grade 2
Sarah Drayton, Grade 3
Elisabeth Sheffield, Grade 4
Harold Stendel, Grade 5
Homer Howard, Grade 6

High School
George Beecher
Carleton Saunders
Helen Post

Louisa Lawton, Shop Teacher

Student Teachers
Kathryn Ash
Priscilla Smith
Elizabeth Miller
Ethel Klein

1931–1932

Primary and Elementary Grades
  Kathryn Ash, Grade 1
  Ethel Carlisle, Grade 2
  Abbie Phillips, Grade 3
  Elisabeth Sheffield, Grade 4
  Lucille Clark, Grade 5
  Ethel Klein, Grade 6

High School
  Homer Howard, Grade 7
  Harry Carlson, Grade 8
  Carleton Saunders
  Helen Post
    Priscilla Smith, Assisting

Louisa Lawton, Shop Teacher

Student Teachers
  Mary Lee Hutchins
  Charlotte Seaman
  Margaret James

1932–1933

Primary and Elementary Grades
  Kathryn Ash, Grade 1
  Charlotte Seaman, Grade 2
  Ethel Carlisle, Grade 3
  Ethel Klein, Grade 4
  Lucille Clark, Grade 5
  Priscilla Smith, Grade 6

High School
  Elisabeth Sheffield, Grade 7
  Harry Carlson, Grade 8
  George Beecher
  Carleton Saunders

Louisa Lawton, Shop Teacher

Alice Bowie, Executive Secretary

Student Teachers
  Cecille Jack
  Rosabelle Englehard
  University of Louisville Students

1933–1934

Primary and Elementary Grades
  Rosabelle Englehard, Grade 1
  Kathryn Ash, Grade 1
  Eunice Jones, Grade 2
  Ethel Carlisle, Grade 3
  Cecille Jack, Grade 4
  Dorothy Winder, Grade 5
  Catherine Cornish, Grade 6

High School
  Elisabeth Sheffield, Grade 7
  Harry Carlson, Grade 8
  George Beecher
  Carleton Saunders

Alice Bowie, Executive Secretary

Student Teachers
University of Louisville Students

APPENDIX II

Arthurdale School

NATIONAL ADVISORY COMMITTEE

Mrs. Franklin D. Roosevelt
John Dewey
E. E. Agger, *Representing Rexford G. Tugwell, Resettlement Administration*
Fred J. Kelly, *Office of Education, Washington, D.C.*
Lucy Sprague Mitchell
Clarence E. Pickett, *American Friends Service Committee*
W. Carson Ryan

STAFF

ARTHURDALE SCHOOL

ELSIE RIPLEY CLAPP, *Director*

1934–1935

Primary Groups
Ethel Carlisle, Grade 1
Eunice Jones, Grade 2
Sara Liston, Grade 3

Elementary Groups
Elisabeth Sheffield, Grade 4
Inez Funk, Grade 5
Katherine Kimble, Grade 6

High School
George Beecher, Head
Adolph Ipcar
Carleton Saunders
Henry Esterley, Assisting

Special Teachers
Fletcher Collins, Teacher of Music and Drama
Harry Carlson, Shop Teacher
Jessie Stanton, Director of the Nursery School
Alice Bowie, Executive Secretary

Harry Timbres, M.D., Physician
Mary L. Shaffer, Nurse 1st Half-Year
Kay Plummer, Nurse 2nd Half-Year

APPENDICES
1935–1936

Primary Groups
Ethel Carlisle, Grade 1
Eunice Jones, Grade 2
Sara Liston, Grade 3

High School
George Beecher, Head
Susan Gross, Grade 7
Nell Rider, Grade 8
Adolph Ipcar
Carson V. Ryan
Carleton Saunders

Elementary Groups
Elisabeth Sheffield, Grade 4
Katherine Kimble, Grade 5
Inez Funk, Grades 5 & 6
Leonard Blamble, Grade 6

Special Teachers
Fletcher Collins, Teacher of Music and Drama
Harry Carlson, Shop Teacher
Kitty Ryan, Librarian

Jessie Stanton, Director of the Nursery School

Alice Bowie, Executive Secretary

M. L. White, M.D., and
Chalmers Wills, M.D., Physicians
Kay Plummer, Nurse

NURSERY SCHOOL STAFF
JESSIE STANTON, *Director*

1934–1935

Head Teacher
Mary Elizabeth Sedman

Senior Teacher
Alice Henry

Teachers
Mabel van Sickle
Argyle Morris
Virginia Williams
Louise Loy

Dietitian
Mildred Bayles

1935–1936

Head Teacher
Mary Elizabeth Sedman
to January 1936
Ethel Wadsworth *January through July*

Senior Teacher
Alice Henry

Teachers
Argyle Morris
Virginia Williams
Louise Loy
Elizabeth Dent
Rudelle Martin

Dietitian
Mildred Bayles

Student Teachers September to June
Assistant Teachers June and July
Glenna Williams
Josephine Harding

APPENDIX III

CURRICULUM, 1934-35

Grade	History	Science	Mathematics	Language	Other Activities
7th & 8th	Life in West Virginia as influenced by mountain environment and natural resources	Introduction to historical geology of the eastern United States	7th Grade Arithmetic 8th Grade Arithmetic	Drama group Writing Reading	Shop Forestry
9th	American history of westward expansion	Plant science and plant environments and relation to soils	Surveying, making use of algebra, geometry, trigonometry	English—group poetry and balladry Formation of drama group	Shop Typing
10th 11th 12th	American history—Reading and interpreting sources for modern history—fusing in the spring with the 9th Grade to produce *The Gold Rush*	Electricity and electrical communication	Accounting and bookkeeping, and School bank	English Building of library service	Typing Work in Nursery School

CURRICULUM, 1935-36

Grade	History	Science	Mathematics	Language	Other Activities
7th	American history of westward expansion	Geology of weather phenomena and use of gauges and formation of physical environment	Arithmetic	Reading and use of library Writing and discussion	Shop Sewing
8th	History of Transportation and Communication	Electricity for power and for communication	Use of mathematical principles in science, shop, everyday calculations, decimals, etc.	Reading and use of library Drama Writing Word study Recording—history work	Electrical shop Sewing Painting
9th	Medieval history—chiefly records as handed down from Roman civilization, as manuscript and type, paper; social life on manor and in towns, crystallized in medieval guild play at Christmas, and guild	Plant Science and study of greenhouse methods Recording of local plant life in book printed by class	Principles—using mathematical symbols and processes in solving problems related to living Study of algebra and the mathematics of	Reading and word study Drama Writing and recording Attention to symbolism	Shop Sewing Painting

CURRICULUM, 1935–36
(continued)

Grade	History	Science	Mathematics	Language	Other Activities
	organization of crafts represented in music (instrument-making)		musical tone relations for constructing a musical instrument		
10th	European history of late medieval discovery and later exploration of the world, including the development of printing in the cultural growth	Biology of local environment and human activity	Principles of uses of mathematics and symbol relations	Language—word study for reference reading. Dialect study	Cooking
					Shop
		Scientific methods of study and thinking preceding and following invention of microscope, plate cultures, etc.	Attention to problems in science	Drama group	Painting
			Bookstore and accounting	Typing	
11th & 12th	American history in 19th century with attention to modern problems resulting from industrialization and centralization	Chemistry of inorganic substances, particularly an investigation of local resources for the glass industry	Economics—taxes, insurance, wealth, costs. School banking; bookkeeping	Development of community newspaper	Cooking
					Shop
				Drama group	Painting
				Typing	

APPENDIX IV

PLAN FOR A RURAL HIGH SCHOOL (GRADES 7 TO 12) AT ARTHURDALE

SEVENTH GRADE

Science—
: Beginnings in the methods of study.
Subjects introduced which would be re-studied more intensively in later years of high school:
: Environment.
Weather conditions and effects of heat, etc., on soil, animal life, etc.
Small garden.
Geology—locally and for oil and steam transportation.

History—
: Westward expansion of the United States and discovery of resources, building, transportation systems.

Language—
: Informal speech and writing.
Plays which grow out of history studies, etc.
Use of library for as much voluntary reading as possible and for history and science studies.

Mathematics—
: Common arithmetic, measuring for shop work, etc.

A discussion of shop work, music, drama, athletics, painting for this class, as well as other classes, brings up first of all the point that there is work to be done in all those lines, and another point that the kind of work to be done depends on several factors: the environment and resources in soil, buildings, stage, shops, and teachers; the cultural background of games, drama, music, songs, stories, lore, dancing; farming, mining, industry; the seasons of the year; and the stage of development in educational experiences at which each individual or group has arrived.

EIGHTH GRADE

Science—
: Some work in the woods and in a small school garden.
Study of electrical communication as a further step in *doing* a science and making use of both shop and laboratory as needed.
Applications of electrical power to houses, motors, transportation.

History—
: The subject of communication as a local problem and a world problem of relations of people.

APPENDICES 403

Language— A continuation of 7th Grade work—as a tool in study or for pleasure in drama, reading, etc.

Mathematics— An advance in simple calculation can be made to applications of measure, to instruments in building, business, and science (surveying, weighing, etc.).

NINTH GRADE

Plant Science— Local botany, garden and field crops, herbs, shrubs, and seedlings.
Share in care of greenhouse and nursery.

Biology— Fertilization, hybridization, selection in plants.
Soil bacteria and protozoa, fungus and insect helpers and pests, balance of animal plant life, nitrogen cycle, etc.

Chemistry— Plant growth and plant foods and products.
Soil, fertilizers, insecticides, herb drugs.

Economics—Mathematics—Costs in production of plants and marketing of nursery and greenhouse stock.
Records and calculations over long period of time.

Language and History—The first step in analysis of language is a study of the history of written records as they are related to alphabets, writing materials, meanings and use of symbols—whether linguistic, phonic, mathematical, musical, etc.
To make a study of records it is useful to consider the study of both history and language, and to build in both with reading in history and literature with emphasis on England and the development of the English language. In later years this background for study of the language and modern language practices and resources and medium of expression is valuable.
Economic organization—structure in Middle Ages.
Dramatic work and music are of direct help in the use of language and in history in such a case as production of a Craft Guild play at Christmas time.
Painting and shop work are indispensable in the study of records and in drama of this sort.
Perhaps the more practical study of writing English comes in preparing a record of science work, etc.

Home Economics—Dealing with agricultural produce is almost as essential here as raising it, and a study with the girls must be done on foods for home use, as well as canning or marketing of specialties in food line.

TENTH GRADE

Animal Science—Biology, especially studying poultry, dairy and bee keeping.
In studying diseases, tests and pests, and the economically

APPENDICES

important bacteria, etc., in dairy products, biology becomes of social value. In addition, the talks of the doctor and the agriculturalist, dairyman, etc., all offer related facts to study.

Chemistry—Analysis of food values in feeds and diets, strengths in disinfectants and chemical changes in foods caused by bacteria or blocked by preservatives and handling of products.

Economics—Mathematics—Marketing of poultry and dairy and bee products and relative costs of production.
Mathematics of store keeping and accounting.
Study of pure food laws.

Home Economics—Food values in planning meals in rural areas where canning, butchering, garden season, and long winters have to be considered.

Language—Recording of scientific and economic studies in form for use in homes.
Study of the technical details of writing in studying the printing press.

History—Activities in the discovery of the world as seen especially in the developments which contributed to the invention of printing and book making.
Processes in making paper, design and casting of type, wood cutting.
Printing, and political changes, economic influences in expansion and beginnings of nationalism.
(Both the shop and art room need to be drawn in on the above studies.)

Music and Drama—The opportunities for singing and playing of instruments and the giving of plays begin to have their own development and to be a community as well as a school activity. The development of arts in the community, as well as of scientific and economic studies, depends on how well the school bridges the gap between the school children and the adults. Most of this has to be done in the later years of high school.

Athletics—Similarly, games and teams begin to be of interest to the community as well as to the school and are the first step in developing good rural recreation, where the gymnasium and stage become the center of activities for the weekends rather than the town movie and dance hall, etc.

ELEVENTH GRADE

Chemistry—Mineral products used in local farming and industry analyzed and tested.
Study of by-products in farm and industry.
After having studied various phases of chemistry in three years of high school, the students should be fairly well accus-

tomed to use of a laboratory and many of the principles of chemical actions.

Geology— This area is full of valuable mineral, oil, and coal deposits, water power, etc., which are the basis of much industry and are the source of products of use in farming and trades, such as glass. The geologic study of the area is thus of value for chemistry, economics, and also the social history of West Virginia people.

Economics—Mathematics—Value of minerals and products such as glassware. Study of economic structure—production and consumption—with a view to understanding problems of West Virginia, and what determines price and value.
School "bank"; bookkeeping.

History— Economic and international.

Language— Job and book printing. Compilation of pamphlets useful to the community or in outside contacts with schools, city markets, etc.

Shop— Craft work in use of mineral resources, such as production of agricultural lime and use of pottery clay and glass materials for glass making and blowing. Here is one field where many of the men of the community can draw on the school or contribute their knowledge and help in such work as the glass trade.

Home Economics—Budget for households.
Studies of standards in foods, rural standards of living and resources.
Contacts with homes and the women of the community.

Drama

Music

Art

Athletics

TWELFTH GRADE

Mechanical Sciences—Related to previous studies in materials, such as lime, concrete, and development of power with coal and water, gasoline, etc.

Chemistry— Fuels, oils, distillations—alcohol from waste produce, etc.
Soybean products.

Economics—Mathematics—Purchase of fuels and electricity for local consumption.
Study in machine invention and machine production as against hand crafts.
School "Bank"; bookkeeping.
Nature of fashions and advertising in marketing produce.

History—	Industrial-social problems of machine age in America which are vivid in this area in coal mining, but also in farming, mills, glass factories, etc. Local government and social organization.
Language—	The study of communication through printing, group discussion, electrical and other machinery, culminates in developing a local newspaper—for which as yet there is no completely satisfactory model. The kind of newspaper has to be worked out in relation to this kind of community, where the newspaper would be not a business but a medium of communication and expression, and in relation to the equipment which is available here.
Shop—	Mechanical shop for work on gasoline and electric motors and machines used in farming or industry. Construction in concrete, wood, etc. Designing and planning.
Home Economics—	Home crafts as possible source of home furnishing and income.

Drama

Music

Painting

Athletics

Note: This plan for development of a high school curriculum is nothing fixed or permanent but, as indicated, must change according to conditions and the stages to which work progresses.

Further: as classes graduate there will be shifts in the types of work needed to be done and the relations between the non-school members of the community.

Already there are graduates who wish to continue school work as student teachers or assistants in various lines of work which have been developed in school. There will thus be need for just as careful attention to post-high school students as to those who are studying their own community in school.

George Beecher
Head of High School

(Note: This Plan for a Curriculum for a Rural High School, as it was originally drawn up, was preceded by the analysis of Chief Local Problems.* The latter was separated from it because we used it as a basis of research into livelihood possibilities before the remainder of the Plan was put into operation. The Plan would have been put into operation in 1936–37; however, in that year the School was transferred to the State and County School authorities. E.R.C.)

---

* See Chapter VII, pp. 348–9.

APPENDIX V

SECOND DRAFT OF MATHEMATICS CHART

PREPARED BY CARLETON M. SAUNDERS, TEACHER OF MATHEMATICS,
WITH THE TEACHERS OF THE ARTHURDALE SCHOOL

SEVENTH GRADE

Activity	Mathematical Principles	Unadulterated Mathematics
Shop Work:	Learning how to measure: Scale drawing Proportion Fundamental processes Areas Fractions Specific gravity	Inventory tests 1. In computation 2. In problem solving Decimals: review of previous work Fractions: four fundamentals covered
Science Work:	(Same as above) Simple metric measurements Tables: humidity, temperature Ratios: in making a rain gauge Formula: in changing C to F, etc.	Percentage Budgets: money and time Using % in buying and selling Using % in saving and earning money
Using School "bank":	Banking	Insurance as means of saving money Simple taxes
History: Progress in Work: Health:	Graphs: showing comparisons, progress, etc., in history and other subjects; in heights, weights, etc.	Learning to understand and to make graphs 1. Picture, line, bar, and circular graphs 2. Examples: a. to show increase in population in U.S. b. Comparison of prices c. Comparison of rate of speeds d. Progress in industries

408 APPENDICES

Activity	Mathematical Principles	Unadulterated Mathematics
		e. Heights and weights of class
		f. Progress of individuals in spelling, mathematics, class work, etc.
Home Economics: Construction of a simple garment	1. Study of divisions on tape measure and how to use tape measure 2. Drafting simple patterns according to individual measurements 3. Checking own body measurements on commercial patterns and making needed alterations before cutting	

EIGHTH GRADE

Activity	Mathematical Principles	Unadulterated Mathematics
Science:	Formula: Ohm's law of resistance Ratios and simple measurements Reading meters Factors	Reading numbers in large denominations Practice in fundamental processes 1. Simple numbers 2. Common fractions 3. Decimal fractions (Correcting and perfecting methods for doing these with accuracy and speed)
Shop: Making magnet for telephone and telegraph Making sending and receiving sets Building model house and	Proportion: Measurements Fractions Areas Circles Volumes Harmonics: alternating currents Relativity: hardness, texture Formula Calculations: inductive reasoning	Terms: Multiplier, multiplicand, product, numerator, denominator, reduction, increase, decrease, equation Practical interpretation of students' need for number: Insurance

APPENDICES

Activity	Mathematical Principles	Unadulterated Mathematics
installing switches, plugs, etc.	Drawing: scale and perspective	Taxes Budgets Keeping accounts
Construction of dam; making shute, wheel, bridge, and generator; depth of water, speed		Interest Drawing to scale Dates Measurements
Trip to Cascade (Coke Furnaces)	Cost, size of furnace, tons of coal, ashes removed, R.P.M., voltage, reading barometer Made chart to report trip drawn to scale, correct proportion	
Made drawings of models showing development in use of steam, electricity, gasoline		
Made frieze of transportation	Graphs: showing growth of various means of transportation; circular, bar	
Home Economics: Construction of a simple garment	1. Study of divisions on tape measure and how to use tape measure	
	2. Drafting simple patterns according to individual measurements	
	3. Checking own body measurements on commercial patterns and making needed alterations before cutting	

NINTH GRADE

Activity	Mathematical Principles	Unadulterated Mathematics
Study of Elementary Algebra for work in the following:		
Surveying:	Equations, factoring, logarithms, trigonometry (ratios)	Elementary Algebra. History of Mathematics to show how its development coincided with that in Science, Industries, Agriculture, Government, Art
Mechanics:	Equations, factoring, logarithms, scale drawings	Algebra
Storekeeping:	Elementary bookkeeping Percentage and proportion	Arithmetic, Algebra
Co-operative Industries	Elementary bookkeeping: Formulas and graphs Business practice forms	Arithmetic
Agricultural Sciences:	Equations (especially, balanced chemistry equations) Formulas	Algebra
Building:		
Building Construction:	Equations, logarithms, scale rule drawings (blue prints) Principles of mensuration	Arithmetic, Algebra
Household Budgets	Insurance, taxes, investment, installments	Arithmetic, Bookkeeping
Shop—Musical Instruments:	Musical scale: fingering board, selection of strings, designing of a suitable resonating body. Metric measures, nodal lines. Relativity: C to B, etc. Pitch vibrations, etc. Proportion	Algebra

APPENDICES 411

Activity	Mathematical Principles	Unadulterated Mathematics
Geography:	Ratios and contour intervals in regard to maps	
Home Economics: Construction of a more complex garment	(1) Same as Grade 8 (2) Working out cost of garment (3) Comparison with ready-made garment in cost	

TENTH GRADE

Activity	Mathematical Principles	Unadulterated Mathematics
Shop— Mechanics: Printing: Electricity:	Printing and study of paper. Size of type. New measure, pica, points ($\frac{1}{72}''$), ems (spaces), vocabulary Fundamental processes—a new measure. Visualize type in reverse—inverse proportion Ratios, proportion, etc. Scale drawings Lever, pulleys, weights, measures, H.P., brake powers, arcs, circles, Geometry, pistons	Origin of Number Roman and Arabic Meaning of fundamental processes. Various ways of doing these and methods of testing them
Bookstore:	1. Double entry bookkeeping based upon the principle of the Equation	Meaning of number Introduction of negative numbers Formulas thermometers
	2. Use of proportion to calculate prices, discount, interest, profit	Mathematics: Vocabulary—function, variable, constant, root, mean, progression, medium, factor, compound, complex
	3. Rigid adherence to necessity of absolute accuracy of arithmetic involved in records	
	4. Business forms	

Activity	Mathematical Principles	Unadulterated Mathematics

Biology:	Metric System: Measurement of micro-organism weights, chemicals and solutions, algebraic formula and trigonometry in calculations—microscope lenses, etc.	Symbols:
		  Compound interest: computation, graph, tables
		  Proportion: means and extremes
		  Graphs: line, circle, straight line (equations), pictogram, bar, square root
		  Taxes, formula
		  Insurance: kinds, theory
		  Budgets: making family budgets
		  Stocks and bonds

Food Analyses:		Metric System: measurement:
		  Length: micromillimeters, bacteria
		  Relations of cm., cc., m.l., gram
		  Graduates for liquid measure in m.l.
		  Estimation of length, size, weight; knowing about what measure is meant when book asks for a road 25 cm. long, etc.

Decimal relations and theory of meter
Pure HO as standard for gram, degree of temperature
Centigrade thermometer and conversion formula
Per cent, proportion
  Solutions:
    1/1000 mercuric chloride as a disinfectant
    N/20 sodium hydroxide
    5% phenol

APPENDICES 413

Activity	*Mathematical Principles & Unadulterated Mathematics*
Dilution:	Stain: saturated solution in 95% alcohol diluted to 10% for use. Fermentation scale .... 10% .... 20% .... 30% .... etc.

Hydrogen-ion concentration:	% of gas formation.
	Scale indicators for % of acid-alkali in solution
	  No. of cc. of normal acid or alkali present in 1000 cc. of the medium, using phenolphthalein as indicator. If it took 17 cc. of the NaOH to neutralize 1000 of medium, it would be written +17° (Fuller's scale)
	Chemical equation and formulae
	  HO, monosaccharide ($C_6H_{12}O_6$)
	  grape sugar
	  disaccharide ($C_{12}H_{22}O_{11}$)
	  cane sugar
	Mathematics of the microscope
	Physical laws of light and refraction, focus, magnification
	Distance between lenses in compound microscope
	Relation of magnifying power to micromillimeter measurements under the microscope
	(Physics text gives algebraic equations)
	Charts, graphs, etc.
	  Economics-agriculture
	    Rates of plant growth, cellulose and sugar formation
	    Value of vegetable growth
	  Fertilizer-water ratios
	    Land values. Tariffs on agricultural products
	Comparative sizes of bacteria, cells, etc.

Home Economics: (10–11–12)

1. Studying Foodstuffs: where found and in what amounts needed

2. Planning daily and weekly dietaries to meet individual needs, as well as family needs

1. Working out the approximate amount of each of the foodstuffs needed daily, and the amounts of food needed to furnish these

2. Tables of measures and abbreviations for liquid and dry ingredients

Activity	Mathematical Principles & Unadulterated Mathematics
3. Preparation of simple breakfast and luncheon menus	3. Actual measurement of food supplies in laboratory
4. Arranging of 100 calorie-portion displays Working out individual calorific requirements	4. Consideration of the calorie as a unit for measuring body heat
5. Studying foodstuffs Marketing	5. Marketing: (1) Teaching the reading of labels (2) Advantages of buying foods in different forms—by weight, measure, number, etc.

ELEVENTH AND TWELFTH GRADES

Economics:
  Taxes
  Agriculture
  Laws
  Patents
  Current Events
  Trade

Chemistry:

  Simple Equations
  (Balances) Symbols
  Conversion of unit of weight and volume
  Metric System
    Thermometers
    Weights, Volumes
  Ratios (Charles's & Boyle's Laws)

School Bank:

  Elementary Bookkeeping:
  1. Double entry bookkeeping involves the principle of the equation
  2. Necessity of absolute accuracy of arithmetic used on bank records
  3. Knowledge of interest formulas and graph work

Home Economics: (10–11–12)

1. Studying Foodstuffs: where found and in what amounts needed
1. Working out the approximate amount of each of the foodstuffs needed daily, and the amounts of foods needed to furnish these

Activity	Mathematical Principles & Unadulterated Mathematics
2. Planning daily and weekly dietaries to meet individual needs, as well as family needs	2. Tables of measures and abbreviations for liquid and dry ingredients
3. Preparation of simple breakfast and luncheon menus	3. Actual measurement of food supplies in laboratory
4. Arranging of 100 calorie-portion displays Working out individual calorific requirements	4. Consideration of the calorie as a unit for measuring body heat
5. Studying foodstuffs Marketing	5. Marketing: (1) Teaching the reading of labels (2) Advantages of buying foods in different forms—by weight, measure, number, etc.

INDEX

Adult Education at Arthurdale, 88, 123, 293, 331–2, 333–4, 336–7; *agencies for, on the homestead,* 337–42; *buildings used by,* 293, 303–4, 331, 341, 363, 377; *athletics,* 362, 379–80; *art,* 253–4; *baby clinics,* 96–7, 189–190, 212–4, 372–3; *clubs: men's and women's,* 87, 112, 118–22, 241, 297, 370, 374, 380; *committees: men's fire,* 118–21; *joint committees: homestead health,* 374, 376; *school,* 358–362; *store,* 374–5; *women's medical committee,* 98, 212–4, 338, 372, 373, 376; *crafts: furniture,* 219, 249–50; *quilting,* 248–9, 341, 352–3, 354; *pottery,* 341, 377; *weaving,* 163, 200, 341; *community activities, 1934–5,* 72, 78–80, 86–8, 96–9, 100–3, 108–14; *1935–6,* 358–61, 362–3, 364–5, 376–380; *drama group,* 256–7, 265–8; *health of adults,* 94–6, 108, 369; *home economics,* 173, 338, 353–4, 363, 370, 376; *library,* 341, 366, 367–368, 378; *"neighboring,"* 335–6; *in nursery school,* 97–8, 172–3, 176–8, 184, 185, 186–7, 189, 190, 197, 211, 214–5, 216, 338; *recreational resources in,* 218, 219; *balladry,* 230–232; *fiddling,* 222; *gospel songs and white spirituals,* 240–2; *mouth-harping and jig-dancing,* 239–40; *music festivals,* 242–8; *square-dancing,* 220–2; *school gardens,* 111–3, 369–370; *school lunches,* 87–8, 113, 338, 375 (*see* Arthurdale; Arthurdale School; Clubs; Community; Cooperatives; Farming; Health; Home and School Relations; Homesteaders; Parent Activity)

Art and Painting, at Ballard, scenery for play, 8th grade, 33–4; at Arthurdale: adults, 253–4; children, 254–5; classes: 4th grade, 146; 5th–6th grade, 160–1; High School, 255–6

Arthurdale Homestead, *a school,* 66–124; *background of,* 68–70; *beginning of,* 70–1; *description of,* 83–4, 85–6; *history of,* 143, 144, 251–2; *location of,* 85, 86; *relations with other towns and cities,* 85–6, 164, 244, 384–8 (*see* Arthurdale School; Community; Homesteaders; Scott's Run)

Arthurdale School, 125–71, 364–5; *Arthurdale, a school,* 66–124; *and the community,* 162–5, 331–2; *and community living,* 384–8; *enrollment of,* 87, 128, 151, 174, 179, 192, 275, 302, 306, 389; *establishing the,* 75–7, 128; *High School,* 273–332; *Nursery School,* 172–216; *preparing buildings for use of,* 77–80, 173–174, 273–4 (*see* Equipment; School Buildings); *a Preston County school,* 151, 386, 388–90; *West Virginia Advisory School Committee's Plan for,* 71–5 (*see* Art and Painting; Children at Arthurdale; Communication; Community; Community School; County Teachers; Curriculum, Appendices III, IV; Drama; Elementary Education; English; Geography; History; Home and School Relations; Home Economics; Industrial Arts; Language; Log Cabin; Mathematics, Mathematics Chart, Appendix V; Playgrounds and Play; Plays; Printing; Programs; Reading; School Bus; School Lunches; Shop; Songs and Singing; Teacher Education; Three R's; Trips)

Assemblies, school, at Ballard, May Day health, 46; at Arthurdale High School, 295 (*see* Arthurdale School; Ballard School)

Athletics, at Ballard, 10–1, 46–7; at Arthurdale, 108–10, 340, 362, 378–381 (*see* Recreation; School Buildings)

Ballads and Balladry, 226–32: "Barbara Allen," 226–9; "Fair Charlotte," 231n; "Young Collins,"

417

Ballads and Balladry (*continued*)
230–1; ballad singing at music festival, 246; children's songs, 232–9: "The Crazy Horse," 237–9; "Mister Frog Went A-Courting," 233–4; "A Paper of Pins," 235–6; "Weevily Wheat," 148–50 (*see* Culture; Music Festival)

Ballard, Mrs. Thruston, founds the Roger Clark Ballard Memorial School, 4–5; assists work of, 24, 25, 29, 30, 42–3, 47, 135 (*see* Ballard School)

Ballard School, Roger Clark—Memorial, beginning of, 6–7; description of, 4–7; a Jefferson County school, 6, 61; building, 4–5, 7; equipment, 7, 8, 10, 47, 58, 59 (*see* Art and Painting; Ballard, Mrs.; Community School; Economics; Elementary Education; Fair; Geography; History; Home and School Relations; Home Economics; Industrial Arts; Language; Log Cabin; Mathematics; Playgrounds and Play; Plays; Printing; Reading; Recreation; School Gardens; School Lunches; Shop; Three R's; Trips)

Biology, at Arthurdale, in Elementary School, 381–2; in High School, 311, 313–4, 323, 350, 369 (*see* Curriculum, Appendices III, IV; Environment; High School; Science; Science Survey, 316–7)

Block Building, in Elementary School: 1st grade, 26, 132, 134; 2nd grade, 28; in Nursery School, 182–3, 188, 195–6, 199, 201–4 (*see* Elementary Education; Nursery School; Programs)

Botany, at Arthurdale, in Elementary School, 381–2; in High School, 291–297, 308–9, 312–3, 327 (*see* Curriculum, Appendices III, IV; Environment; High School; Science; Science Survey, 316–7)

Chemistry, at Arthurdale High School, 294, 310, 314–5, 318–22, 348, 353, 383 (*see* Curriculum, Appendices III, IV; Environment; High School; Science; Science Survey, 316–7)

Children at Arthurdale, in Nursery School: description of, 180–1, 183, 186–7, 201–10; physical condition of, 68–9, 93, 97, 176–8, 185, 186, 214–215; in Elementary School, health of, 68–9, 93–4, 154, 155, 159; interests of, 129, 131, 132, 133, 134, 136–7, 138, 141, 142–3, 145, 146, 147, 153, 154, 155, 156, 158, 159, 160; adults' efforts for, 116, 128; learning with community, 131, 135; summer activities, 108, 109, 379–80, 381–4 (*see* Arthurdale; Elementary Education; Food; Health; Nursery School; Playgrounds and Play; Plays; Songs and Singing)

Choral Speaking, Arthurdale High School, 288–9, 295 (*see* English; High School; Poetry)

Christmas, at Arthurdale, first, 101–103; carols, 242, 259, 263–4; plays, 255, 259, 263–4; toy-making by parents, 185

Clinics, in Kentucky: at Ballard: preschool, 45–6, 63; Jefferson County, 12; Louisville, 12, 44; at Arthurdale, baby clinics, 96–7, 189–90, 212–4, 338, 372–3, 376 (*see* Health; Physical Examinations)

Clubs, civic and social, 118, 122; men's, 87, 112, 118, 220, 241, 297, 337, 370, 380; men's fire committee, 118–21; women's, 121–2, 337; women's medical committee, 98, 212–4, 338, 372, 373, 376; joint committees: homestead health, 374, 376; store, 374–5; school, 358–62 (*see* Health; Homesteaders)

Communication, 268–72, 306–7, 315, 326 (*see* High School; Newspaper; Printing)

Community, activities, 1934–5, 79–80, 86–8, 100–3, 110–3, 115; 1935–6, 337–342, 357–8, 362–4, 369–70, 385; summer, 107–10, 377–80; bringing—into the work of the school, 331–2; interest in the log cabin, 150–1, 383; newspaper, 268–72, 322, 341, 353; Nursery School help on—problems, 173; relations with other communities, 85, 164, 244, 385–8 (*see* Adult Education; Arthurdale; Clubs; Community School; Co-operatives; Culture; Farming; Health; Historical Tradition; Livelihood Enterprises; Music Festivals; Parent Activity; Rural Areas; Scott's Run; Songs and Singing; Young Adults)

Community Education, 62–5, 67–8, 76–7, 80–1, 169–70, 355–6, 364; *County teachers become interested in*, 161–5; *earlier work of Friends*

INDEX 419

Service Committee in, 68–70; *learning by living*, 123–4, 297; *Nursery School and*, 172–3, 183, 184, 185, 186–7, 197–8, 210–2, 215–6; *prerequisite conditions for*, 80–1; *requires a year-round program*, 384; — *is social education*; Arthurdale, a School, chapter II, 66–124; Community and School Life, chapter VII, 333–91; Cultural Resources and Opportunities, chapter V, 217–72; *this report useful to*, 391; *what is* —, 89 (*see* Adult Education; Arthurdale School; Ballard School; Clinics; Clubs; Community; Community School; Co-operatives; Culture; Environment; Farming; Food; Health; High School; Home and School Relations; Home Economics; Homesteaders; Livelihood Enterprises; Milk Testing; Nursery School; Parent Activity; Rural Areas; School Gardens; School Lunches; Social Education; Teacher Education; Young Adults)

Community School, *Arthurdale School*, chapter III, 125–71; *Ballard School*, 1–65; *beginning, on homestead*, 86–88, 89, 99–124, 126–32, 173–80, 273–279; *County teachers in a*, 151–60, 161–5; *everyone's school*, 79–80; *health the concern of*, 90–2; *an instrumentality for community education*, 66–7; *idea of a*, 6, 9, 48, 49, 76–7; *a laboratory for the community*, 172–3, 183, 184, 186–7, 197, 215–6; *learning about a, in Kentucky*, 67, 80–1, 125, 126–7; *organizing subject matters for use in a*, 171, 273–332: *language*, 51–3, 167–9, 326–30; *mathematics*, 49–51, 323–4, Appendix V (Mathematics Chart); *parents' activity in Nursery School*, 80, 174, 176, 177, 186, 188, 191–2, 195–6; *parents' education*, 97–8, 172–173, 176–8, 185, 186–7, 189, 190, 197, 211, 214, 216, 338; *participation by parents in a*, 79, 87–8, 98, 111–3, 130, 359, 383; —'*s relations with its families*, 7–8, 9, 10–1, 14, 40–2, 44–5, 46–7, 61–2, 191–2, 210–2; *social education work of a*, 4, 15, 48, 49, 62–5, 66–7, 67–8: *at Ballard*, 7–8, 10–4, 41–2, 42–7, 57, 58; *at Arthurdale: see* Clinics; Health; School Gardens; School Lunches (*see also* Adult Education; Arthurdale; Community; Community Education; Culture; Curriculum; Elementary Education; Environment; High School; Home and School Relations; Home Economics; Livelihood Enterprises; Nursery School; Parent Activity; Rural Areas; Social Education; Teacher Education; Young Adults)

Co-operatives, *Arthurdale Co-operative Association*, 199, 250, 272, 338, 346, 351, 352, 353, 375; *Arthurdale Co-operative Store*, 140, 175, 199, 200, 272, 304, 338, 357, 374–6; *First Farm Co-operative*, 110–1, 280, 297, 338; *Mountaineer Craftsmen Co-operative Association*, 70, 78, 85, 110, 173, 175, 178, 199, 201, 219, 249, 250, 304, 341, 370, 377, 387

County Teachers, *in Kentucky: invited to Ballard School*, 6; *courses offered to*, 53; *at Arthurdale*; — *assigned to the school*, 154–5, 389; *become interested in community education*, 161–5; *education of, in work*, 151, 152, 153, 156–7, 161; — *as teachers of*: *3rd grade*, 153–4; *5th grade*, 155–6; *156–8*; *6th grade*, 158; *5th–6th grade*, 154–6, 158–61 (*see* Arthurdale School; Elementary Education; Programs; Teacher Education)

Culture, *cultural resources at Arthurdale*, 217–72 (chapter V); *in rural areas*, 60–1; *a school the center of, in rural areas*, 217–8; *Scotch-Irish traditional culture, at Arthurdale*, 218–9 (*see* Art and Painting; Ballads and Balladry; Communication; Drama; Fiddling; Furniture-Making; Historical Tradition; Mouth-Harping and Jig-Dancing; Music; Quilting; Songs and Singing; Square Dances)

Curriculum, 288, 311; *of High School*, *1934–5*, Appendix III; *1935–6*, Appendix III; *for a rural High School*, Appendix IV; *idea of socially functioning studies and*, 4, 47–8, 56–7; *organizing subject matters for use in a community school*, 171, 273–332; *organization of work in the High School: 1934–5*, 276–98; *1935–6*, 306–31; *plan for a, drafted by the West Virginia Advisory School Committee*, 73–4; *Science Survey*, 316–7; *staff study of subjects: language*, 51–3, 167–9, 326–30; *mathematics*,

INDEX

Curriculum *(continued)*
49–51, 323–4, Appendix V; *teachers and,* 279–80 *(see* Biology; Botany; Chemistry; Choral Speaking; Drama; Elementary Education; English; Geology; History; Home Economics; Language; Library; Livelihood Enterprises; Mathematics; Music; Newspaper; Plays; Poetry; Printing; Programs; Science)

Dentistry, *in Kentucky:* at Ballard, 12, 13, 44; *Jefferson County dentist,* 12, 44; *at Arthurdale,* 90, 96, 108 *(see* Health)

Dewey, John, 9, 48 *(see* Foreword by, vii)

Drama, *at Arthurdale,* 256–7; *adult, group,* 265–8; *High School, group,* 257–65, 363 *(see* Dramatic Play; Plays; Songs and Singing)

Dramatic Play, *at Ballard: 1st grade,* 26; *2nd grade,* 28; *4th grade,* 31; *at Arthurdale: Nursery School,* 167, 182–3, 188–9, 195–6, 201–4, 209–10; *1st grade,* 134, 135; *2nd grade,* 138, 142 *(see* Nursery School; Plays, Programs)

Economics, *geography, Ballard High School,* 57–8; *resources studied: at Ballard,* 15–6, 53–8; *at Arthurdale,* 314–5, 348–55, *in High School,* 280, 281, 325, 348, 355, Appendix IV (Curriculum for a Rural High School), Appendix V (Mathematics Chart) *(see* Environment; High School; Livelihood Enterprises; Social Education; Young Adults)

Elementary Education, Ballard and Arthurdale, *art,* 254–5; 4th grade, 146; 5th–6th grade, 160–1; *block building,* 1st grade, 26, 132, 134; 2nd grade, 28; *buildings for,* at Arthurdale, 1934–5, 78–9, 85–6, 129, 138; 1935–6, 301, 302; dramatic play, 1st grade, 26, 134, 135; 2nd grade, 28, 138, 142; 4th grade, 31; *enrollment of,* at Arthurdale, 128, 151, 302, 389; *equipment,* Ballard, 7; Arthurdale, 78–9, 87, 128–30, 146–147; *geography and maps,* at Arthurdale, 2nd grade, 141; 5th grade, 158; 5th–6th grade, 160; *history,* 3rd grade, 22, 153–4; 4th grade, 22, 28–32, 58–9, 142–5, 146, 147–51, 251–3, 382–3; 5th grade, 156–7; 5th–6th grade, 22, 35–9, 155, 159–61; 6th grade, 158; *home economics* (study of food), 1st grade, 24–5, 132–5; 2nd grade, 27, 139, 140, 141; 3rd grade, 153, 163; 4th grade, 29–30; *industrial arts,* 2nd grade, 26–7, 136–7, 138, 139; 3rd grade, 153–4, 163; 4th grade, 28, 30, 129–30, 143–8, 150–1; 5th grade, 155–6, 157–8, 164; 5th–6th grade, 38, 59, 160–1; 6th grade, 156, 158; *language,* at Arthurdale, 166–7; group stories, 1st grade, 135; 2nd grade, 140; *mathematics* (arithmetic), at Arthurdale, 154, 155, 158, 165–7, 324; at Ballard, 1st grade, 26; *physical condition of children,* at Arthurdale, 68–9, 93–4, 154, 155, 159; *playgrounds,* Ballard, 10–1; Arthurdale, 4th grade, 142–3; *plays,* 4th grade, 31–2; 5th–6th grade, 38–39, 40; *pottery,* 5th–6th grade, 161; *reading,* Arthurdale, 163, 166–7; 3rd, 4th grades, 166–7, 290; 5th grade, 155; 5th–6th grade, 35, 154; 6th grade, 158; *school gardens,* 63, 369–70, 381; 1st grade, 25, 42–3, 132–5, 381; 2nd grade, 27, 381; 4th grade, 29–30, 150; *science,* in summer activities, Arthurdale, 381–2; *shop,* 4th grade, 29, 145, 147–8; 5th grade, 155–6, 157; 5th–6th grade, 161; 6th grade, 156; *singing,* 1st, 2nd, 3rd grades, 232–9; 4th grade, 149–50, 232, 234; 5th grade, 229, 232–3, 235–7; 5th–6th grade, 232–3, 235–7; 6th grade, 226–9, 235–7; *spelling,* Arthurdale, 155, 158, 163; *summer activities,* 381–3; *trips,* 1st grade, 24, 131, 132–4; 2nd grade, 28, 137, 138, 139, 140, 141, 142; 4th grade, 29, 148; 5th–6th grade, 38, 160; 6th grade, 158; Three R's in, 8, 127, 154, 155, 158, 159, 163, 165–7 *(see* Arthurdale School; Ballard School; School Buildings)

English, *at Arthurdale,* 168, 278, 283–284, 287–8, 328–9 *(see* Ballads and Balladry; Choral Speaking; High School; Language; Library; Reading; Songs and Singing)

Environment, *at Ballard:acquaintance with,* 3–4, 5, 8–9; *country fair,* 43–4; *Kentucky,* 15–21; *region,* 53–8 *(see* Ballard School; Elementary Education; Health; Historical Tradition; History; Home and School Relations; Kentucky; Programs); *at*

Arthurdale: educational use of: in cultural resources, 217–72; *in school programs:* Nursery School, 181–3, 187–8, 195–6; Elementary School, 131–61; High School, 273–332; *new elements in our understanding of,* 170; *people and,* 71–2, 83, 84, 85–6, 125–8, 170–1, 173, 197–8, 217, 241, 273, 347–8, 355–64; *and education in rural areas,* 14, 62–8, 125–7 (*see* Arthurdale; Arthurdale School; Children at Arthurdale; Clubs; Community; Community Education; Community School; Co-operatives; Culture; Economics; Farming; Health; Historical Tradition; Home Economics; Homesteaders; Livelihood Enterprises; Outdoor Theater; Parent Activity; Parks; Recreation; Rural Areas; Science; Scott's Run; Songs and Singing; West Virginia; Young Adults)

Equipment, School: *Ballard,* 7, 8, 58; *Arthurdale: Nursery School,* 77, 79–80, 130, 152, 172, 173–6, 178–80, 182, 193–4, 195, 208–9, 284; *Elementary School,* 78–9, 87, 128–30, 146–7; *High School,* 78, 129, 289–91, 292, 293, 294, 295, 303, 320, 323 (*see* School Buildings; Science)

Fair, Ballard Country, 42–3; Kentucky State, 6–7, 28–9 (*see* Ballard School)

Fairfax, Colonel John (first owner of land at Arthurdale, friend of George Washington), 144, 251–3 (*see* Historical Tradition; Log Cabin)

Farming, *at Ballard:* 4H Club, 42, 46; *in school programs,* 1st grade, 24–5, 26, 135; 2nd grade, 27; *at Arthurdale: on the homestead,* 110, 339, 363–4, 369 (*see* Co-operatives; School Gardens; School Lunches); *in school programs:* Nursery School, 205–8; 1st grade, 132–5, 381; *young adults,* 339; *High School greenhouse,* 346, 351; *livelihood enterprises,* 350–2 (*see* Biology; Botany; Food; Health; Home Economics; Livelihood Enterprises; Science; Young Adults)

Fiddling, *at Arthurdale,* 222; *fiddlers' contest:* in Kentucky, 55–6; at Arthurdale music festival, 245; *fiddle-making,* 223–6, 307–8; *fiddle-tune:* "Soldier's Joy," 222n, 223; *fiddles exhibited,* at music festival, 225 (*see* Square Dances)

Food, *eating problems,* Arthurdale Nursery School, 173, 178–9, 186, 189, 195, 373; *nutrition needs,* at Ballard, 41–2, 63; at Arthurdale, 90–1, 93–4, 96–8, 159, 186; studied in school programs: 1st grade, 24–5, 132–5; 2nd grade, 27, 139, 140–1; 3rd grade, 153, 163; 4th grade, 29–30; High School (Ballard), 57; *school gardens,* 63, 135; 1st grade, 25, 42–3, 135, 381; 2nd grade, 27, 381; 4th grade, 29–30, 150; *woman's — exchange* (Ballard), 43–4; *young adults* (*see* Farming) (*see* Co-operatives; Farming; Health; Home Economics; Livelihood Enterprises; School Gardens, School Lunches)

Friends Service Committee, American, 92, 387, 389; work in Monongalia County, West Virginia, 68–70

Furniture-Making, 70, 201, 219, 249–250 (*see* Co-operatives; Culture)

Geography, economic, Ballard High School, 57; Arthurdale, 5th grade, 158 (*see* Maps and Map-Making)

Geology, at Arthurdale High School, 285–6, 292, 294, 309–10, 322–3; Curriculum, 1934–5, 1935–6, Appendix III; Curriculum for a rural High School, Appendix IV (*see* Curriculum; Environment; High School; Science; Science Survey, 316–7)

Greenhouse, botany work in High School needs a, 292, 295; first forms of, 295, 304; location of, in New High School building, 303, 304–5; young adults use, 339, 349, 351 (*see* Botany; Curriculum; Curriculum, 1935–6, Appendix III; Curriculum for a rural High School, Appendix IV; Environment; High School; Science)

Groupings and Grades, at Arthurdale, Elementary School, 128, 159, 167; High School, 279–82, 284, 294 (*see* Curriculum; Elementary Education; High School; Interests; Three R's)

Gugler, Eric (first architect of Arthurdale), 70, 71, 77, 299

Health, in Kentucky: *at Ballard: health work,* 10–4, 40–6; *nutrition needs,* 41–2, 63; *physical examinations,* 11–2, 40–2, 63; *physiology courses,* 46, 62; *pre-school clinics,*

Health (continued)
45–6, 63; *woman's food exchange*, 43–4; *Jefferson County: clinics*, 12; *dentist*, 12, 44; *nurse*, 11, 12, 44; *Kentucky: State Board of Health*, 44, 45; *State Tuberculosis Association*, 10, 11–2, 41, 45, 46; *Louisville clinics*, 12, 44; *at Arthurdale: baby clinics*, 96–7, 189–90, 212–4, 338, 372–3, 376; *agencies in adult education*, 337–9; *committees: homestead*, 374, 376; *women's medical*, 98, 212–214, 338, 372–4, 376; *eating problems at the Nursery School*, 173, 179, 186, 189, 195, 373; *efforts to meet — problems, 1934–5*, 89–92; *1935–6*, 163, 368–76; *medical services on the homestead*, 87, 91–2, 94–5, 97, 98, 189–90, 213–4, 337–9, 369, 370, 372–3, 374, 376; *nursing*, 91, 93, 96–7, 108, 176–8, 194, 213–4, 337–9, 370–1, 372–3, 376; *nutrition needs*, 68–9, 90, 91, 93–4, 96–7, 159, 186; *physical condition of: Nursery School children*, 93, 97, 176–8, 185, 186, 189, 194, 195; *Elementary School*, 68–9, 93–4, 154, 155, 159; *High School*, 94, 276, 284; *young adults*, 94, 343–4; *adults*, 94–6, 108, 115; *physical examinations: adults*, 87; *daily inspection of children at school*, 91, 176, 184, 194; *at Nursery School*, 214–5, 337; *physicians on the project: Timbres, Harry, M.D.*, 91, 92, 94–95, 98, 108, 189–90; *founds homestead health committee*, 374; *White, M. L., M.D.*, 92, 369, 370, 376; *Wills, Chalmers, M.D.*, 92, 213, 372–3; *physiology courses*, 366, 369, 375; *practical nursing, WPA course in*, 213, 339, 370–1, 376; *rural areas, — of*, 90 (see Adult Education; Children at Arthurdale; Clinics; Community; Community School; Cooperatives; Farming; Food; Home Economics; Homesteaders; Milk Testing; Nursery School; Parent Activity; Playgrounds and Play; Recreation; School Gardens; School Lunches; Scott's Run)

Herbs, *as medicine*, 6th grade (Ballard), 39–40; *as livelihood enterprise* (Arthurdale), young adults, 351, 354 (see Livelihood Enterprises; Programs)

High School, *at Ballard*, 22–4, 32–4, 57–61; *at Arthurdale, 1934–5*, 273–298; *1935–6*, 305–32; *building for, 1934–5*, 78, 80, 85, 273–4, 275; *1935–6*, 301, 303–5; *enrollment*, 111, 275, 306, 389; *equipment*, 78, 79, 129, 273, 275, 289–91, 292, 293, 294, 295, 303, 306, 320, 325; *groupings and grades*, 279–82, 284, 294; *physical condition of students in*, 94, 276, 284; *young adults in*, 315, 339, 341, 344–5, 347–8, 351; *used by adults*, 293, 303–4, 331, 341, 377 (see Athletics; Biology; Botany; Chemistry; Choral Speaking; Curriculum; Curriculum, 1934–5, 1935–6, Appendix III; Curriculum for a rural High School, Appendix IV; Drama; Economics; English; Environment; Geology; History; Home Economics; Interests; Library; Livelihood Enterprises; Mathematics Chart, Appendix V; Milk Testing; Music; Newspaper; Physiology; Plays; Printing; Programs; Science Survey, 316–7; Young Adults)

Historical Tradition, *at Ballard*, 21, 22, 23, 29, 30–2, 33, 36–40, 53–6, 58–9; *at Arthurdale*, 125, 251–3; *homesteaders' traditional culture*, 219–49; *pioneer program of 4th grade*, 143–5, 147–51, 251–3, 382–3 (see Environment; Fairfax; History; Homesteaders)

History, 324–6; *in school programs, at Ballard*: 21; 3rd grade, 22; 4th grade, 22, 28–32, 58–9; 5th–6th grade, 22, 35–9; 6th grade, 22; High School, 22–4, 32–4, 58–9; *at Arthurdale*: 3rd grade, 153–4; 4th grade, 142–5, 146, 147–51, 251–3, 382–3; 5th grade, 156–7; 6th grade, 158; 5th–6th grade, 155, 159–61; High School, 261–3, 285, 296, 324–6 (see Curriculum; Appendices III, IV; High School; Kentucky; Programs; West Virginia)

Home and School Relations, *at Ballard, relations with the families*, 7–8, 10, 12, 14, 40–2, 44–5, 46–7, 61–2 (see Ballard School; Clinics; Community School; Environment; Fair; Food; Health; Parent Activity; Recreation; School Gardens; School Lunches); *at Arthurdale, shared living and working*, 79–80, 86–9, 112–3, 130, 185, 214, 337 (see Adult Education; Arthurdale School; Christmas; Clinics, Community School; Cul-

INDEX 423

ture; Health; Home Economics; Log Cabin; Parent Activity; Plays; Recreation; School Gardens; School Lunches; Square Dances); *teachers as neighbors and community members,* 81, 122, 334-6, 337, 385 (*see* Clubs; Co-operatives; Farming), *visits: of parents to school,* 97, 176, 184, 185, 186-7, 194-6, 338, 358-62 (*see* Clinics [baby]); *of teachers to homes,* 174, 177-8, 185, 187, 190, 197-8, 211-2, 213, 338 (*see* Arthurdale School; Children at Arthurdale; Community Education; Economics; Environment; High School; Homesteaders; Nursery School; School Buildings; Social Education; Teacher Education)

Home Economics, *at Ballard:* 13-4, 41, 46, 63; *in school programs (study of food):* 1st grade, 24-5; 2nd grade, 27; 4th grade, 29-30; High School, 57; *at Arthurdale: Elementary grades (study of food),* 1st grade, 132-5; 2nd grade, 139, 140, 141; 3rd grade, 153, 163; *High School,* 280, 281, 298, 307 (*see* Curriculum, 1935-6, Appendix III; Curriculum for a rural High School, Appendix IV); *girls (older),* 104, 183, 298, 338, 377; *housekeepers,* WPA course of training as, 339, 371-2, 376; *women's,* 173, 338, 339, 363, 369, 370, 376; *canning,* 113, 338, 353-4, 370, 375; *school lunches,* 87-8, 113, 338, 370, 375 (*see* Adult Education; Ballard School; Elementary Education; Food; Health; High School; Milk Testing; Nursery School; School Gardens; Science; Young Adults)

Homesteaders, at Arthurdale, *background of: pioneer,* 143, 150-1, 253, 383; *racial,* 116, 218-9 (*see* Culture); *Scott's Run,* 81-3, 92-6, 99-100, 101-2, 356-7; *description of,* 84-5, 100, 112-3, 114-8, 128, 130, 133-4, 137, 148-9, 184, 185, 187, 191-2, 197-8, 211-2, 230, 241-2, 243-4, 245, 247, 248, 253-4, 265-8, 283, 335-6, 366, 378 (*see* Ballads and Balladry; Fiddling; Jig-Dancing; Mouth-Harping; Songs and Singing; Square Dances); *jobs and trades,* 115 (*see* Arthurdale; Children at Arthurdale; Community; Co-operatives; Farming; Parent Activity; Recreation; Rural Areas; Young Adults)

Indian Life, studied in programs (Ballard), 3rd grade, 22; 7th grade, 23; (Arthurdale), 3rd grade, 153-4 (*see* Elementary Education; Environment; Programs)

Industrial Arts, *at Ballard: country fair,* 43; *course for teachers,* 53; *log cabin, building of the,* 58-9; *repairs, home and school,* 58; *in school programs:* 2nd grade, 26-7; 4th grade, 28, 30; 5th-6th grade, 38, 59; High School, 33-4, 57, 59; *at Arthurdale:* 342-3; *crafts: block printing,* 219, 254, 341, 377; *furniture,* 70, 201, 219, 249-50, 377; *pottery,* 104, 241, 252, 254, 277; *quilting,* 121, 219, 248-9, 341, 352-3; *weaving,* 163, 254, 341; *livelihood arts,* 350-4; *in school programs:* 2nd grade, 136-7, 138, 139; 3rd grade, 153-4, 163; 5th grade, 155-6, 157-8, 164; 5th-6th grade, 160-1; 6th grade, 156, 158 (*see* Adult Education; Art and Painting; Culture; Historical Tradition)

Interests, *of children, in school programs (Ballard),* 4th grade, 30-1; 5th-6th grade, 37-8, 39; 8th grade, 33; *(Arthurdale),* 1st grade, 131, 132, 133, 134; 2nd grade, 131, 136-7, 138, 141; 3rd grade, 153; 4th grade, 129, 142-3, 145, 146, 313, 382; 5th grade, 155, 156, 157-8; 5th-6th grade, 155, 159, 160; 6th grade, 156, 158; *High School students,* 277-8, 279-80, 281, 282-6, 294-6, 308-9, 329; *County teachers,* 153, 156-7, 161-5; *young adults,* 344, 345, 346 (*see* Elementary Education; High School; Young Adults)

Jefferson County, Kentucky, *Board of Education,* 4, 6, 7, 9, 11, 62; *Clinics,* 12; *dentist,* 12, 44; *nurse,* 11, 12, 44 (*see* Kentucky)

Jig-Dancing, 240, 246 (*see* Culture)

Kentucky, *Board of Health,* 45, 46; *description of,* 15-21; *history, studied in school programs:* 21; 3rd grade, 22; 4th grade, 22, 28-32, 58-9; 5th-6th grade, 35-9; 7th grade, 22-23; 8th grade, 23, 32-4, 58-9; *State Tuberculosis Association,* 10, 11-2, 41, 44, 45 (*see* Elementary Education; Environment; Jefferson County; Programs)

INDEX

Language, 51–3, 167–9, 326–8; *and the curriculum*, 169; *studied in classes:* Elementary grades, 166–7; High School, 283–4, 286, 287, 288, 328–30; *used: in Nursery School, in discussion*, 205–8; *dramatic play*, 201–3, 209–10; *group stories*, 205, 209; *1st & 2nd grades, group stories*, 135, 140 (*see* Ballads and Balladry; Choral Speaking; Dramatic Play; English; Nursery School; Plays; Poetry; Songs and Singing)

Library (*Ballard*), fiction-lending, run by parents, 62; (*Arthurdale*) *School and Community* —, 289–91, 306, 366–8, 377–8; *circulation*, 341, 366, 368; *course (WPA) in — training and service to shut-in mothers*, 341, 367–8, 378; *equipment*, 289–91, 306, 367, 377; *location in new High School building*, 303; *used by: adults*, 341, 366, 367–8, 378; *children*, 290n, 368; *classes:* Elementary, 367; High School, 366–7, 368; *young adults*, 290n, 341, 377–8 (*see* Elementary Education; High School; Reading)

Livelihood Enterprises, listed, 350–4; study of economic resources of environment for young adults, 347–9, 350, 354–5 (*see* Economics; Environment; High School; Young Adults)

Log Cabin, *at Ballard*, 58–9; *at Arthurdale* (the Fairfax) *and the 4th grade*, 143, 144–5, 147–51, 251–3, 382–3; *community interest in the*, 150–1, 383 (*see* Arthurdale; Elementary Education; Environment; Historical Tradition; Industrial Arts; Parent Activity; Programs)

Maps, *of Arthurdale*, 7th–8th grade, 283; *of West Virginia*, 5th grade, 160; study of, 2nd grade, 141 (*see* Elementary Education; Geography; High School; Programs)

Mathematics, *reviewed*, 49–51, 323–4; Chart, drafted by teachers, Appendix V; *studied in classes: Elementary grades* (arithmetic), 26, 154, 155, 158, 165–7; *High School*, 279, 280, 281, 284, 308, 310, 314, 354 (*see* Curriculum; Curriculum; 1934–5, 1935–6, Appendix III; Curriculum for a rural High School, Appendix IV; Elementary Education; High School; Science; Science Survey, 316–7; Three R's)

Milk Testing, at High School, 314, 323, 331, 352, 354, 369, 375, 383–4 (*see* Food; Health; High School; Home Economics; Livelihood Enterprises; Science; Science Survey, 316–7; Young Adults)

Mouth-Harping, 239–40; at music festival, 246 (*see* Culture)

Music, *at Ballard*, 1st grade, 26; old fiddlers' concert, 55–6; *at Arthurdale: ballads*, 226–32, 246; *fiddling*, 222, 223, 245; *fiddle-making*, 223–6, 307–8; *instrument-making*, 225–6, 307–9; *mouth-harping*, 239–40, 246; *music festivals*, 242–8; *songs and singing*, 232–9, 240–2, 248, 259, 261–2, 263–4; *square-dancing*, 220–2, 246–7 (*see* Culture; Drama; High School; Plays)

NYA-WPA, 147, 168, 272, 276, 305, 314, 344, 345, 346, 376, 390; *courses in library work*, 341, 367–8, 378; — *housekeeping*, 339, 371–2, 376; — *practical nursing*, 213, 339, 370–1

Newspaper (at Arthurdale), 268–72, 322, 341, 353; and magazine (at Ballard), 59–60 (*see* Adult Education; Communication; Culture; High School; Livelihood Enterprises; Parent Activity; Young Adults)

Night School, for the older girls and boys, at Arthurdale, 103–7, 183, 305, 343–4 (*see* Young Adults)

Nursery School, at Arthurdale, 1934–5, 172–92; 1935–6, 192–216; *block building*, 182–3, 188, 195–6, 199, 201–204; *buildings used by*, 1934–5, 79–80, 173–4; 1935–6, 192–4, 301, 302; *children*, 180–1, 183, 187–8, 198, 201–210; *dramatic play*, 182–3, 188–9, 195–6, 201–4, 209–10; *environment used in*, 181–3, 187–8, 195–6, 198–212; *eating problems*, 173, 178–9, 186, 189, 195; *equipment*, 77, 79–80, 130, 172, 173–6, 178–80, 182, 193–4, 195, 208–9, 284; *health: baby clinics*, 96–7, 189–90, 212–4, 338, 372–3, 376; *daily inspection of children at school*, 91, 176, 184, 194; *physical condition of children*, 93, 97, 176–8, 185, 186; *physical examinations*, 214–5; *as laboratory for the community*, 172–173, 183, 184, 186–7, 197, 215–6; — *for other teachers and visitors*,

INDEX

190–2; language: discussions, 205–8; in dramatic play, 201–3, 209–10; group stories, 205, 209; parent education, 172–3, 185, 186–7, 197, 216, 338; fathers, 184, 187; mothers, 97–8, 176–8, 214–5 (see Clinics); playgrounds, 174–5, 182, 208–9, 301; trips, 194, 195, 198–201; visits: parents to school, 97, 176, 184, 185, 186–7, 197, 214–5, 338; teachers to homes, 174, 176–8, 186, 187, 190, 197–8, 211–2, 213, 338 (see Arthurdale; Community School; Food; Health; Home and School Relations; Parent Activity; School Buildings)

Outdoor Theater, 261–3, 292–3, 296, 377 (see Culture; Drama; High School; History; Plays)

Parent Activity, at Ballard, in school and community: country fair, 42–3, 63; health: 10–4, 40–6, 63; nutrition needs, 14, 41, 63; pre-school clinics, 45, 47, 63; physical examinations, 11–2, 40–1, 63; physiology courses, 46, 62; school gardens, 25, 30, 42–3, 63; school lunches, 8, 10, 41, 63; woman's food exchange, 43–4; home and school relations, 7–8, 10, 12, 14, 41–2, 44–5, 61–2, 64; PTA, 8, 12, 40–1, 45, 47, 56, 62, 63; recreation, 42, 47, 56, 62, 63; support of the school, 4–5, 6; at Arthurdale: in community and school, 79, 80, 97–8, 130, 174, 188, 191–2, 194–5, 331, 335–6, 370, 376; civic organizations: clubs: men's, 87, 112, 118, 220, 241, 297, 337, 370, 380; women's, 121–2, 337; committees: men's, fire, 118–21; joint: school, 358–62; store, 374–5; education, at Nursery School, parents', 172–3, 185, 186–7, 197, 216, 338; fathers, 184, 187; mothers, 97–8, 176–8, 214–5; health: baby clinics, 96–7, 189–90, 212–4, 338, 372–3, 376; committees, homestead, 374, 376; women's medical, 98, 212–4, 338, 372, 373, 376; physical examinations, 214–5; school gardens, 111–3, 369–371, 381; school lunches, 87–8, 113, 338, 370, 375, 383–4 (see Farming; Home Economics); recreation: athletics, 362, 379–81; crafts: block printing, furniture-making, quilting, pottery, weaving (see Adult Education, Culture); "good times": ballads, Christmas festivities, drama, fiddling, jig-dancing, mouth-harping, music, music festivals, plays, songs and singing, square dances (see Adult Education; Christmas; Culture); in school programs, 133, 134, 137, 138, 148–9, 150–1, 163, 195–6, 271, 285–6, 383 (see Arthurdale School; Elementary Education; High School; Nursery School); visits of parents to school, 97, 176, 184, 185, 186–7, 194–6, 338, 358–62 (see Home and School Relations; Nursery School) (see Arthurdale, Community Education; Community School; Environment; Homesteaders; School Buildings)

Parks on the homestead, High School plans for, 292–3, 296 (see High School)

Physical Examinations, adults, at Arthurdale, 87, 214; children, 214–5; daily inspection at school, 91, 176, 184, 194 (see Clinics; Health)

Physiology Classes, at Ballard, 46, 62; at Arthurdale, 366, 369, 375 (see Ballard School; Health; High School)

Plant Nursery, 292–3, 351 (see Economics; Environment; High School; Livelihood Enterprises; Young Adults)

Playgrounds and Play, at Ballard, 10–1, 46–7, 62; at Arthurdale, 108, 109, 378–80; 4th grade, 142–3; Nursery School, 174–6, 182, 208–9, 301; plan for, 74 (see Arthurdale School; Athletics; Ballard School; Health; Nursery School; Recreation; School Buildings)

Plays, at Ballard: 4th grade, 31–2; 5th–6th grade, 38–9, 40; 8th grade, 32–4; at Arthurdale, adult, 87, 266–8; High School, 257–65, 296, 325 (see Christmas; Drama; Dramatic Play; Outdoor Theater)

Poetry, at Arthurdale, 7th–8th grade, 284, 286; High School, 287–8 (see Choral Speaking; English; High School; Language; Programs)

Pottery, at Arthurdale, 5th–6th grade, 161; for girls and women, 104, 341, 377; clay products as livelihood enterprise, 352, 354 (see Adult Education; Elementary Education; High

INDEX

Pottery (continued)
School; Livelihood Enterprises; Young Adults)

Preston County, West Virginia, *Arthurdale School, a — school*, 76, 151, 386, 388, 389; *Board of Education*, 76, 98, 131, 151, 386, 389; *Board of Health*, 90, 323, 386; *teachers:* 76, 129, 145, 154-5, 389; *interest of, in community education*, 161-5; *programs taught by*, 153-61; *Shaffer, Kenneth* (Assistant Superintendent of Schools), 361, 386, 387n; *Watson, Paul* (Superintendent of Schools), 361, 386, 387n (*see* Arthurdale School; County Teachers; Elementary Education; West Virginia)

Printing, 269-71, 272, 306, 312, 315, 325-6, 327-8, 353, 354 (*see* Curriculum for a rural High School, Appendix IV; High School; Livelihood Enterprises; Newspaper; Young Adults)

Programs, at Ballard, *plans for*, 8, 14-15; *developed through study of resources*, 15-21, 53-9; *1st grade*, 24-6, 42-3; *2nd grade*, 26-8; *3rd grade*, 22; *4th grade*, 22, 28-32, 58-9; *5th grade*, 22; *5th-6th grade*, 22, 35-40, 59; *6th grade*, 22; *7th grade*, 22-3, 58-9; *8th grade*, 23, 32-4, 58-9; *9th grade*, 23-4, 59-60; *High School*, 57-8, 59-60; *at Arthurdale: 1st grade*, 131, 132-5, 324, 381; *2nd grade*, 131, 136-42, 381; *3rd grade*, 153-4, 163, 166-7; *4th grade*, 129-30, 142-51, 166-7, 251-3, 381-3; *5th grade*, 155-8, 164; *5th-6th grade*, 154-5, 158-61; *6th grade*, 155, 156, 158; *7th grade*, 309-10, 324, 325; *7th-8th grade*, 282-6, 308-9; *8th grade*, 310; *9th grade*, 311, 312-3, 325-6, 327; *10th grade*, 311, 313-4, 325, 327-8; *11th-12th grades*, 314-315, 318, 319-22, 325, 327-8 (*see* Curriculum, 1934-5, 1935-6, Appendix III; Curriculum for a rural High School, Appendix IV; Science Survey, 316-7) (*see* Art and Painting; Arthurdale School; Ballard School; Biology; Botany; Chemistry; Choral Speaking; Drama; Elementary Education; English; Geography; Geology; Groupings and Grades; High School; History; Home Economics; Industrial Arts; Interests; Language; Library; Mathematics; Mathematics Chart, Appendix V; Milk Testing; Music; Newspaper; Physiology; Plays; Printing; Science)

Progressive Education (*Ballard*), *children's reactions to*, 8; *course for local teachers in*, 53; *teachers' background of*, 9; (*Arthurdale*) *advice of Committee on School and Community Relations*, 71

Quilt Making, at Arthurdale, 121, 219, 248-9, 341, 352, 354 (*see* Adult Education; Culture; Livelihood Enterprises)

Reading, *at Ballard*, 35, 62; *at Arthurdale*, 163, 166-7; *adults*, 366, 367-8, 378; *in school programs:* in Elementary School, 163, 290, 366, 367, 368; *3rd & 4th grades*, 166-7, 290n; *5th grade*, 155; *5th-6th grade*, 154; *6th grade*, 158; *young adults*, 367-8, 377-378 (*see* English; High School; Language; Library; Poetry; Three R's)

Recreation, *at Ballard*, 10-1, 42-3, 46-47, 56, 62, 63; *at Arthurdale*, *athletics*, 106, 108-10, 340, 362, 378-81; *ballads*, 226-32; *Christmas festivities*, 101-3, 185, 242, 255, 259, 263-4; *drama*, 87, 256-68, 296, 325; *entertainments*, 340, 363; *fiddling*, 222-4, 245; *mouth-harping and jig-dancing*, 239-40, 246; *music festivals*, 242-8; *library*, 290n, 341, 366, 367-8, 377-8; *outdoor theater*, 261-3, 292-293, 377; *songs and singing*, 232-9, 240-2, 259, 261-2, 263-4; *square dances*, 100-1, 220-2, 246-7; *summer activities, children*, 379, 380, 381-3; *adults and young adults*, 108-10, 376-80 (*see* Adult Education; Community School; Culture; Parent Activity; Young Adults)

Roosevelt, Mrs. Franklin D., 70, 72, 121, 245; member of National Advisory Committee of Arthurdale School, Appendix II

Rural Areas, *acquaintance with*, 3-4, 5, 8-9, 14; *health facilities in*, 90; *a Nursery School in*, 172-80, 215-6; *the school the center of culture in*, 217-8; *social-education work of a school in*, 62-5; *study of resources of*, 15-21, 53-8, 273, 314-5, 318, 331-332, 348-54 (*see* Arthurdale; Environment; Kentucky)

INDEX

School Buildings, at Arthurdale, *old buildings on homestead used as, 1934–5*, 77–80; *equipment available*, 78–9, 87, 128–31, 146; *plans for new: by West Virginia Advisory School Committee*, 74, 299; *by teachers with architects*, 71, 76–7, 299–300, 302; *site and grouping of new*, 301; *separate:* Nursery School: *1934–5*, 79–80, 85, 173–4, 199–200; *1935–6*, 192–4, 301, 302; *equipment of*, 77, 79–80, 129–30, 152, 172, 173–6, 178–180, 182, 192, 193–4, 199, 208–9, 284; Primary and Elementary: *1934–5*, 78, 85–6, 129, 138, 155, 159; *1935–6*, 159, 301, 302; *equipment of*, 78–9, 87, 128–30; High School: *1934–5*, 78, 80, 84, 85, 107, 129, 273–4, 275, 283; *1935–6*, 301, 303–5; *equipment of*, 78–9, 129, 273, 274–5, 295, 303; *art room, 1934–5*, 254; *1935–6*, 303; *library, 1934–5*, 290, 366; *1935–6*, 303, 304, 366; *equipment of*, 289–91, 306, 366–7, 377, *printing room*, 303; *science greenhouse, 1934–5*, 295, 304; *1935–6*, 303, 304–5; *science laboratory, location*, 303, 304; *equipment of*, 274, 291, 292, 293, 294, 303, 304–305, 320, 322–3, 331; *made by parents*, 341, 359, 383; *shop, 1934–5*, 78, 107, 274; *1935–6*, 303; *Recreation Building, 1934–5*, 85, 100, 102, 245, 258; *1935–6*, 247, 301, 304, 362, 377, 378–9; *School Center building, 1935–6*, 199, 301, 304, 362–3, 377; *doctor's office, 1934–5*, 86, 87, 107; *1935–6*, 304, 369; *home economics rooms, 1934–5*, 87, 88, 113; *1935–6*, 301, 304, 370; *School lunch room, 1935–6*, 199, 301, 304; *School office, 1934–5*, 78, 79, 85, 107; *1935–6*, 301; — *used by adults, parents, young adults* (see Adult Education; Elementary Education; High School; Home and School Relations; Log Cabin; Nursery School; Parent Activity; Science; Young Adults) (see Arthurdale School; Community School; Elementary Education; Outdoor Theater; Playgrounds and Play)

School Committee, Arthurdale School: *homestead*, 358–62; *National Advisory*, Appendix II; *West Virginia Advisory*, 71–5, 360–1, 387, 388

School Gardens, *at Ballard*, 63, 135; *in school programs*, 1st grade, 25, 42–43; 2nd grade, 27; 4th grade, 29–30; *at Arthurdale*, Nursery School, 205–208; *in school programs*: 1st grade, 132–5, 381; 2nd grade, 381; 4th grade, 150, 381–2; High School (see Botany; Greenhouse; High School; Livelihood Enterprises; Science); — *and School lunches*, 111–3 (see Adult Education; Co-operatives; Elementary Education; Farming; Food; Health; Parent Activity; School Lunches)

School Lunches, *at Ballard*, 8, 10, 41, 63; *at Arthurdale: mothers prepare*, 87–8, 113, 338, 370, 375, 382–4; *new plans for*, 369–70; *Nursery School eating problems*, 173, 178–9, 186, 189, 195 (see Adult Education; Food; Home Economics; Nursery School; Parent Activity; School Gardens)

Science, *Arthurdale High School*, 291, 298, 307, 309–23 (see Curriculum, 1934–5, 1935–6, Appendix III; *for a rural High School*, Appendix IV; *interest in, of: adults*, 304, 331, 341, 383; *adults make equipment for*, 341, 359, 383; *young adults*, 106, 315, 339, 345, 384; *greenhouse: Botany work needs a*, 293, 295, 303, 304–5, 312–3, 339, 351; *laboratory* (Science room), 291–2, 293, 294, 303, 304, 322, 383; *outdoor* —, 285, 291, 292–3, 296–297, 306, 313–4; *plans for*, 292–3, 294, 297–8, 309–1, 314–5, 322–3, 331 (see Chief Local Problems, 348–9: Livelihood Enterprises, 350–4; Mathematics Chart, Appendix V; Science Survey, 316–7); *special sciences: Biology:* Elementary School, 381–2; High School, 311, 313–4, 323, 350, 369; *Botany:* Elementary School, 381–2; High School, 289, 291–7, 308–309, 312–3, 327; *Chemistry,* High School, 294, 310, 314–5, 318–22, 348, 353, 383; *Geology*, 285–6, 292, 294, 309–10, 322–3; *Milk Testing*, 314, 323, 331, 352, 354, 359, 375, 383–4 (see Arthurdale; Community School; Co-operatives; Economics; Elementary Education; Environment; High School; Livelihood Enterprises; Mathematics; Physiology; Plant Nursery; School Buildings; Young Adults)

Scott's Run, 68–70, 71, 81–3, 99–100, 101–2, 209–10, 387; *and Arthurdale*,

Scott's Run (*continued*)
70–1, 83–5, 101–3; *effects of life in, on: children*, 68–9, 91, 93–4, 96–7, 142–3, 145, 154, 155, 166–7, 176–8; *older boys and girls*, 94, 284; *young adults*, 94, 103–7, 276, 305, 343–7; *adults*, 84–5, 100, 112–3, 114–8, 121, 123, 128, 184, 185, 187, 356–8, 364; *Mrs. Roosevelt visits*, 70; *work of Friends Service Committee in*, 68–70, 389 (see Adult Education; Arthurdale; Children at Arthurdale; Community; Community Education; Community School; Health; Homesteaders; Young Adults)

Shop, School, *at Ballard, beginning of*, 8; *course to teachers*, 53; *home and school repairs*, 57, 58; *used in school programs:* 4th grade, 29; 8th grade, 33; *at Arthurdale, 1934–5*, 78, 107, 274; *1935–6*, 303; *used in: making fiddles*, 223, 224, 225; *in school programs:* 4th grade, 145, 147–8; 5th grade, 155–6, 157; 5th–6th grade, 161; 6th grade, 161; High School, 262, 274, 280, 282, 284, 285, 286, 296, 308, 310, 323, 324, 327; *with young adults*, 104, 105–6, 139, 290n, 345 (see Arthurdale School; Ballard School; Elementary Education; High School; Mathematics; Night School; Programs; Young Adults)

Social Education, *the basis for community education*, 68–70; *the work of a community school*, 4, 15, 48, 49, 62–5, 66–8, 89, 123, 124, 126–7; *community education,* — (see Community Education: Arthurdale, a School, 66–124; Cultural Resources and Opportunities, 217–72; A Rural High School, 273–332; Community and School Life, 333–391); *industrial arts as —*, 342–3; *social studies in school programs:* 1st grade, farms and farming, 24–6, 132–5; 2nd grade, village study, 26–8, 136–42; 4th grade, pioneer study, 28–30, 143–5, 147–51, 253, 381–3; High School (Ballard), 57–60; (Arthurdale), 280, 281, 310–1, 314–5, 325, 326, 331–2, 333, 336–7; *socially functioning studies*, 47–53; *tested in action*, 170–171; *study of resources of the environment*, 15–21, 53–6, 348–54 (see Adult Education; Arthurdale; Arthurdale School; Ballard School; Clinics; Clubs; Co-operatives; Community School; Economics; Elementary Education; Environment; Farming; Food; Health; Home and School Relations; Home Economics; Livelihood Enterprises; Nursery School; Parent Activity; Recreation; School Gardens; School Lunches; Teacher Education)

Songs and Singing, *children's songs*, 232–9: "Mister Frog Went A-Courting," 233–4; "The Crazy Horse," 237–9; "A Paper of Pins," 233n, 235–236; "Weevily Wheat," 148–50; *gospel songs and white spirituals*, 240–242; *music festivals*, 246; *singing schools of the region*, 240, 248 (see Ballads and Balladry; Culture; Music; Music Festivals)

Square Dances, 100–1, 220–2, 246–7 (see Fiddling; Mouth-Harping and Jig-Dancing; Music Festivals)

Stanton, Jessie (Director of the Harriet Johnson Nursery School of the Co-operative School for Teachers, New York, Director of the Arthurdale Nursery School), 77, 80, 102, 103, 172, 173, 174, 181–2, 185, 186, 187, 188, 192, 194, 195, 196, 215, 302 (see Nursery School)

Subject Matters, *language*, 51–3, 326–330; *mathematics*, 49–51, 323–4, Appendix V; *organizing — for use in a community school*, 170–1, 273–332; *socially functioning*, 47–9, 52–3 (see Art and Painting; Culture; Drama; Elementary Education; History; Home Economics; Industrial Arts; Language; Mathematics; Plays; Poetry; Printing; Programs; Science; Songs and Singing)

Summer Activities, *1935*, 107–10; *1936*, 376–84

Teacher Education, *shared living and working*, 78, 79, 81, 84–5, 167–8, 174–175, 177–8, 197–8, 210–2, 223–6, 243–244, 297, 380–1, 382–5; *in: Christmas festivities*, 102–3, 185; *baby clinics*, 212–4, 372–3; *plays*, 87, 88; *recreation*, 100, 108, 220, 362, 363; *school gardens*, 111–3, 360–70; *school lunches*, 86–8; *square dances*, 100–1; *teachers and the community* (at Ballard), 43, 61, 62, 64; (at Arthurdale): *teachers as neighbors and community members*, 89, 122, 161–5, 335–6; *in: clubs*, 87, 161–2; *their committees: fire*, 118–22; *homestead health*, 373–4; *store*, 374–5; *school*,

INDEX 429

358–62; *farming and farm co-operative*, 110–1; *teachers learning through study of organization of subjects for use in community education (see* Elementary Education; High School; Subject Matters); *study of people and environment, resources of environment (see* Environment); *visiting (see* Home and School Relations); *training of local teachers (see* County Teachers)

Three R's, in Ballard School, 8; Arthurdale School, 127, 154, 155, 158, 159, 163, 165–7 (*see* Arthurdale School; Ballard School; Elementary Education; Mathematics; Programs, Reading)

Trips, Nursery School (Arthurdale), 194, 195, 198–201; 1st grade, 24, 131, 132–4; 2nd grade, 28, 137, 138, 139, 140, 141, 142; 4th grade, 29, 148; 5th–6th grade, 160; 6th grade, 158; High School (Arthurdale), 285, 291, 292, 296, 310, 313, 319; teachers, 53–55 (*see* Arthurdale School; Ballard School; Elementary Education; Environment; High School; Nursery School; Programs)

Wagner, Steward (second architect of Arthurdale), 299, 300, 302, 303

West Virginia, *Advisory School Committee,* 71, 75, 360–1, 387, 388, 390; *plan for new school at Arthurdale,* 72–5; *Cox, Floyd B.* (Superintendent of Schools, Monongalia County), 361, 387n, 388; *Monongahela Valley,* 69, 285, 387; *Monongalia County,* 69, 71, 191, 387, 388; *Morgantown,* 68, 72, 80, 81, 86, 103, 173, 191, 219, 221, 229, 239, 250, 251, 253, 256, 268, 276, 346, 363, 387, 388; *Preston County,* Arthurdale a school of, Board of Health, Assistant Superintendent and Superintendent of Schools, teachers of (*see* Preston County); *State Normal School,* 388; *State Supervisor of Nursery Schools, Miss Bonar,* 191; *studied in school programs;* 3rd grade, 153–4; 4th grade, 142–5, 146, 147–51, 251–3, 382–383; 5th grade, 156–7; 5th–6th grade, 155, 159–61; 6th grade, 158; High School, 261–3, 285, 296, 324–6, 355; *towns related to Arthurdale School:* Albright, 380; Brown's Mills, 253; Burke, Bretz, 174, 386; Dellslow, 248; Dogtown, 220, 223, 382, 386; Fairmont, 388; Gladesville, 386; Laurel Point, 244; Masontown, 81, 84, 86, 174, 386; Mount Zion, 248; Reedsville, 81, 85, 86, 109, 110, 195, 201, 242, 244, 245, 251, 362, 363, 379, 383, 385–6; Terra Alta, 86, 388; *Trent, W. W., the Hon.* (State Superintendent of Schools), 75, 76, 387n; *University of,* 230, 358, 361–2, 387, 388; *Agriculture Department,* 110, 111, 289, 350, 351; *Chappell, Louis W.,* 230, 246; *Chemistry Department,* 318; *Education, Department of,* 72, 360, 361, 387; *Geology Department,* 352; *Library,* 289, 319, 367

Young Adults, 275–6, 305–6, 342; *agencies for adult education shared in by,* 337–42; *art,* 255–6; *athletics,* 106, 109, 340, 362, 379–80; *construction work on the project,* 105–6, 276, 340, 344, 345; *drama,* 263, 340; *English* (Night School), 104, 106–7; *farming,* 339, 346; *fiddling,* 222–4, 339; *furniture-making,* 341, 377; *High School:* 276, 306, 315, 344–5; *— and post-High School work,* 347–8; *Science: laboratory,* 106, 345, 383–4; *greenhouse,* 339, 351; *School grades,* 94, 106; *History* (Night School), 104; *home economics,* 104, 107, 183, 338, 369, 377; *housekeepers, WPA course in,* 339, 371–2, 376; *jobs* (Arthurdale Co-operative store), 141, 276, 305, 344, 346; *library,* 290n, 341, 377–8; WPA — course, 341, 345, 367–8; *mathematics,* Night School, 106; assistant in, 344; *mouth-harping and jig-dancing,* 239–40, 246; *livelihood enterprises,* 347–55: *milk testing as a,* 352, 354, 383–4; *newspaper* (printing) *as a,* 353; *plant nursery as a,* 351, 384; *Night School,* 103–7, 305, 344, 345; *nursing, WPA course in practical,* 213, 339, 370–1, 376; *NYA-WPA activities,* 168, 272, 276, 314, 344; *pottery* (for girls), 104, 341; *problem of the,* 276, 305–6, 343–7; *psychological adjustments and health of,* 94, 103–5, 107, 343, 344; *shop,* 345: *Night School,* 104, 105–6, 290n; WPA, 147; *square dances,* 100–1, 220–2, 246–7; *summer activities, 1934–5,* 108–10; *1935–6,* 376–80, 383–4; *use of school buildings,* 303–304, 362

9442